Soviet Soft Power
in Poland

THE NEW COLD WAR HISTORY
Odd Arne Westad, editor

This series focuses on new interpretations of the Cold War era made possible by the opening of Soviet, East European, Chinese, and other archives. Books in the series based on multilingual and multiarchival research incorporate interdisciplinary insights and new conceptual frameworks that place historical scholarship in a broad, international context.

Soviet Soft Power in Poland

Culture and the Making of Stalin's
New Empire, 1943–1957

PATRYK BABIRACKI

The University of North Carolina Press   Chapel Hill

Set in Miller by Westchester Publishing Services
The paper in this book meets the guidelines for permanence and durability
of the Committee on Production Guidelines for Book Longevity of the Council on
Library Resources. The University of North Carolina Press has been a member
of the Green Press Initiative since 2003.

Jacket illustration: The USSR's Moiseev song and dance ensemble performs in
Warsaw (1947), POLISH PRESS AGENCY / Jerzy Baranowski

Library of Congress Cataloging-in-Publication Data

Babiracki, Patryk, 1978–
Soviet soft power in Poland : culture and the making of
Stalin's new empire, 1943–1957 / Patryk Babiracki.
pages cm—(The New Cold War history)
Includes bibliographical references and index.
ISBN 978-1-4696-2089-3 (cloth: alk. paper)
ISBN 978-1-4696-5478-2 (pbk.: alk. paper)
ISBN 978-1-4696-2090-9 (ebook)
1. Soviet Union—Relations—Poland.   2. Poland—Relations—Soviet Union.
3. Propaganda, Soviet—Poland—History.   4. Soviet Union—Foreign relations—1945–1991.
5. Soviet Union—Cultural policy.   6. Imperialism—History—20th century.
7. Power (Social sciences)—History—20th century.   I. Title.
DK67.5.P7B28 2015
303.48'243804709045—dc23
2014034903

Portions of chapters 2 and 3 appeared as "Between Compromise and Distrust:
The Soviet Information Bureau's Operations in Poland, 1945–1953," *Cultural and
Social History* 6, no. 3 (September 2009): 345–67. Used with permission.

To the memory of my Grandmother
To my Mother
To my Wife

Contents

Illustrations, Tables, and Figures

ILLUSTRATIONS

TABLES

FIGURES

Acknowledgments

This book had an unusual beginning. For the greater part of my life, history as a discipline did not really appeal to me. Although I grew up in Poland, a country where the study of the past assumes a supreme importance, my lyceum teacher numbed any budding excitement for the subject through emphasis on memorization of dates and events. Moreover, among my family and friends, we talked about music, art, philosophy, travels, and all sorts of trifles, but politics carried as little weight as the Euro cup; so while the world held its breath in 1989–91, as incredible as it may sound, I failed to appreciate the great drama of postcommunist transitions while living in the middle of it all. Then, when I was an undergraduate at Portland State University, my professors Lawrence Wheeler and Michael Reardon changed my life by introducing me to the problem-oriented study of the past, structures and poststructures; ironically, though, no living historian stirred my historical passions as much as the late philosopher Michel Foucault. During a research internship at the Wilson Center in 2000, I had the good fortune to work for Professor Jeffrey Brooks, whose scholarship I came to admire. The great thing about being a cultural historian, I thought later, was that I would never have to touch politics. And without the complex history of mass political parties and democratic processes, Russian and Soviet politics seemed both simple and dismissible. In that sense, this monograph has been an exercise in humility, an extended act of massive catching up and proving myself wrong.

This monograph grew largely out of my fascination with a world that no longer exists. It was also born out of questions about a dark, distant decade, and the controversial beginnings of an era, at the dusk of which I grew up. I felt energized and occasionally defeated by the challenge of writing about Soviet-Polish interactions in the decade after World War II. It was hardly advantageous, from an academic standpoint, to have grown up in a society that had experienced Russian domination for centuries. I tried to turn that familiar sense of Russian proximity to my own advantage, by using it to locate the subjects of my study as accurately as possible in their distinct, though entangled, cultural contexts—"finding my feet" with them, as Clifford Geertz has called it. I made my best effort to question my own assumptions about the period I thought I had known.

And I went on an offensive against the received knowledge, as it were, by trying to reconstruct within the story the views of its often demonized Soviet participants. I thank the many people who helped me at least try to live up to the task.

The topic proved far more convoluted than I had ever imagined it would be. Thinking about Soviet-Polish links in the postwar decade compelled me to confront the extremely complicated issue of Polish-Jewish relations. Then I had to ensure that my discussion of this important problem did not overwhelm the chief focus of my study. That was perhaps the hardest task, because the controversies and emotions surrounding the subject make it nearly impossible to make a statement without qualifying it with dozens of others. In working through this aspect of the story, I also incurred many debts.

I owe my greatest debt to Jeffrey Brooks, who read many drafts of the book and supported me tirelessly along the way. Through his patient guidance and truly generous feedback he has provided me with inspiration, cheer, and a sense of what good scholarship is about. Jeff helpfully encouraged me to start my book by thinking about the sources, not about Michel Foucault. I am thankful to Paul Kramer for lively and stimulating conversations about empire and transnational history. Mark Blyth, Charles Gati, Peter Jelavich, Kenneth Moss, David Narrett, Alfred Rieber, Daniel Treisman, and the two anonymous readers at the University of North Carolina Press offered many penetrating criticisms and constructive comments on subsequent draft versions of the manuscript. I wish to express my profound gratitude to them.

During the nine years of work on this monograph, I met many people who influenced my thinking, facilitated access to sources, or simply expressed their enthusiasm for the project. In Baltimore, outside of seminars, I exchanged ideas with Albert Beveridge, Karen Brooks, Gülru Çakmak, Georgy Cherniavskyi, Lars Maischak, and Caleb McDaniel; Justin Roberts and I shared ideas and good laughs. In Moscow, I discussed my project with Professors Albina F. Noskova and Tatiana V. Volokitina. Andrew Janco, Benjamin Loring, and Andrey Shlyakhter made great companions within and outside the archive walls. During subsequent trips to Warsaw, I greatly benefited from the guidance of Professors Andrzej Paczkowski and Jerzy W. Borejsza. In 2008–9, I took up a yearlong position at the University College Dublin; there, fellow Russianist Judith Devlin offered a warm welcome and invaluable support, while friends Balázs Apor, Julia Eichenberg, and John Paul Newman showed me around the Irish pubs. In other places, Sandra Freels helped me to identify several obscure Russian texts, while Wade Jacoby and Mary Nolan generously commented on a paper that significantly informed this book.

I continued thinking about Soviet soft power under the salutary influence of the vast Texas sky. Friends and colleagues at my academic home at the University of Texas at Arlington have created a supportive environment for further research and writing. Elisabeth Cawthon, Stephanie Cole, John Garrigus, Donald Kyle, Stephen Mazlish, Christopher Morris, David Narrett, Steven Reinhardt, and Sarah F. Rose shared their experience, always offering a good word in the hallways and over lunches. I thank especially the two subsequent chairs of the Department of History, Robert Fairbanks and W. Marvin Dulaney, for their encouragement and flexibility in granting me two research leaves; both Bob and Marvin understood that no amount of sky-inspired thinking can replace taking another trip to the archives.

Further research took me to Warsaw, Vienna, Washington, D.C., Budapest, and Berlin. In each of these Cold War capitals, I was surrounded by friends and acquaintances whose informed interest, insights, or companionship helped me to finish the book. Among them are Jan Behrends, Birgit Beumers, Marta Bucholc, Jens Gieseke, Eva Fodor, Tomasz Gromelski, Michael Hamlin, Hope Harrison, Kristof Jacobs, Jacek Kochanowicz, János M. Kovács, Christophe Lécuyer, Attila Melegh, Olena Palko, Valentina Parisi, Christine Philiou, Ann Philips, William Pomeranz, Natalya Rostova, Marci Shore, Anna Sobór-Świderska, Iryna Vushko, and Vladislav Zubok. Friends Marsha Siefert and Alfred Rieber have given me several opportunities to rehearse my ideas; they read and commented on parts of the manuscript and have supported me emotionally and intellectually in very meaningful ways.

I am grateful to my closest friends Constantin Katsakioris, Damien Kempf, Mariusz Lisiecki, Miron and Maciej Musiał for good cheer and companionship unrelated to the book—their positive effect on my social-scientific endeavors must not be overlooked.

I am likewise indebted to the many people who helped me gain access to various materials. Foremost among them are the staff at the Russian archives GARF, RGASPI, RGALI, and RGANI; in Polish archives, the AAN, the AMSZ, and the Mickiewicz Museum of Literature, and Filmoteka Narodowa; the Lenin Library in Moscow, Warsaw's Polish National Library, and the BDIC in Nanterre—a West European treasure trove of East European sources. In the United States, I wish to thank the Interlibrary Loan staff at the University of Texas at Arlington; the people at the Slavic Reference Service of the University of Illinois Urbana-Champaign, and Jan Adamczyk in particular, for responding so quickly to my often obscure last-minute requests; Angela Cannon of the Library of Congress, for solving the mystery of the missing microfilm reels; Michelle Kamalich and Dagne Gisaw of the Woodrow Wilson Center Library for ordering these microfilms, and so many other items, so quickly and on such short notice. Librarian Janet Spikes also helped me on several occasions, often sharing her enthusiasm for the project together with her own East European stories. Alexandra Shaheen, my research assistant at the Wilson Center, found much useful material for this book and helped me design the figures. Support staff at the various research institutes created friendly and truly utopian environments in which I had nothing to worry about except scholarship. Among them were Susanne Fröschl, Maria Nicklas, and Claudia Zimmer (IWM); Lindsay Collins and Lauren Crabtree (Wilson Center), Agnes Forgo, Eva Gonczi, and Angelika Papp (CEU-IAS); Stephanie Karmann and Roxanna Noll (ZZF). Barbara Richardson read two versions of the manuscript, catching the missing articles and critiquing my writing style.

Research for *Soviet Soft Power* would not have been possible without the financial support of many institutions. The Social Science Research Council enabled me to carry out preliminary three-month research in Moscow in the summer of 2005. The Fulbright-Hays DDRA Program of the U.S. Department of Education, as well as the IARO Program of the International Research and Exchanges Board (IREX) generously funded my research in Russia in 2005–6; the Fulbright-Hays grant subsequently sponsored my five-month research in Poland. The Johns Hopkins University, my doctoral alma mater, supported my research in 2007 in the form of a grant from the Stulman Program in Jewish Studies, which made it possible to spend a summer in Poland. Over the course of rewriting, I realized that many of the histories I was trying to weave together go back to the last years of World War II. I had to find out more, and a scholarship from the Polish History Museum enabled me to spend two months in Warsaw's Central Military Archive in the summer of 2009. The materials formed the basis of chapter 1, which I further researched and wrote as a Józef Tischner Fellow in Vienna's wonderfully welcoming Institut für die Wissenschaften vom Menschen (IWM) between July and December of 2010. I was fortunate to have spent the three summer months of 2012 as a Title VIII Scholar at the Woodrow Wilson Center's Kennan Institute, where I researched and wrote chapter 5. In 2012–13, I spent a delightful academic year at the Institute for Advanced Study of the Central European University in Budapest. Although I wrote mostly in my office, or in the luxurious Raoul Wallenberg Guesthouse, some of my clearest thinking occurred while strolling the streets of Budapest and staring at the Art Nouveau facades, or walking across the Chain Bridge that spans the city center and the Buda Hills. Finally, I used the first months of the generous postdoctoral fellowship in Germany from the Volkswagen and Andrew W. Mellon Foundations to work on the final, mostly technical stages of the book. During my successive stays at Potsdam's Zentrum für Zeithistorische Forschung, Jan Behrends and Jens Gieseke have been kind and accommodating hosts. None of these organizations (or people) are, of course, responsible for the views expressed in this book.

I wish to thank Chuck Grench, the editor at the University of North Carolina Press, for believing in this book from the start. Together with his assistants Alison Shay, Lucas Church, and Katherine Fisher, and later the project editor Paul Betz, he patiently helped me navigate through the bewildering first-time publication process, sharing his good advice along the way. I am likewise truly grateful to the series editor Arne Westad for his continued support.

Sections of chapters 2 and 3 appeared under the title "Between Compromise and Distrust: The Soviet Information Bureau's Operations in Poland, 1945–1953," in the journal *Cultural and Social History* 6, no. 3 (2009); I thank the editors for permission to republish it here.

Finally, I am deeply thankful to my family, especially my mother Barbara, who inspired in me wonder about the world and love of books, and who recommended my first Bulgakov novel; my late grandmother Maria-Magdalena, who tolerated my fascination with Russia despite her own contempt for "the East"—a sentiment that she traced to her own experience of the violence that accompanied the Soviet liberation of Poland; my godfather Andrzej for emotional support over the years, gifts of books, books, and more books. My parents-in-law Rosemonde and Bernard and my two *belles-soeurs* Diane and Margaux repeatedly relieved stress and provided logistical and babysitting support many times, in different parts of the globe. My wife Séverine has been my absolute greatest source of support from the beginning to the end: as a scholarly sister-in-arms, a kindred spirit, a fellow expat and globetrotter, and the mother of our son Xawery, she shared in the joys and frustrations of her husband's writing, sometimes putting her own projects on hold. I owe *her* my deepest thanks. I wish to dedicate this book to the memory of my grandmother, to my mother, and to Séverine, for everything they have done for me— they were and are the three women of my life.

Soviet Soft Power
in Poland

INTRODUCTION

Empire's Shades and Shadows

On August 20, 1953, Soviet journalist Nikolai Bubnov hurried to meet the Soviet ambassador to Poland, Georgii M. Popov. Poland's capital, having been razed to the ground during World War II, was still rising from the ruins. The Soviet embassy occupied a spacious building in the city center on Aleja Szucha 2/4. When Bubnov entered, the ambassador received him immediately. His suit jacket undone, trousers hanging well below his bulging belly, Popov paced nervously back and forth "like a lion in a cage." Although the two men were meeting for the first time, the ambassador ignored formal introductions. He made straight to the point, "heatedly" telling Bubnov about the situation in Poland. "You see, *redaktor*, each day in Brest we're handing over to the Poles thousands of wagons of grain," Popov said, referring to a town on the Soviet-Polish border. "And they? If they keep acting this way, they'll turn all of Poland into shit." Bubnov listened in silence, aware that Popov had been a powerful Party functionary before assuming diplomatic duties in Poland.[1] On the very same day, the Soviet government admitted to a successful detonation of a hydrogen bomb—Bubnov learned firsthand about the explosive nature of culture in Soviet-Polish relations.

The diplomat was widely known for his rude demeanor and irascible temperament.[2] Popov's indignation over Poles' lack of gratitude for Soviet grain shipments seems misplaced; the USSR derived enormous economic advantages from its new vassal state, which paid for the grain many times over.[3] Bubnov waited. It was clear that Popov was not angry over a mere grain loan. Art threw Popov over the edge of civility—an invitation to a recent exhibition of Polish art. The gallery featured a painting by nineteenth-century Polish master Jan Matejko titled *Bathory at Pskov*. It depicted envoys of the sixteenth-century Muscovite tsar Ivan the Terrible, paying homage to the Hungarian-born king of Poland Stefan Batory. As other Soviet observers were quick to point out, the scene shows an invented aftermath of a real conflict—the two rulers negotiated the outcome of the Polish block-ade before a victor emerged.[4] In later parts of his career, Matejko had produced his vast, panoramic canvases depicting periods of Poland's glorious past with a strong sense of purpose. He wanted to give solace to his compatriots when Poland disappeared from the European map as a result of partitions by Russia, Prussia, and Austria in the late eighteenth century. But recently, Popov had heard a disturbing (and untrue) rumor that "some artists" had added to the painting an image of the Russian tsar, whose face ended up nearly touching his own ambassadors' protruding bottoms. Highly offended, the diplomat passed his own ticket on to his beleaguered guest. Out of "a sense of national pride," Bubnov, too, refused to attend the exhibition.[5]

Banal as it may seem to us today, in the rarified climate of the Stalinist empire this abortive Soviet-Polish encounter in the Warsaw museum revealed deeper tensions between the two countries' elites over the form, content, and role of culture behind the "iron curtain." Culture, in turn, reflected important rifts over the meaning and functioning of the new Soviet empire that Stalin and his East European allies had built during the preceding decade. The Soviet dictator had been dead for five months now, and the overwhelming sense that life would not be the same amplified conflicts that had built up during his last years. Lavrentii Beria, the chief of the notoriously repressive Soviet security police, had been arrested and shot soon afterward. That summer, Poland's minister of defense Marshal Konstantin Rokossovskii, a Soviet citizen of Polish origin, proposed a gradual removal of omnipresent Soviet officers from the Polish armed forces. Likewise, the head of the country's infamous security police Stanisław Radkiewicz began hinting at the institution's "incorrect and unjust methods of work," which, in the regime's euphemistic language, meant torture, terror, and other forms of coercion.

But both events, most certainly encouraged by Moscow, constituted a weak and secret undercurrent of the empire's political life. On the surface it was business as usual; few outward signs suggested that Stalin's hardline cronies in Poland, still firmly in power, would change their ways. Soviet officers continued to staff top posts in the Polish army. Arrests of people accused of plotting against the regime hardly abated. The authorities launched an aggressive campaign against the Catholic Church—for many Poles, a most sacred institution.[6] Stalin's "gift" to the Polish people, the layer cake, Moscow-style skyscraper that would become the Palace of Culture and Science, was rising fast in Warsaw's very center. Even as it echoed early twentieth-century American architectural designs, cre-

Warsaw, 1953. Palace of Culture and Science under construction.
Courtesy of Polska Agencja Prasowa.

ating certain ambiguities, the monumental building, based directly on skyscrapers overlooking Moscow and Riga, symbolized an unequivocal Soviet intrusion and the Polish communists' overt commitment to the Stalinist reorganization of space.[7] Just before seeing the ambassador, Nikolai Bubnov relished the view of its already towering skeleton, noting with a certain pride that when finished, the palace would be more than 100 meters high.[8] Simultaneously, its architects were drafting plans for a new building of the Soviet embassy. The opulent neoclassical structure with a sizable portico supported by four columns would evoke the lavish Russian palaces of the eighteenth century. It would sit on an artificial hill overlooking the adjacent Polish Ministry of Defense and the Presidential Palace, the Belvedere, across the street. Erected, like the Palace of Culture, in 1955, it reminded all passersby that the momentum of Stalinism had outlived its prime mover by at least two years. It also projected the confidence and glamour of centuries-old, Russian imperial might.

Yet for those same Polish passersby, enough had changed in the country's political and social life by 1955 to mitigate even the ominous presence of Stalin's ghost. Surely, that life continued to be defined by Poland's close relationship with the USSR. But paradoxically, as a result of pressure from Moscow and domestic social and political ferment, daily life was becoming noticeably different. The authorities implemented "the new course" in economic policy, geared to increase the availability of notoriously scarce consumer products on the market. The security apparatus had been downsized and restructured; its powerful director Radkiewicz now held the unenviable post of minister of State Farms. By 1955, restrictions on freedom of speech had loosened up in Poland far more than in the Soviet Union, as members of the cultural and political establishment themselves became embroiled in debates over the excess limits of censorship. In November 1955, the Theater of the Polish Army in the Palace of Culture and Science staged *The Wedding*. Stanisław Wyspiański, the author of this heavily symbolic drama from 1900, had conceived it as a veiled critique of contemporary Polish society that he deemed too passive to struggle for its own independence. Anti-Russian overtones were even more palpable in Adam Mickiewicz's *Forefathers' Eve*, staged in Warsaw four months earlier; there, the Russian tsar and his officials, cavorting against the architectural landscape on which the new Soviet embassy was modeled, are unmistakably in the service of the devil himself.

■ We have thus transported ourselves to the familiar juncture between two historical eras known as "Stalinism" and "the Thaw"—the latter term taken from the title of Soviet writer Ilya Ehrenburg's novel first published in the spring of 1954. In historiographic terms, that year also marks a contact point between two narratives of Soviet-East European relations after World War II. The first is the story of Sovietization, that is, the recasting of East European life and institutions on the Soviet model. The building of Warsaw's Palace of Culture belongs here. Starting in 1948, Soviet authorities and their East European allies transplanted monoparty rule, command economies, leader cults, and an artistic method known as "Socialist Realism" onto new terrains. Though the war had galvanized the support of East European societies for left-wing politics, the communists implemented their programs by riding roughshod over many national traditions, cultures, customs, and institutions.[9] We now know that Stalin was acting in response to the growing international tensions between East and West, while fulfilling important domestic objectives and far-reaching imperial ambitions along the way. The Red Army liberated countries for Poland from the German occupation and simultaneously became the chief instrument of the communists' rise to power. The Soviet troops had to stay, as Stalin told the Polish communist leader Władysław Gomułka in 1946, when Gomułka dared to point out the inauspicious propaganda effects of Soviet troops' presence. "The point is," Stalin said, that the anti-communist partisans "would not kill you."[10] Unlike in Czechoslovakia, where the communists succeeded in making alliances with intellectual opponents and the population at large, and very much as in Hungary and Germany, in Poland, they rose to power largely thanks to Soviet support.[11] They would not have been able to maintain that power without deception and coercion; their actions brought on the suffering of countless innocent individuals and spilled an ocean of blood.

The second chief narrative relates the undoing of Stalinism, communism, and empire. In some ways, the process is incomplete. The Russian embassy still overlooks the Belvedere from its artificial hill. The embassy's website claims that the building belongs among the most beautiful in the Polish capital, and it may well be so.[12] The Palace of Culture continues to grace (or disgrace) the center of Warsaw; though placed next to a flashy, modern, capitalist shopping mall, it still dominates—being twice the height that Bubnov had imagined it would be. During late socialism, the joke went that its top floor offered the best view of the Polish capital because from this place only one could not see the building itself. Perhaps the most radical aspect of post-Stalinism was that the police stopped arresting the joke-tellers. The very fact that Soviet ambassador Popov merely refused to go to an offensive exhibition—as opposed to initiating investigations—was a sign of changes to come.

In a watershed moment during the Twentieth Party Congress in February 1956, Nikita Khrushchev denounced Stalin as a "brutal" and "capricious tyrant who pretended to be a god."[13] In Poland, the abatement of arbitrary police terror went hand in hand with the growing, though certainly limited, freedom of speech. It was followed by the demise of the Stalin cult, the ousting of Stalinist hard-liners from power, and the dismantling of collective farms. During the October 1956 plenum, Władysław Gomułka became the leader of the Polish Party. The Polish communists reinstalled Gomułka without consulting Moscow—something that could not have happened under Stalin. Furious, Khrushchev flew to Warsaw, in another unprecedented step, since Stalin simply summoned his East European protégés. But eventually, the two leaders struck a deal. The Soviets would grant Poland a degree of autonomy in internal affairs—thus sanctioning Poland's "national road to socialism," which had been anathematized in 1948. In turn, Gomułka pledged to fend off any real and potential dangers to socialism; in keeping his word, he disappointed those who had hoped for more liberal reforms. But unlike his Hungarian counterpart Imre Nagy, who proclaimed a multiparty system and thus provoked the Soviet invasion, Gomułka avoided a similar catastrophe. While the leaders of the great powers largely changed the terms of the Cold War, the new type of Soviet-Polish relations Gomułka forged with Khrushchev also framed broader possibilities for anticommunist resistance in Poland until the system's dying days in the "year of miracles," 1989.

Remarkably, of the two stories, neither Stalinism nor the Thaw quite clarifies why Ambassador Popov fulminated in his office in late August 1953. And neither story explains fully the scale and intensity of anti-Soviet sentiment among Poland's cultural elites, which erupted within two years of the Soviet leader's death and included even those who had been genuinely committed to friendship with the USSR during the preceding decade. For key agents of empire have remained largely in the shadow of the momentous and often violent changes wrought by the Soviet Union in Eastern Europe. What we know about the Soviets in this era of bourgeoning empire—during the process of widespread Sovietization—touches little on culture and meaning. And the familiar story of the impact of Sovietization on East European cultures deals only obliquely with the Soviets.

■ This is the first book in any language to examine both sides of the story of Soviet-Polish cultural interactions during the troubled and little-known postwar decade.[14] It builds on both classic accounts of Soviet-East European relations, new works on Sovietization, and recent studies that recognize the Soviet and Polish communists' limited successes in meeting their stated objectives.[15] Some have argued that the leaders in the Kremlin and their plenipotentiaries abroad Sovietized Eastern Europe because they could not conceive of doing otherwise.[16] In her gripping story about Sovietization of Eastern Europe, Anne Applebaum stressed the methodological and efficient nature of the process; rational and systemic in their approach, the Soviets "applied only those techniques which they knew had a chance of success."[17] Others, like Vladimir Pechatnov, blamed the pervasive inefficiency of Soviet totalitarian bureaucracy for the feeble influence of foreign propaganda.[18] Conversely, according to another account, East European leaders "self-Sovietized" their countries with minimal guidance and support from the East.[19] Here I show that the Soviets participated actively in shaping Poland's culture and cultural relations between the two countries. Yet many Soviet officials displayed a much greater sensitivity to local conditions than has been acknowledged.[20] They also experienced a great deal of confusion about what was expected of them.

At its core, this book reaches far beyond the extent to which Poland did or did not become Sovietized. The most successful empires in history have managed to balance out the universalist drives from the center with the particularistic demands from the peripheries.[21] While the USSR was different from the ancient empires and prerevolutionary Russian imperial state, the challenges that Soviet officials confronted in their new sphere of influence were essentially the same. I ask how Soviet-Polish cultural contacts affected stability in the Soviet Bloc, without assuming that the terms of Sovietization were the only issues at stake. In moving beyond what I call "the Sovietization paradigm," and in focusing on the Soviet experience of cultural outreach, I hope to contribute to our understanding of the USSR as an imperial state during the crucial, formative decade of the Cold War.[22] Zbigniew Brzezinski has most famously argued that Stalin's charisma and ideology sustained what he labeled the "Stalinist interstate system"; as the former withered away and the system became more elastic after the Soviet leader's death, the "unity of ideology and power dissipated," threatening the bloc's cohesion.[23] Drawing on previously classified archival documents from Russia and Poland, as well as insights from "New Cold War History," I show that culture played a crucial and wide-ranging role on all levels of Soviet-Polish interactions. For all the ink spilled about Stalin's charisma or credo in traditional histories, what often mattered the most in Soviet-Polish cultural relations was something we are not supposed to care about: the picture on the book jacket.

We know that the Soviet Bloc communists tried to resolve the imperial tension in several ways. Most obviously, the Kremlin capitalized on postwar chaos by offering the communist order as an alternative. As Andrzej Paczkowski has pointed out, the Soviet leaders built a mutually beneficial, sovereign-vassal relationship with the Polish communists.[24] The Polish communists then co-opted other Poles by offering them numerous opportunities and concessions to the society at large. Publicly, Polish and other East European communists elevated all things Soviet—and Stalin in particular—to the status of the sacred; those who failed to prove their commitment to friendship with the USSR, found themselves excluded from the "invented community of the new communist nation."[25] Like their counterparts in the USSR and other East European vassal states, Polish masses and scores of intellectuals participated in the cult.[26] That the USSR guaranteed Poland's postwar security and the inviolability of its new western borders mattered even to members of the anticommunist intelligentsia.[27] But over time, the communist effort to transform East European institutions, cultures, and societies made the most procommunist, even pro-Soviet Polish elites rapidly lose enthusiasm for the Soviet Union. Writing in the 1960s, Polish science-fiction writer Stanisław Lem compared the USSR to a repulsive dragon; in contrast to the devil himself, this loathsome and unappealing creature had nothing to offer to the population it terrorized, not even worldly pleasures in exchange for one's soul. Lem's view was certainly a retrospective one, and large segments of the Polish cultural elites immediately after the war hardly shared it. Yet most did by 1956. Examining the Soviet side of imperial consolidation can help us to understand why.

The world we shall delve into was an empire of heavily guarded state borders. International travel within the Soviet Bloc was a privilege few enjoyed, and fewer still dared to dream about traveling to the West. Under communism, borders "were always taboo, a murky topic . . . simply a magical affair," confessed one Polish man trying to explain his urge to walk around his country's internal perimeter after 1989.[28] As Vladislav Zubok observed, a Soviet intellectual living under Stalin had a greater chance of seeing a total solar eclipse than meeting a foreigner.[29] Yet precisely because the communists restricted travel on an unprecedented scale, even the limited cross-border contacts within the Soviet Bloc and with the outside world carried tremendous weight. Those who traveled abroad variously experienced fear, excitement, pride and shame; those who did not travel physically imagined going to faraway places through literature and film. Poland felt the constraints of travel most pointedly. The Soviet-Polish border became the strictest crossing point of any Soviet Bloc country. In fact, Soviet troops guarded it with the same ferocity as they did the border between East and West—the so-called "iron curtain."[30] In recent years, scholars have explored the significance of borders and the impact of border crossings within the context of totalitarian communist regimes.[31] By focusing on the least travel-friendly (and least explored) decade in the history of Soviet-Polish relations, I ask: What did international travel signify and offer to people who crossed the Soviet-Polish border during the gestation of Stalin's new empire?

■ In the shadow of terror and Sovietization accompanying Poland's "revolution from abroad," a less-known project of persuasion through culture came to life. This book tells the story of how it was carried out in the ever-shifting middle ground, between the Soviet Union and Poland, the USSR's strategically important and certainly most rebellious vassal state. These fascinating and often flawed new cultural initiatives—never truly micromanaged by Stalin, though necessarily sanctioned by him—arose out of the efforts of Soviet propagandists and their Polish interlocutors: Soviet and Polish Party and government bureaucrats, political officers in the Soviet-sponsored Polish army, artists, intellectuals, and scientists. Their goal was to persuade the masses in both countries that, despite the long-standing mutual mistrust, resentment, and all-out hatred, the two nations shared a common, peaceful destiny as neighbors, friends, ethnic Slavs, and communists.

The task of winning over Polish society to the idea of mutual friendship was extremely ambitious. Russia had partitioned Poland in the eighteenth century and, together with Prussia and Austria, erased it from the European map. Incorporated into the Russian empire, Poles, especially the elites and the all-important Catholic Church, suffered notorious persecutions. More than a century later, the newly independent Poland fought an offensive and ultimately victorious war with the civil war-weary Bolsheviks in 1919–21. Nearly two decades later, the Soviet and German prime ministers signed a mutual nonaggression pact; the subsequent, simultaneous invasions of Poland from West and East in September 1939 crushed the country's overconfident but completely unprepared armed forces in no time. Each occupying power launched an assault against the Polish elites, whom they arrested, incarcerated, murdered, or deported to faraway labor camps. Perhaps the most brazen instance of wartime criminality was the shooting of nearly 22,000 bound, unarmed army officers, policemen, and civil servants. In April 1940, the Soviet security police, the NKVD, put bullets through the backs of their victims' heads in the forest near Smolensk.[32] This hefty historical baggage together with the excesses accompanying the Soviet liberation and ongoing postwar persecutions made Soviet-Polish unity a nearly impossible task. Still bleeding, the wounds of many Poles would take a long time to heal. Yet the propagandists' main goal was to explain to the population why they should now turn this difficult page in history and move on.

From our postcommunist vantage point, we know now that the Soviets failed to maintain their sphere of influence for many reasons. But where culture was concerned, failure was not a forgone conclusion even in the

1940s. The Russian Empire was a cauldron of radical ideologies, but it gave its middle- and upper-class Russians and Poles a common experience of modernity. Empire created a tangled web of enmities and friendships. It meant the tsars, but also Tolstoy; it involved repression through Russification, but it also gave birth to the Ballets Russes. The Soviet state policed and purged, but it also co-opted Sergei Prokofiev to serve its goals. And, along with crude propaganda, it created an enormous audience of cultural consumers with whom the elites from all over Eastern Europe were eager to engage. To assume, as has often been the case, that the moral price of collaboration and collusion necessarily excluded satisfying cultural cooperation is to take much for granted.

Certainly, the Soviets too had myriad reasons to distrust the Poles. Poles were Catholics and Latin, and therefore nineteenth-century apologists of empire thought them to be "traitors" of the Slavic "race." They invaded Moscow in the early seventeenth century; then, in the nineteenth, they rebelled twice against the tsarist rule. Dostoevsky caricatured Poles as stingy buffoons, and saw them as corrupted morally by their Catholic faith. Tolstoy portrayed them as naive, if pathetic, minions of Napoleon, ready to die for the French leader who cared little about them. Gogol saw Poles primarily as oppressors of Ukrainians. In the interwar era, Soviet propaganda depicted Polish political and cultural elites as forces of reaction.[33] Soviet pupils in the 1930s knew *Ivan Susanin*, a renamed version of Mikhail Glinka's 1836 opera *A Life for the Tsar*. Set in 1613, it tells of a peasant who saves the newly elected Russian tsar by leading the invading Poles into a trap. Stalin, a veteran of the Soviet-Polish war, liked this opera more than any other; his daughter Svetlana remembered that he relished especially the final scene, in which the outwitted Poles freeze to death in a forest.[34]

Against these apparent odds, the Soviet-Polish cultural initiatives sprang out of practical considerations, many of which communists on both sides shared. The Soviets had decades of experience of cultural outreach to Western countries. Now, the Soviet side tried to reduce the costs of empire by supplementing brutal coercion with a kind of influence that today is known as "soft power," or "the power of attraction." Joseph Nye, who coined the term, also observed that "although all power depends on context—who relates to whom under what circumstances—soft power depends more than hard power upon the existence of willing interpreters and receivers."[35] Particularly the interpreter, as Marsha Siefert has insightfully pointed out, implies "a person who is willing to speak both languages, understand both cultures, in order to explain one to the other," suggesting that not just anyone can play that role.[36] This knowledge as well as individuals' willingness and ability to convey it to others derives largely from their experience of a political-social-cultural crossroads. As sociologist Karen Barkey observed, social actors who operate at the "boundaries of systems at the interstices of different groups and who can learn from both, connect them, find analogies between them, and exploit the best practices and beliefs of each end up innovating," a precondition of imperial longevity.[37] Such people existed on both the Soviet and Polish sides. They traveled between the USSR and Poland, despite the tough restrictions on international travel; in some cases, they changed passports and national identities as well. By enlisting the intellectual energies of the Polish elite who were sympathetic to communist ideas, Soviet propagandists hoped to gain a hearing with broader Polish audiences. Projecting soft power involved efforts to shape public foreign opinion, popularize the USSR via propaganda, mobilize the masses for the shifting political goals, and legitimate Soviet hegemony. But none of these concepts fully captures the extent to which the Soviet attempt at mastering the power of attraction simultaneously affected—and undeniably molded—Soviet minds and institutions.[38]

Culture was at the heart of the Soviet soft-power initiatives in three interrelated senses. Most broadly, it was an effort to give meaning to the political, economic, and social transformations undertaken under the aegis of Moscow.[39] Cultural anthropologist Clifford Geertz has described culture as "webs of significance" that "man himself has spun," thus suggesting that all human activity resulting in production or consumption of meaning is a form of cultural interaction.[40] Geertz's broad definition frames major questions pursued in this study. In the communist world these webs of significance more closely resembled a tightly woven fabric. The meanings of a theater play, a paper delivered at a scientific congress, a random wall graffiti, and, say, a plaque displayed in a greengrocer's window spoke to one another more directly than they would have in a Western liberal democratic society. For one thing, they were part of one physical space, characterized by the communists' incursions into all spheres of human activity, private and public, as well as their claims to total power over society. They also constituted an identifiable ideological territory, defined by the purportedly scientific, therefore predictable and interconnected, Marxist explanation of world-historical processes.

The communists created and maintained a system in which affirmation or rejection of their power and the official ideology became the public measure of man; privately, and especially in the context of postwar terror, these standards became an inescapable point of reference to all individuals behind the "iron curtain." The philosopher Leszek Kołakowski, himself a devout Stalinist in his early years, pointed to the surreal quality of such a semantically interconnected world. Books of even irreproachably Stalinist authors disappeared from bookstores when they fell into disfavor: "as in all magical thinking," he wrote, "an object connected in any way with the evil spirit was contaminated forever and must be cast out and blotted from memory."[41] This was a common experience. People who fell out with the authorities suddenly felt a social vacuum developing around them; employers fired them for seemingly inexplicable reasons, friends stopped calling, and acquaintances who saw them approach on the sidewalk crossed the street to avoid contact. This fear of guilt by association, even the most innocent kind, isolated people in communist systems from one another but also, in an unexpected way, drew them together via common experiences. As David Crowley and Susan E. Reid observed, under socialism, "everyday life was not opposed to ideological life. On the contrary, it was a fundamental site of ideological intervention."[42] The world acquired extraordinary characteristics under Stalin. This is what writer and son of high-ranking Kremlin official Viktor Erofeev meant when he wrote that "life itself was literary back then."[43]

To Stalin and his East European cronies, culture writ large represented both a fertile experimental terrain for social engineering and a convenient tool for legitimating their power. Theoretically, Marxists understood culture as a broad sphere of human activity distinct from and largely epiphenomenal to the material world. According to the view derived from Marxist dogma, culture formed part of the frothy "superstructure," which, in turn, reflected but never influenced the true motor of history that was the economic base. Some theorists today define culture as a "shared system of beliefs and customs" in a given community, including "higher aesthetic pursuits and day-to-day human interactions."[44] Marxists would have agreed. But they would also dismiss strictly national contours of culture, seeing one's values, customs, language and, above all, consciousness, as determined by one's class—or by one's relationship to the means of production. That view clashed frontally with the traditional Polish approach. Facing the assault on state institutions and their disappearance, Polish elites used culture to nurture the society and preserve national identity.[45] In practice, though, both Soviet and East European communists departed from and adjusted Marx's original precepts to their own needs. Stalin had already reconciled communist internationalism with the de facto mobilizing power of nationalism by the 1930s, and the East European leaders followed suit whenever they could. Challenging an established axiom, the

Soviet leader granted certain autonomy to the superstructure in 1952. In postulating that the evolution of language, in fact, fails to keep up with the logic of economic development, Stalin merely proved the obvious. Most important, officially aiming to "transform" bourgeois mentalities into proletarian ones, communists also sought to create a docile public that would perpetually affirm their rule. For instance, Stalin and his East European surrogates developed their own notorious "personality cults." And although their emotional, quasireligious character ran in the face of Marxism's claim to a scientific status, their transformative yet legitimating purpose was consistent with the communists' revolutionary goals.

Lastly, the communists perceived culture to be the sum total of all artistic output, from literature to painting and opera, to performances of folk ensembles. In the early revolutionary years and throughout the 1920s, the Bolshevik plan to forge a purely proletarian culture benefited from a truly democratizing energy. Marginalized in the prerevolutionary arts market, avant-garde artists such as Marc Chagall and Wassily Kandinsky temporarily gained prominence as the Bolsheviks established state patronage of the arts. The Soviet authorities showered artists with privileges until the alliance between them and the avant-garde fell apart in the early 1930s. Pressured to affirm the Party line above all else, writers, painters, and playwrights who survived the Stalinist onslaught were recruited from the masses and encouraged to create for them.[46] This same tension between genuine democratic impulses driving large sections of intellectual, artistic and political elites, and their gradual implication in harnessing culture in the service of the repressive regime, characterized the situation in Poland after World War II. In the West, especially in America, the transition from hot war to Cold War helped forge an alliance between artists and governments.[47] Artists, shaken by the seemingly indescribable horrors of war, defied figuration; liberal-democratic governments actively supported abstract expressionist art as a freer, and therefore quintessentially "Western" form of artistic expression, as opposed to the official Soviet prescription for party-affirming realism. In postwar Poland, both cultural and political elites willingly embraced broadly understood realism in the name of bringing art to the masses. They, like their West European counterparts, denounced vague abstraction, believing that realism better engaged the pressing social problems of the day.

Culture, therefore, meant stories, tastes, memories, and institutions; but above all, it meant the people who operated within those badly tangled webs of meanings and mandates. The Poles and Soviets who wielded soft power— using culture as a means to gain influence and establish unity—often felt vanquished or betrayed by the very forces they tried to master. This book is about them.

■ This study is based on sources from multiple archives in Russia and Poland. Most of these have never been used as historical documents. In order to provide context, corroborate archival findings, and also to construct a more coherent narrative, I relied on existing literature and published primary sources, especially several collections of documents, a few diaries, periodicals and numerous memoirs.

The book is organized chronologically into five chapters. Chapter 1, "From Sel'tsy to Siedlce," tells of the Polish communists' learning experiences on the Eastern front in 1943–45. Trying to convince the anti-Soviet and often anti-Semitic Polish soldiers that the Soviet-sponsored army units represented a genuine national force, they created a propagandistic formula that would constitute the basis of their broad cultural strategy in the immediate postwar years and an eventual source of conflict with the Soviets. Chapter 2, "Postwar Hopes and Promises," examines the Soviet-Polish negotiations over the terms of cultural initiatives in the immediate postwar years. Despite frictions, opportunities for dialogue and compromise abounded, giving few reasons to doubt that a mutually satisfying approach might be worked out. Chapter 3, "Soft Power on the Sidelines," shows how Soviet cultural interventions, increasingly aggressive and insensitive to Polish conditions, alienated even those Polish communists and cultural figures who were Stalin's most loyal allies. Chapter 4, "Unlikely Heroes," zooms in on Moscow's failure to co-opt Polish officials and writers by letting the latter publish contemporary Polish fiction in the USSR. Chapter 5, "Soviet Soft Power and the Polish Thaw," examines the changes in Soviet-Polish cultural contacts during the immediate post-Stalin years 1953–57.

1

FROM SEL'TSY TO SIEDLCE

We resembled a great laboratory, in which methods for political work of the fighting Army have been worked out. . . . From our ranks arose an entire group of leading state and social activists in the Reborn, Democratic Poland.
—Lieutenant Colonel Władysław Maskalan to Colonel Piotr Jaroszewicz, July 4, 1945

■

The White Eagle flows above us
Our banner is white and red
onto the battle field, the field of glory
our division, forward march.
—Leon Pasternak, "We, the First Division," 1943

THE JOURNEY OF THE APOSTLES

On the bitter cold Moscow morning of May 12, 1943, six men embarked in an open, half-ton truck and sped off toward the sunrise. They headed to the region of Sel'tsy, a swampy pool of the Oka River near Riazan. Marian Naszkowski and the handful of other Polish communists in the car felt tired but overjoyed, thrilled by their newfound roles as makers of history.[1] In a few days, they would be setting up a recruitment camp for the Kościuszko Division. Named after Poland's eighteenth-century revolutionary hero who stood up to the oppressive policies of Catherine the Great, this was to be the country's first Soviet-sponsored military unit to fight its way home under the wings of the mighty Red Army.

Jerzy Putrament's eastward journey toward the red, rising sun constituted a symbolic landmark on his larger political odyssey, which was not unusual for men of his generation. He had been born in 1910 to a "Russified Polish" mother and a "Polonized Lithuanian" father, as he would remind his audiences in future years.[2] Only one year older than Czesław Miłosz, Putrament met his younger colleague at the University of Wilno, where the two began a complicated, love-hate relationship that lasted throughout their lifetimes. In his *Captive Mind*, Miłosz recounted the

Sel'tsy, 1943. Wanda Wasilewska speaking to the soldiers of the Kościuszko Division. Standing in the background are General Zygmunt Berling (left) and Włodzimierz Sokorski (right). Courtesy of Polska Agencja Prasowa.

meeting with the boorish, provincial, and recalcitrant anti-Semite Jerzy Putrament whom he branded after World War II, "Gamma, A Slave of History." Miłosz felt offended "by his behavior, his piercing voice—he just did not know how to speak in a normal tone—and by the opinions he uttered."[3]

Putrament's affiliation with right-wing student organizations lasted for only one year in 1930–31; while he himself minimized this episode in later autobiographical accounts, it colored Miłosz's memories of him for decades to come.[4] Putrament had been attracted to the Right for many reasons. He admired the strong, charismatic leader of the university's right-wing youth organization. He liked the latter's clear sense of hierarchy. He had few reasons to sympathize with communism, which, as a son of a Polish officer, he associated with fear during the Polish-Soviet war of 1920. He liked the lavish corporate dress and colorful, bombastic ceremonies of his organization.[5] Putrament claims to have broken with the nationalist youth organization, the "All-Polish Youth," disgusted at the difference between their right-wing ideologies and the brutal methods with which they implemented them.[6] Putrament prided himself on ending his affiliation in

1932, only after it dominated the student political scene at the University of Wilno. For that reason, as his biographer pointed out, it is difficult to read this choice as a result of Putrament's opportunism.[7] It was also a rare moment in which the young writer's independence triumphed over the pressure from a force majeure. By the time the Soviets occupied Eastern Poland in 1939–41, Putrament was a committed communist, surprising the most radical Poles with his pro-Soviet zeal—in one case, trying to convince the poet Adam Ważyk and a few others to sign a statement condemning selected "traitors and renegades."[8] Back in 1939–41, the Soviets had been Nazi accomplices in the partition of Poland. Now the Red Army was defeating the Germans. After the Red Army's strategic victories at Stalingrad and at Kursk many people worldwide came to admire Stalin and the Soviet system. And Putrament, once a bellicose chauvinist turned Soviet collaborator, now traveled east to become a willing interpreter of Soviet soft power.

Besides the chill, their fatigue, and a common purpose, the passengers in that speeding half-ton truck shared a sense of relief. It stemmed from the long period of anticipation that had preceded their journey. Facing an invasion by Germany and the USSR in 1939, scores of Polish communists, sympathizers, and intellectuals chose to escape east, hoping to become useful one day. While some of them ended up dead or in the camps, others saw their desires fulfilled in the Soviet Union. The "Red" L'vov, a former Polish city (named Lwów in Polish) in Western Ukraine, turned into a cultural capital of Poland's progressive avant-garde between the fall of 1939 and summer of 1941, even as the NKVD continued to arrest people with suspicious backgrounds left and right. After the German invasion of the USSR, Polish activists and cultural figures followed the patterns of Soviet relocation into the depths of the country meant to spare the country's industrial infrastructure and governing institutions from the bombings. Many enlisted in the Red Army either as political officers or for combat duties.[9] Others, after months of doing odd jobs, often in remote corners of the Soviet Union, cut their teeth in propaganda work in the Comintern or Polish-language information outlets in Moscow, Saratov, Ufa, and Kuibyshev.[10] Like Putrament, they were able to use their previous experience as cultural organizers, and some made their wartime media debuts. Like an answered prayer, these men at last became useful; the events of the recent past offered them the exhilarating chance to link their talents and utopian dreams directly to the cause of Poland's liberation. The Red Army's offensive in the winter of 1942–43 raised questions about the fate of the continent after the defeat of the belligerents in this war. Poland's central location in the "heart of Europe," smack between the USSR and Germany, suddenly turned it into a focal point of interest for Stalin and the leaders of Western powers.

In March 1943, Stalin gave his support for the creation of the Union of Polish Patriots (ZPP). Led by Wanda Wasilewska, the charismatic daughter of the socialist Leon Wasilewski and wife of Ukrainian writer Aleksandr Korneichuk, the leftist activists spread the word about the ZZP. Stalin used the organization to create an alternative center of power to the London-based Polish government in exile. Ostensibly established on a broad leftist platform meant to represent Poles in the USSR, the ZZP was actually an organization dominated by Polish communists.[11] The organization's press organ, *Wolna Polska* (Free Poland), founded in Moscow, became a creative outlet to individuals who had previously worked in other editorial posts. Both the Union of Polish Patriots and its mouthpiece provided the Polish activists with a clear sense of mission and an unprecedented feeling of cohesion. *Wolna Polska* also spread the word about the ZPP to the Poles dispersed throughout the Soviet Union. Two newspapers, *Wolna Polska* and *Nowe Widnokręgi*, became interactive forums for discussing the role that the scattered Polish community should play in World War II after the breakthroughs on the Eastern Front.

Stalin and the Polish communists worked to create a center of power that would rival the political and military forces loyal to the Polish government in London. A vision for the country's postwar development was most likely still vague in the mind of the Soviet leader. All the same, Stalin saw that a Soviet-sponsored Polish organization with its own military units as a potential asset in at least three ways. First, it would allow Stalin to speak on behalf of a visible, institutionalized Polish community in the Soviet Union during the inevitable negotiations with the other leaders of the great powers over the postwar order—and thus, it would help legitimize Soviet geopolitical interest as a Polish claim. Second, there was a functional advantage to having such an organized political community ready for a potential power contestation in Poland, whatever its exact nature might be. Third, the symbolic weight of associating the Polish left with the agents of victory on the Eastern Front and the liberating Red Army furnished the communists with a weapon against Polish skeptics.[12] The communists could thereby claim credit for the victory. They could also create a visible precedent for Polish-Soviet friendship, thus showing everyone that the impossible can be done.

As they were leaving Moscow behind, Naszkowski felt the growing anxiety that his fellow passengers shared. Given the complexity of the task they were about to begin, their fears were well-founded. The Polish communists in the USSR gained a powerful patron in the Kremlin. Most of them managed to rationalize Stalin's purges of Polish communists in 1938, to justify the Soviet-Nazi nonaggression pact and their joint invasion of Poland in 1939, and even the Stalinist labor camp system. In the spring of 1943, Stalingrad seemed to embody the virtues of Stalinism more than the Gulag reflected its flaws; in any case, the Party knew best what it was doing and, after all, mustn't one break the eggs in order to make an omelet? The Polish radicals' faith in the iron laws of history and in the correctness of the All-Union (Bolshevik) Communist Party (VKP(b)) was matched by their unflinching belief in the infallibility of Stalin. Those few who needed still more reasons to justify their cooperation with Stalin summoned their sense of political realism sweetened by his promise of a truly free, democratic Poland, which they all yearned to see.

The bitter twined with the sweet. No Polish communist doubted that Stalin's patronage would soon prove to be a serious liability. The ambitious young men riding to Sel'tsy knew that most of the recruits they would try to mobilize for battle under the Soviet aegis knew better than to give Stalin a second chance. After marching into Polish territory in September 1939, the NKVD had arrested these future recruits along with 300,000 other Polish citizens as proven or suspected enemies of Soviet power. The captives and their families rode in cattle wagons into the depths of the Soviet Union; upon arrival, they suffered incredible hardship in the labor camps. Their anti-Soviet sentiments and deep distrust of Polish communists were hardly mitigated by their sudden release or by the news of the new military formations. On the contrary, the biggest question in their minds was whether the Kościuszko Division was really Polish.[13] Anti-Semitic prejudice, often intertwined with anticommunist sentiments, was common among these inhabitants of historically multiethnic lands. It rankled them to see Jewish officers in the division. Also, many of the men knew and few doubted that the 22,000 missing Polish citizens—in some cases, their family members, friends, or neighbors—had been murdered by the Soviets in 1940, not the Germans. The recruits had hoped to join the other Polish deportees released on Stalin's orders during the brief moment of Soviet-Polish rapprochement that followed Hitler's invasion of the USSR. Stalin granted Polish General Władysław Anders permission to form an army to be evacuated via Iran in the summer of 1942. Fiercely patriotic and loyal to Poland's London government, the Polish deportees wanted to enlist to fight on the Western Front, but thousands missed their chance due to long distances, wartime chaos, and the obstinacy of the local Soviet authorities. Some people succeeded in contacting the Anders Army on time, but—as was the case with Józef Sigalin, the future coarchitect of Warsaw's Palace of Culture and Science—the enlistment commission rejected them on account of their Jewish background.[14] They did not wish to embrace Polish-Soviet friendship, but they saw the Kościuszko Division primarily as their way to fight the Germans and thus earn their way home.

Naszkowski grew nervous as he anticipated the upcoming confrontation with his distrustful compatriots. There was more though. Like his fellow "apostles," as they later became known by the self-serving chronicles of the communist regime, he was keenly aware that the division ought to become the poster child for a new Poland—a clear contrast to the authoritarian, socially oppressive regimes of the interwar era, yet unmistakably Polish; friendly with the great power in the east but never Soviet-like.[15] Theirs was an ambitious vision: to transform the old Polish society with its social divisions, anticommunist political traditions, and inter-ethnic resentments into a microcosm of a new, better society that would show everyone that a total overhaul of liberated Poland would be possible and, indeed, desirable. Naszkowski, Putrament, and others keenly felt the high stakes involved. With nervous excitement, as they approached their recruits in Sel'tsy, they accepted the hard, cold, heady fact that the fate of this great experiment depended largely on them.

MICKIEWICZ AND BRONIEWSKI IN THE KILLING FIELDS

Sel'tsy surprised the newly arrived men with its onion-domed church and richly decorated window frames—a typical, picturesque Russian village. Yet, filled with excitement at the historic moment, the communist activists tended to see the familiar: the name Sielce (a Polish rendition of Sel'tsy) reminded them of Siedlce, a town back home. Not so to the future rank-and-file soldiers, in whom the camp by the Oka River, deep inside the Soviet territory, "provoked distrust."[16] The military camp lay a few kilometers outside the village. Within days after arrival, Naszkowski found himself standing "with a pounding heart," in front of "a scowling, distrustful, silent crowd of people."[17] In a system that resembled the Soviet one, political officers were responsible for the ideological education of the troops. Naszkowski became one of them. Others included Putrament and Wiktor Grosz, a Polish-Jewish radical activist who had transferred from the Red Army. Their task was to transform the recruits who poured into the camp into "conscious fighters for a People's Poland."[18] The quasi-religious

Sel'tsy, 1943. Soldiers of the Kościuszko Division await the show of the field theater. Sitting from the left are Vladislav Sokolovskii, Włodzimierz Sokorski (only partially visible), Wanda Wasilewska, Zygmunt Berling, division chaplain Wilhelm Kubsz. Second from the right is correspondent Janina Broniewska. Courtesy of Centralne Archiwum Wojskowe, Poland.

language with which the Polish political officers enshrined their early experiences in Sel'tsy reflected their political zeal in working with the recruits and their commitment to the socialist cause. But the references to apostles, missionaries, and converts hardly capture the extent to which Naszkowski and his Polish and Soviet comrades had to transform themselves in order to connect with the skeptical recruits.

Adam Bromberg, the future book publisher, also worked as a political officer in the Kościuszko Division. He recalled his task without mincing words:

> The commanders of units with more expensive technical equipment were so-called pops—Soviet officers carrying out the duties of Poles. They imposed the Soviet style [of command]: the cursing, the threatening at every step and without a reason, just in case. The soldiers pretended that they did not understand the Russian language, and the "pops" did not know Polish, and thus could not do without the mediation

of a political officer. The job of the political officer was also to ensure that the Soviet commander would not drink constantly, that he would not do something foolish, and that he would command.[19]

The Poles clearly delighted in the hilarity of the acronym "pop" (*pełniący obowiązki Polaka*), for the word also refers to a Russian priest. In referring to themselves as "apostles," however, Polish political officers took *themselves* quite seriously.

Major Włodzimierz Sokorski, who became Colonel Zygmunt Berling's deputy commander for political affairs (a structural arrangement also borrowed from the Red Army), arrived in the camp from Georgia a few days after Naszkowski.[20] He was born in Aleksandrovsk, in Zaporozhian Ukraine, to a noble mother and a blacksmith father. He grew up among Russians, Ukrainians, Poles, Jews, and Tatars. Sokorski spoke Polish at home and claimed bilingualism, though Putrament later recalled Russianisms in Sokorski's prose. Spanning the Russian and Polish cultures, Sokorski made a natural bridge between Soviet authorities, commanders, and Polish troops—he was perfectly pedigreed to interpret Soviet soft power, and perfectly willing to do so.[21] Yet there was no small irony in that this child of multicultural borderlands with an aristocratic background was now to promote a vision of a new, tolerant though ethnically homogeneous, classless society. Sokorski's self-described fondness for his noble grandfather Platon Poleski-Szczypiłło, "an extraordinary character," might help explain how he saw his own role in the Kościuszko Division. "On the one hand, a sincere Polish patriot who donated funds for Polish schools and the Catholic Church," he told an interviewer in the early 1990s; "on the other hand, he demonstrated a near absolute loyalty to the tsarist court."[22]

Given their precarious standing in the eyes of soldiers, political officers had to walk a delicate line between affirmations of commitment to the national cause and their pro-Soviet loyalties. In private, they drew inspiration from both sources. Naszkowski thought of himself as a Polish "revolutionary." Chapaev, the fictional Civil War–era Bolshevik commissar in Dmitri Furmanov's novel, served as a secret role model to Jerzy Putrament.[23] Such comparisons would hardly have been comforting to the Polish troops. The idea, in Naszkowski's words, was to strike the right balance between the "flexibility" necessary to attract the soldiers, and "a rotten compromise with nationalism."[24] The architects of the Kościuszko Division had already showcased the Polish credentials of the new units in order to appeal to the new soldiers. The division marched under the aegis of the officially nonpartisan Union of Polish Patriots. The presence of the Red Army officers of Polish ancestry was to highlight the unit's Polishness even more. Another means to this end was to select some Polish national heroes, symbols, and traditions, while scrapping others. Thus Tadeusz Kościuszko and the patrons of future Polish divisions were chosen for their contributions to the struggle for Polish independence.

The eagle remained as the Polish emblem, but the crown was gone, and the predator's hostile gaze turned West, not East, just like the symbol of the Piasts (the first Polish dynasty)—to symbolize the new direction in foreign policy. Wanda Wasilewska is said to have telephoned the writer and leftist activist Janina Broniewska in the second week of May 1943, with an order to design the soldiers' uniforms "for tomorrow." After a mad search through Polish artist Paweł Ettinger's old historical albums, the journalist found the right image: an eagle with open wings, his head turned leftward, signifying the West.[25] Although Ettinger's eagle seemed somewhat stout and clumsy, Broniewska found it practical and down-to-earth. Fitting the troops was her next challenge. Though embarrassed to ask for advice from a fresh convert to the pro-Soviet cause, the journalist-turned-political instructor had to ask Colonel Berling about the required measurements for uniforms. Berling, a former officer in Poland's interwar army, recited the formula in one breath.[26] The efforts paid off, "[Our] first Polish uniforms and peaked cap with an eagle" reminisced one soldier, brought him closer to motherland. "It was an awful joy. We wanted to cry from joy."[27]

This symbolic framework sufficed only for the start. Sokorski, Putrament, and the growing cohort of other political officers were on their own in convincing the troops that they would go to battle for a good cause. The ZPP issued only general ideological enunciations and provided little guidance on the specific argumentation to be used with the new recruits. Likewise, their subsequent statutes consistently summoned political officers to deepen the soldiers' commitment to issues such as Soviet-Polish friendship, the ideals of the ZPP or the Polish Committee of National Liberation (PKWN) and democracy, but provided no precise formulas for addressing soldiers' doubts.[28] During daily conversations with soldiers the political officers had to address the key problem of the sudden about-face in Soviet-Polish relations. In blaming tsardom and the Polish bourgeoisie for the centuries of antagonism between the two "peoples," Naszkowski and others seconded the editors of *Pravda*.[29] They blamed the failed elitist government policies for the disastrous defeat of 1939. The political officers also juxtaposed the alleged cowardice of the Anders Army with the

Kościuszko Division: the former was said to "flee from confrontation with the enemy," while the latter was taking a direct route to the front side by side with the Red Army. The prospect of reaching Poland without making detours must have been no small temptation to those recruits who abhorred the USSR. According to the new scenario, the presence of Red Army officers in the new military unit as well as Soviet military equipment symbolized the disinterested help of the USSR's government; as such, it marked a new page in the history of Polish-Soviet relations.[30]

The predominantly atheist political officers believed in a paradise on earth. To their own bitter amusement, they found that performing political conversions among soldiers involved rubbing shoulders with the Lord. While the authorities banned the official "call to prayer" during morning muster (a tradition in the Polish military), they tolerated religious songs as part of soldiers' unofficial repertoire. Naszkowski's secretary and most of the other new recruits were known to be praying in private. Eager to meet the soldiers halfway, the division's political commanders even fetched a priest. Father Franciszek Wilhelm Kubsz had been a German prisoner until Soviet partisans abducted him and a number of other captives. Realizing that they had freed a man of the cloth, the bearded guerrillas were apparently glad to hand him over to the Poles. The chaplain conducted holy Masses in front of a makeshift altar, initially set up in front of the division's general staff. "Even our bigwigs participated, whether they wanted to or not," recalls Naszkowski, adding that while some shed tears during the ceremony, others "stoically endured it."[31] The irony was great in Naszkowski's case. The thirty-one-year-old graduate of several Catholic schools, having turned to communism two-thirds into his life, now found himself praying again—this time as a sacrifice for the cause of communism.[32]

In their attempt to reconcile the new politics with old-fashioned "Polishness," the communists turned the war-torn marshlands of western Russia into a classical stage. They kept the old national anthem, "Dąbrowski's Mazurka," to underscore continuities with ancient patriotic traditions. Indeed, as a story about Napoleon's Polish legions longing to become reunited with their homeland, it struck the perfect note to the troops in training who were stranded in the foreign land. Maria Konopnicka's somber *The Oath* (Rota) also enjoyed its renaissance as the Kościuszko Division's official anthem. It had been written in the nineteenth century to mobilize the nation against the Prussian oppressors. Now, despite its "anachronism" and nationalistic overtones, the communist activists found that the talk about "the German" who "shall not spit in our face" had useful contemporary relevance—its mandatory singing became part of the morning and evening "apel" starting May 30, 1943.[33] As with the anti-German rhetoric in *Pravda*, the demonization of the Germans helped generate hatred and a fighting spirit, while also diverting attention from Polish-Russian animosities. As the soldiers sought to find and fix their division's identity, they revived an array of military songs from before World War II. *The First Brigade* had originated in Józef Piłsudski's units. Although the work evokes martyrology and heroism, and direct anti-Russian themes are absent, its Piłsudskiyte pedigree sat uncomfortably with the new anti-London orientation. It took the thirty-three-year-old revolutionary poet Leon Pasternak less than one hour to write new lyrics to the song; by cutting some of the pathos and by mentioning themes such as "the shortest route to Warsaw," the division's "courtly poet" helped the communists incorporate this powerful piece of military tradition into the new ethos.[34]

At this highly unusual training camp, the sound of Polish poetry replaced the noise of frontline battles, for in order to help the soldiers "believe in the Polishness of this division," the political officers set up a field theater.[35] With Władysław Krasnowiecki being the only Polish actor in Sel'tsy, Naszkowski and others combed through the division looking for the talented and the daring.[36] The repertoire included recited works of radical poets such as Władysław Broniewski and sympathizers like the lyrical Julian Tuwim (member of the Skamander group before the war).[37] The readings also featured long-deceased classical authors like Adam Mickiewicz.[38] Poets like Pasternak and Lucjan Szenwald, the official chronicler of the division, would write the lyrics to the songs. Adam Ważyk, a radical poet in his late thirties who also worked as a political officer, would prepare the mise-en-scène, while music would come from Adam Barchacz. For people like the actress Ryszarda Hanin, this modest theater was a springboard to an artistic career. For the communists, it was a means of creating a myth of their own success—through stories "about the soldier-wanderer who was being transformed in the division into a proud, conscious fighter for a free Poland."[39] It was also another lesson about how to reconcile multiple sets of contradictions: the old and the new, the national and the international, the Russophobic and the pro-Soviet.

Jan Karol Wende, then a young political officer, later claimed having been reprimanded for reciting to the soldiers the march-like communist and fiercely patriotic poems of Poland's revolutionary poet Władysław Broniewski during one morning muster in the Sel'tsy camp.[40] The Soviet Pole Józef Gawroński took Wende and Antoni Alster aside, at first to tell them he had not had contact with "the country" before the war, but that "after September" he met many Polish writers, journalists, and artists during his stay in Soviet-occupied L'vov. Even though he had never met Broniewski in person, he "knew his poems quite well."[41] But, he added, "the L'vov affair completely distorted my image [of him]. Today someone remarked to me that our army is advertising the poet who left us."[42]

Gawroński was referring to Broniewski's arrest by the NKVD during a staged brawl in Soviet-occupied L'vov on the night of January 23–24, 1940.[43] The poet had been the revolutionary bard of Poland between the wars—the country's Mayakovsky, as it were, but with a nationalist twist. Members of the Polish Left would chant his poems to boost their morale in dingy prison cells. The poet had traveled in Soviet Ukraine during the great famine of 1932–33, a disaster most likely exacerbated by Stalin himself. He then wrote enthusiastic reportage upon his return—pampered during his trip, like so many Western visitors to the USSR, he refused to see the tragic events.[44] But he was also a veteran of Piłsudski's Legions and the Polish-Soviet war; "Polak-Katolik-Alkoholik," he introduced himself to those whom he thought would get the joke.[45] His complicated biography, notorious lack of self-discipline, and rebellious temperament clashed frontally with the mechanism of Soviet terror and landed Broniewski in several Soviet prisons (during his stay in Soviet L'vov, Broniewski was said to have talked out loud about "red imperialism."[46] Released after thirteen months, Broniewski remained a communist but lost his taste for the USSR. He joined the Anders Army—so deeply reviled by the Left—and evacuated to the Middle East. He amused himself and his compatriots with light poems about the benefits of masturbation. His later wartime work was censored by the British government, in order to protect the image of its new Soviet ally. Broniewski roused their indignation, his poems seething with a militant will to defend the eastern territories of Poland against being ceded to the USSR.[47]

Quiet up to that point, Alster then protested Gawroński's cynical stance. He told Wende and Gawroński how he and others had "yelled out" Broniewski's poems while being clubbed by Polish prison guards. He recited Broniewski's early revolutionary poems, while Gawroński watched "with consternation." Encouraged, Wende brought his volume of poems, too, and "Broniewski was again present in Sel'tsy."[48] However much inspiration the two men drew from that passionate aside, Wende's sentiments were wrong. Physically and ideologically, Broniewski was moving ever farther from the camp, and not even considering coming back to the new Poland. But his early poetry would live on in the shadow of early conflicts over the form and content of culture in communist Poland.

"This was totally unlike the Red Army," *Sunday Times* correspondent Alexander Werth opined during his visit to the Sel'tsy camp on July 15, 1943.[49] The Russian-born, British journalist referred to the open-air Catholic Mass that launched one of the most unusual spectacles that the surrounding ancient pine forest had ever seen. The freshly minted recruits of the Kościuszko Division took their military oath on the 533rd anniversary of the Battle of Grunwald, in which the Poles, Lithuanians, and also Russians, Tatars, and Czechs defeated the Teutonic Knights. Thousands of former Gulag inmates, now soldiers in the Soviet-sponsored, Soviet-trained, and Soviet-equipped division received Holy Communion in front of a richly decorated altar. Wanda Wasilewska and General Zygmunt Berling, the unit's commander, oversaw the two-hour parade that followed; Soviet and Polish officers accompanied them on the grandstand, draped with Polish, Russian, British, American, Czech, and French flags. The omnipresent Polish symbols and emblems gave the vigilant Werth enough reasons to see, despite constant expressions of gratitude to the Soviet Union, "no suggestion that this was anyway a Russian show."[50] Impressed at the sight of thousands of soldiers parading in Polish uniforms deep inside the Soviet territory, the scores of once skeptical foreign journalists concluded that the new forces coming from the East were real, strong, and to be reckoned with."[51] Only insiders knew that the military orchestra playing the Polish anthem consisted of recently "borrowed" Red Army musicians dressed up in Polish uniforms.[52] While Naszkowski laughed about it affably over the years, he would also have admitted that the Soviet presence in the division left many of the rank and file ambivalent.

Convincing the troops to pledge loyalty to the Soviet Union and to the Red Army proved to be a challenge for political officers; after all, such an oath institutionalized Poland's political dependence on the great power.[53] Enormous frictions were caused by the overwhelming presence of Red Army officers throughout the division. According to data for July 6, 1943, 66 percent of the officers who served in the Kościuszko Division came from the Red Army. Their percentage varied by units as the Polish formations expanded. Red Army proportions also fluctuated by periods—on March 15, 1945, 52.7 percent of the 29,372 officers in the 330,000-man strong Polish Armed Forces (Wojsko Polskie) were Red Army officers. They constituted 40 percent of all officers who served in the Polish units during the war.[54] Especially in the beginning, in 1943 and 1944, these were often men with Polish names—offspring of Polish insurgents against

Sel'tsy, 1943. The soldiers of the Kościuszko Division are taking an oath. Wanda Wasilewska is standing directly behind. Father Wilhelm Kubsz can be seen on the far right. Courtesy of Polska Agencja Prasowa.

tsardom who had been sent to Siberia and stayed, and children of Polish participants in the October Revolution.[55] One of them, a gray-haired captain, Jan Zawadzki, spoke "immaculate Polish of the past century." He still treasured old editions of works by Polish Romantic poets Adam Mickiewicz and Juliusz Słowacki.[56] By now, however, most of these Soviet officers were well integrated into the Soviet system; with memories of anti-Polish purges in 1937–38 still fresh, they were suspicious, confused, and ill at ease in this strange new place.[57] The sense of alienation was even more true of those ethnically Russian officers without any historical connection to Poland.

From the outset, the large proportion of Red Army officers seemed to contradict the official argument about the "Polishness" of the division. The communist activists explained the conspicuous near absence of pre–World War II Polish officers as due to the "cowardly" flight of the Anders Army to Iran. Echoing the Soviet scenario and contrary to the facts, the politi-

cal officers worked hard to popularize the view that the Polish officers murdered in the Katyn Forest were, in fact, victims of the Germans. While the
top brass of the political apparatus like Sokorski knew the truth, its lower
echelons like Piotr Jaroszewicz simply found it more difficult to believe the
Nazis' story. The soldiers had to make up their minds between the two versions, and heard with horror the gruesome rumors of Nazi cruelty that
spread among the Soviet population.[58] In this context, the presence of Red
Army officers indeed appeared to be a blessing. Thus Naszkowski and
others exploited this ambiguity, also using the Polish origins of many
Red Army officers to persuade the soldiers of two things: first, the Red
Army commanders of Polish origin were the nation's long-lost sons who
had at last become reunited with their kin; and second, the soldiers
should be grateful to the Soviet government for making experienced officer cadres accessible to the Poles.[59] Thus they praised Soviet generosity
and mediated Soviet soft power, yet they simultaneously minimized the
Sovietness of the Red Army officers in their midst. Soviet authorities and
Polish communists generally downplayed their internationalist rhetoric;
instead, they appealed to their citizens' nationalism and patriotism in
order to mobilize them for the war. So at a time when the premium for
one's national identity was at its all time high, these "Soviet Poles" found
themselves stretched between two different worlds. Institutionally and
culturally firmly in the USSR, they now had to expose their Polish roots;
their role as hybrids, the "inbetweeners," "cultural insiders," to use Paul Gilroy's term, was to make the new system work.[60]

Yet differences between the Red Army officers and Polish recruits
quickly made themselves felt in the regimented atmosphere of the camp.
The political officers responded by adjusting *both* sides of the conflict:
through "teaching" the Soviet commanders "about Poland," and "trying to
create a bridge between them and the soldiers," while working on the anti-
Soviet complexes of the troops.[61] The interactions between the two groups
continually caused frictions and misunderstandings that the activists had
to learn how to resolve and also had to explain to the rank and file. The
vast majority of the Red Army commanders had no knowledge of the Polish language and little appreciation for the Poles' national traditions, history, or symbols. Well used to hearing about the Polish "Pan" (a contemporary Polish form of address, but also a legacy of feudalism, aptly rendered
as a cross between "a mister" and "a master") as their worst enemy, they
were now forced to learn the dreaded language (mandatory in the Polish
units), and sing Polish patriotic songs like Konopnicka's *The Oath*.[62] Most
Soviets responded to these new conditions by isolating themselves from

the Polish soldiers. Naszkowski's commander in the First Infantry Regiment, Lieutenant Colonel Vladislav Kozino, preferred to transfer rather than argue with Poles over the need to accommodate the practice of religion among soldiers. Others relaxed their discipline: they took to drinking alcohol or abusing subordinates, thus creating further resentments and creating more work for the political officers.[63]

"WHAT ARE WE FIGHTING FOR?"

When initially asked about the future shape of Poland, the political officers answered the recruits in training somewhat abstractly. Democracy, with wide-reaching agricultural reform in the nationalization of big industry, was hardly a concrete plan, but Włodzimierz Sokorski recalls "our imagination could not reach further ahead."[64] The ZPP's "Ideological Declaration" had been the most-used official guideline for discussions about postwar Poland. It spoke of a parliamentary democracy based on progressive forces, economic modernization and realizing ideals of social justice.[65] But it was disturbingly vague in depicting the political system to be installed in Poland on the morning after liberation. The issue of Poland's future borders, still unresolved by Stalin and the Allies, hung heavily over the heads of the soldiers, most of whom had left their homes, farms, and families in the disputed territories of former Eastern Poland. The anticipation of combat and the steady advances of the Red Army brought immediacy to the questions about the exact shape and nature of postwar Poland. Once the call to military service at the front began, the Polish soldiers increasingly demanded to know more about the kind of Poland for which they would be spilling their blood. By the fall of 1943, a newly created Polish Corps subsumed the Kościuszko Division and several others. The thirty-five-year-old Sokorski became its deputy commander for political affairs. Shuttling back and forth between the Polish communists in Moscow and the noncommunist Berling (the Polish general had no communist affiliation at the time), he also mediated regularly between his military commander and the political officers, the soldiers, and Soviet supervisors, trying to ameliorate the conflicts over clashing visions and interests.[66] Shortly before the Polish Corps marched off to the front, Sokorski the middleman unexpectedly found himself thrust into an experiment in accommodation that set new limits on the margin for compromise and revealed the shifting constellation of power among Poles in the USSR.

The debate about the future boundaries and political system of Poland unfolded between August and November 1943. The political exchanges among the army's custodians have most often been analyzed as a struggle between two distinct political visions: that of the army's military including some members of the political leadership on the one hand, and of the communist section of the ZPP on the other. Yet these exchanges were also important on several other levels. As a dialogue between the military leadership and rank-and-file soldiers, the fierce exchanges showed the urgency with which the former had to confront issues that were far beyond their ability to resolve. On the question of political systems, Berling, Sokorski, and others repeatedly affirmed their "democratic" credentials and fashioned themselves as guardians against both "fascism" and Soviet-style revolution or central economic planning. But in a document called "What We Are Fighting For" (later labeled "Theses number 1"), dated September–October, 1943, Sokorski and Deputy Commander for Political Affairs (and longtime communist activist) Jakub Prawin also suggested that the army would play a dominant role in maintaining a postwar order through a so-called organized democracy.[67] In doing so, they overreached their competencies and created dangerous ambiguities.

The most heated discussions took place only at the top.[68] But Berling and Sokorski also reached out to tell the soldiers something concrete and optimistic about Poland's disputed eastern borders. During a meeting of the division's political department on August 9, 1943, for example, Berling quoted his conversation with Stalin to set the tone of the official propaganda line. The Soviet leader had allegedly told Berling that "if the relations with the Soviet Union are friendly, [and] if Poland is democratic," then two- or three hundred kilometers would not be an issue. Stalin's assurance, confirmed elsewhere by Wasilewska, was naturally ambiguous: he did not specify which one of the "friends" would have to make the compromise. But the anecdote made it onto the pages of *Żołnierz Wolności* on the very next day. Sokorski also used Stalin's statement, though more obliquely, to convey a positive message to the soldiers in the Second Division.[69]

The communists were quick to respond to perceived heresies. Earlier, in the summer of 1943, Poland's chief communist ideologist Alfred Lampe had visited Sel'tsy. The camp, he said caustically (and to Sokorski's dismay), "smelled of the First Brigade more than the First Division," referring to the musical repertoire and maybe the ideological ambiance.[70] Lampe himself doubted the expediency or possibility of transplanting Soviet political culture onto Polish soil.[71] But clearly, the methods used to woo Polish skeptics to the division struck him as extreme as well. On September 28, he wrote to Roman Zambrowski that the very appearance of "Theses number 1" was a very "sad symptom."[72] By the beginning of November, Roman Zambrowski and Hilary Minc, both former Communist Party of Poland (KPP) members working in the corps, repudiated Sokorski's views and outlined their own vision in the so-called "Theses number 2." They vaguely condemned any attempts to impose single-party rule in a free Poland. While repeating many of their opponents' democratic postulates, they identified the ZPP *and* the Polish Armed Forces as agents of "consolidation" of Polish democracy. They cast the communists as champions of parliamentary democracy who, at the same time, would have a decisive voice in defining the country's new course after the war.[73]

The communists in the ZPP also punished the dissenters. By January 1944, Sokorski was released from his responsibilities as deputy commander for political affairs. Shortly thereafter, he was excluded from the main board of the ZPP. Charges against him included "spreading ideological foment in the army," and propagating slogans of single-party rule and "directed democracy," both at odds with the line of the ZPP.[74] He was sent to work at a remote railway station and in 1944–45 was forced into a role of labor union activist in Georgia; according to Jaroszewicz, it was only Wasilewska's intervention with Stalin that saved Sokorski from hard labor or death.[75] As one of the few genuinely Polish pro-Soviet field officers, Berling became temporarily irreplaceable, and stayed on at his post. But politically, Berling found himself increasingly irrelevant. Sokorski was replaced by Aleksander Zawadzki—the former miner and veteran of the Soviet-Polish war (fighting, like Berling, against the Bolsheviks), turned Comintern agent in Poland, now officiated as chair of the ultraclandestine Central Bureau of Polish Communists (CBKP). The Central Bureau, created on Berman's initiative in January 1944, had the goal of coordinating the communists' activities in the USSR, in Poland, and in the army.[76] Having to cosign all decisions made by the General, Zawadzki effectively subjected Berling to communist control.

For those who participated in the debate or watched it from the sidelines, the exchange, or rather its conclusion, imparted invaluable lessons. They discerned quite clearly that real power in this ever-uncertain, changing world ultimately lay with the communists backed by Stalin. The exchange showed just how quickly the alarmed communists in the ZPP were able to turn the dissenting views to their own political advantage. Sokorski and other political officers undoubtedly took note of the dangers of playing the Polish national card. Co-opting parts of the national tradition could be useful in advancing one's immediate goals, but trying to distance oneself from Stalin's center of power could make one guilty of right-wing heresies.

It is possible that the polemic about Poland's future political system had an even more arcane dimension. If we are to believe Piotr Jaroszewicz, who claims to have found out about this hidden information long after the events transpired, the NKVD actively nurtured Berling and Sokorski's military-dictatorial aspirations. He points to the agency's high-level operative Iurii G. Zhukov as a direct source of the misfired intrigue. Zhukov had been Berling's personal guardian during the Pole's internment in the USSR between 1939 and 1941. Zhukov was then the USSR's plenipotentiary for the formation of foreign military units in the Soviet territory.[77] As such, Zhukov accompanied the colonel to the Kościuszko Division where, together with other agents of the secret police apparatus, he held a close watch on the unit's leadership. According to Jaroszewicz, as soon as the question of power in Poland appeared on the horizon, Zhukov (or his superiors) decided to make a bid. The agent Zhukov, the argument goes, envisioned himself as the future dictator's chief political adviser. Had they succeeded, Zhukov would have been the ultimate winner: as someone who had access to a discrete body of compromising materials on key figures in Poland's future administration, he would have been able to wield massive power from backstage.

Perhaps the most revealing and compelling aspects of Jaroszewicz's account are his insights on the attitudes of the NKVD operatives toward the Poles. The secret police agents were well aware of Stalin's constantly shifting policies regarding Poland. They were also the same men who had only very recently unleashed bloody terror against Poles in the Soviet Union at the massacre in Katyn Forest. Strong institutional instincts inspired distrust within the hearts of the NKVD agents, even against the "good," pro-Soviet Poles. In Stalin's Russia today's friends were often tomorrow's enemies and it was understandable that the NKVD men expected shortly to be called to persecute the Poles. The psychological switch from killing to kindness and cordiality was difficult to make. Zhukov (and possibly his superiors) thus appear to have made a double bet: first, on Berling and Sokorski's success in imposing their vision of Poland's postwar order; and second, on Stalin's sanction to another purge of Polish communists in the near future. They miscalculated on both counts, but unlike the political losers Berling and Sokorski, Zhukov denied all involvement in the affair and suffered a minor demotion.[78] It is difficult to tell whether Jaroszewicz's story is true: it is based on compelling deductive reasoning, but little factual evidence. However, if the entire debate did originate as an NKVD ploy, then presumably, both Berling and Sokorski learned through their own experience that Soviet-Polish friendship was a game too big, too complex, and too risky to be played solo.

And the soldiers, what did they fight for, after all? The 11,500 men in the Kościuszko Division left for the front at the end of August 1943, just as the political battles above their heads were about to begin. For now, they were the only ones to face the Germans, leaving the other units behind. The optimistic but evasive statements coming from Sokorski, Berling, and others in August and September would have been an unlikely source of frontline inspiration. At the end of the day, hatred toward the Germans, constantly incited by political officers, and perhaps the sense of a historical mission provided the main drive. Most soldiers' dreams of leaving the inhospitable, foreign land coincided with the urge to reach Poland by the shortest possible route, and to see her free.

One of the few Soviet rank-and-file soldiers of Polish descent, Feliks Opolski, had no clue who Tadeusz Kościuszko was when he arrived in Sel'tsy. The swarms of mosquitoes and forced inertia had made life unbearable in the camp for "politically uncertain" elements near Lake Bornoe. Having earlier been rejected by the Anders Army as a Soviet citizen, Opolski concluded that it was "bad to be a Pole" in the USSR.[79] The Kościuszko Division turned out to be a godsend; he quickly learned *The Oath*, and enjoyed singing it twice daily, hoping that his parents' motherland would offer him a better life than the one fate had chosen for him. Similar hopes drove the thirty-two-year-old Karol Ozimek, a former deportee to Soviet Central Asia, who relished genuine hopes that his material conditions in the new Poland would improve. "They explained lots of things to us during the political meetings," he reminisced four decades later, "but what I liked the most was that once we beat the Germans, reach Berlin, and win a democratic Poland, I will receive land that I have never had, but of which I have always dreamed."[80]

The first Polish soldiers faced the enemy on October 12–13, 1943, at the Battle of Lenino, near Smolensk—a confrontation that later became the cornerstone of the communist heroic myth of origin.[81] For many reasons, the two-day battle turned out to be an operational fiasco, and the division lost 30 percent of its men. Again, Wasilewska's phone call to Stalin and the unit's subsequent withdrawal saved it from bleeding to death. The inexperienced soldiers fought well nonetheless, showing much courage and bravado, many advancing with their backs straight while holding their fire. They were proud to be fighting Hitler's troops side by side with the awesome Red Army. To the new troops in training back at camp, the Kościuszkovites became heroes. For Stalin and the communists, the battle counted as a political victory, because the drama behind Lenino brought much publicity to the Polish units on the Eastern Front. It put them on the radar of Western leaders, increasing the representative weight of the ZPP and giving Stalin a better negotiating position for the upcoming Great Powers conference in Tehran.[82]

ALMOST IN POLAND

The death of the Polish prime minister Władysław Sikorski in a mysterious airplane crash on July 4, 1943, took the political officers in the Kościuszko Division by surprise. Jerzy Putrament claimed to be even more astounded at the military authorities' silence that followed this important event. He later saw it as the first symptom of the evasive "propagandistic style that started to dominate," and that would "cause so much damage in the days to come."[83] The political officers lost even more room for maneuver during the six months after the incident, just at the time when their jobs became even more complex. Following the affair with Sokorski, the communists in the secret CBKP became even more concerned about the potential threat of ideological freelancing in the corps to their own power. Alarmed by the possible consequences of ideological laxity, the communists in the CBKP began, in January 1944, to shape the corps' political apparatus according to their ideological line. While on the surface, the acceptance of the "ideological declaration of the ZPP" was all that was required from potential political officers, the communists promoted many party members into the ranks of the political officers. In so doing, they strengthened their position in the corps by transforming more men and women in the state institution under the official aegis of the ZPP into available and willing interpreters of the party line.[84]

Within this heated political atmosphere—defined by the often conflicting demands of Soviet observers like Zhukov, the Polish communists, and the rank and file—the sheer numerical imbalance between their ranks and the soldiers put even more pressure on the political officers. By mid-March 1944, the entire corps would number some 40,000 troops. As new recruits poured in from the liberated territories, the Polish force expanded by several divisions. On March 16, the decree issued by the Presidium of the Supreme Soviet of the USSR transformed these divisions into the First Polish Army. By then, they were 78,000 men strong.[85] The ranks of the "brain and soul" of the Polish units, as Wanda Wasilewska nicknamed the political officers collectively, grew much more slowly.[86] From only 7 in May 1943, the number of political officers reached 333 in January 1944, with scores of future instructors in training. By May 1944, as a result of more aggressive recruitment and training, the Political Officer Corps would include 1,000 instructors.[87] Those political officers making it through the screening and accelerated educational courses had to double and triple in number to produce a compelling, coherent message that would please everyone.

The Polish units continued to advance west in the footsteps of the Red Army. On train and on foot, they passed destroyed villages and the scorched forests. The freestanding walls and chimneys scattered here and there reminded Naszkowski that "the Hitlerites have been here."[88] By January 1944, the newly trained "Jan Henryk Dąbrowski" Second Infantry Division and several smaller units of the Polish Corps joined the Kościuszkovites in the frontline zone, near the village of Laptevo, in the snow-covered Smolensk region. Marian Naszkowski had spent Christmas there, breaking the traditional Polish wafer—the symbolic body of Christ—with the soldiers, while chanting Polish and Soviet war songs. He greeted the new units a few days later but then had to leave Laptevo for the newly vacated Sel'tsy camp; Adam Bromberg was to replace him at his post.[89] The birthplace of the Kościuszko Division on the Oka River became home to the Third Division in the making, named after Romuald Traugutt, a hero of the January Uprising of 1863; the now-seasoned propagandist Naszkowski was summoned to train new ranks of the perennially scarce political officers.

Between Sel'tsy and Laptevo, daily life in the Polish Corps gave the political officers plenty of occasions to hone their problem-solving skills. The political officers took it on themselves to help overcome the "mutual distrust and disrespect" between Polish soldiers and Soviet field officers, still strong at the beginning of 1944.[90] The Red Army officers continued to separate themselves from the social life of the units, refusing to learn Polish. Many abused alcohol, in part as a response to the strange circumstances in which they found themselves. This, in turn, created organizational difficulties and demoralized the troops. For example, upon questioning, a soldier who showed up drunk to guard duty stated that if his commander Nesterov could drink, so could he.[91] Soviet officers in the Second Light Artillery Regiment drank notoriously, and a certain Major Muzelf, the commander of the Sixth Infantry Regiment, beat his subordinates' faces while intoxicated. "With commanders like this, we shall perish," some soldiers complained gloomily.[92] There is little doubt that many soldiers welcomed the occasion to drink, but the fact that Soviet commanders gave them the excuse by setting the pace made the tasks of the political officers all the more complex.

The Polish authorities were able to send the hard-drinking culprits back to the Red Army, but the scale of the phenomenon left the impression that the lack of discipline was systemic. For those offenders who stayed, communist activists tried to organize free time "to pull them away" from drinking. They tried to "bring them closer to Polish problems and help them in their work as unit commanders in order to facilitate friendships between them and their units."[93] By March 1944, former Red Army officers attended mandatory classes in Polish language, history, geography, and economy.[94] With the same goal and also to "emphasize the Polishness" of the army, the army leadership organized a common celebration of Easter holidays.[95] It is not clear whether this made the Red Army officers feel more at home, but they were impressed with the panache of these religious ceremonies.[96] The political officers' routine, their simultaneous attempts to influence the behavior of the Soviet commanders and minimize the biases of their Polish subordinates, created experiential baggage that informed their later propagandistic habits.

Crossing into the new environment in the Soviet Belorussian Republic furnished the political officers with new propagandistic challenges. In a twisted turn of history, Laptevo, the new home to the Polish Corps, lay close to the Katyn Forest where the NKVD had gunned down more than 4,000 of the 22,000 captured Polish officers. Having broken diplomatic relations with the Polish government over this issue, the Soviet authorities had set up the Burdenko Commission to look into this matter in the fall of 1943. Another strange coincidence was that the Burdenko Commission (composed only of Soviet citizens) announced its findings within a few days after the Polish troops arrived in the Smolensk region. The commission confirmed the official Soviet version of events, claiming that the Germans had committed the crime.[97] The announcement and the proximity to the site of the massacre raised new questions and opened up old wounds among soldiers. The division's authorities managed to pass over in silence General Sikorski's tragic death in faraway Gibraltar in July 1943, but to ignore confronting the all-sensitive Katyn issue while among the ancient trees that witnessed the well-known mass murder proved impossible. As a consequence, the slaughter at Katyn dominated interactions between political officers and soldiers in early 1944.[98]

The political officers thus faced a whole new challenge: how to assuage the Polish troops. At the end of January 1944, leaders of the political apparatus, with the assistance of the NKVD, organized ceremonies to commemorate the victims. The events, which included sending delegates to the Katyn Forest, a holy Mass, and somber speeches, turned into a series of rallies against the Germans and the Polish government in London.[99] Many soldiers who found it difficult to trust the Germans' insistence that the Soviets had slaughtered their countrymen went out of their way to participate—even chipping in their last money for the purchase of a new tank, to be called "For Katyń." Yet a large portion of those who had experienced Soviet camps had reservations about the evidence presented by the Burdenko Commission. According to Zawadzki's report, soldiers framed their case this way: "I was not there, I don't know," adding, "My father, or a relative died in prison in the USSR," as if to explain why they would not give the Soviets the benefit of the doubt. They asked: "Why wasn't there an international commission?" In addition, a "significant percentage" of soldiers continued to declare their support for the London government. Their resentments against attempts to discredit it often went hand in hand with hostility toward the Soviet Union.[100] In dealing with those who had experienced Soviet cruelty directly, or who had lost their loved ones, the political officers reached the limits of Soviet-Polish compromise on the Katyn issue. Not surprisingly the story, even in the version that falsely attributed the murders to the Nazis, disappeared from the official discourse after the war.

Laptevo was an awkward location for another reason. Only three hundred kilometers from Poland's prewar boundary, Laptevo lay in the antechamber to many of the soldiers' family farms. Together with rapid breakthroughs at the front, the troops' joyful anticipation of return further complicated the work of the political officers who had to explain with renewed energy why these lands would no longer mean home. On January 11, 1944, the Soviet government issued a statement confirming its acceptance of the Curzon Line as the future border between the USSR and Poland, thus drawing renewed attention to this sensitive issue. The high diplomatic negotiations about the border continued, and the Polish government in London continued to refuse to recognize the ceding of Poland's eastern lands to the USSR.[101] Unsurprisingly, the Soviet claim to a large part of Poland's former territory "caused quite a stir and difficulties among soldiers."[102] Corporal Więckowicz from the First Battery of the Fourth Armored Regiment expressed the despondence of many: "We are going to have to give up our machine guns, there is nothing to fight for anymore."[103] Others spoke openly about "Soviet imperialism."[104] Even those soldiers who accepted the new borders, largely thanks to the promised compensation in the West, voiced nostalgia and continued to talk about newly liberated

Western Ukraine and Belorussia as "our territory."[105] Some who accepted the Curzon Line recoiled at giving up the city of Lwów.[106] Other soldiers expressed relief at the prospect of not having to deal with "those Ukrainians or Belorussians" anymore.[107] Such attitudes show that political officers efforts to transform the mentalities of the soldiers were partial at best. Xenophobia contradicted the lofty ideals of many communists. And even those soldiers who rationalized Poland's altered borders mourned, at heart, the country's territorial losses. The political officers could see once more that emotional attachments and deep-seated sensibilities resisted appeals to reason, and would not change overnight.

By the time the Polish units reached the Bug River, part of the Curzon Line, two things were clear. The soldiers could safely wager that whether they liked it or not, it was only now that they were crossing the borders of the new Poland. And the political officers knew that a new set of challenges would take over their lives. In this redrawn, devastated country of theirs they would have to prove their Polish credentials both to the new recruits and to the masses of suspicious civilians.

EX ORIENTE LUX

Codenamed "Bagration," after a Russian prince who perished in a battle against Napoleon, the Red Army's summer offensive began on June 23, 1944.[108] The troops in the right wing of the First Ukrainian Front crossed the Bug River by the third week of July.[109] Further north, armies of the left wing of the First Belorussian Front provided cover and support. Selected Polish artillery units participated in the first strike. The entire First Polish Army, now more than 100,000 strong, forced the Bug on the night of July 22–23, in the second strike of the First Belorussian Front. Accompanied by ceremony, the historic crossing of troops met with the strains of an orchestra, their standards unfurled as the Polish population flocked to the river's western banks to greet the liberators in Polish uniforms— the kind they had not seen since 1939.[110] For the officers, soldiers, and local population, the event brought tears of joy, feelings of pride, and the anxiety of anticipation. Most had a sense that their lives in the new Poland would never be the same as before the war. Soldier Adam Bromberg remembered how in the territories surrounding Lublin, "people looked under our caps with incredulity, asking, with tearful eyes, if we were really Polish. In Chełm women ran toward us with flowers, and threw themselves on our necks."[111] But Bromberg, a Lublinite, was tense. He knew that most Jews in the area had been murdered; in his house there now lived a certain

Dr. Milewski, the prewar leader of Lublin's right-wing National Democrats, and "my father's greatest enemy."[112]

For the commander of the First Belorussian Front, Konstantin K. Rokossovskii, the entry to Poland marked an ambiguous return.[113] Born to a Polish father and a Russian mother in the Pskov Province, he had lived near Warsaw as a child. But his Polish was weak and, like many other Soviet Poles in the commanding posts of the new Polish Army, he identified chiefly with the Soviet system he now represented. Having enlisted with the tsarist army during World War I, he moved over to the Bolshevik side in 1917. During the Great Purges in 1937, Rokossovskii had been arrested by the NKVD as a Polish and Japanese spy and tortured, escaping the dark fate of other top commanders only by a hair's width—largely thanks to renewed Japanese hostilities in China. He never mentioned the painful experience in public, but his unflinching loyalty to Stalin came from the inevitable conclusion that his margin for error as a Soviet citizen and a top military man was exceedingly small.[114]

The armies' rapid advance past the Curzon Line radically improved Stalin's negotiating position vis-à-vis the Allies. From now on leaders of the great powers could do little but accept the terms of the Soviet-Polish relationship dictated by the Soviet leader. Recognizing the redrawing of Poland's boundaries according to the anticipated scheme was one of these terms. The deal struck at the Yalta Conference in February 1945, deprived Poland of some 50 percent of its territories in the East, and provided compensation in the West. Three years before Poland's borders would be closed to mass human traffic, the state itself moved some two hundred kilometers westward. Another forced concession was the acceptance of the succession of bogus coalition governments, largely handpicked by Stalin and dominated by the communists. Between July 22, 1944, and January 1, 1945, the PKWN ruled. In January 1945, Stalin transformed it into a Provisional Government of the Republic of Poland, without consultations with Western Allies. Finally, the rigged elections of January 1947—made possible partially due to loopholes in the Yalta agreements—lifted the communists to power and created an institutional basis for the future totalitarian state.

In the meantime, Stalin and the Polish communists skillfully exploited the presence of the loyal armed forces to subdue the widespread opposition against communists in Poland. As the front moved west, the Red Army assumed unlimited power over territories that far exceeded the need for frontline operations, helping the Polish communists set up the new administration. In the summer of 1944, special units of the NKVD began arresting and deporting entire detachments of the Home Army—the actual army of the Polish state—frequently after fighting together on the same side against the Germans. Some 48,000 people were deported to the USSR from Central and Northeastern Poland in 1944–45, about 20,000 of whom were Home Army soldiers.[115] Later, the Soviet-trained, Polish security forces took over the hunt for the remaining Home Army units and other opposition groups, thus earning the hatred and distrust of the society at large.

After the crossing of the Bug, the communists had to shift gears in their propaganda work in several ways. Most important, they had to make the case for their own Polishness and for the benefits of Polish-Soviet friendship to millions of their skeptical compatriots. Both arguments proved a hard sell. The Red Army's defeat of the Germans on the Eastern Front played well into the hands of the communists, and so did the participation of the Polish units in the liberation of its homeland. But the fact that a relatively large number of the top communists had arrived from Moscow caused their Polish credentials to be suspect in the eyes of many. The communists knew that their numerous enemies translated the acronym of their party, the Polish Workers' Party (PPR), as "Russia's Paid Servants" (Płatne Pachołki Rosji). They, like well-oriented Allied diplomats and Stalin himself, realized that they had very little support in Polish society.[116] The Soviet collusion with Hitler in the 1939 attack against Poland, the murky circumstances of the Katyn murders, and the loss of Poland's eastern territories constituted fresh wounds. The planned repressions against Poland's legitimate government institutions and supporters created deep resentments, while the spontaneous violence and robberies committed by marauding Red Army soldiers created a new set of propaganda challenges. Nothing attenuated the Poles' grief over their losses: not the noticeable shift to the political left in Polish society after World War II, not the overall disenchantment with the quarreling and ineffective government in London, and finally, not the society's craving for stability that pushed so many to cooperate with the new power. Instead, a sense of moral outrage over the actions of the communists and the fear of a "new occupation" defined the overall mood.

The officers who continued political work in the First and the newly created Second Polish Army (consolidated, with other procommunist units, into the Polish Armed Forces, or Wojsko Polskie) confronted head-on these novel, more complex conditions.[117] The internal reports of the political department from the summer and fall of 1944 give a sense of the kinds of problems they faced. The documents suggest that the soldiers who had been recruited at the earliest stages, and especially the Kościuszkovites, largely identified themselves with the esprit de corps of the new army and with the new government.[118] Both these reports and later memoir literature explain the troops' transformation by the irresistible power of communist ideals and the effectiveness of the political apparatus. There is no reason to minimize either factor. Yet it also mattered that the most senior soldiers were simply exposed to the communist propaganda the longest. They also had the most time to reconcile themselves with the changing circumstances beyond their control, and to reflect on their prospective careers in the new Poland. To many troops and officers, the chance of employment, privilege, or prestige after the liberation must have inspired as much loyalty to Poland's new masters as did the two-year history of common struggle. Piotr Jaroszewicz was one such soldier who suffered through the Soviet camps, then joined the new military units and enjoyed a stellar career in the communist power structures. A former teacher, he advanced from the rank of private in 1943 to political officer, to deputy commander of the First Army for political affairs and deputy minister of defense by February 1946—and this was only a beginning.[119]

The fresh recruits, on the contrary, presented a new though familiar challenge. Most of them came from the newly liberated territories of western Ukraine, Belorussia (regions of L'vov / Lwów, Tarnopol, Volhynia) and the western side of the Bug River, primarily Poland's Lublin and Warsaw voivodships. Officers in the political department identified "pronounced anti-Soviet and anti-Semitic tendencies" especially among the arrivals from Western Ukraine. These were also the people who found the question of borders "to be painful." The reason was neither emotional attachment nor political conviction, but practical considerations: unwillingness to swap "the fertile Podolian lands" for Western Poland.[120] As a result of a mandatory draft announced on August 15, 1944, the communists mobilized 110,210 soldiers in the territory between the Bug and Vistula rivers in the second half of 1944; they included 84,677 privates and 21,330 officers.[121] On July 30, 1944, the new chief commander of the Polish Armed Forces, General Michał Rola-Żymierski, appealed to all soldiers of the Polish underground to enter into the ranks of the new army.[122] Given the simultaneous NKVD arrests of the Home Army, the commander's decision is difficult to interpret. Some suggest his overarching goal was to create the largest Polish Army possible, believing that the new members could be reformed.[123] A number of Home Army soldiers answered the call. A report from September 9, 1944, written from across the river in a burning Warsaw, described these fresh recruits as questioning the legitimacy of the new government, with "condescension" toward fellow soldiers from the procommunist underground and "surprise" about the presence of Jews in the army; as such, they became another source of trouble for political officers.[124] The latter relied on discussions and persuasion in fighting such attitudes. The chief of the First Army's Political Administration, Piotr Jaroszewicz, explicitly warned against using "methods of police control" in working with former Home Army soldiers.[125] At the same time, they found that organizing symbolic ceremonies and especially Catholic Masses was the most effective way of winning over the skeptics.[126]

Given the long, tangled nature of Polish-Jewish relations, the divisive legacy of the Nazi and Soviet occupations coupled with the official emphasis on the Polishness of the army, the relatively large number and visibility of ethnic Jews in the leading posts of the military units also created tensions. Initially Jews were excluded from enlisting. Yet, they were generally better educated and, as seasoned communists, considered by Soviet officials more reliable than ethnic Poles. They were also thought to be more dependable for other reasons. "We trust Jews more," the recruiting NKVD official told Adam Bromberg in 1943, "A Jew will not go over to the German side."[127] For all these reasons, Jewish officers played important roles in the army's political apparatus.[128]

Jewish journalists also figured conspicuously in the editorial staffs of the division, corps, and army newspapers. Leading figures in the units' "cultural work" were also Jewish. The communist poet Lucjan Szenwald worked as the Kościuszko Division's chronicler; the film director Aleksander Ford headed the Polish Army Film Unit Czołówka (assisted by Jerzy Bossak, Stanisław Wohl, and Ludwik Perski, who were also Jewish); Jan Cajmer directed the division's orchestra, while Leon Pasternak took on the job of the division's theater director.[129] Anti-Semitic tendencies among the soldiers caused indignation among political officers, but many simultaneously realized that the Jewish cohorts in their midst sometimes hurt their cause. To avoid conflicts, Jews were encouraged to Polonize their names. Those who made it through the enlistment commission, remembered Bromberg, "pretended to be Sarmatians" or the mythical progenitors of Slavs, that is, non-Jews. But some failed to put on a convincing act—Zambrowski's pronunciation, wrote Bromberg, "was even more Jewish than my face."[130]

This prominence of ethnic Jews in the political-cultural apparatus certainly cannot explain Polish anti-Semitism. Had there been no Jews in the army at all, it is still likely anti-Semites would claim that the army was a Jewish institution.[131] But the conspicuous role Jewish communists played as cultural mediators between Soviet authorities and Polish troops helped perpetuate the cycle of misperception and mistrust that already characterized Polish-Jewish relations during the war. There was thus a profound irony in the position of the Polish Jews within the cultural apparatus of the army. Since Polish-Jewish communists were better educated than their Polish peers, and more experienced with work in the communist underground—at once deeply patriotic and committed to a Soviet-Polish alliance—these new recruits were well suited to mediate between the two sides. They were the perfect "willing interpreters" of Soviet soft power. And yet, their Jewishness, which had likely pushed them to study harder and embrace the emancipatory communist ideals in the first place, now proved a disadvantage in their roles as cultural power brokers.

From the Soviet perspective, too, the Jewish presence among political officers raised a concern. Vladislav Ivanovich Sokolovskii served as one of the few Red Army officers in the political apparatus. In the spirit of the times, Jerzy Putrament described the thirty-two-year-old captain as "a clever, tiny, blond-haired Soviet Pole from the Minsk region."[132] A namesake of the famous Marshall Vassilii Sokolovskii, the young political officer became both important and visible in the life of the Polish units—a rare photograph of the audience at a performance of the Kościuszko Division's theater shows him sitting in the first row, next to Sokorski, Wasilewska, Broniewska and Berling (see illustration 3).[133] Perhaps the most important of Sokolovskii's functions was to inform the Soviet authorities about the political situation among the Poles. On the eve of the Polish Army's entry into Poland, June 14, 1944, Sokolovskii sent a lengthy report to Moscow in which he expressed dissatisfaction with the large numbers of Jews among political officers. His main argument was that the Polish Army "commanded by Jews" would not be credible to the Polish population. The document is replete with anti-Semitic language and assumptions—including references to "Trotskyists," "careerists," and "Zionists" from the standard repertoire of Stalinist rhetoric.[134] But the Soviets appear to have been really worried: although there was nothing new about the ethnic composition of the political cadres, the report was sent on the eve of the Polish Army's entry into Poland. Various forms of anti-Semitism survived the war in all the European countries where large Jewish populations had lived before the Holocaust; in Poland, resentment and violence against Jews proved the most intense.[135] It was a time when appearing too Soviet or too Jewish—in either case, not Polish enough—would be particularly costly for the communists.[136]

Few more painful and controversial events exist in the history of Soviet-Polish relations than the Warsaw Uprising, which broke out on August, 1, 1944. It was the tragedy of its thirty thousand active participants that in order to prevent the Soviets from liberating the city they had to fight the vastly preponderant Nazi force. Soviet propaganda played up the recklessness of the Home Army commanders, who sent their troops to near-certain deaths, and risked the lives of thousands of civilians. In the meantime, the Red Army stood on the other side of the Vistula and watched the insurgents perish for six weeks. Much of recent historiography focused on Stalin's exact reasons for waiting with his aid to Warsaw, and on the drama of the Home Army soldiers.

Arriving one week after the outbreak of the disastrous Warsaw Uprising, Berling's troops lived through a tragedy as well. A burning Warsaw greeted the soldiers, but they could only watch and wait. Everyone around them seemed to be engaged in frantic activity. The newly recruited Home Army soldiers deserted in droves to help the bleeding capital. Entire units of Home Army soldiers managed to cross over to their side, demoralizing Berling's troops with depressing stories from beyond the river. While Adam Bromberg found it hard to comprehend the unilateral decision of the Home Army's top command, neither he nor his fellow soldiers understood "why we are not coming to the rescue."[137] Many soldiers shared Bromberg's bitterness. "Why are they taking Warsaw away from us?" they asked in the following days, "we were fighting, moving forward, and they turned us back from the very walls of Warsaw."[138] Other troops expressed their hopes that the rescue operation be accelerated; as the political officers learned, "they dream about bearing the name 'heroes of Warsaw'."[139]

During the infuriating and dispiriting six-week delay, then, Berling's soldiers raised unsurprising questions about the rationale of Stalin and his commanders. But the troops knew so little, the political officers found it easy to steer their beliefs toward the irresponsibility of the Home Army commanders who had ordered the doomed uprising in the first place—a view that some soldiers eagerly spread among the population in the liberated Praga district.[140] The soldiers' inability to see the profound dilemma of the Home Army leadership together with the substantial, almost universal erosion of faith in the country's Western allies, who allowed Poland's capital to bleed to death, helped the political officers far more than Stalin did damage to their cause.[141]

In contrast, frequent abuses by Soviet officers and soldiers on the western side of the Bug ensured that political officers had their hands full. In the last months of the war, some 53 percent of the officer corps (15,492 men) consisted of cadres from the Red Army.[142] Only a small minority of them eventually integrated well into the Polish military. Some joined more experienced Polish soldiers and together denigrated the newly drafted rookie troops.[143] The rest isolated themselves from the Poles finding it difficult to adapt to the new conditions, and to get used to the cold welcomes from some Polish officers. The specter of their uncertain futures after the war spoiled their moods. Some officers continued to refuse to socialize with the Poles or to learn the language, or both.[144] In a report dated September 1944, political officer Major Zygmunt Okręt euphemistically pointed out "only partial successes" among staff officers, largely from the Red Army, who "constitute as if a separate group, and their ties with the rest of the officers and the rank and file are weak."[145] Many Soviet officers vented their frustrations by resorting to heavy drinking. Cases of mistreatment of the Polish rank and file by their superiors from the Red Army became notorious; as such, they demoralized the soldiers and weighed heavily on the work of political officers.[146]

Soviet interactions with the Polish population also provided a considerable amount of extra work to those political officers who continued to march on. There already exists a substantial literature documenting this dark underbelly of the Soviet liberation of Eastern Europe. Red Army troops dismantled entire factories and terrorized local populations, often while drunk, by raping women, confiscating private property (bicycles, watches, food, etc.), and sometimes killing those who resisted. While Berling's soldiers requisitioned property from fellow Poles as well, the Soviets appear to have done this far more conspicuously, intensively and frequently. Warsaw was still fighting at the time when Red Army soldiers began to uninstall and ship off factory machinery in and around the Praga district, and confiscate bicycles, food, musical equipment, clocks, and clothes. In mid-September 1944, the weary political officers complained that such acts, together with arrests of the Home Army troops by the NKVD, undermined the work of the army's agitation squads, eroding the otherwise "very positive" attitude toward the liberating Russians.[147]

By spring 1945, Piotr Jaroszewicz had advanced to the rank of deputy chief of the Political Department of the Polish Armed Forces.[148] On July 25, 1945, he received one of the numerous troubling reports that described some of the excesses of the Soviet soldiers in Poland. The chief of the First Army's Political Department, Colonel Władysław Maskalan, described fourteen cases of "marauding and transgressions," adding that they took place on a "massive scale." He pleaded for intervention, explaining that the abuses "result in strong anti-Soviet sentiments, not only among the Polish population but also among soldiers."[149] NKVD arrests of the Home Army likewise left a trace of "deep bitterness" in Polish towns and villages.[150] In a report from late August 1944, Lieutenant Colonel Roman

Zambrowski reported that soldiers had found an image of PKWN members, on which Wanda Wasilewska's eyes had been poked out.[151] Though politically irrelevant by then, Wasilewska's name—and, clearly, her face as well—continued to symbolize uncompromising devotion to Stalin. Hundreds of political officers who worked in the army in these last months of the war stayed on as permanent instructors. They had survived and benefited from propaganda boot camp. Explaining Soviet misdeeds to anti-Soviet Poles left them experientially enriched for the work to come. The widespread Soviet abuses no doubt compounded many Poles' feelings of impotence vis-à-vis the tide of change from the East, thus discouraging direct resistance. But these same abuses also created an enormous political liability for the Kremlin and for the Polish communists, who would then use soft power to defuse the seething resentments for decades to come.

The storied Polish Army led by Zygmunt Berling became an important link between Moscow, the Polish communists, and Polish society on a far larger scale. Scores of people in the new Poland who would be charged with explaining the nature of the Soviet-Polish relationship to the Poles would draw on the experience of the First Army; often, they would be the same people who would negotiate this very relationship with Soviet supervisors and peers. Outwardly, of course, the "national front" strategy designed by Stalin for the communist parties and enforced since 1941 framed the parameters of PPR policy.[152] But with their on-the-ground experience in the Polish Army created in the USSR, the Polish communists and future "willing interpreters" of Soviet soft power relied on their experience with real people and methods of work. Their world became a crucible of commitment to honoring Polish particularism and, more broadly, to gaining a degree of reciprocity for Poland that would persist even in the face of the changing directives from Moscow. Soviet patronage of Polish communists made honoring this commitment hard at times, for purely technical reasons. The first batch of Polish money printed in Moscow in late 1944 contained glaring Russianisms. The Poles' joy turned into horror as they discovered the error that would have spoiled so much of their work—and destroyed the first impressions; that they chose to withdraw the new currency temporarily, and with heavy hearts, shows that they knew what was at stake.[153]

Two months after the German defeat, the Soviet Pole Lieutenant Colonel Maskalan compared the First Army's Political Department, which he headed, to "a great laboratory in which methods for political work of the fighting Army have been worked out." More important, Maskalan pointed out that "from our ranks arose an entire pleiad of leading state and social activists in the Reborn, Democratic Poland."[154] Though Maskalan did not say it, widespread Polish hostility to their rule forced the communists to staff the expanding state administration largely with political officers plucked from the First Army.[155] Some of the top party men responsible for cadres and policies in all areas of the reviving country, including the security services, had served as political officers during the war.[156]

Political officers and editors of army newspapers became instrumental in the administration of Polish culture on all fronts. For example, Captain Stefan Matuszewski, editor of the Third Division's newspaper, became the de facto chief of the Department (later: Ministry) of Information and Propaganda. This was the main information outlet of the PKWN, TRRP, and TRJN between September 1944, and early 1947; its employees, frequently with direct links to the First Army, later filled posts in other institutions administering culture.[157] Officers from the First Army made up the entire team of *Rzeczpospolita*, the PKWN's press organ.[158] Aleksander Ford would become the head of Film Polski, while the "military-civil dual power would decide the future of Polish cinematography."[159] Jakub Berman, who supervised Polish affairs (and therefore the army) in the CBKP during the war was a member of the ruling triumvirate in the postwar decade. Hilary Minc, another member of the trio, responsible for the economy, had also been the first chief of the Political Department in the Kościuszko Division and then a political officer.[160] Berman, in addition to heading up the security police, ruled the culture and security services. He had direct experience defending the Polish communists' nationalist formula against Soviet criticisms in the work of the ZPP.[161]

Following the fall 1943 "theses" controversy and his subsequent demotion, Włodzimierz Sokorski returned from his exile in Georgia in 1945; by 1948, he was vice-minister of culture, and became minister in 1952. Jerzy Putrament served as Poland's ambassador to France immediately after the war and later directed the Polish Writers' Union (first, as general secretary, then as vice-chair). Marian Naszkowski served as Poland's ambassador to the USSR from 1947 to1950, and was vice-minister of defense from 1950 to 1952. Zygmunt Modzelewski, another "apostle," preceded Naszkowski as ambassador to the USSR in 1945. Between 1947 and 1951 he served as Poland's minister of foreign affairs.[162] Jan Karol Wende served as vice-minister of culture in 1944–45 before being appointed as ambassador to Yugoslavia.[163] Another political officer, Paweł Hoffman, edited several cultural periodicals under Stalinism and in 1950 became the chief of the Culture Department of the Polish Central Committee.[164] In 1949, Wende, Putrament, Hoffman, and former political officer Edward Ochab became part of the twenty-two-person Committee for Cultural Cooperation with Foreign Countries (KWKZ), the Polish equivalent of Soviet VOKS.[165]

The poet and noted translator of Apollinaire, Adam Ważyk, stands out as one of the willing interpreters of Soviet soft power. He returned to Poland as a political officer of the Soviet-sponsored Polish Army: "Small, wearing a uniform and boots and a huge Nagant pistol by his side, he seemed like a caricature."[166] Unlike most of the rank-and-file soldiers he had trained and even the younger poets who turned into radical Stalinists during the immediate postwar years, Ważyk came into the corps as a firm believer. He would serve as secretary in the newly reactivated Professional Union of Polish Litterateurs and, in the years following the war, coedited several important literary journals.

In this military laboratory, the Polish organizers of the country's political and cultural life also had ample opportunities to learn how to deal with their Soviet patrons. The seasoned KPP members who had survived Stalin's purges or labor camps were hardly naive. They knew that the facade of friendship covered up a complex web of tenuous relationships that they would have to negotiate on a daily basis. Leftist sympathizers like Putrament who had traveled to the USSR had also come to know the Soviet reality "from the kitchen stairs."[167] Still, the experience with the army was something entirely new. For the first time, the new world beckoned. Eager to seize it, the Polish communists knew they could do so only with Soviet help. Yet Stalin was fickle and far away, and Soviet officials like Zhukov and his kind showed less tolerance of Poles' particularities than did their master in the Kremlin. The NKVD recruited some Poles as informants ("everyone knew about Jaroszewicz," claimed Bromberg); all Red Army officers filed reports to the NKVD; and every prominent Polish officer was followed by a shadow "friend" from the Soviet security police or military counterintelligence.[168] These people made their own judgments, wrote reports, and wove intrigues of their own. They were products of the Soviet system who had a superficial understanding of Polish affairs, cultural idiosyncrasies, and language. These Soviet interventions both undermined the Poles' pretense to independent action and simply proved counterproductive to the Polish communists' attempts to establish legitimacy. Thus, the Poles chose to keep these "friends" at arm's length. As they set out to rebuild their country's life and culture, the communists were open to advice from Moscow. And as long as it did not imperil their position in Poland, they were eager to interpret Soviet soft power.

It took the Kościuszko Division thirteen months to cover the fifteen hundred kilometers between Sel'tsy and Siedlce. Until spring 1943, the village in the heartland of European Russia and the town near Warsaw shared little of note. Barely anyone would have cared to comment on the vague similarity of names. But after Sel'tsy became home to the Soviet-sponsored Polish Army, Poles came to relish the way in which one place evoked the other. Away from home in a suddenly friendly but still foreign land, they seized upon the phonetic affinity to dream the two places closer physically as well. They drew courage from this imagined connection, encouraged by Polish political officers determined to convince thousands of newly recruited Polish troops—many of whom were arrivals from Soviet labor camps—that the USSR could truly serve as their second home. Sel'tsy and Siedlce formed two landmarks on the route of Berlin-bound troops. Perhaps more important, these two locations symbolized the newfound link, even kinship, between the Soviet and Polish nations. The Soviet village and the Polish town also formed markers within the new cultural topography that the political officers constructed for practical ends.

For the political officers, the stretch between Sel'tsy and Siedlce marked the beginning and the end of a two-tiered experiment. One part of the challenge required molding their communist enemies into their friends; the other involved finding a common ground with their foes. How did the experiment turn out? "Flows the Oka flows, as broad as the Vistula," went the famous song written by Leon Pasternak; but how many of the Polish soldiers who chanted it on the march really saw and felt the resemblance?[169] Did those who began to feel at home in the Sel'tsy camp continue to believe it as they watched Warsaw burn from across the Vistula River in August 1944, helpless to intervene? Prevented, as they were, by the Soviet military command from coming to the rescue, how many Polish men suffered for how many days, watching their homeland burn from the viewpoint of their new "home?" Statistics do not tell us what percentage of this army of anticommunist skeptics transformed into hardened backers of the communist regime. But one thing is certain: while some Polish troops came to embrace the new political reality and ideals, others parted ways with the communists as soon as they had the opportunity to do so.

Still, the military cultural experiment proved useful. Experience gained in the Soviet-backed Polish Army shaped the Polish propagandists' initial negotiating positions vis-à-vis the Soviets, having provided them with a sense of what would and would not work effectively to sway hearts and minds in Poland. Hundreds of people in the middle and upper levels of the state and communist hierarchy during the postwar decade had access to the treasure trove of the Polish Army's experience with propaganda between 1943 and 1945, either directly or secondhand. They drew conclusions from this experience that may have been easy or difficult to accept. But in the conditions of a desperate struggle for legitimacy, for the individuals "who made the weather" under the new regime, as Putrament described them later, failing to consider what succeeded, what failed, and what misfired in propaganda work on the way from Sel'tsy to Warsaw (and Berlin) was not a viable option.[170] Both the communists and propagandists drew one sure lesson from their experience in the years immediately preceding the Soviet takeover: in forging the future Polish-Soviet friendship, relating to Polish society was as important as listening to Moscow. Their experiences with anti-Communist, anti-Soviet, and often anti-Semitic recruits sobered communists. They carried the weight of their country on their shoulders. They saw it as a matter of life and death to prove to their compatriots that they represented a credible, truly Polish force. Conversion of the Poles was anything but guaranteed. Given Poland's deeply contrary popular opinion and the precariousness of their position, the future interpreters of Soviet soft power had to get used to the idea that establishing communism in Poland would be a long, gradual process.

2

POSTWAR HOPES AND PROMISES

April is the cruelest month, breeding
Lilacs out of the dead land, mixing
Memory and desire, stirring
Dull roots with spring rain . . .
—T. S. Eliot, "The Waste Land," 1922

■

There are few people here, the streets have been tidied up, the trees are green
despite everything. The shoots of wild vine revived on a completely scorched house;
solicitously, they try to embrace the bullet holes.
—Jerzy Putrament, "Warszawa w lecie" (Warsaw in the Summer)

CRUELTY AND CULTURE

It was mesmerizing to watch Poland's return to life. The revival gave new strength to the exhausted people who set out to rebuild the country. Involvement in constructive activities injected moral confidence in those who would not have fathomed working with the communists a few years earlier. For leftists like Jerzy Putrament, the wild vines around bullet holes in devastated Warsaw contrasted with the darkness of the averted apocalypse; more than a simple vital sign, they spelled a promise of a radiant future under socialism. Henryk Różański still wore a political officer's uniform in the fall of 1944. Informally, he served as Hilary Minc's assistant for economic affairs in the nascent state administration temporarily set up in Lublin. He was struck by the "strangeness" of the small town, which, "removed from the frontline only by 60 to 100 kilometers, pulsated with life, as if the war carried on some place faraway." Crowds of men and women moved through the streets "lazily" and without haste, like "vacationers;" though Różański spotted many soldiers, they no longer carried combat equipment. Here, too, "life was becoming more intense." The daily press came out regularly, cinemas and a theater opened up, as did several restaurants and cafés. The postal service resumed its work and issued its first

Warsaw, spring 1945. Courtesy of Polska Agencja Prasowa.

stamps; one of them pictured Tadeusz Kościuszko.[1] Amid the contrasts and contradictions of the immediate postwar years, most Poles could only guess what the future would bring them.

The exact nature of Soviet involvement in Poland's culture likewise seemed unclear after the war. Earlier in the Sel'tsy camp, Putrament had described Major Vladimir Ivanovich Sokolovskii as a "Soviet Pole." By 1946, the thirty-five-year-old Sokolovskii had crossed back over to the Soviet side, working as a journalist for *Wolność* (*Freedom*), the newspaper of the Northern Group of the Red Army for the Polish population. The journalist's mission in postwar Poland actually threatened to undermine the Polish communists' bid for power. On February 5, 1946, exactly one month before Winston Churchill symbolically divided the world with an "iron curtain," Sokolovskii interviewed the Polish undersecretary of state, Jakub Berman. The official "number two" in the Polish Workers' Party (PPR), responsible in the Politbiuro for ideology and the security apparatus, was the éminence grise among Polish communists. The reporter asked why the local press gave so little coverage to Soviet help in rebuilding Poland's homes, farms, and schools. By contrast, he inquired, why did they give so much attention to the United Nations Relief and Rehabilitation Administration's reconstruction aid? Enriched by the political experience in the Kościuszko Division's Political Department, Sokolovskii must have known the answer to his own question: the Soviet presence in Poland enabled the Polish communists to survive, but in many ways, it also severely cramped their style.

Indeed, Sokolvskii's "interview" was a form of intimidation, an implied threat to let Berman know what some Soviet observers would have wanted the Poles to publish. As a second tier official in the Communist Party of Poland (KPP) who "kept his distance from the Soviet Union" at the time, Berman had survived the purges of the party in the 1930s. He had risen to power after the change of tide in 1941 forced Stalin to look for loyal Polish communists. The Pole's political savoir faire and intellectual prowess catapulted him to the top echelon of the communist elite. Only his Jewish background is said to have prevented him from being offered the top post, though given how comfortable he felt operating backstage, he might have refused it even if invited. Now, as Stalin's trusted man and one of the brightest of the country's communists, Berman was not to be bullied by middling officials like Sokolovskii.[2] At first, before meeting the journalist in person, Berman had responded in writing. Now, speaking "off the record," with his usual self control, the gray-eyed official explained that he could only do so much; after all, some individuals who worked in the press "do not represent the policy of the Polish government on this issue." But Berman went beyond defending himself. It would be "very inexpedient," he said, to publicize the Red Army's help to the Polish population. However, should concrete new cases come to his attention, Berman would ensure that they did appear in the press. The Polish official then requested that *Wolność*, Sokolovskii's Soviet employer, cease publishing articles on Poland's domestic issues and limit its coverage to Soviet internal affairs. Moreover, he suggested, discontinuing the daily newspaper altogether and publishing an illustrated weekly instead might best serve the interests of Soviet propaganda.[3] Berman skillfully used the opportunity to convey his own message back to the Soviet side. His response, measured as an archer's aim, put Sokolovskii artfully in his place at a time when the power of Soviet liberators on Polish soil was virtually unchecked. Though Berman and Sokolovskii may not have shared the same approach to winning over the hearts and minds of the Polish masses, they were still able to engage in a dialogue concerning the differences that divided them.

Though there was nothing dull about the winter of 1944–45 on the Eastern Front, the immediate postwar years in Poland resembled T. S. Eliot's April. Having survived six years of brutal German occupation, Poles now mixed memories of wartime hardships, suffering, and sacrifice with the euphoria of their newly gained freedom, and with joyful anticipation for a better future. In the official communist parlance, the country was a

"People's Democracy"—a left-wing coalition government distinct both from "bourgeois" and Soviet forms of rule.[4] In 1944–46, several political groups competed for the right to lead the effort of physical, social, and economic reconstruction. Most Poles hoped that the far-reaching reforms promised by each would eventually bring a more egalitarian and prosperous society than the one that the Nazis had ripped apart and driven underground in September 1939. Over time, such hopes led many to accept more easily the inevitability of communist rule.

But as they sought to monopolize power in Poland, the communists resorted to cruelty—a physical reality in the East European wasteland of 1944–47—and to many people, cruelty spoke louder and meant much more than political bantering and conflicted states of mind. The Polish communists enjoyed the vast advantage of Stalin's patronage. The Soviet leader had provided those who fled to the USSR with material and institutional support; he gave them the Kościuszko Division-turned-Polish Army, which helped liberate Poland and fought in the battle of Berlin. He personally crafted the Polish Committee of National Liberation (PKWN), which in early 1945 transformed into the Provisional Government of the Republic of Poland, and, in so doing, he secured the power ministries for his most trusted communist activists. But like them, the Soviet leader realized that the communists' position in society was precarious. Members of armed anticommunist resistance, "the forest boys," attacked communists, Soviet officials, and sometimes Jews, whom they associated with Soviet power. Thousands of partisans were grouped into dozens of paramilitary organizations, which included the demobilized Home Army soldiers and several extreme right-wing formations. Like Maciek, the hero of Jerzy Andrzejewski's novel *Ashes and Diamonds* (later turned into a film by Andrzej Wajda), they heroically claimed their vision of a noncommunist Poland on moral grounds. The NKVD detachments actively hunted down the armed opposition. In responding to these desperate acts of terrorism with terror of their own, they perpetuated a vicious cycle of violence. They also further damaged the reputation of Polish communists even as they helped them to achieve the preponderance of power in the war-ravaged country.

The victorious Red Army units played a key role in the communist takeover as they secured the liberated territories and handed them over to the communists. Some marauders also raped and pillaged, evoking widespread public outrage. Having spent the war in occupied Poland, the leader of the PPR (a de facto reactivated KPP), Władysław Gomułka, knew that overt Soviet support and its unintended consequences weighed down the communists' claim to be an independent force, a precondition for public legitimacy. In 1944, writing to the chief of the recently abolished Communist International, Georgii Dimitrov, Gomułka pointed out that "the mistakes that the Soviet organs have committed with regard to the Poles (deportations) have influenced public opinion . . . ; given these attitudes, there is a danger that we might be accused of being Soviet agents and subjected to isolation."[5] Soviet leaders understood their Polish comrades' dilemmas, but the best they could do was to dress up the sinister NKVD troops as Red Army soldiers in the spring of 1946.[6] By the end of the war, the communists found themselves in a double bind: they depended on Soviet help, but publicly had to dissociate themselves from it in order to maintain their Polish credentials. Many communists remembered this dilemma from the laboratory setting of the Soviet-sponsored Polish Army, in which even the skeptics depended on them for a return to Poland. Now they had to face doubts and hatred from a population of twenty-four million.[7] Grim realists, the ruling communists knew that relinquishing violence amid the real-life, bloody struggle for survival would be difficult.

As Soviet-trained and supervised Polish security forces increasingly took over the fight against the resistance from the Soviets, a full-scale civil war ensued. Under Berman's Politbiuro, overseen and directed by Stanisław Radkiewicz, a Kościuszko Division veteran, in 1944–48 the newly created Bureau of Public Security arrested tens of thousands of people.[8] Ostensibly created to provide security, the communists used it to hunt down opposition members. The creators of the notorious security apparatus recruited new employees largely from the *Armia Ludowa* (People's Army, or AL), the demobilized communist underground resistance force.[9] The institution offered new possibilities of social advancement to the previously disadvantaged peasants and workers. It allowed them to move to towns, gain minimal education, and improve their material lot. It also opened up new opportunities to remaining ethnic Jews, who had been second-class citizens before the war. Some communists may have deliberately placed Jews in prominent leadership positions in order to channel anticommunism into anti-Semitism.[10] Others, aware of Polish anti-Semitism, may have considered Jews in the security force as more reliable employees.[11] And some Jews may have sought access to power partially out of hatred for the anti-Semites.[12] But one suspects that many communists—Soviet and Polish—would have preferred to build Polish communism without Polish Jews, had there been such an option.[13] As in the Soviet-sponsored Polish Army, the relatively large numbers of ethnic Jews, especially in the higher echelons of the party and the security police, weighed down the communists' efforts to legitimate themselves.[14] As in Hungary at that time, the ethnic composition of communist institutions contributed to the misperception that the political conflict between communists and the society at large ran along ethnic lines, which further discredited the regime.[15] Fear mixed with bias, and distrust toward Jews came in many variants. As Krystyna Kersten observed, many people did not think that "the Jew was the enemy" per se; what irked them was that "the enemy was a Jew."[16] At the same time, the Jewish prominence in communist power structures easily played into the hands of vocal conspiracy theorists who equated Jews with communism and vice versa.[17]

In short, the Polish communists correctly saw a direct correlation between their ability to cast themselves as an autonomous political force, friendly with but independent from Moscow, and their popular legitimacy. Hoping to relax the tense political atmosphere and even win the elections to the Sejm scheduled for early 1947, they had to tread carefully the hair-thin line between public affirmations of friendship with the Soviet Union and what might be seen as endorsements of the Soviet way of life. They felt dismayed by the uncurbed activities of the NKVD in Poland; repeatedly, they complained directly to Stalin about the crimes committed by Red Army soldiers and about insufficient consideration for Poland's national economy.[18] In the case of *Wolność*, the medium was the message: as an undisguised Soviet commentary on Polish affairs, it begged the obvious questions about the Kremlin's intentions in Poland and about the scale of Soviet meddling in Polish culture. Its publisher, the Red Army's Political Department, also drew unwelcome attention to the ambiguous presence of Soviet troops in Poland.

Audaciously, Edward Osóbka-Morawski, the Polish prime minister and member of the Polish Socialist Party (PPS), had telephoned Marshal Konstantin Rokossovskii, the commander of the Northern Group of the Red Army earlier in 1945 with the request to shut down cancel the newspaper.[19] More remarkably, Berman, a member of the PPR's Politbiuro, did so at least twice. A month after his conversation with Sokolovskii, he petitioned the Soviet ambassador Lebedev directly.[20] Having overseen the Polish Army in the Soviet Union as member of the Central Bureau of Polish Communists, Berman knew better than his Soviet interlocutors about how to appeal effectively to his countrymen during this moment of political transition. More important, as a trained lawyer with intimate knowledge of the Soviet context, Berman also knew where to stop. After an NKVD general had once kindly offered to let Berman "see for himself" the good conditions enjoyed by the arrested Home Army soldiers in Soviet camps, Berman, who was concerned about the effect of the arrests on Polish public opinion, fell silent.[21] But this time, as he considered the fate of *Wolność*, no such threat hung over him, and though Berman promised to renew the contract, he possessed the means to renege on it by taking the confrontation behind the scenes.

The Soviet military administrators perceived these Polish attempts to close *Wolność* as "harmful." Doing so, they argued, would not only have vindicated the "anti-Soviet elements," it would also have left the aggressive Western press with no Soviet counterpoint. Having cornered Berman into renewing the publishing contract, Lebedev and his colleagues seemed unconvinced that the paper had harmed the communists' cause in Poland. Ultimately, the Soviets chose also to distribute the newspaper through their own channels: the publisher and the commandants' offices.[22] These military institutions dispersed all across Poland were officially charged with securing frontline communication, but in fact actively took part in setting up the new communist administration.[23] Set on reaching the Polish public on their own, the distributors of *Wolność* sometimes came into conflict with the provincial administration by forcing it to buy large quantities of the paper and distribute them at the latter's own expense. The commandants' offices set up their own newspaper kiosks to sell Polish newspapers at a higher price because they included a "free" copy of *Wolność*. These were often the Polish newspapers, such as *Życie Warszawy* (*Warsaw Life*), which they had obtained free of charge from the local distributor. Provincial officials complained to the Ministry of Propaganda and Information that Soviet officers distributed copies of the newspaper in local cafés, demanding advance payments.[24] Overtly intervening in Polish press politics, the Soviet officials were undercutting the cause of Polish communists on all levels. The Poles had reasons to obstruct Soviet efforts in return.

By the time Berman pleaded with Lebedev over *Wolność*, Churchill had publicly captured East-West tensions by speaking out about "the iron curtain." The metaphor was apt: it evoked isolation, iron, and Stalin—the "man of steel" who stood behind them.[25] But in compartmentalizing developments in the Soviet sphere of influence into a uniform pattern, the figure of speech glossed over internal schisms between ostensive Soviet Bloc allies in the cultural sphere. It failed to capture the sense of indeterminacy that characterized the relationships in the East. Soviet and Polish propagandists, ostensibly together on the path toward socialist transformation, had a long way to travel before understanding each other. They also had reasons to think and hope that despite their differences, a mutually satisfying approach to Soviet soft power could eventually be worked out.

As historian Wiesław Władyka wrote recently, in the Polish mass media before 1948, "Two Polands battled against each other . . . one that wanted to continue [the traditions of] the Second Republic, and one that desired its revolutionary destruction."[26] That black-and-white picture captures the basic contours of a well-known story. Yet a closer look reveals that Soviet interventions forced Polish newspapers editors to negotiate a variety of visions for postwar Poland. Whether printed or withheld from publication, stories about the future of the Soviet-Polish relationship came in many tones of gray.

Soviet efforts to reach Polish audiences through the press in the immediate postwar years extended well beyond haggling over the distribution of the Red Army's *Wolność*. Besides policy "recommendations" at top government and party levels, they included a network of mid-level government, social, and cultural institutions such as Glavlit (censorship), the Telegraph Agency of the Soviet Union (also known as TASS); the All-Union Association Mezhdunarodnaia kniga (MK) charged with distribution of Soviet newspapers; the All-Union Society for Cultural Relations Abroad (or VOKS); the Red Army's Political Department, as well as the Soviet Information Bureau. Most of these institutions cooperated with one another or exchanged staff members on initiative from above. The Soviet embassy in Poland provided some administrative and political support to these organizations, mostly through the offices of its secretaries and cultural advisors, who also communicated Moscow's policy "suggestions" to cultural and political leaders.

Major K. I. Orlov worked as a representative of the Soviet Information Bureau (Sovinformbiuro) in Poland. Distinct from the similar-sounding Communist Information Bureau (established in 1947), the Sovinformbiuro was the most important channel of Soviet intervention in Polish mass media in terms of size, scope, continuity, and political weight. Established on June 24, 1941, two days after Hitler's invasion of the Soviet Union, its responsibilities included informing Soviet audiences about developments at the front, informing foreign audiences about life in the Soviet Union and the war effort, countering Nazi propaganda, and providing financial and organizational support to five antifascist committees.[27] After a number of structural changes, in 1945 the Sovinformbiuro consisted of sixteen departments. It employed 350 people on a full-time basis and 161 field correspondents, a number that remained roughly the same during the following decade.[28] Among them were the brightest stars of Soviet journalism and literature, such as I. Ehrenburg, B. Polevoi, K. Simonov, M. Sholokhov, V. Grossman, M. Shaginian, N. Tikhonov, and many others. In addition, the organization worked with about 1,500 freelance authors, about 100–140 per individual department.[29] In January 1945, the Sovinformbiuro produced materials for Soviet diplomatic posts, its own field offices, and local social organizations in 42 countries and a year later in 55 countries.[30]

In 1945, the Central Committee of the All-Union (Bolshevik) Communist Party (henceforth, VKP(b)), restructured the Sovinformbiuro to serve the goals of Soviet foreign policy.[31] Besides intelligence gathering, which officially became the organization's responsibility only in 1947, changes included new departments for socialist countries. The Sovinformbiuro's goals, as outlined in June 1945, were: "To inform foreign audiences about the political and economic life of the USSR, about the national, social, and cultural achievements of its peoples as well as propaganda to convey Soviet views of the more important questions of international life."[32] The Sovinformbiuro was to mold foreign public opinion.

While the departments working for capitalist countries were much bigger, large issues were also at stake for those working in the Soviet sphere of influence. "We should take particular care," continued the authors of the restructuring document, "to inform about these issues: government propaganda organs, democratic organizations, and the press in Finland, Poland, Czechoslovakia, Romania, Bulgaria, Yugoslavia, as well as press organs in Germany."[33] The managers of the Sovinformbiuro tried to accomplish this goal by placing their own news articles in local foreign presses through the institutional field offices.

Sovinformbiuro's field office in Poland was set up in 1944 and began working at top capacity in 1945. A "Department of Poland and Czechoslovakia" was created in Moscow in February 1945 to serve offices in both countries, as well as newspapers published by the Red Army and, to a lesser extent, Polish radio.[34] The institution's work was structured vertically. The organization's representative in Poland reported to the head of "his" department in Moscow. Simultaneously, he implemented his superior's decisions and advised him on their feasibility. The department heads as a rule reported to the deputy director of the Sovinformbiuro in Moscow. At the top of the chain of command was the director of the agency who made his decisions on the basis of general policy and consulted with the Central Committee.[35]

Writing to Solomon Lozovskii, his boss and the director of the organization at the end of 1946 (and, simultaneously, deputy minister of foreign affairs), Orlov reported that in following the general directives, he worked throughout the year to: "continually suggest to the Poles the thought that only in friendship with the USSR will they achieve peace and economic prosperity, that any other path spells trouble for them; . . . to promote the economic and military power of the USSR; to dispel the slanderous statements about the backwardness of the Soviet culture and technology; . . . to navigate political reefs, in order not to complicate the situation of the PPR with insufficiently considered articles (keeping in mind the question of the collective farms, life in L'vov, etc.); and to unmask the reactionary essence of the Anglo-Saxons' foreign policy."[36]

Orlov captured well the Sovinformbiuro's general goals in Poland for the half decade after the war, that is, to use the press to convince Poles to look eastward for comfort and for an inspiring example in rebuilding their lives, culture, and economy from the ruins of war.[37] He also aptly described some of the major constraints on the full popularization of the Soviet Union in the Polish press as well as the political difficulties inherent in postwar Poland. The sensitive questions included Poland's loss of its eastern territories and cultural centers, such as the cities Wilno and Lwów (rendered later in Russian as Vil'na and L'vov), and the prospect of Soviet collective farms, word of which trickled across the border. The Sovinformbiuro officials correctly surmised that mentioning collective farms would be seen as an attempt to impose the most unpleasant aspects of the Soviet system in Poland. In 1945, Orlov included the collective farms among unacceptable materials. He explained that, "The collective farm is a bugbear with which the Home Army (AK) is scaring the Polish peasant. It is too early in my opinion to explain the role of the collective farms. It could bring the opposite results. Consequently, I ask that you avoid the terms 'collective farms,' 'collective farm workers,' and so on. Instead, write 'peasants,' 'villages,' 'peasant farms,' and so on."[38]

Orlov speculated, at the end of 1946, that the circumstances for publishing material on the collective farms would become "more favorable" after the elections to the Sejm in 1947.[39] Stalin officially opposed introducing collective farms in the new satellite states until the fall of 1947. The local communists adopted the policy in 1948–49 and began implementing it only in 1950.[40] Aware that collectivization was a sensitive issue in Poland, Orlov had made efforts to alert the seemingly indiscriminate bureau in Moscow to this fact; in so doing, he took on the role of a "willing interpreter" of Soviet soft power. Another compromise Orlov requested was a temporary concession to the Poles' reading habits and traditional anti-Soviet bias. The Polish intelligentsia, explained Orlov, "consider us Russians to be Asians, and themselves to be the bearers of high Western culture."[41] For that reason, he added, the concept of the friendship of the Slavic countries was very unpopular among them. Slavic friendship was one of the official slogans under which Stalin consolidated his empire in East-Central Europe. Consequently, Orlov suggested avoiding explicit praise of the Soviet government so that the intelligenstia would not be put on guard. The Sovinformbiuro, he suggested, also had to consider the population at large, which the interwar government had been "poisoning" with anti-Soviet "slander."[42]

To wean the Poles from their anti-Soviet notions, Orlov suggested first sending general articles to "familiarize the Polish reader with how the USSR had grown stronger, with our economy, strength of the Red Army, our attitude toward the 'little peoples' and so on," and to complement these with current news about the USSR.[43] In addition, Orlov requested that Moscow avoid sending articles by authors with Jewish names or at least to provide their pen names, since "anti-Semitism has deep roots here" and might thus be an obstacle in promoting the Soviet Union.[44] The form of delivering the news also had to be changed: after "hundreds" of meetings with editors in 1946, Orlov advised the Moscow office that the "political immaturity" of the Polish reader required the articles to be short, clear, and full of examples.[45] The Soviets continued the tactics of adjustments later, as they tried to gain the sympathy of new groups of readers, such as peasants or women, by catering to their interests and reading habits.[46] But Soviet officials from other East European countries were also pleading for help. Valerian Zorin, then ambassador to Czechoslovakia, remarked in June 1947, that Sovinformbiuro's articles were of such low quality, "that they are barely used even by the leftist press."[47]

Certainly, Orlov's main concern was to avoid topics that might cause Polish communists to lose potential votes. The major was no fighter for freedom of the press; indeed, when Soviet observers in Poland supported the notion that the press should be centralized on the Soviet model, Orlov came close to condoning it explicitly.[48] Yet, however temporary and interested his approach may have been, the Soviet official's ability and willingness to see things from another perspective constituted a remarkable phenomenon. Soviet officials' actions in Eastern Europe after the war often hurt the Soviet cause. In particular, their insistence on implementing Soviet institutional structures and cultural practices has been explained as their inability to imagine another way of organizing a society.[49] Orlov's keen insights suggest that at least some Soviets imagined alternatives to blind Sovietization. He and others like him embodied the human potential for turning Soviet soft power into a force that carried genuine appeal to the Poles. Moscow was not ready to listen.

Yet, in his efforts to implement this surprisingly nuanced approach to the Polish press, Orlov faced two chief difficulties. The first stemmed out of the Soviet inability to deliver high-quality materials. This impotence, in turn, reflected staffing shortages caused by the war and, no doubt, the priorities of the Soviet authorities during the period of transition from war to peace. During the postwar years, Sovinformbiuro officials had to grapple with their organization's internal deficiencies as did others working in Soviet institutions whose purpose was to shape foreign opinion.[50] Officials at all levels of the organization realized how poorly the Soviet Information Bureau was faring in comparison with Western channels of propaganda and information, including in the sensitive region of East-Central Europe.[51] Orlov's personal problem was his inability to read Polish, which prevented him from translating the Soviet articles himself or fully appreciating the character of the Polish press. Inadequate funds precluded hiring more translators, which impeded the distribution of the articles among provincial newspapers, whose staffs did not know Russian. The articles that arrived in Russian—about two-thirds of the total in mid-1946—were often badly written.[52] Often transmitted by teletype, they frequently contained typographical errors. If they were shipped by plane instead, they were notoriously late. At best, all these factors rendered the Soviet articles old news. At worst, they turned them into poor reading material. In either case, Sovinformbiuro's institutional inertia combined with bad timing impeded Orlov's plans for capturing the hearts and minds of Polish audiences and gave Polish communists plenty of excuses to get their news from elsewhere.

Orlov's second problem was that in trying to improve the appeal and long-term effectiveness of Soviet press propaganda in Poland, he had turned his face against the prevailing political winds back home. Increasingly at the time, Soviet institutions were subject to purges; fear of repressions for unsolicited action effectively discouraged independent initiative in the bureaucratic ranks. Soviet society at large became the target of a mounting nationalist propaganda that sought to eradicate empathy toward foreigners. So despite his appreciation for Polish sensibilities, and often against his better judgment, Orlov had little choice but to prioritize his second, overarching goal: getting as many articles into Polish newspapers as possible. This must have been an incredibly frustrating process since the more Orlov pressured the Poles into accepting Soviet articles, the more likely he was to convey the impression that Soviet demands were unreasonable.

Yet many of Orlov's Polish editors—lacking their communist bosses' years of training in the Comintern—still honored prewar notions of journalistic professionalism and the nationalist formula that worked in the Polish Army commanded by Zygmunt Berling. These editors resisted Orlov's efforts to plant Soviet articles in the Polish press.[53] The political climate in Poland was conducive to such independent initiatives. Between 1945 and 1947 the press was relatively free, though even then the communists actively strove to control it as much as possible without losing their official democratic credentials. They had the advantage of controlling paper distribution, which enabled them to severely restrict the press of the Polish Peasant Party, their chief competitor.[54] The national market was dominated by newspapers of various parties, mostly the PPR and PPS, as well as the cooperative Czytelnik (the Reader). The latter was set up by the PPR as a tactical move to win over the noncommunists; as such, it promoted a broad range of democratic ideals until its submission to the party line in 1948.[55] There were also numerous local publications that retained some independence longer than the larger central ones.

Most often, editors refused Soviet material citing the potential political risk of provoking Polish readers. In October 1946, for instance, Orlov reported to Moscow that he had recently met with Wiktor Borowski, the editor of Czytelnik's central organ *Życie Warszawy*. When Orlov asked why the Sovinformbiuro's materials had disappeared from Borowski's paper, the Pole replied with the "theory" that avoiding articles about the USSR could help "neutralize" the petty merchant before the elections to the Sejm.[56] This was a common excuse for rejections. Referring to Roman Werfel, the editor of the central organ of the PPR *Głos Ludu* (People's Voice), Orlov observed that he "is as scared of the anti-Soviet citizen as the devil is of incense."[57] At a time when excessive tolerance toward foreigners could have earned any Soviet official a demotion or a jail sentence, Orlov's militant language can be seen as a safety net. But it could just as well have arisen from genuine frustration with those Poles who seemed to surreptitiously undermine the Soviet official's work.

The powerful editor and director of Czytelnik, Jerzy Borejsza, embodied a chief obstacle to Orlov's mission. Having worked in the propaganda apparatus of the Union of Polish Patriots, and served as captain in the Red Army during the war, Borejsza arrived in Poland on August 1, 1944. Initially he chaired *Rzeczpospolita* (The Republic), an organ of the PKWN;

like all other members of the editorial staff, Borejsza wore the uniform of the political officer of Berling's Army.[58] A committed communist with connections to the top PPR officials, Borejsza embraced an independent vision of a nonviolent, "gentle" revolution in culture. Its goal was to be the creation of a new socialist society, but without the excesses and bloodshed that characterized the Bolshevik power grab. This seeming contradiction reflected the larger contrasts of life in postwar Poland. When Jerzy Putrament, his deputy at the journal, talked about his boss's "triple and quadruple life," he captured the impressions of many other contemporaries who admired his natural, stupendous energy.[59] Adam Bromberg remembered that "Borejsza had seven telephones, three government lines, two secretaries, while he worked eighteen hours per day." No matter the hour, a visitor would see him with a phone receiver in his hands, often bragging that he "must call Jakub, Bolesław, Wiesław."[60] That energy partially reflected Borejsza's nature, but it also stemmed from the man's genuine hopes for achieving a better society through culture—a socialist, non-Soviet society to be built with a degree of Soviet support. Borejsza cultivated his larger-than-life image of Polish culture's powerful éminence grise. He used his position as a middleman in several ways. Known as a man who could get things done for his writer friends and for strangers seeking employment whom he came to like, Borejsza could also be obstructionist, occasionally depriving the more radical communists of printing paper, which he hoarded for his own publications.[61] He employed several former Home Army officers in the crucial areas of his enterprise, such as management, printing, distribution, and finances. Earlier, he had convinced these runaway passengers from the last German transport to Auschwitz to share his vision of culture.[62] Able to connect with anyone in the divisive world of postwar cultural politics, Borejsza was an able and willing interpreter of Soviet soft power.

Veterans of the Soviet-backed Polish Army had a decisive influence on the country's reviving cultural life.[63] In fact, Orlov's failures in controlling the output of the Polish presses resulted, in large part, in their clout and Borejsza's patronage. Though Borejsza assured Soviet officials of the editors' support, the scrappy Poles undeniably dragged their feet when it came to publishing Soviet materials. Indeed, Borejsza's recent biographer has likewise concluded that the energetic press magnate deliberately avoided subjecting his titles to the control of censorship; intimately familiar with Soviet institutions, he knew how counterproductive such censorship would be in Poland.[64] In Bromberg's words, "while still in Lwów Borejsza taught us how to keep quiet about what we did not like and to do what we can do."[65] Soviet reprimands had only a temporary effect, according to Orlov.[66] The Soviet representative also reported that some publications, notably those of Czytelnik, openly published "anti-Soviet articles," although it is unclear what he meant by that.[67] Soviet officials and top leaders from Sovinformbiuro were all suspicious about the Polish communists' good intentions.[68] They nevertheless tolerated the Poles' insubordination, hoping that things would change after the elections in January 1947. "It will become clear who was really worried about this," wrote Orlov, referring to the Polish editors' argument about scaring the masses with Sovinformbiuro's articles, "and who used this excuse as a cover for his personal antipathy toward our country."[69]

At the same time, when articles proposed by the Sovinformbiuro officials failed to elicit the Poles' interest, the organization's representatives directly pressured the editors to accept the articles. In 1945, Orlov mentioned "other Soviet employees" who helped him to do this. He probably had in mind the officials at the Red Army's Political Department. The ambassador to Poland, Lebedev, often refused to intervene when asked by the Sovinformbiuro representative to force an article through, but he helped occasionally.[70] Although Lebedev's position as official representative of a foreign government theoretically constrained his actions, a few years later, Lebedev would feel no compunction about overstepping his competences and weaving top-level intrigues in the Polish Politbiuro.[71] Therefore, his occasional refusal to assist Sovinformbiuro officials resulted probably from his lack of time. Another time, Orlov mentioned that the adviser Iakovlev tried to "exert influence" on Borejsza through the PPR to get him to publish more about the Soviet Union.[72] But like the ambassador, Iakovlev also seems to have been unreliable: despite the fact that he had offered his help earlier, he was of no assistance on numerous other occasions.[73] Such a lack of support from Soviet officials caused Orlov further headaches, empowering the Poles who sought to sustain their culture without interventions from abroad.

Indeed, Jakub Berman's exchanges with Sokolovskii and Lebedev show that the top communists in Poland protected their sphere of cultural autonomy. And when they acquiesced to Soviet demands, they often did so only temporarily.[74] The acceptance rate for Sovinformbiuro's articles in 1946 hovered around 50 percent—the same as in South Africa and the United States![75] Yes, suspiciousness was hardwired in the Soviet institutions' modus operandi, but in this case the Soviet officials had it right. Orlov, infuriated by their independence, described these editors as "hiding their heads in the sand."[76] It must be pointed out that the growing institutional pressures forcing people like Orlov to make less than empathetic assessments of Polish intentions proved counterproductive in the long run. Most of the editors, including Borejsza, disagreed with Orlov not on whether the Soviet experience in building socialism should be publicized, but rather when and how it should be done. As Jerzy Putrament, the communist fiction writer, former political officer in the Kościuszko Division, party activist, and editor of *Dziennik Polski* (the Polish Daily), pointed out in his letter to the Central Committee: praising the USSR magnifies the conviction among all Poland's social classes that "our government and party are only puppets in Moscow's hands."[77] Other editors would have agreed with him wholeheartedly. In sum, the Soviets were on the mark when they pointed to anti-Bolshevik bias among the Polish population. But at the same time, Soviet domestic pressures (and possibly their own anti-Polish prejudices) prevented them from giving local communists the benefit of the doubt. This historical, and especially institutional, distrust weighed down the Soviet outreach activities. The Soviets often complained of lack of resources and understaffing. And those Soviet officials who could have been editing Sovinformbiuro's articles instead kept busy breathing down the Poles' necks.

Yet it is unlikely that anyone other than Stalin himself could have created the conditions for more sensitive cultural outreach to Eastern Europe. Soviet officials in Moscow knew about Sovinformbiuro's problems from periodic reports and personal briefings. Interrogated by a Central Committee Commission in the summer of 1946, one functionary told A. A. Kuznetsov and others that one of the reasons behind the low publication rate has been "our very awkward and untactful approach to the Polish Press." The Sovinformbiuro had been sending articles in Russian, "but the Poles have great honor, more than other nations," he explained; they complain, and "always find a convenient excuse to reject our materials."[78] Historian A. S. Stykalin described those who supervised foreign propaganda outreach in Moscow as "extremely shortsighted," for squandering, through their "intolerance," potential alliances in the new sphere of influence.[79] But precisely at that time, Stalin reintroduced terror within his inner circle in order to reassert his authority after the war.[80] To a large extent, Sovinformbiuro's ineffectiveness resulted from the fact that the top officials feared ruining their careers as much as the people further down the chain of command did. Indeed, since they had more responsibility, they also had much more to lose.

"Few phenomena spelled the onset of socialist-realism, and hardly anything suggested that nearly all literature would go in that direction," commented a historian of contemporary Polish literature, in referring to the immediate postwar years.[81] Indeed, many Polish and some Soviet contemporaries had reasons to see good potential for postwar cultural cooperation in realms that extended beyond the press. That was also the case with Germans and Soviets in the Soviet Zone of Occupation further west.[82] Decades after this period, Polish artists and intellectuals often explained their collusion with the homegrown Stalinist regime by citing the slow, nearly imperceptible nature of the cultural transformation. When they enlisted, the project purported to make culture accessible to the masses; yet, accommodating one compromise after another, they "yielded, little by little, to the magic influence of the New Faith," using their talents to legitimate the communist party-state.[83] With a few notable exceptions, scholars have explained Polish intellectuals' paths toward and away from complicity with the communist regime by focusing largely on these domestic dynamics. But the acquiescence of the members of the intelligentsia who straddled the moral-ideological fence also reveals their assumptions about the acceptable nature of Soviet culture or, at least, Poland's safe distance from Soviet incursions.

The poet Czesław Miłosz became world famous for his prose work *The Captive Mind*. Published in 1951, it was a scathing critique of his fellow writers who succumbed to and lent their talents to the support of the Stalinist regime. But before the work about the "New Faith" came out, and thanks to Jerzy Putrament, Miłosz, one of Poland's greatest moral authorities of the twentieth century, worked for the diplomatic corps of the new Poland.[84] Miłosz's position as a cultural attaché to the Polish embassy in Paris allowed him to seek asylum in France in 1951. During those years, Miłosz was one of many intellectuals who, without fully condoning the activities of the Polish communists, found a modus vivendi with them.

The years 1944–47 forged and encouraged a cultural symbiosis between the Polish communists and intelligentsia as no other period had before. Swaths of skeptical and suspicious intelligentsia members coexisted with the communists in a tenuous arrangement grounded in mutual compromises. As Miłosz pointed out, "this was to be the era of the NEP [New Economic Policy]. Liberalism was the word in cultural matters."[85] Julian Tuwim thought likewise: himself about to leave New York for Poland, he was urging his old literary friends to do the same, persuading them in his letters

Warsaw, 1946. Jerzy Borejsza (left) and Jakub Berman (middle) greet the poet Julian Tuwim who arrived from the United States. Courtesy of Polska Agencja Prasowa.

that the new Polish authorities would not dictate to writers what to write.[86] Although the communists frequently resorted to violence and illegality in politics at the time, they avoided unnecessary conflicts with the artistic establishment because they desperately needed the approval and voices of Poland's educated elite in order to acquire legitimacy among broader social strata. Those intellectuals who survived World War II—and in some sectors they counted only 30% of the prewar number—were divided on a range of issues having to do with the role of culture in society, its form and relationship to the Soviet model. Accordingly, the communists used a dual strategy of drawing the "old intelligentsia" to the communist cause while training the new intellectual cadres at a fast pace.[87]

Jan Karol Wende had been a political officer in the Polish Army commanded by Berling; in February, 1945, he was vice-minister of culture and the Polish government's plenipotentiary in the Cracow region, responsible for building the new administration. Later he recalled how the editor of *Dziennik Polski*, Jerzy Putrament, arrived at his door in early February with a note from Jakub Berman. Its content sheds light on Putrament's role at the time and shows the determination of the communists: "We would wish to devote much attention to Cracow's intelligentsia," Berman wrote, asking to facilitate any initiatives Putrament might undertake in this direction. "One must not spare any means to win over a healthy portion of the intelligentsia and simultaneously move on to an ideological offensive."[88] Everyone knew that the conquest of the city's conservative intelligentsia would be difficult. But at this time when institutions of higher education and libraries lay in ruins, even nonleftist intellectuals throughout Central Europe sought to establish cultural contacts with the USSR. This included sections of Cracow's ostensibly anti-Soviet intelligentsia who participated actively in the work of the Polish-Soviet Friendship Society (Towarzystwo Przyjaźni Polsko-Radzieckiej, or TPPR).[89] Had they suspected that such cooperation would eventually curtail the autonomy of science, they would most certainly not have shown such initiative.

For their part, members of the Polish artistic elite were facing truly agonizing dilemmas at that time. Most of the elder generation abhorred the communist establishment. Few, too few according to later observers, shunned the communists altogether. Gustaw Herling-Grudziński was one of them. Eventually, some, like Jerzy Andrzejewski (later nicknamed "Alpha" in Czesław Miłosz's *Captive Mind*), weakened and lent their names to the communist cause in exchange for comfort and privilege; others, like Miłosz himself, at first supported the system and then escaped abroad. In most cases though, the choice was hardly a Manichean one. In the immediate postwar years, it was still possible to believe that Poland would be spared Stalinism. And working as a national writer of leftist convictions was the norm rather than the exception by European standards. Marxism was in the air, and being on the correct side of history was an enormous temptation, as was the need to return to normalcy. As the communists assumed more and more power, the new régime was becoming the only vehicle for positive action. Intellectuals correctly saw the triumphant communist state as a genuine opportunity to "democratize" culture and to devote themselves to the rebuilding of Poland's cultural and social life; this possibility to do good things made it much easier to justify compromises with immoral people.[90]

As a result, the Polish authorities were able to impose some thematic taboos, mostly related to Polish and Soviet political histories. Artists during that time were still far from embracing the "socialist optimism" of the later Stalinist era. But they had to accept some compromises: "in order to write, sing, make films, one had to forget about the Soviet camps, about the Ribbentrop-Molotov pact, about Katyń, about the bravery of the Home Army soldiers and their leaders, and about the Soviet army standing by dying Warsaw."[91] Among contemporary subjects that were off-limits to artists, historian Marta Fik mentions Stalin's "advisory" role in creating the "July Manifesto." Published in July 1944, the document was the Polish communists' message to the public, presenting their platform as a moderate one and the only social changes needed as those that were in genuine demand. The communists shielded from view Stalin's role in its creation because doing otherwise would reveal their intimate links with the Soviet leader, and thus further endanger their precarious standing in Poland. Other taboos included the "trial of the sixteen," the Home Army leaders who were invited to Moscow under false pretenses, imprisoned, and subjected to a three-day show trial; subsequently, a few were released, but most faced hard labor sentences, and some were likely murdered by the Soviet authorities.[92] The rather long list of taboos also included voicing resentment against the West's "betrayal" of Poland's anticommunist government, that is, its eventual capitulation on the Polish question, the rigged referendum of 1946, and the elections of 1947.[93] At that time, the communists also frowned upon experimentation in the arts. But those who managed to circumvent the most sensitive issues retained a wide field for artistic maneuver. They did so by focusing on Polish historical and Western classical themes, resorting to artistic ambiguities, and sharing in the generally accepted European realist genres.

Perhaps more important, what did the Polish cultural elites really know about the USSR? The few Polish communists who had been there, and who survived the purges, left enigmatic accounts of their impressions.[94] Miłosz himself pleaded ignorance. "Russia began to figure in our conversations ever more frequently," he wrote, denoting an interest that arose in the late 1930s. "We lived less than a hundred miles from the borders of the Soviet Union, yet we had no more knowledge of it than did the inhabitants of Brazil. The border was hermetically sealed."[95] Such statements must be read with a grain of salt since traditionally they have served to justify leftist intellectuals' support for the murderous Stalinist regime.[96] Marci Shore has offered a more compelling explanation. In her account of Warsaw writers' "life and death in Marxism," she traced the Polish intellectuals' infatuation with a dream of social justice and with Soviet Russia as well. "For these poets," she wrote in the context of the 1920s, "the Revolution spoke in the words neither of Marx nor of Lenin, but of Vladimir Mayakovsky," the towering Soviet poet with a thundering voice who visited Warsaw several times during this decade.[97] The dream overshadowed both the ominous clues behind Mayakovsky's suicide in 1930 and the more dystopian signs coming from Stalin's Russia.[98] Many writers and poets who observed the USSR from a safe distance liked what they saw. Those who traveled to the

USSR disregarded the obvious for the same reasons that so many Western "political pilgrims" to the birthplace of socialism did: because they wanted to believe, or because in criticizing the Soviet Union they risked professional marginalization back home.[99] After World War II, there were more causes for concern—rumors about Katyn were one. But Polish writers and the reading public genuinely felt eager to rediscover Chekhov and Dostoevsky. These and other Russian classics had been unavailable in the interwar era, while in the nineteenth century, the Polish elites translated them from the French—for it was "unbecoming for the patriots to know the language of the partitioning state."[100] And the longed-for victory over Germany coupled with irresistible democratic slogans in literature and the arts buttressed the Soviet claim to be the only alternative to the discredited cultures of the West.

And Soviet cultural officials did little to destroy such impressions. The Soviet embassy was the main nexus of Soviet-operated cultural forces in Poland. Immediately after the liberation of Warsaw, it was located at 13 Wileńska Street, in one of the least ravaged parts of the city's Praga district on the eastern side of the Vistula.[101] Besides the obvious representative functions, diplomatic work, and less conspicuous espionage duties, embassy officials were charged with strictly cultural work popularizing Soviet culture in Poland, coordinating such efforts on the part of various Soviet organizations, and coercing cultural cooperation from Polish leaders. Between 1944 and 1948, the main cultural operative at the embassy was Vladimir Grigorevich Iakovlev (b. 1908). He was an important figure in this Soviet "cultural nomenklatura," and an illustrative one at the intersection of the parallel cultural hierarchies. During his tenure in Poland, he was a close associate of the Soviet legate Nikolai Bulganin (he served only a few months in 1944) as well as the latter's successor, the ambassador Viktor Lebedev (1945–51), with whom he shared highly sensitive government information and even duties.[102] At the same time, Iakovlev was the cultural adviser to the Soviet embassy and the representative of VOKS in Poland. Later, most cultural work of the embassy was shifted to the second and third secretaries and the cultural attaché, perhaps on Iakovlev's request in August 1948.[103] In the meantime, lower-ranking diplomats such as Vladimir Peutin, I. Kuznetsov, and Iurii Safirov assisted Iakovlev in mediating between Moscow, Polish elites, and society.[104]

In 1945–46, Soviet officials were testing the waters—looking for opportunities to engage the intellectuals, assessing the risks of hasty actions, and forming alliances. Courting the even mildly sympathetic Polish intellectuals became an element of their daily routine. Writing in 1946, Peutin, the

Soviet embassy's second secretary, singled out the writers Julian Tuwim and Jarosław Iwaszkiewicz as potentially useful in the future. Both were members of Skamander, a group of avant-garde poets active between the wars. Tuwim had been one of those enchanted by Mayakovsky. Tuwim suffered from loneliness during his wartime stay in the United States, and had been one of the first to send a congratulatory note to the newly formed Kościuszko Division.[105] The perception that such highly regarded artists supported the new regime became a decisive argument for young, zealous people to do the same. Decades later, a Polish Stalinist writer attested to this, saying the poets' involvement triggered an avalanche-like effect among writers.[106] In his report, Peutin focused on Tuwim's self-avowed sympathy for the USSR and Polish-Soviet contacts. "I believe it is extremely necessary," he concluded, "that we pay utmost attention to him, particularly since Tuwim's relationship with VOKS has been a long tradition."[107]

By the fall of 1945, Goslitizdat started to prepare an edition of Iwaszkiewicz's collected works, extending an implicit promise to other prominent writers who would choose to consider friendship with the USSR.[108] Another time, upon learning about Iwaszkiewicz's trip to the Soviet Union, Peutin wrote to Moscow that he considered it "absolutely necessary" to show him "maximum attention in the full meaning of the word, and in the way that VOKS can do it." The stakes were high: Iwaszkiewicz had already managed to go to Paris in his new capacity as chair of the Polish Writers' Union and allegedly was slightly offended that nobody from Moscow had taken the initiative to invite him yet.[109] In his correspondence with VOKS officials, the beleaguered Peutin berated them for failing to take advantage of other opportunities for showing even the most meager signs of interest in Soviet culture throughout Poland.[110] As late as February 1948, VOKS officials debated about how to win over two visiting Polish musicians; the honoraria of conductor Grzegorz Fitelberg and violinist Eugenia Umińska were said to be low, and their expectations, rather high. It is, perhaps, no wonder: having toured all of fin-de-siècle Europe and cooperated with the famous Ballets Russes, the sixty-nine-year-old Fitelberg had seen it all.[111] The Poles' moods apparently improved after VOKS put them up in a better hotel. "Why didn't you give them this hotel in the first place?" Deputy Foreign Minister Andrei Vyshinskii's handwritten comment asked on the report.[112] Vyshinskii had been chief prosecutor and mastermind of the 1930s show trials; "his past as a Menshevik together with his Polish and bourgeois background made him particularly servile and obsequious in his dealings with Stalin," noted one British diplomat after the war.[113] Thus, Vyshinskii's question strikes a disingenuous chord; he must have known that for lower-ranking officials, daring to decide to treat bourgeois musicians to a nice hotel—even from allied socialist countries—incurred risks.

Along with K. I. Orlov from the Sovinformbiuro, there were embassy functionaries who made a considerable effort to understand the specificities of the Polish audience. In late 1945, the Polish Ministry of Foreign Affairs had complained to the Soviet embassy that in a long Soviet film about the defeat of Germany, no Polish units had been mentioned.[114] There was no apparent danger in forging compromises with East European foreigners; after all, every Sunday evening, Soviet intellectuals attended screenings of American films at the Spaso House, the residence of the ambassador of the United States in Moscow.[115] From the perspective of Stalin and the Polish communists, the value of the Soviet-sponsored Polish Army had been more symbolic than strategic; now, the erasure of the Polish soldiers' role in the German campaign deprived the Polish communists of substantial symbolic capital. Unlike the unresponsive Soiuztorgkino official who failed to edit the film, the mid-level diplomats learned their lesson. Writing to VOKS in January 1946, the second secretary of the Soviet embassy, V. Peutin, argued that the photographic exhibit titled "The Red Army's Art of Warfare" was unfit for public display since "there is no mention of the Polish units." Only a single photograph with the caption "Red Army liberated Warsaw" contained a glimpse of a Polish politician. "We cannot show such a photograph here right now," wrote Peutin, anticipating the Polish outrage at what they would certainly perceive as their marginalization in the story of liberation. Had [Lidiia] Kislova been able to read the Polish press, chided Peutin, referencing a VOKS official, she would have known about the Polish point of view on the issue. "We have to take into account this purely Polish perspective."[116] Like Orlov, earlier in July 1946, Peutin also warned against a hasty popularization of collectivization.[117] Clearly, the Soviet ability and willingness to accommodate Polish sensibilities was more than a monopoly of one man.

Soviet-Polish cultural exchanges, organized largely by VOKS and the TPPR, were "modest" during this period. The Poles downplayed the dominant role of the USSR in Poland's international cultural contacts, while the Soviets emphasized the partner-like nature of the relationship.[118] Contacts between the Soviet and Polish intelligentsia helped foster the notion that cultural cooperation satisfying to both sides would be possible in the future. The Soviet writer Fedor Panferov was one of the few Soviet intellectuals to visit Poland in the immediate postwar period. Known for his novels about the Soviet countryside, the writer, who had been mentored by Maxim Gorky, also looked to French and Polish nineteenth-century realists for inspiration.[119] Yet the date of Panferov's visit, occasioned by an invitation from the TPPR in early April 1946, was a strange time in the USSR. Two months earlier Winston Churchill had menacingly talked about the "iron curtain." Dark clouds had been gathering over the literary journals *Star* and *Leningrad* since the late summer of 1945; by August 1946, a resolution condemning the work of the journals on ideological grounds would also attack the poet Anna Akhmatova, the writer Mikhail Zoshchenko, and intimidate artistic elites at large. Yet in April nothing would presage the onset of the Cold War: no all-out campaign in the Soviet press followed Churchill's Fulton speech, while throughout 1946 and even into 1947, "*Pravda* gave half its space on foreign affairs to stories about peaceful relations and antifascism."[120] Soviet and Western administrators in occupied Germany continued to coexist and even cooperate on good terms even into 1947.[121] Many of the Soviet visitors to Poland continued to act as bona fide cultural intermediaries between the two countries. But in making sense of their visits and navigating through the conflicting signals from their two masters, the party and the state, the Soviet travelers were on their own.

Panferov's impressions from his trip to Poland betray his confusion about what was expected of him. They also reveal a sense of genuine hope for closer cultural ties with a range of Poland's writers. He met with luminaries of Polish culture—Leon Kruczkowski, Władysław Broniewski, Leon Pasternak, and others. During a reception at the house of a former "apostle" from the Kościuszko Division and now Poland's minister of foreign affairs, Zygmunt Modzelewski, he met Jaroszław Iwaszkiewicz. Panferov noted that many "of the most sincere of our friends are being drawn toward France." Among Soviet writers, Boris Pasternak enjoyed great popularity. Panferov recounted "discussing" with his fellow writers the professional life of Soviet literati. He "disagreed" with the Poles' view that most Soviet writers were servants of the state, and that the method of socialist realism merely served as a "universal comb" for literature. Still, despite their differences, Panferov felt the Poles were full of warmth and respect toward him. Clearly, the feeling was mutual. Panferov wrote an emotional account of his meeting with the famously introspective, left-leaning but hardly pro-Soviet writer Zofia Nałkowska. One can only wonder how Mikhail Suslov, the notoriously dry director of the Soviet International Department, felt when he read Panferov's grand finale, in which he claimed "we parted almost as friends."[122] Most likely alluding to Panferov's emotional investment and his apparent fondness of open debate, an official at the Soviet embassy in Warsaw commented that "Panferov initially failed to understand his mission in Poland."[123]

A sense of déjà vu may have added a layer of confusion to Panferov's experience. In his report, Panferov wrote that, earlier in Polish literature, "symbolist and formalist . . . currents" dominated, "almost everything just as in our country in 1919–24."[124] Thus, Panferov's report framed his positive if artistically varied experience abroad as a developmental stage in the progress of history toward communism. From Panferov's vantage point, it only made sense that the Poles would build the new system gradually. But conspicuous in its absence from the report is another historical parallel. Ten years earlier, in 1937—the dark year of the Great Purges—Fedor Panferov had dedicated the fourth volume of his novel about collectivization to two men who were subsequently arrested. This unfortunate coincidence had made the writer fear for his life until he met with Stalin, who spared him.[125] Now, the upbeat tone of the report and Panferov's relatively unconstrained conduct in Poland suggest that the writer hardly anticipated a return to the dark period of the Soviet past that he, and many others, would soon revisit.

A COLD WAR BATTLEGROUND

Between 1944 and 1948, Poland evolved from a more or less free marketplace of ideas to a Cold War battleground. Writers of all persuasions—artists and journalists alike—had front-row seats in the skirmish over Poland's national identity. The tensions between Polish communists, editors, and officials from the Sovinformbiuro continued after the PPR's victory in the rigged elections in 1947, but not always for the reasons that the latter were able or willing to identify correctly. The stolen victory gave the Polish communists a springboard for consolidation of power. But the simultaneous onset of the Cold War also unexpectedly complicated their relations with agents of the Soviet soft-power project in Poland. Having swallowed up the PPS in 1948 (after which it renamed itself the Polish United Workers' Party, or PZPR), the communists quashed these major voices of opposition. Although the PPR gained a decisive voice in matters of the press by mid-1947, even by mid-1948, the party control was not absolute.[126] The frantic race to publish more newspapers than the opposition made it difficult for the communists to pick their editorial staffs carefully, especially in the provinces.[127] The provincial party journalists were the least qualified. Moreover, they enjoyed the most independence as a result of their distance from Warsaw. Some journalists continued to adhere to prewar no-

Warsaw, 1947. The USSR's Moiseev song-and-dance ensemble performs in Warsaw. Courtesy of Polska Agencja Prasowa.

tions of professionalism. Such journalists resented the imperative to sugarcoat reality and tried to avoid doing so.[128] Sometimes the communists themselves rejected the Sovinformbiuro's articles for political reasons—in order not to preempt a propaganda campaign they had planned for a different time, or simply to avoid compromising the party newspaper with Soviet-looking or badly written journalism.

Though the Soviet approach to its East European satellites evolved slowly in the postwar years, 1946 stands as a turnstile. Stalin took an increased interest in these countries' internal affairs in mid-1946, when, unexpectedly, several West European communist parties lost parliamentary elections.[129] In the new circumstances, those communists in East-Central Europe who openly embraced "national roads to socialism" appeared to pose an additional threat to the global constellation of communist forces. The Soviet side increasingly pushed for centralization of the communist movement and institutionalized these plans through the formation of the Communist Information Bureau (Cominform) in the fall of 1947.[130] The latter was a Soviet-led organization responsible for coordinating activities of foreign communist parties. The Stalin–Tito split in the summer of 1948 and the Kremlin's ongoing problems in taming the nationalist insurgencies in Soviet-East European borderlands eventually provided other impulses to consolidate the Soviet sphere of influence.[131] Soviet leaders quickly condemned any aspirations to autonomy on the part of the foreign communists. Among those singled out was the PPR secretary Władysław Gomułka. In 1948, he was accused of a "nationalist deviation," and removed from power.[132]

The Polish communists' subsequent crackdown on Czytelnik and the downfall of the indefatigable Borejsza resulted naturally from their new-found ability and need to eliminate independent spirit in their ranks. It reflected their frustration with Borejsza's extraordinary drive. As Bromberg noted, "He [Borejsza] had too much energy and initiative. Jakub, Bolesław, Wiesław could not have kept up with him. They could not match him, they had to get rid of him."[133] But the closing of Czytelnik also shows that despite their noncompliant attitude toward lower-level Soviet officials, the Polish communists' ultimate obedience to Moscow was unflinching. In October 1947, the Secretariat of the PPR issued a decision excoriating Czytelnik's work. Among other things, the cooperative was accused of weak popularization of Soviet experiences in building socialism. It is unlikely that the Poles issued the decision as a result of Orlov's interventions. If this were true, it would have come earlier. It is more probable that a confluence of the interests of top Polish and Soviet leaders saw Borejsza's power in the publishing world waxing and his concept of gradual ("gentle") cultural revolution as a threat to the communist party's political hegemony.[134] The Soviet authorities called for a greater ideological uniformity in Eastern Europe in September 1947, thereby giving the Poles a green light to cut down further on autonomous activity in the public sphere. By 1948, the acceptance rate of Sovinformbiuro's articles jumped to 81 percent. But as the following years would show, the significance of the remaining, un-published 19 percent also grew, exacerbating conflict and paralyzing any constructive dialogue concerning propaganda. Growing anti-Semitism in the USSR had worked against Borejsza as well. In Bromberg's apt words, "for Moscow, he was too fast, too savvy, and, worst of all, scored one success after another. But the Jews were supposed to be responsible for mistakes, failures, and defeats, not successes."[135] Still, Borejsza lived in a world different from his Soviet acquaintance and analogue, the cultural busy-body Ilya Ehrenburg, who was also Jewish; partly for that reason, and in part due to a different temperament, Borejsza had too much confidence in himself to conform. Up until this time, he had set the tone of the "gentle revolution" in Polish culture. From now on, as the revolution was acquiring a coercive course, he would be struggling to keep up with it.

The mounting Cold War raised the stakes for the Soviets in appealing to the hearts and minds of the Poles. The Polish communists' ascent to power made the more orthodox Soviet officials' working conditions more propitious. So it is startling to see that despite their militant rhetoric and efforts to intervene in Polish cultural affairs, even the most inflexible Soviet bureaucrats approached cultural relations with Poland from a position of relative weakness.

For one thing, their associates in Moscow forced the Soviet officials into passivity by dragging their feet in providing material, administrative, and political support to Soviet *kulturträger* in Poland. Just as Sovinformbiuro functionaries in Poland, the cultural officials at the Warsaw embassy battled to secure adequate material support from Moscow. The ostensive indecisiveness on Moscow's part baffled and angered officials like V. Kuz'menko, convinced as they were that the crux of their jobs was to popularize Soviet culture in Poland. Integrating and promoting Soviet culture was particularly pressing at this time, insisted Kuz'menko, who led a VOKS delegation to Poland in June 1946, in the face of the might and allure of British, American, and French propaganda in Poland. The Soviets had to step up their presence in order to compete. VOKS needed much more money to do its job there, he argued, and much more attention from the Agitation and Propaganda Department in the Central Committee. More Soviet books had to become accessible to the Polish mass public. Indeed, embassy reports suggest that Mezhdunarodnaia kniga, the Soviet institution responsible for distributing Russian texts abroad, worked unevenly. In 1947, for instance, the organization supplied less material than in 1946, preventing the Soviets from meeting the high demand for Stalin's works, Soviet textbooks, and Russian classics. Many of these works were likely purchased by Polish communists who wanted to please the Soviet authorities.[136] Demand for high-quality Russian classics can be explained by the fact that few of them were being published in Poland at the time.[137] Mezhdunarodnaia kniga bureaucrats were widely criticized by outside officials who had to deal with this organization. The Soviet embassy also complained to the Soviet Ministry of Foreign Affairs about this matter.[138] Seemingly, the interventions had no effect.

According to Kuz'menko, more cultural exchanges had to be arranged since, as the recent delegation learned, even the most progressive members of the Polish intelligentsia had "the most confused, inaccurate, and harmful" impressions about Soviet cultural and scientific life. In addition, argued Kuz'menko, reactionary elements in the Polish government helped to maintain such impressions by promoting anti-Soviet policies and tolerating similar behavior. Here Kuz'menko singled out the minister of education, Czesław Wycech from the Polish Peasant Party (PSL), who failed to condemn nationwide student demonstrations conducted under "anti-Soviet and antigovernment" slogans at the beginning of May.[139] Kuz'menko's strong urge to disseminate Soviet culture in Poland may seem portentous of things to come; but his sense of impotence and insecurity vis-à-vis Western organizations and Polish opposition shows that he was hardly in a position to intimidate anyone in Poland at that time.

Embassy officials shared Kuz'menko's concern about the effect of the Western cultural presence in Poland. Western governments and private organizations spent considerable resources to expose Poles to their culture and propaganda. Although the U.S. government slashed funding for propaganda operations overseas in 1945–47, it revived the initiatives in 1947–48.[140] Even with these variations in funding, the "Anglo-Saxons" were still considered a formidable competitive force by the representatives of all major Soviet institutions. Vladimir Peutin did note that the U.S. propaganda operation in Poland, coordinated by the United States Information Service, was more modest than the British operations.[141] Still, one Sovinformbiuro official, in his report to Marshal Zhukov from early 1946, claimed the Information Service was expected to be mightier than its predecessor, the Office of War Information.[142] In a world on the brink of polarization, this is what mattered. Throughout 1947, Americans inundated the editorial offices of Polish newspapers with press bulletins, materials, and photographs. They were able to offer 65 films to Polish distributors (who accepted only 20), while the American embassy set up a special screening room for 150 people on its premises. With envy, Soviet officials like Iakovliev and Peutin deemed the British Council a dynamic propaganda institution. They noted the presence of British libraries and activities of other "well-staffed" organizations; they followed the upcoming exhibitions, the high circulation of enemy journals, the availability of books in English, and their popularity.[143] By contrast, the MK's director complained to G. M. Malenkov (and urged him to let Stalin know) that in 1945 alone he needed at least 10,000 copies of each Russian book title he carried in order to satisfy the export demand throughout Europe; the 200–500 copies he had were, he argued persuasively, hardly enough even for the single vassal state of Yugoslavia.[144] Deep anxiety about not being able to match their foes' propaganda prowess was another factor that prodded the MK to seek support from Moscow ever more desperately. In 1947, the Soviet embassy in Poland arranged a special screening room just like its American counterpart. The trouble was—as VOKS Chair Vladimir Kemenov admitted to the minister of Soviet cinematography, Ivan Grigor'evich Bol'shakov—there were no movies to show.[145] At this crucial stage, the Soviets were one of many contenders for Polish hearts and minds. Jealous of the Western propaganda capacities and anxious about the Anglo-Americans' influence on Poland, the Soviet functionaries appear surprisingly vulnerable. Neither from the Polish perspective nor from their own did they seem bound to win one of the most important Cold War battles in East-Central Europe.

To the chagrin of the mid-level officials, Moscow remained generally inert throughout the first half of 1947. The Polish communists' seizure of power at the beginning of 1947 and their subsequent slow but steady attempts to curtail Western influences in cultural life seemed to present the Soviet officials with new possibilities for asserting their own agenda. In a letter to top party and state Soviet authorities in April 1947, Iakovlev opined, "We do not take advantage of even a fraction of the available opportunities for strengthening the influence and authority of the Soviet Union among the broad Polish masses." Poland required redoubled efforts, he added, since anti-Soviet sentiments were particularly strong there.[146] Iakovlev identified several reasons for this. Primarily, the Soviet government's lack of attention to the Polish situation resulted in poor performance by propaganda organizations such as VOKS. In a bitter tone, the diplomat pointed out that his government managed to send to Poland "hundreds of thousands of tons of grain," but ensuring that VOKS sent out artists and cultural figures as well as sufficient propaganda materials to Poland "turned out to be absolutely impossible."[147] A few artists did visit Poland that year, notably the Moiseev and Aleksandrov music ensembles, which toured the country with "stunning success," but generally Soviet sojourns in Poland in 1946–47 were few and far apart.[148]

From Iakovlev's perspective, the USSR was losing the battle for the Poles' hearts and minds by doing too little. Iakovlev's criticisms reflect a justifiable sense of frustration, which he shared with Soviet officials working for other East European countries, including the Soviet Zone of German Occupation.[149] In a broader sense, Iakovlev's remarks also underscore his awkward position as a willing but impotent interpreter of Soviet soft power.

Though Polish authorities actively filtered out some Soviet material, they also hoped to receive helpful culture and propaganda, anything they could use to effectively influence public sentiment. As a result, an unusual alliance emerged from Polish and Soviet officials' exasperation with Moscow and their craving for more resources that would help them make a case for Soviet-Polish friendship. Authors of a memo to the Polish Ministry of Foreign Affairs from October 4, 1945, explicitly stated that "popularizing in Poland the enormous cultural achievements of the Soviet Union" was an issue that carried great political weight.[150] Soviet cultural impoverishment

Warsaw, 1947. Polish President Bolesław Bierut (left) and Soviet Ambassador Viktor Lebedev watch the performance of the Moiseev Ensemble. Courtesy of Polska Agencja Prasowa.

after World War II was well-known. But the sheer absence of Soviet initiatives such as youth celebrations, music festivals, and the like, was becoming an embarrassment to the Polish communists. In Moscow, mid-level Polish embassy officials Henryk Wolpe, a historian of literature, and "young and still full of energy" former teacher Aleksander Juszkiewicz made this point on repeated occasions during their meetings with Soviet government officials in 1946 and 1947. The communist musicologist Zofia Lissa, also working at the Moscow embassy, made separate requests in December 1946 for more visits of Soviet musicians and artists to Poland during the current season.[151] In most cases the Soviet response was sympathetic, generally noncommittal and at best only partially satisfying.[152]

To the Polish politicians interested in building communism—be it national or Stalinist—the Soviet cultural presence in Poland had direct implications. Part of the Poles' proactiveness may have stemmed from what Zbigniew Brzezinski called "competition in loyalty to the USSR," that is, ostentatious displays of commitment to the Soviet Union made in the presence of Soviet officials, usually at the expense of others.[153] The Polish demands for more material could easily be read as assertions of loyalty and obedience. But some Polish communists ardently sought, within the Soviet Union's cultural output, sound alternatives to the recovering domestic cultural scene and to the potentially threatening aggressive Western propaganda. And greater Soviet involvement had the potential of disproving those skeptics who scrutinized Soviet culture through the pejorative prisms of the Stalin cult, production novels, paintings of tractors, as well as prisons and Siberia. Access to good material would have allowed the beleaguered politicians to recast their negative image as "agents of Moscow" into a more positive mold: that of close affiliates of a culturally able military superpower. Not surprisingly, as Soviet influence expanded throughout Eastern and Central Europe, the early postwar period saw a great rise in demand for Russian classics and early Soviet avant-garde writings; yet the Soviets sent mostly political brochures that nobody bothered to read.[154] Conversely, for the Polish communists, bad Soviet propaganda "poured water into the mill of reaction."[155] The fact that they believed they could get something better testifies to the great potential of cultural cooperation after the war.

Ultimately, these early years contained a great irony: just as the Soviet authorities gained the political means to export Soviet culture to the most defiant of its vassal states, the tense political climate and barren cultural landscape at home would prove to be a major obstacle to success. Thus the Soviet officials' complaints about lack of material support from Moscow may have served as symbolic affirmations of good will, but in the substantive sense they seem somewhat misplaced. The canon of acceptable classics was shrinking by the day in the USSR; sending off even seemingly innocuous Soviet and Russian works could have reflected extreme imprudence.[156] The case of Soviet films underscores the problems with supply that Soviet officials were facing. VOKS Chair Kemenov's July 1947 complaint about not having enough films to show constituted the tip of an iceberg of structural problems that the Soviets were facing at the time.[157] In 1946, 60 percent of the big screen showings were Soviet films, but the repertoire tended to consist of the same dated films and could not compete with the frequently changing and often more interesting offerings from the Western propaganda organizations, especially American ones.[158] This is not surprising, given how few films Soviet studios produced after the war: 18 in 1945, 22 in 1946, 22 in 1947, 16 in 1948, and even fewer in the subsequent two years. Peter Kenez aptly characterized these years as a period of "film hunger." Many of the films listed in the statistics, according to him, "were only filmed versions of theatrical performances," and could not even count as real films.[159] Soviet literary output was likewise hitting an all-time low due to strict censorship laws and the repression of artists.[160] Later in the summer of 1947, Iakovlev complained, "It has been for a year now that Poland has been forgotten by our artists."[161] Thus, a chief and ongoing problem the willing interpreters of Soviet soft power were facing was the Soviet inability to deliver the goods. Hunger requires food. In 1947, the Soviet regime struggled to feed its own citizens with bread and culture alike; the Soviet authorities shipped grain to Eastern Europe during the postwar famine, depriving Soviet peasants of bread, but as for motion pictures, there was simply nothing to steal (see appendix B, figure B. 5).[162] Yet, paradoxically, so long as the Soviet "film hunger" left the Polish communists starving for more Soviet films, the potential for future cooperation also seemed real.

Above and beyond unmet cultural needs, strong political reasons also prevented the Soviet government from putting its full weight behind an overt propagandistic campaign in Poland. Top Soviet policy toward Eastern Europe after World War II was fraught with contradictions. Although Stalin pursued policies that would allow him to gain control over the region deftly and aggressively, he followed no specific "blueprint" for the Sovietization of Eastern Europe.[163] Soviet leaders pursued pragmatic goals in the region, but ideological tenets also appear to have influenced their actions. The Soviets' policy comprised a mixture of active and reactive measures, of rigidity and flexibility. The resulting contradictions created confusion about the exact nature of Soviet cultural policy as well. In particular, with respect to their goals, Soviet mid-level officials both at home and in Poland seem to have been torn between conflicting demands from two directions—the party and the state.

On the one hand, the party gave these Soviet functionaries a clear idea about which ideological line to pursue in Poland. Their knowledge may have come from their propagandistic experience at home and from their general sense of Soviet foreign policy at the time. It is more likely though that their clear ideological stance came directly from the top party officials at the International Department of the Soviet party's Central Committee.[164] The Central Committee's International Department shared in the ideological control of a range of state, social, and cultural institutions working abroad, including the Soviet embassy and VOKS.[165] Mid-level officials working with Poland were pressured to accomplish two things: (a) pay attention to acts of nonconformity with the Soviet model, and then report them to Moscow; and (b) bring the situation in Poland into conformity with the Soviet model.

But through its unresponsiveness and lack of support, the Soviet Ministry of Foreign Affairs (MID) forced its representatives in Moscow to have doubts about what exactly they were supposed to be doing, and how. Surely, Stalin's many concerns—about the escalating conflict with the West, about postwar domestic recovery, and about the Soviet political takeover in Eastern Europe—pushed problems of cultural exchange with the region into the background of his agenda. For this reason, it is likely that before the beginning of 1947, the MID officials had no clear policy with regard to Poland. In addition, excessive Soviet interventions in Polish culture could have been construed as violations of the Yalta-Potsdam agreements and thus to some extent explain the passivity of the MID. Especially when it came to intervention, the embassy officials had their hands tied: they were official agents of the Soviet state who for all intents and purposes had to preserve the appearances of their host country's sovereignty.

These mixed signals from the party and the state to all Soviet cultural bureaucrats in Poland fueled mid-level Soviet officials' tremendous frustrations. They were confused, and rightly so. Unsure what to do, some visitors, such as the writer Fedor Panferov, took the personal initiative of relying on their own instincts in deciding how to carry themselves abroad. Like Panferov, who chose to be open and friendly, they nurtured the promise of a sustained international dialogue, leaving those few who feared Poland's cultural Sovietization with paltry arguments.

After the founding of the Cominform, it took several months for Soviet propaganda initiatives to gain traction within Soviet institutions, but Soviet reports for the second half of 1947 and for the first half of 1948 were slightly more upbeat. Earlier on, in April 1947, Iakovlev had mentioned having recently learned that the Soviet Communist Party was preparing a decision about the intensification of Soviet propaganda in Poland.[166] In May, the PPR began working on turning the Polish-Soviet Friendship Society into a mass organization.[167] Most likely as a result of the Cominform conference, the Secretariat of the PPR's Central Committee issued a decision "On the question of propaganda of Polish-Soviet friendship and the activity of the TPPR" in October 1947. The resolution was designed to involve the local party organizations in actively helping the Friendship Society. According to the document, mass media and cultural institutions gave inadequate attention to Soviet themes.[168] Iakovlev himself encouraged the leaders' interest in the organization. For example, he was the main initiator for putting the report of the Friendship Society's party organization on the agenda of the Secretariat.[169] Several performance groups, athletic teams, and cultural figures visited Poland as a result of these efforts.[170]

The celebrated Soviet writer and journalist Ilya Ehrenburg's visit to Poland in the fall of 1947 signaled Moscow's rekindled interest in cultural cooperation. Ehrenburg has rightly been considered one of the most intriguing figures of the Stalinist cultural landscape. His ability to make himself useful to the brutal regime's propaganda machine in exchange for a chance to live his beloved cosmopolitan lifestyle—all this at a time of rapidly growing isolation and official xenophobia—astounded many observers, and so did his ability to survive Stalin's numerous purges in the ranks of cultural elites. Ehrenburg was Jewish, and his ability to function internationally in the atmosphere of growing anti-Semitism after the war, in particular, raised questions about the moral price he paid for these privileges. Yet it is clear that the writer suffered from having to lie on many occasions, even to his dearest friends; and it was precisely his "protean nature," his indispensability to Stalin that allowed him to help many others, and even save their lives. Like many in the USSR, Ehrenburg hoped that "life would be better, sounder, more just" after the war. And just like the others, the journalist quickly grew disillusioned. Ehrenburg had made his name writing furiously anti-German articles meant to mobilize Soviet society, and the Red Army soldiers especially, for the war. He also became involved in initiatives meant to publicize the Holocaust in the USSR. But the war was over. Now, as Stalin tried to work with East German communists and appeal to the hearts and minds of "his" Germans, Ehrenburg's reputation and his new efforts stood in the way of the Soviet leader's plans—and much of Ehrenburg's output from 1945–46 has been doomed to the drawer.[171]

Ehrenburg's postwar travels throughout Eastern Europe reflect the contradictory forces and commitments in his life. His trips in the summer and fall of 1945 can be seen as part of his effort to return to Stalin's graces. His reports from Romania and Yugoslavia "helped to camouflage the nature of these new governments," and affirmed the benevolent scenario promoted by *Pravda*. He arrived in Poland in 1947, for the first time, after the war. Writing about his trip twenty years later, he recalled the baggage of anti-Polish prejudice that had weighed him down on his first trip there in 1928. This may have been a retrospective effort to justify the tendentious, politicized journalism that grew out of his early journey.[172] But this time around and long after his visit ended, Ehrenburg felt at home: "this is a dry fact, but it says a lot" he reminisced.[173] The comment, issued in the circumlocutory parlance of the Brezhnev era, nevertheless contained more than a grain of truth. The writer was probably referring to the changing political landscape, which, whether he liked it or not, made his country and Poland increasingly part of the same world. And, like everywhere else in Europe, Ehrenburg had close friends in Poland, whom he was happy to see. One of them was the Polish writer Julian Tuwim, whose thoughtful essay about what it meant to be Polish and Jewish at the same time, Ehrenburg translated into Russian and quoted to others throughout his life.[174]

In August 1948, Iakovlev informed his bosses that measures had been taken to improve the situation with visiting artists. First, the Soviets re-routed a group of Soviet youth performers on the way back home from Czechoslovakia, which apparently had a "positive effect." Another group of artists was directed to Poland on the orders of Zhdanov, who, in turn, responded to a request to that effect from Władysław Gomułka. Indeed, it was Iakovlev who had prodded Gomułka to make the request; the labyrinthine manner of eliciting the Polish "initiative" shows just how much the Soviet authorities cared to appear unassertive.[175] By 1948, the TPPR had a vibrant and energetic publishing house, producing visual and print propaganda about the USSR and often sending the material to the Polish press. It also had a sizable library of Russian and Soviet books both in the original and in Polish translation, which it acquired with the help of the VOKS.[176] Soviet officials observed with glee that works by both Russian and Soviet composers became more popular in Polish philharmonics; others pointed out that their works were becoming "more important to the success of particular concerts."[177] Another report from 1948 claimed, "It is now difficult to find a theater in Poland that has not staged at least two–three plays by Soviet authors."[178] Poles actively sought out Soviet theater and music, the report noted, and that demand should be satisfied by sending Soviet specialists to Poland.[179] But in order to take full advantage of the improved circumstances, Iakovlev wrote in August 1948, the embassy still needed a fixed apparatus of at least two people who would concentrate solely on the questions of propaganda.[180]

"In the autumn of 1947," wrote historian Jan C. Behrends, "the TPPR already had 500,000 members and the Soviet Union cult had become a part of everyday Polish life."[181] The PPR certainly launched a vigorous pro-Soviet propaganda campaign via the Polish-Soviet Friendship Society; however, the minimal direct Soviet involvement continued to disappoint the Poles. The Polish government continued to face difficulties in engaging the Soviets even in mid-1948. In mid-February, upon receiving from the Poles "the first realistic project of cultural exchange ever presented by the Polish Embassy," the Soviet government effectively failed to fulfill it without officially rejecting it.[182] The Polish embassy adviser Janusz Zambrowicz had recently replaced Juszkiewicz as second secretary. A geographer by training and "a sensationalist" by temperament, until recently, he had served as head of the Soviet Department in the Ministry of Foreign Affairs. "He had no political past," recalled Naszkowski, "but he committed himself fully and enthusiastically to the new reality."[183] After another exasperated attempt to direct Soviet artists to Poland, Zambrowicz bitterly pointed out to a Soviet official that most such visits to date had been "accidental" in character. By that he meant that most Soviet artists stopped in Poland on the way to someplace else, but rarely made the country a destination in its own right.[184] Appearing to be a Soviet afterthought, the Poles may have believed that they were of least importance to the Soviets. But in fact, regular complaints about Soviet passivity flowed to Moscow from many East European countries and the Soviet Zone of Occupation in Germany.[185] Similarly, despite several official Polish entreaties concerning the presence of the Soviet delegation during the famous Congress of Intellectuals in Defense of Peace in Wrocław at the end of August 1948, by as late as June 17, 1948, the Poles had not received a definite answer.[186] Since direct Soviet involvement in Poland's political and economic affairs was well under way, how can we square Soviet passivity in Polish cultural exchanges with its overtly interventionist practices in other spheres? Mid-level cultural contacts continued to be stifled on several fronts: by the secondary importance given to cultural interactions, by major postwar institutional reshufflings, and no doubt also by ongoing Soviet confusion about top-level demands and the fear of taking independent initiative. Add to this the divisive nature of the Polish question in East-West relations, and clearly the Soviet government wished to show great caution about ostensive displays of soft power in this country.

Few historians have given full credit to the Polish side, which exhibited great initiative and interest in importing Soviet culture during this early postwar period. Eventually the Polish government was no more successful in securing the desired materials from Moscow than were the Soviet cultural workers in Poland; they won some concessions, but still not nearly enough to meet their tremendous expectations. In effect, Polish officials who wanted to lure the Polish intelligentsia away from Western culture or impress Polish mass audiences with Russian or Soviet culture were virtually helpless. In April 1948, for example, an adviser at the Polish embassy, Janusz Zambrowicz, told the MID official A. M. Aleksandrov that despite previous interventions in that regard, "Polish radio has not been receiving any materials for a while now, which forces it to patch its programs with English and American records."[187] At this point, Soviet government officials were still willing to admit openly that they themselves were to blame for inadequate support.[188] But very soon Soviet institutional mechanisms would lock all responsibility for failure on the Polish side, as well as sanction the existing sense of imperialistic entitlement among some Soviet visitors to Poland, thus making similar give-and-take dialogues virtually impossible.

If the Soviets offered little direct cultural support to the Poles, they nudged them ever more heavily to turn to ideological orthodoxy in that sphere. Only a few months after his first postwar visit, Ehrenburg had the chance to return to Poland; this time, the role he had to assume would prove much more challenging. The World Congress of Intellectuals in Defense of Peace in Wrocław, Poland, in August 1948, constituted a watershed in the evolution of Soviet-Polish cultural relations. Jerzy Borejsza is known to have thought up the congress, while the Polish and French communists acted as the official hosts; however, as Krystyna Kersten suggested convincingly, the initiative was likely to have originated in Moscow—it occurred only one year before Stalin launched the Soviet campaign for world peace, and therefore at the time when preparations for the campaign were already under way.[189] The congress was therefore meant to impress world public opinion with the unifying power of communism. For many Poles, including Borejsza, the event was "a chance to preserve links with the Western world."[190] It brought together hundreds of participants, including the most famous representatives of the left-wing intelligentsia, such as Pablo Picasso, Paul Éluard, and Aldous Huxley. In an excited but fraternal atmosphere, delegates spoke about peace and unity, criticizing fascism and the traditional apoliticism of intellectuals. Then Aleksandr Fadeev, the head of the Soviet Writers' Union, launched an unexpected attack against the West. He spoke about a "lightning war against the decadence of literature and art in the West," and he called Jean-Paul Sartre a "hyena writing on the typewriter." The Poles panicked when they realized that Fadeev was torpedoing the congress with his divisive rhetoric. Shocked, some French delegates seemed paralyzed in their chairs; other participants, such as Aldous Huxley, were seen leaving the hall. Borejsza, now slowly falling from grace, called Berman, who, in turn, telephoned Molotov, pleading to save the event. Though the charming and famously diplomatic

Wrocław, August 1948. Polish visitors to the Soviet book stand at the World Congress of Intellectuals in Defense of Peace. Courtesy of Polska Agencja Prasowa.

Ilya Ehrenburg softened the damaging effect of the earlier speaker's remarks, many insulted Western delegates had already left. The tottering World Peace Congress showed East European leaders quite forcefully that the cultural transformation in the Soviet Union's new sphere of influence would have to accelerate.[191]

But even the Polish Stalinists were not ready to copy the Soviet models. A row over Tadeusz Hołuj's play, *A House Near Auschwitz*, staged four months earlier, illuminates the disheveled state of cultural unity in Soviet-Polish relations on the eve of the congress. On March 27, 1948, when Ambassador Viktor Lebedev declared the play "ideologically erroneous," Jakub Berman would have none of such criticisms.[192] Even two such close political allies met the limits of common dialogue in a shocking verbal row.

Had the drama been about the Holocaust, Lebedev's reservations could easily be explained in terms of his reluctance to put Jews in the center of the story. But *A House Near Auschwitz* is not about Jews. Hołuj has a Polish man, Jerzy, fall in love and move in with Maria, wife of Jan, a communist activist who had been imprisoned in Auschwitz. Jerzy's mother, Franciszka, had signed the *volksliste* to keep a house near the crematorium; from that house, filled with the stench of burned human flesh (not

Wrocław, August 1948. Aleksandr Fadeev speaking at the World Congress of Intellectuals in Defense of Peace. Jerzy Borejsza is sitting next to him. Courtesy of Polska Agencja Prasowa.

identified as Jewish), she runs rescue operations in which Jerzy is involved as well. But one day, Jerzy cowers from fulfilling his assignment to pick up a runaway prisoner who, though he does not know it, happens to be Jan. Jerzy's responsibility as the sole breadwinner for his beloved Maria and her daughter helps him to justify his failure to show up for the risky mission to save an anonymous escapee.

Hołuj's play is therefore a drama about making excruciating moral choices in extreme circumstances. Woven into the story are uncomfortable questions about one's own responsibility for these choices: as Jan tells his coconspirator, "even the best kind of person can be a total scoundrel. We all know many good people after all—for instance, the Germans. They love their families, children, country, they never hurt anyone—not with their own hands, that is."[193] Jerzy's vacillating, morally ambiguous role makes it difficult to classify *The House Near Auschwitz* as anti-German; but that "the Germans" do figure as responsible en masse for the murders of other human beings may have posed a problem on the eve of the creation of the German Democratic Republic. One scholar described the play as a "parable about the ethical blandness of the human condition, about the blurring of black-and-white schemas in the gray fog of the everyday, which is as far from heroism as it is from the hell of self-torture."[194] It irked Hołuj that after the war, Poles and Europeans conveniently understood their world to be neatly divided into criminals, heroes, and victims. In his play, Hołuj intended to zoom in on the "third world" in-between—the one inhabited by "people who wanted to survive, save their loved ones, who worked someplace, had personal lives, considered themselves Polish, helped the needy as long as it did not endanger their lives or the lives of those close to them." His artistic intention was to destroy their inner peace.[195] Many Polish critics rejected this dramatic excursion into the world of grays on the grounds that it lacked the necessary social context (the political affiliation of the partisans was unclear); or humanized the "traitors" such as Jerzy.[196] It was also a world that hardly fit into the Manichean universe of Stalinist values in the early Cold War.

Perhaps most important to the Polish communists, *The House Near Auschwitz* symbolized a glass not half empty but half full. They were fighting for the soul of every young writer at the time; in the mass of artists who were escaping into historical themes to avoid censorship or self-loathing, and amid the battle for the hearts and minds of intellectuals, a commentary on a contemporary subject by a freshly minted PPR member such as Hołuj came as a small victory.[197] The play was no paean to communist ideology, but it did not reject communism either. Although not expressly about class struggle, this drama about Auschwitz, through its marked absence of references to Jews, helped the Polish communists both "de-Judaize," "Polonize," and politicize the memory of the Holocaust—and turn it into a weapon in the struggle for legitimacy.[198] Leon Kruczkowski, then deputy minister of culture and the arts and a playwright who was preoccupied with similar issues, gave his support. Władysław Gomułka and "several other people from the leadership" attended the premiere in Warsaw's Polish Theater, directed by Arnold Szyfman. *Głos Ludu*, PPR's central press organ, organized a discussion after the performance.[199] And now, on March 27, 1948, the Soviet Ambassador Lebedev dared to criticize the play.

Jakub Berman was known for his stoicism; now, responding to Lebedev, the "number two" within Poland's ruling triumvirate was "furious." Defiantly, he defended the Poles' decision to stage the play. Berman made a menacing reference to top the Polish communists' "working directly under comrade Stalin's directions," and the reference was no bluff.[200] Berman and others felt they had a mandate to snub mid-level Soviet bureaucrats from the Sovinformbiuro, Glavlit, and even the ambassadors; Poland's cultural bureaucrats believed they could pull the Soviets by their noses. As for the Soviets, despite the pressure on them to show vigilance at all times by inventing Polish cultural diversions, Polish sabotage of Soviet culture and cultural interventions was not all in their heads.

Remarkably, the frictions between hard-line top Soviet and Polish wardens of new culture in the Eastern Bloc echoed the debates over the nature of Poland's cultural revolution. Here, too, Hołuj's play had its place. Mocking those critics who demanded a more decisive ideological stand from the playwright, Jerzy Borejsza proposed a seemingly more acceptable scenario. In his article titled "Krochmalism czy realizm?"—literally, "Starch-ism or realism?" referring to the product used to stiffen laundered clothes—the proponent of the gentle revolution wrote:

> Franciszka does not accept the Volksliste . . . and condemns her only son for cowardice. She disowns him (Gorky's Mother would have done so). There is no priest in the play, all the Auschwitz prisoners belong to the Left. Jan returns home, his daughter takes his mommy and daddy by the hand and says: I want you to be together. . . . Jan and Maria embrace each other. They kiss. Then, Franciszka enters, heading a detachment of militia or of Bureau of [Public] Safety. She orders the arrest of her son. A People's trial is taking place. Jerzy is being escorted in handcuffs: he has been sentenced to fifteen years of prison. Or, another alternative: a death sentence. A shot. A dead body falls on the ground.[201]

This would be neither theater nor realism, argued Borejsza, it would be "Krochmalizm." Yet this scenario involving the heavily "starched-up" characters probably approximated the version that the angry Ambassador Lebedev would have preferred to see.

CONCLUSION

Ghastly phantoms of war and nebulous specters of the future haunted Eastern Europe in the first years after the victory over Germany. The Poles, for one, began rebuilding their lives to the tunes of the funeral march, Glenn Miller's "Chattanooga Choo Choo," the national anthem, and the ever-louder strains of the "Communist International." Millions of Soviet citizens, including the cultural elites, awoke from their wartime nightmare feeling entitled to a world without fear, which had poisoned their lives for decades. Yet Stalin quickly disabused his people of such hopes. When he unleashed another wave of terror against them, he made it clear that he owed nothing to anyone. Confusion now ruled the area between Sel'tsy and Siedlce, turning the blood-soaked crime scene of heinous German atrocities and the terrain of a unified anti-German offensive into a land of daily contradictions. The lives of most Soviets and Poles plunged and rolled on this turbulence. And the concerted effort to survive the war and beat the Nazis descended into cacophony.

Cacophony ruled the day. The leaders of the great powers laced the postwar international order with key paradoxes. This was true especially of Soviet-Polish relations. The provisions of the Yalta treaty stipulated that Poland should be both democratic and friendly to the USSR.[202] And yet anyone aware of history, or of the moods among the Poles in 1945, knew that such conditions could not be met for long. Did Stalin therefore intend to bolshevize Poland from the beginning, even before the United States announced the Marshall Plan? Scholars have been debating this question for decades. Quite recently, historian Alfred Rieber suggested that Stalin had labored under a number of "illusions," which enabled him to believe that it would be possible to uphold "People's Democracy," or a left-wing parliamentary system, for at least ten years.[203] Others have pointed to the fact that Stalin could not have afforded a democracy next door: a democratic Poland destabilized the situation in the USSR's western borderlands and was likely to complicate Soviet hegemony over the all-important Germany.[204] Furthermore, the Soviet leader appears to have been heavily invested in ideology, to have been too committed to territorial expansion. But the Soviet economy and military were in shambles; it was hardly in Stalin's interest to antagonize the Allies too soon by violating the Yalta agreements. He had a flexible timeline. He held back his men from interfering overtly in Polish institutions. The Soviet leader also discouraged some overeager Polish communists from manifesting their pro-Soviet orientation. And, at the same time, he consistently supported the Polish communists in their bid for power. Contradictory impulses, interests, and commitments pulled the notoriously secretive Soviet leader in different directions; it is, perhaps, no wonder that everyone else in the communist chain of command experienced a form of political-ideological schizophrenia. Certainly, the resulting simultaneous boldness and bashfulness behind Soviet involvement in Polish affairs contributed to the sense of uncertainty that so many Poles felt immediately after World War II.

Scholars have debated for decades the exact nature of the East European political systems in 1945–47. Was this People's Democracy merely one of the many myths that the Soviet and East European communists have used to gloss over the violence and deceit that often accompanied their rise to power? Or was it a really existing arrangement?[205] In Poland, a coalition government did exist from 1945 to early 1947, but the communists dominated it heavily. These Poles, with Stalin's support, constantly resorted to violence, coercion, and deceit to eliminate their rivals. Some scholars in the debate espouse a noteworthy nuanced middle ground. They suggest that a People's Democracy in Eastern Europe was both a reality *and* a myth—because while parliamentary mechanisms were indeed in place, the existing international circumstances made them unsustainable in the long run.[206] But the opposite claim can also be made: that while such democratic mechanisms did function to some degree, the Soviets and Polish communists violated them and disemboweled them—killing their power—which turns the middle-ground interpretation on its head; Poland was *neither* a People's Democracy *nor* a dictatorship of the proletariat in these early years. Like so many other things at that time, the reality was something amorphous, something in-between.

Even more than in politics and economics, the Soviets displayed a mélange of aggressive overtures, tactful involvement, and plain inaction in their approach to Polish culture. On the whole, the mid-level Soviet officials and cultural figures often mixed the desire to intervene with the prudent impulse to disengage. Thus, the Soviets' approach frequently contributed to the confusion about the future of Soviet-Polish cultural relations. But the Poles' resulting disorientation mixed with a potent postwar optimism. Their perceived sense of open ground easily fostered hopes that a Soviet-Polish modus vivendi in the cultural sphere could be sustained. In this way, cultural cooperation had a hopeful start in Poland after the war.

Early on, leading Polish communists also managed to ignore or resist unwelcome Soviet initiatives due to their own strengths and the relative Soviet weaknesses. A rather large middle ground—created by Soviet flexibility on cultural affairs and the Polish elites' interest in selected forms of Soviet cultural fare—raised hopes on both sides that cultural cooperation might prove to be a mutually beneficial project. The years 1945–47, though short and troubled, witnessed the emergence of a genuinely symbiotic relationship between Soviet and Polish elites in the all-important cultural sphere—the kind of relationship that characterizes successful empires. The human potential that drove this fledgling cooperation could have forcefully sustained Soviet soft power and the long-term interests of the Soviet empire at large. Instead, the potential was squandered. As the Kremlin pushed for ever more radical and aggressive interventions in Polish culture, the Soviets alienated even the most dedicated Polish Stalinists, preventing them from wholehearted participation in the cultural consolidation of Stalin's new empire.

By mid-1948 Stalin decided to tighten the ideological screws by isolating the Soviet sphere of influence from the outside world. Fadeev's jeremiad against Western writers at the Wrocław Congress suggested that Stalin, the *vozhd'*, put his weight behind the most orthodox observers of East European cultures. Thus, the new gnarled grip of orthodoxy reconfigured power relations between the Soviets and the Polish political and cultural elites. The promise of cross-cultural exchange died a quiet, rapid death in the years that followed. As confusion, *krochmalizm*, and the cult of Stalin took its place, Soviet-Polish struggles over culture retreated behind the scenes.

3

SOFT POWER ON THE SIDELINES

Nothing is ever lost in nature—except fulfilled hopes.

■

Nothing is ever lost in nature—except people.
—Stanisław Jerzy Lec

RED CHERRIES, MEN IN BLACK, AND
"THE LAND OF THE WHITE EAGLE"

"Only now, after I have visited more than forty countries across the world, I remember the quivering and anxiety with which I was crossing the Soviet border for the first time in my life."[1] Writing these words nearly half a century after the fact, former diplomat Iurii Vladimirovich Bernov still passed over in silence the reasons behind his fears on that Poland-bound train.[2] It was 1952, the apex of Stalinist terror and state-sponsored xenophobia. The former chair of the Sovinformbiuro, Solomon Lozovskii, was languishing in the Lubyanka jail. Lozovskii and fourteen other members of the disbanded Jewish Anti-Fascist Committee (JAFC) had "disappeared" in 1948 and 1949. They endured torture and indignities at the hands of the MGB (the former NKVD, and future KGB); these innocent social figures, artists, and intellectuals who had worked during 1942–45 to secure international Jewish support for the Soviet war effort were now forced to confess that they were American spies.[3] The non-Jewish (indeed, notoriously anti-Semitic) minister of state security, Viktor Abakumov, had been fired in 1951 for having failed to prove their invented crimes; subsequently, his friends and allies were purged from the MGB.[4] Most JAFC members would be executed in the summer of 1952. In 1950, Stalin ordered several top-ranking officials shot to death for procedural breaches in the so-called Leningrad Affair. Thousands of their allies, acquaintances, and subordinates suffered dismissals, trials, and hardships as a result—the authorities found some individuals "unreliable" because they corresponded with

Warsaw, Marszałkowska Street, October 7, 1948. A group of lecturers in front of a mobile cinema showing a Soviet adventure film during the Polish-Soviet Friendship Month. Courtesy of Polska Agencja Prasowa.

close relatives in the United States.[5] The "anticosmopolitan" campaign waxed and waned; although journalists and editors vilified Jews particularly ferociously, anyone with links abroad, or anyone who knew someone with foreign ties, risked arrest.[6] Bernov did not know that Stalin was planning another top-level purge of his closest associates.[7] He did know that almost nobody traveled internationally. Aware of this unique opportunity to see a broader world, and also of the potential risks, the thirty-year-old

Bernov must have known that as he traveled westward, he was also moving upstream.

Debriefed and encouraged by the Soviet ambassador Arkadii Sobolev soon after his arrival in Warsaw, Bernov set off for the city of Szczecin, where he was to assume the post of vice-consul. The port city on the Baltic Sea had been German before and throughout the war. Within new borders east of the Oder River, it was still in ruins, with "signs of American and British bombing raids visible everywhere."[8] But the three-story structure of the consulate lay far from the city center, in a neighborhood that had been inhabited by German aristocrats and officers of the Wehrmacht. An area that housed no industrial enterprises, it was therefore spared by the Western Allies' fire. With its garden full of flowers and exotic plants, fragrant cherry trees, walnuts, plums, grapes, and a heated swimming pool, the villa was like a luxury resort within a lush oasis—a dreamlike sensual cornucopia on a barren landscape of dearth, drabness, and destruction. With its "cozy, comfortable interior" the building was, in Bernov's view, "perfectly suitable" as a workplace and a dwelling for the consular staff. An important industrialist from Berlin had allegedly built the villa for his lover, whom he was visiting regularly.[9] Now, with its latent Chekhovian symbolism of the cherry tree, and the authority of the Red flag displayed in front, the consulate represented the ambiguities and possibilities of the gestating Soviet-Polish friendship.

By the time that Bernov arrived in Poland, the Red flag symbolized the essence of Soviet-Polish relationship far more than did the humanism of any Chekhov story. Stalin's desire to control Eastern Europe gradually resulted in the Sovietization of the region. It is unlikely that the Soviet leader made a one-time decision to Sovietize Eastern Europe. But his gradual pressure on the local communists to gain control over their respective societies, and to conform to his wishes, left them with few other alternatives.[10] For Stalin, too, the integration of the East European institutions with the mighty bureaucracy of the Soviet state may well have meant the most efficient short-term means of controlling them.

Sovietization brilliantly expressed Russia's ancient messianic zeal, and a sense of mission in the world now channeled into the effort to spread the revolution abroad—a set of political ideas that Vladislav Zubok and Constantine Pleshakov dubbed the "revolutionary-imperial paradigm."[11] The new empire validated the Soviet system and helped Stalin reassert his power at home. It gained him new supporters—officers and officials who reaped enormous material advantages from the postwar imperial spoils.[12] Recalling his stay in "the Land of the White Eagle," as he called Poland, alluding to the country's national emblem, Bernov betrayed no imperial hubris. But he felt pleasantly tickled when Polish passersby greeted him on the streets of Poznań with unusual respect, which he explained to himself as being based on his status as a "representative of a friendly great power."[13]

Tortuously though consistently, sometimes under Stalin's direct oversight or at other times with his tacit approval, Polish leaders were turning Poland into a Soviet replica.[14] Having destroyed the opposition, Poland's communists now ruled a mono party-state. At the time that East German, Czechoslovak, Hungarian, and Bulgarian leaders increasingly relied on mass repressions, the Polish leaders turned to intimidating the society in a more arbitrary but no less effective fashion, making anyone vulnerable through what Andrzej Paczkowski has termed "generalized terror."[15] Campaigns against senior Church and military officials were under way. Poland's centralized economy now served the interests of the USSR. The country was in the grip of the industrial Six-Year Plan. While the Polish communists would not even have mentioned collectivization in the immediate postwar period, now they were coaxing and coercing Polish farmers to turn over private land to the collective farms. Soviet officials directly administered Poland's key sectors—the military and the economy. In 1952 Stalin personally set out to edit Poland's new constitution, making his mark on a sacred document of an allegedly sovereign state.[16]

Remarkably, even during the apex of Stalinism, the Polish brand of socialism stood out in the Soviet Bloc. The communists launched an attack on the Catholic Church relatively late, in 1949; and even though the party-state tried to divide and disembowel it, Poland's Catholic hierarchy retained both the popular support and a certain institutional autonomy that other religious leaders in the Soviet Bloc failed to secure.[17] University professors retained much of their traditional autonomy. No Stalin statue has ever stood on any of Warsaw's squares. Writers and artists who fell in with the authorities risked marginalization, not execution or even a labor camp. Still, these forms of distinction brought little consolation to most Poles, who saw the Soviet-sponsored regime as an occupying power. The "invented friendship" between Soviets and Poles, to use Jan C. Behrends's formulation, meant little more than precisely that: wishful thinking of Polish and Soviet communists—and in some cases, not even that.[18] Tellingly, the only reason why Polish pedestrians greeted the astonished Iurii Bernov during his stroll in Poznań, as the diplomat learned quickly, was that, seeing a man clad in a black overcoat, white collar, and dark hat—standard apparel of Soviet diplomats at the time—they mistook him for a Catholic priest.[19]

Much has been written about the successful implementation and excesses of Polish Stalinism, a period roughly between late 1948 and early 1954. Many scholars have emphasized how well Poland's new masters handled that challenge through a gradual recasting of the domestic cultural life into the Soviet mold. Jacek Trznadel, a former Stalinist writer, suggested years later that given Polish writers' critical role in society, simply too many embraced socialist realism, the officially sanctioned artistic doctrine. Zbigniew Jarosiński, a noted scholar, estimated that in the literary community there were hundreds of "zealous" practitioners of "the method."[20] Czesław Miłosz had defected to France in 1951. Poland's leaders such as Jakub Berman promoted a widespread apotheosis of Stalin and put the country's president Bolesław Bierut on a pedestal. Sokorski and Putrament seconded Berman as they implemented his decisions through the Ministry of Culture and the Polish Writers' Union.[21] When the Soviet leader had turned seventy in December 1949, "everyone" wrote about him, including Maria Dąbrowska, Zofia Nałkowska, and Jarosław Iwaszkiewicz, the country's literary giants, middle-class noncommunists and—or perhaps therefore—great moral authorities.[22] Yet outward displays of Poland's most upbeat Stalinist propaganda say little about the efficacy of Soviet soft power. They reveal even less about the motivations of people in the USSR and in Poland who wanted to save face and find fulfillment within the framework of the phony friendship.

This chapter shows that developments in the USSR and Poland's forced transformations of 1948–54 affected Soviet soft power in a couple of ways. First, as Stalin unleashed a new wave of terror in the USSR, the Stalinist administrative machine shoved effective Soviet soft power initiatives to the sidelines—paralyzing independent initiative, empowering opportunism, and promoting low-quality, aggressive propaganda on behalf of the Soviet state. Second, most Polish cultural figures and functionaries found little fulfillment—and often much shame—in their roles as impresarios of Stalinism, with its adulation of the Soviet leader, pseudo science, and senseless propaganda. They found themselves increasingly unwilling to interpret the culture that the Soviets were forcing them to accept. Coercion took hold over Polish culture; as a result, the hitherto open Soviet-Polish confrontations over meaning and form in all spheres of cultural activity moved to the back stage.

In the early 1950s, Roman Werfel, the editor in chief of *Trybuna Ludu*, asked Jakub Berman: "Comrade Jakub, do you really think my readers will notice that you've switched that sentence over from one paragraph to another?" He recalled his boss's sad smile and his reply: "Your readers probably won't, but there are certain readers who might."[23] Werfel's reminiscence is both striking and credible, as it runs counter to the prevalent tendency within the genre to blame the bosses for Stalinism's excesses. It also helps to highlight a rarely acknowledged point, namely, that the ostensible fervor with which some of the top Polish communists such as Berman set out to Sovietize their country's culture was largely due to fear.[24]

Hard-liners like Berman certainly sought to overhaul Poland's culture from the beginning of their struggle for power. Their desire to control institutions of culture, knowledge, and propaganda—in short, those of meaning-production—was a direct cultural corollary to the communists' political aims. Those included the discrediting of the opposition, legitimating themselves in society, and mobilizing the populace for participation in the larger social and economic upheavals. Yet even the hard-liners resisted Sovietizing culture fully, hastily, or both. The Polish communists' limited influence on Poland's culture through mid-1947 (even late 1948) can be largely explained by their physical inability to carry out any drastic changes. But the delay until late 1949, with the sudden push for a full-fledged transformation of Poland's artistic institutions and methods on the strict Soviet model, reflected their unwillingness to do so earlier. True, in the heyday of Stalinism, Poland's communist president Bolesław Bierut tried to convince the poet Władysław Broniewski to rewrite the country's national anthem (the offer was rejected). Yet, shortly after the war, Bierut, together with other dignitaries, had been regularly spotted attending Catholic Mass. No doubt, it took some cynicism and a very stiff upper lip for Bierut to undergo such an ideological makeover. But the reasons why the communist endured the sermons in the first place were very much practical in nature. The communists may have enjoyed a formal monopoly on power, but the hearts and minds of most Poles were unlikely to be won over anytime soon. The same was true of most of the artistic and intellectual elites, on whom the communists depended so much.

Now renowned as a patriot, Władysław Gomułka defended Poland's separate road to socialism at this sensitive juncture. When Moscow changed the strategy and the postulate fell into disfavor, in the wake of the Cominform conference, the recalcitrant party chief was accused of "right-wing, nationalist" deviation and, together with several other East European communists, Gomułka moved downstream. He was eventually ousted from power. Yet, as his Jakub Berman's biographer Anna Sobór reminds us, Berman's public views on the matter hardly differed from Gomułka's even as late as the spring of 1948. Indeed, many other future Stalinists could have been attacked on the same charges; only by sacrificing Gomułka did they manage to avoid his fate.[25]

Poland's top communists and cultural bureaucrats had many reasons to be afraid even after the ritualistic sacrifice of Gomułka. "Number two" among the hated Polish communists, responsible for the sensitive areas of culture, ideology, and security, Berman bore the additional burden of working within the rarified atmosphere of Polish and Soviet anti-Semitism after the war. Later, the arrests and subsequent show trials of East European communists such as Rudolf Slánský, in 1951–52, were largely anti-Semitic in character, and Berman justifiably felt he could be next.[26] The danger became clearer in Poland in 1949: due to pressure from the USSR, the security services initiated purges in the Polish Army; fourteen officers from the army's Intelligence Department, all of them Jewish, were arrested.[27] All Polish communists would have risked their positions by failing to notice the cues from Moscow; Poland's Jewish communists, and especially Berman, could have been most eager in implementing the Kremlin's instructions, and still risk losing their lives. In order to stay in power and to stay alive, Jewish communists throughout Eastern Europe turned to promoting anti-Semitism. Writing in 1952, the Yugoslav communist Milovan Djilas observed that "the Hungarian leadership is most anti-Semitic in its propaganda today for the simple reason that it is composed of Jews." The Hungarian communists used this tactic to "prove" that they have "freed" themselves from the alleged "Jewish cosmopolitan mentality," and prove their faith to Stalin—not only by following their master's directives but also guessing his wish to rid communist institutions of Jews.[28] The Polish communists reacted differently to the anti-Semitic signals from Moscow. They feared that by transplanting the anticosmopolitan campaign on their native soil they might be facilitating attacks on themselves; instead of adopting the racist undercurrents of "anticosmopolitanism," they reinterpreted it as a struggle against bourgeois, Western, and *traditional* Jewish values—and largely focused on a struggle against Zionism. Although in some respects the Polish authorities did validate anti-Semitic views of some Poles, Poland's anti-Zionist campaign turned out to be significantly less intensive than in the other countries of the Soviet Bloc.[29] Berman appears to have been less concerned with proving his break with his Jewish roots to anyone; perhaps he felt that having an openly Zionist brother, about whom he deeply cared, would have made such efforts futile.[30] But he did play a role in supervising anti-Semitic purges in the Polish Army.[31] As such, Berman, together with other Jewish communists, was caught up in the same paradox as his Hungarian comrades: promoting racist policies from which they had themselves suffered in their youth, and digging his own grave at the same time.

Jerzy Borejsza's fate served as an example to those who wanted to stay afloat in the fast currents of Poland's cultural politics. His name had long been associated with cultural moderation and independence, but the ominous signs he read around him by 1949 made him nervous. The Soviet embassy secretary Evgenii I. Dluzhinskii found the Pole visibly "agitated" when Borejsza arrived at the embassy at the end of the year. Borejsza complained that Berman had refused him a visa to the USSR. He wanted to know why Soviet correspondents from Poland meticulously passed over his name, even though he had been the chief organizer of the events they were covering. He explained to Dluzhinskii that he was displeased to see his name mentioned in Ralph Parker's book *The Conspiracy Against Peace*, which was published in Russian translation in the Soviet Union in October 1949.[32] Parker was a Stalinist sympathizer who set out to prove that the reason behind the breakup of the antifascist coalition lay with the politics of Western powers, and not actions of the Soviet state. The work was widely publicized in the Soviet press as part of the stepped-up campaign against the West.[33] But Parker's book depicted Borejsza vividly and at length discussing his own plans for the Polish publishing system in 1948, thus undercutting Borejsza's authority and security.[34] The Pole smelled intrigue against himself, and he traced it to Wanda Wasilewska in Moscow, but he had no evidence to back up his claims. Though sick from a serious car accident suffered a year before, Borejsza was probably safe from physical harm: his brother Jacek Różański was making a brilliant career in the torture chambers of the security police.[35] But even this important relation could not avert Borejsza's rapid downfall after the autumn 1947 about-face in Poland's cultural politics. Once a fearsome champion of a "gentle revolution" in Polish culture, the towering Borejsza was reduced to political irrelevance, a monument to a bygone era and a living antihero to those who wanted to hold on to power or rise through the ranks.

Among figures who paid heed to Borejsza's fall were Włodzimierz Sokorski and Jerzy Putrament. Few knew more about the tactical advantages of cultural moderation than these two political veterans of the Soviet-backed Polish Army. By 1948–49, their sharp instincts, fear of going under like Borejsza, and a keen ability to adapt to new circumstances propelled them into positions of power. After three years of political isolation at home and abroad, Sokorski became vice-minister of culture in 1948. Only a few months earlier, he had moved into a comfortable apartment at 6 Aleja Róż (Avenue of Roses), an elite neighborhood of Warsaw within walking distance to the Belvedere. The model (albeit architecturally and ideologically confusing, and considered "monotonous and appallingly boring") Marszałkowska Residential Quarter (Marszałkowska Dzielnica Mieszkaniowa) would rise nearby in the early 1950s.[36] At this address Sokorski became neighbors with Jerzy Borejsza and other members of the cultural elite, including Władysław Broniewski, Antoni Słonimski, Stefan Żółkiewski, Leon Kruczkowski, and Jan Kott.[37] Putrament assumed the powerful chairmanship of the all-important Polish Writers' Union after returning from a diplomatic post in Paris in 1950 (where he served as ambassador and as something of a spy for the Soviets).[38] The two both reported to Berman and also depended on him; both implemented the instructions of Poland's chief ideologue with well-known zeal, delivering lengthy fire-and-brimstone lectures (replete with Stalinist "newspeak," awkward Russianisms, and even entire interjections in Russian) to the increasingly powerless artists.[39] Putrament, in particular, became notorious after Czesław Miłosz excoriated him at length in his brutal critique of postwar Polish intellectuals coming to terms with Stalinism, *The Captive Mind*. As "Gamma, The Slave of History," Putrament struck some readers as "the only true Bolshevik" among Miłosz's barely disguised protagonists.[40]

Decades after the Stalinist frenzy, in both distinct and contradictory ways, each man denied truly believing in the merits of Sovietization. Putrament, in his memoir of 1970, recalled the "importunate and mechanical proclamations, according to which everything from over there is more than the best, that it is sacred." Reminiscing about what he claimed were counterproductive forms of promoting Soviet-Polish friendship, the writer bewailed them as a result of underfunding for socialist realism and "the bureaucratization" of Poland's life. The former admirer of Chapaev did acknowledge his own role in the popularization of socialist realism, justifying such efforts with his alleged faith in the "inner merits of Soviet people," whom he had met during his stays in the USSR.[41] By contrast, Sokorski claimed to have actively protected Poland's culture from the interventions of domestic and foreign Stalinizers. In a 1991 interview, the former official aligned himself with the influence of his maternal grandfather, a nobleman from Western Ukraine. According to Sokorski, he was "an extraordinary figure. On the one hand, a genuine Polish patriot, who gave funds for Polish schools and the Catholic Church. On the other hand, he demonstrated nearly absolute loyalty to the tsarist court."[42] Sokorski crafted his lineage well. Poles had accepted this form of collaboration ever since the period of partitions; it even received its own name, "Wallenrod-yzm," after the hero of Adam Mickiewicz's 1828 narrative poem *Konrad Wallenrod*, in which the main hero, a Lithuanian brought up by the Teutonic Knights, rises to the rank of Grand Master and destroys the order from within. Due to his self-professed skepticism about the relevance of Soviet experience to Poland, Sokorski claims to have led a double life: while giving "fiery speeches on socialist realism," he recalls, "I left the artists alone."[43] Both writers, therefore, distanced themselves from the orthodox policies of the Stalinist era, but are they justified?

Like many communists after the war, Putrament had initially supported a moderate policy in cultural affairs. It is difficult to verify what the writer really thought in 1948–53; neither his deeds in these years nor the words of others about him betray the latent skepticism about orthodoxy he claims. In contrast, Sokorski, a man who liked to exaggerate, seems to have really tried to minimize the impact of Soviet interventions in subtle but significant ways. During his tenure, deeply humanistic and established writers such as the revolutionary Władysław Broniewski, the less committed to communism Julian Tuwim, and even completely apolitical lyrical writer Leopold Staff received state prizes, while the socialist realists placed second and, like Wiktor Woroszylski, third.[44] Some artists later blamed Sokorski for forcing them into ideological orthodoxy, but recent works reveal that their own enthusiasm and opportunism, not the minister's, drove them to collude in the cultural initiatives of the party-state.[45] Sokorski's record in the Polish Army under Berling's command attests to his ability to handle conflict with higher powers; Putrament, despite major shifts in his circumstances, outlooks, and loyalties, eventually and unwaveringly almost always sided with the strong. Soviet observers complained about Sokorski's lack of Sovietizing enthusiasm.[46] Certainly, the decision to award state prizes belonged to the Politbiuro, but Sokorski's word mattered a great deal. And the pattern of awards hardly constitutes an indubitable proof of subversive activity on Sokorski's part, but for Putrament, even such evidence, or any Soviet complaints against him, are revealingly difficult to find.

It is a fascinating study in individual temperaments, comparing the two men's abilities to see clearly and act boldly when put to the test. Putrament's full complicity with the oppressive Polish regime cannot be attributed to the appeal of Soviet soft power. His biographer suggests that, on the contrary, the bureaucrat's "ideological zeal" provided him with confirmation of the choice to embrace communism that he had made "semiconsciously" earlier in his life—though he also adds that the writer became slightly more cynical over time.[47] In all likelihood, fear had played a negligible role in Putrament's journey toward the "New Faith"—after all, he had already lived through wave after wave of fear in wartime in the USSR and had developed a thick skin.[48] Yet later, once Putrament was in power, he was certainly not immune to the anxiety of losing that power, which all top officials across Eastern Europe shared. This anxiety, combined with the writer's evident inner need for social confirmation, perhaps best explain Putrament's choices. His ability to join the winning side at the crucial moment makes good material for the untalented writer's unheroic biography. But as has been shown, Putrament's perceptiveness also made him keenly aware of how to win over his society to the idea of Soviet-Polish friendship. It was a characteristic feature of the Stalinist empire that it discouraged others from drawing on Putrament's insights; perhaps it was the writer's weakness that prevented him from trying harder to convey his experiences to others.

In the years to come, many Polish writers, artists, scientists, and intellectuals colluded with the consolidating Stalinist regime. Among them, few drew inspiration from direct interactions with Soviet culture and society. Scores of Polish true believers in the superiority of the Soviet system had traveled to the USSR in the 1930s; ironically, they perished at the hands of NKVD agents in the late 1930s, often without knowing why. Like the Polish writer Aleksander Wat, those few who survived prison and exile in the USSR generally lost their Sovietophilic enthusiasm, withdrew from cultural life, and emigrated back to Poland.[49]

Even the literary servants of the Polish communists lacked the mandatory enthusiasm for the Soviet Union. Sokorski's neighbor from 6 Aleja Róż, Władysław Broniewski, became famous for his *Word About Stalin*, written for the seventieth-birthday celebrations of the *vozhd'* in 1949. Indeed, few artists outdid the poet in lending their talents and services to the affirmation of communism; as Mariusz Urbanek pointed out, Broniewski became "one of the visiting cards of the new power."[50]

But there was nothing obvious or natural in Broniewski's postwar role as bard of Stalinism. In 1920, Broniewski had fought with Józef Piłsudski against the Bolsheviks. In his verses from the 1920s and 1930s, he had managed to combine fervent patriotism with the plight of Poland's persecuted minorities and downtrodden working class, while praising the revolution at the same time. In January 1940, the NKVD arrested Broniewski in L'vov on false charges. In prison, he shared a cell with Aleksander Wat; the two also shared a hope for a socialist but non-Bolshevized Poland.[51] There, in a dingy Soviet penitentiary, Broniewski had composed in Russian (but refused to write down) the sarcastic poem "Human—That Sounds Proud" (Chelovek—eto zvuchit gordo). In this poem Broniewski describes an NKVD prisoner who prays to "a faded crimson star"—thus reflecting Broniewski's deep disillusionment with the system he had earlier praised and admired.[52] Following his release from prison, Broniewski evacuated to the Middle East with the Anders Army; talking to friends in Jerusalem during the last months of the war, he often revisited memories of his Soviet imprisonment. Broniewski had difficulties accepting the new Poland, some recall, and hardly thought about returning home. Then he learned that his wife Maria, long considered a victim of Auschwitz, had survived. The man whose talents Poland's Stalinist regime would soon co-opt, at last decided to return home. But, as his recent biographer emphasizes, Broniewski's choice was hardly a result of his sudden conversion to communism. The poet left for Poland in the summer of 1945 in order to be with his beloved woman, hoping he would be spared performing "the mandatory drumbeating" for the authorities.[53] Ironically, the communists defined Broniewski's contribution to Polish literature precisely around his "drumbeating." Why did he write "A Word about Stalin"? In part, because he could not have known about the enormity of Stalin's crimes, suggests Broniewski's biographer; more cynical observers speculated that Broniewski came to appreciate Stalin, having received from the communists a villa and a car.[54]

The most militant of Poland's Stalinists came from the ranks of the youngest generation. Some were still in their late teens when they embarked on the project of building a socialist society. Young, angry writers like Wiktor Woroszylski earned the nickname "pimpled ones" on account of their youth; one of many anecdotes about the origin of this collective moniker points to the writer Zofia Nałkowska, who coined it out of resentment toward her younger, less accomplished and often untalented, but more privileged literati colleagues.[55] In poetry, the "pimpled ones" would settle for nothing less than what seemed to them like revolutionary Vladimir Mayakovsky. In prose, they were the chief motive force behind the popularization of Soviet-style fiction devoted to the industrialization of Poland and collectivization of agriculture. That they rarely received national first prizes for their output reflects the cautious approach of the authorities. The late, Nobel Prize–winning poet Wisława Szymborska, now widely known for her unassuming, intimate verses, jump-started her career with poems about Lenin and industrialization. And among these most zealous supporters of the Stalinist regime, in all areas of cultural activity, we find the lodestars of future opposition to communism: historian Bronisław Geremek, philosopher Leszek Kołakowski, and activist Jacek Kuroń. Ryszard Kapuściński became a journalist in the late 1950s; by now, his beautiful and riveting reportage from the hellholes of the world have been translated into thirty-five languages.[56] One of Kapuściński's most famous collections of essays, *Imperium*, is based on his travels in the moribund Soviet Union in 1989–91.[57] The famed reporter, too, had started out as a poet in the literary vanguard of Poland's Stalinist front: an eager activist in the ZMP, the Polish youth organization, and a self-described mentee of Broniewski and Woroszylski. And then there was Kapuściński's Soviet inspiration. "The eighteen-year-old Rysiek," noted his biographer, had entered the "two worlds, that of literature and the kingdom of the New Faith," by way of ascending the poetic "'staircase' of Mayakovsky's stanzas."[58]

Many have speculated about what exactly drove these youngsters into their uncompromising positions. Even despite these efforts—with a notable amount of discourse coming from the perpetrators themselves—no clear, single answer exists. The democratic, humanistic slogans of communism coupled with the system's energetic support for the arts are said to have appealed to some.[59] Others cite an experience, ineffable by today's standards, of living in a charged universe of moral imperatives that fused Poland's potent romantic tradition with the sudden spiritual void brought about by Poland's wartime defeats (in the September 1939 campaign and in the Warsaw Uprising of 1944). One of the "pimpled ones," Tadeusz Konwicki, declared that in such a world, a middle ground was unthinkable, and the utopian promises of the new ideology were hard to resist.[60] Though most of the neophytes later denied being aware of Stalin's crimes during their youth, it is likely that at least some knew of the atrocities but dismissed them. The about-face *was* possible, journalist Teresa Torańska reminds us, pointing to Poland's General Wojciech Jaruzelski. Jaruzelski had survived the Stalinist camps, having been deported to the USSR with his family. Yet when he arrived in Poland with the Soviet-sponsored Polish Army, Jaruzelski became a career military man and a recalcitrant defender of the system until today.[61] The same ideological about-face was true of Piotr Jaroszewicz, another veteran of the Polish Army in the USSR. But claims to ignorance about the brutality of Stalin's rise seem vastly overstated, particularly in the case of journalist Kapuściński. He must have known, argues his biographer, as Kapuściński came from Eastern Poland where "'one knew' who the Soviets were and what they were doing after

17 September 1939."[62] Wiktor Woroszylski, who hailed from Grodno in Eastern Poland must be measured against the same standards.[63] But many of Stalin's young devotees came from other parts of Poland, and not everyone may have known the brutal reality behind the Soviet occupation of Eastern Poland in 1939–41. For them, unlike for Broniewski, the red crimson star continued to shine.

Did these young men and women, boys and girls, in some cases, fully understand the cost and consequences of Sovietization? Are we really amazed that militant youth became the most eager advocates of Poland's Sovietization, when *as a group* they had the least direct exposure to the Soviet system, methods, and "way of life?" For the Soviet propagandists and promoters of soft power, these young militants may have promised easy victory. But after 1948, when Soviet incursions into Polish life became more aggressive, Soviet cultural ambassadors would in time be forced to admit: the "pimpled ones" also presented the greatest unknown.

SOVIET CULTURAL OFFENSIVE

Communist leaders from other East European states were jealous when, on November 6, 1949, the Soviet Marshal Konstantin K. Rokossovskii became Poland's minister of defense. He himself was surprised.[64] Following his appointment, Soviet officers took over the vast majority of top posts in the Polish Armed Forces—far more than in any other East European vassal state (even Hungary and Romania, which had fought against the USSR during the war, as well as Bulgaria).[65] The day that Rokossovskii assumed control of the country's armed forces—the second strongest in the Soviet Bloc after the USSR—was also, somewhat perversely, the thirty-second anniversary of the October Revolution. But this circumstance was the least of the Soviet Pole's PR problems. For despite his affable character and stunning appearance—he was tall, handsome, classy, and looked well in his Polish uniform—this hero from Stalingrad fought a losing battle, his poor Soviet-trained tongue at war with certain Polish consonants.[66]

Adam Bromberg, working for the Polish Army's Political Department, was given the Herculean task that resembled his earlier duties as political officer: "to convince the nation (*naród*) in twenty-four hours, that it should rejoice" from Stalin's unexpected "gift" and "come to love the brave Red Army soldier."[67] Bromberg panicked—the rest of his propaganda team comprised only Jews, including fellow-veterans from the Soviet-sponsored Polish Army, plus one Soviet adviser to boot—but they all set to work, and

Warsaw, February 1949. Soviet Marshal Konstantin Rokossovskii is visiting Warsaw for the celebrations of the thirty-first anniversary of the creation of the Red Army. Accompanying him is the former Kościuszko Division political officer and architect Józef Sigalin. Courtesy of Polska Agencja Prasowa.

one million copies of the joyous brochure spurted out of the press on the following morning.[68] Without knowing it, Rokossovskii himself provided the humor that ultimately helped offload the stress: in one of his first public speeches in Polish, the Marshal made so much verbal effort that "he raised his eyebrows higher and higher as he was reading out the villainies of the American imperialists," until his face reached an expression of "constant surprise," which, as Bromberg points out correctly, was later commemorated in numerous portraits.[69] In the long run, however, Rokossovskii's controversial appointment was no laughing matter to anyone; for, even though the top communists liked the idea that he would share responsibility for their decisions, they and most Soviet officials had to bend over backward to spruce up the Soviet marshal's nearly nonexistent Polish biography. In the Polish communist propaganda, Rokossovskii thus became "a symbol of Soviet-Polish alliance."[70] Most Poles saw the appointment as a blatant violation of Poland's sovereignty. Some even saw Rokossovskii's appointment as the first step in the Soviet incorporation of Poland.[71]

Rokossovskii's promotion to Poland's top military post was certainly the most obvious sign of direct Soviet meddling in Polish affairs. Statistics show that the tempo of Soviet interventions in the Polish cultural sphere picked up the pace in the second half of 1948 (see appendix B, figures B.1, B.3–B.8). The scrupulousness with which Soviet officials collected such data suggests just how much these individuals were preoccupied with their mission. Polish radio was the first to respond to the new initiatives. In the second half of 1948, Polish radio increased by three times the number of hours devoted to discussions of Soviet subjects, from about 3 hours per month to 10–11 hours per month. Although these numbers were still insignificant relative to the length of the Polish broadcast, the 300 percent increase suggests an important shift. The number of hours of Soviet and Russian music on the radio went up from 15.5 hours to 39 hours per month. In addition, the number of hours that combined Russian/Soviet music with a discussion of Soviet or Russian subjects skyrocketed from 15 hours in June to 65 hours in December 1948.[72] In 1950, Polish radio aired a total of 1,290 hours of programs dedicated to Soviet and Russian subjects, including 856 hours of music, 380 hours of discussion, 30 hours of news programs "Novosti dnia," and 24 hours of programs in Russian language.[73] This took place during a rapid expansion of radio networks in Poland.[74] In 1947, only 5 Soviet cultural delegations visited Poland, but by 1948 the number went up to 14, and in 1949 the delegations had reached 18. Conversely, only two Polish cultural delegations went to the USSR in 1947, but in 1948 there were 9 and in 1949—12.[75] In 1950, a total of 31 Soviet delegations visited Poland.[76]

Soviet cultural authorities worked up other forms of Soviet propaganda less rapidly, but ultimately with equal consistency. The breakthrough came at the beginning of 1949 as part of a broader trend to augment the Soviet symbolic presence in Poland through representations of Soviet political, cultural, and economic models and, by implication, Polish dependence on the Soviet Union. The direct impulse for more active Soviet involvement in the Polish cultural sphere may have come from the Soviet Ministry of Foreign Affairs. On March 21, 1949, the head of the ministry's Fourth European Department, Stepan P. Kirsanov, sent his "Suggestions for Intensifying the Soviet Union's Influence on Cultural Life in Poland, Czechoslovakia, and Other East European Countries" to Andrei Vyshinskii, Andrei Gromyko, and Valerian Zorin. The key problem, he argued, was that Soviet propaganda directed toward these countries had still not been given the appropriate state priority. Kirsanov suggested concentrating the entire propaganda effort in the hands of one agency, the Soviet Information

Bureau (the suggestion was never implemented). A more active approach would also be necessary, he pointed out, a shift from merely catering to the needs of local communists to intervening more actively. Kirsanov's other suggestions included streamlining the onerous bureaucracy involved in international exchanges, expanding the competences of ministries and organizations that would allow them to get involved in the process, as well as increasing cultural exchanges between the Soviet Union and its new satellites. Last, Kirsanov stressed the necessity of putting more pressure on East European Communists to decisively cut off their countries' cultural ties to the West.[77] The official's marked emphasis on Poland attests to the country's strategic importance in the Soviet plans; however, Soviet cultural engagement with Poland as well as with Czechoslovakia, Bulgaria, Rumania, Hungary, and Albania also left much to be desired—and for quite similar reasons.[78]

It is difficult to say to what extent this document spurred the Kremlin's interest in East European propaganda or simply coincided with it. Stalin remained the ultimate power broker after World War II. However, the Soviet bureaucracy was enormous, and the Soviet leader delegated much of the decision making to numerous commissions and committees; Mikhail Suslov, who, as chief of the International Department had gained control over staffing issues in the MID by the beginning of 1949, also influenced the organization's approach to East European affairs.[79] Kirsanov's report certainly foreshadowed more aggressive Soviet involvement in Poland's cultural life. In all of 1947, Soviet organizations exported 77,900 books: copies of Russian and Soviet nonfiction and belles lettres, and children's literature; in 1948 the figure went up to 160,300; in 1949 it was 539,200. By 1950 it was 1.3 million, in 1951—1.8 million, and in 1952—2.3 million.[80] Throughout all of 1948, the USSR sent across the border 617,600 copies of books of all genres; only in the first quarter of 1949 did the number goes up to 804,700.[81] The figure amounted to 3.3 million for the entire year of 1949.[82] The increase in exported periodicals was stunning: 21,812 copies of journals and newspapers in 1948 and 83,157 copies in the first quarter of 1949.[83] With the help of Polish publishers, Mezhdunarodnaia kniga published the following numbers of titles of Soviet books in Polish: 54 in 1947, 110 in 1948, 229 in 1949, and as many as 303 titles in the first half of 1950.[84] Soviet organizations exported to Poland 31 films in 1945, 69 films in 1946, 96 films in 1947, 150 in 1949, and 182 in 1950, thus appropriating roughly half of the big-screen exposure, measured by the number of screenings. The number of viewers of these films also went up from 12 million people in 1945 to 79 million in 1951.[85] In 1947, only 1 Soviet and 4 Russian plays were staged in Poland, where a total of 47 performances were staged to audiences of 31,000 people. In 1948, the totals included 521 performances of 16 Russian and 14 Soviet plays to audiences totaling 314,000. By 1949, the number went up to 29 Russian and 34 Soviet plays, as a staggering increase in the number of performances reached 10,000 and the number of viewers—3.5 million people (see appendix A, table A. 2).[86] Exhibitions of Soviet and Russian art became more frequent.[87] Membership in the Polish-Soviet Friendship Society (TPPR), another institution aiming to attract Poles to the USSR grew exponentially.[88] The government organization KWKZ (structurally mirroring the All-Union Society for Cultural Relations Abroad, or VOKS) took over cultural exchanges in July 1950.[89] Never before or after the four-year period that followed was the Soviet presence in the Polish cultural sphere so strong.

FRICTION

Czesław Miłosz recounted an incident from 1945, in which a well-known, elderly Soviet journalist visited Poland and toured several provincial cities. Miłosz writes: "This recurrence of sterile hopes amused him and he was flattered to be a representative of a country ruled according to infallible predictions; for nation after nation had indeed become part of its Empire, according to schedule." Miłosz detected a "compassionate *superiority*" in the man's smile, comparable to the feeling of a housewife for "a mouse caught in her trap."[90] Some Soviet visitors to Poland after the war indeed displayed the supercilious demeanor of the anecdotal guest. Yet their reactions to the cultural changes in the country, even in 1948–54, were much more diverse than the émigré writer's story and even recent literature would lead us to expect.

Marxist ideology may have informed some Soviet visitors' impressions of Poland, but most anchored their opinions in the more concrete frameworks of personal experience. Guests such as the writers Ilya Ehrenburg, Fedor Panferov, or the pianist Iakov Zak, who had already been to the country between the wars, generally praised developments in Poland's culture. The Soviet writer Nikolai Tikhonov, who visited Poland in 1950, recognized and recorded the transition to strength he had witnessed. "When it comes to general observations, . . . there is a sense that the air became clearer—there is fresh air." In comparison with Warsaw in 1935, he wrote, "it is a straight-out different world. One can see it in the people on the streets, their conversations, and so on."[91] Clearly, Tikhonov enjoyed his stay. Other writers and artists traveled to confront the negative national stereotypes that had been popularized in the USSR before the war. Gripped by stage fright, members of the Ukrainian Ivan Franko Theater group who visited in early 1951 were anxious to see whether the Poles would "display the condescending attitudes toward the Ukrainian people that had been inculcated in their heads by the Polish nobility during the rule of the previous governments."[92] Their series of performances turned out to be a self-described success (internal reports often identified failures as well). Like Panferov earlier, many artists experienced a strange feeling of familiarity: the state of Poland's artistic life reminded them of the years 1923–24 in the USSR, "when Constructivism was thriving on the scene."[93] For some visitors, such "time travel"—to use Ann Gorsuch's metaphor for analogous visits in the later period—may have indeed proved gratifying. In the atmosphere of terror against artists in the USSR, Soviet travelers to Poland were pressured to criticize "foreign influences" in official reports from Poland; yet many Soviets visiting Eastern Europe must have felt genuine nostalgia for the period of artistic experimentation buried in their pasts. Perhaps even those who paid lip service to the xenophobic party demands of the moment felt a degree of envy that the Poles were partaking in a cultural ferment that was denied to them.

Soviet visitors to Poland in these years often registered their puzzlement, but not arrogance. Visiting Wrocław in 1950, Tikhonov enjoyed the exhibit on Mickiewicz and Pushkin. He only took issue with the display titled "The Cult of Pushkin in Russia," commenting that "cult" was not, in his opinion, the most felicitous word to describe the phenomenon.[94] The writer Anna A. Karavaeva and literary scholar A. S. Miasnikov arrived in Poland in the spring of 1952 on official business. In 1935, Karavaeva had found the "gentry-dominated" (*panskaia*) Poland to be dark and "gloomy." She had also seen firsthand the destroyed state of Warsaw from the plane to Paris in 1945. Now, returning to what she saw as sunny, socialist, prosperous Poland, she was overjoyed.[95] Both visitors observed interest among Polish writers in the works of Dostoevsky. They reported that their Polish counterparts had a "superficial" grasp of socialist realism. But while on a mission to promote the "typical"—that is, the chief, albeit vague, characteristics of "socialist realism"—what vexed them most were their hosts' indulgence in seeming clichés. Lengthy discussions of "the Russian soul" or of "the unstable Russian mind," often based on the Poles' readings of Dostoevsky's works such as *Crime and Punishment*, seemed standard fare. To Miasnikov's relief, the Poles warmly welcomed his talks on Russian and Soviet literature. But he found it "very interesting," and even perplexing, "that during my lecture on socialist realism, they applauded Lenin, Stalin, and *Tolstoy.*"[96] Both visitors agreed that helping Polish writers find their voice required a "very careful" approach because the Poles "are very sensitive to mentorship." Consequently, Miasnikov discouraged lecturing "in our interactions with Polish writers," since "the members of the old intelligentsia still do not understand many things."[97] Miasnikov acted as Moscow's guide as he urged his bosses to consider a more sensible soft-power policy. At the time, however, the Soviet system put a premium on pride, passivity, and opportunism; Miasnikov's call, remarkable in its honesty, remained without an echo.

Unlike most Soviet artists, the country's government officials viewed the developments in Polish culture in concrete, strategic terms. Now that the Soviet party *and* government officially supported westward cultural expansion, even those diplomats who earlier refrained from riding roughshod over Polish sensibilities became, willy-nilly, agents and enforcers of Sovietization. In practice, the officials understood their mission to encompass three goals. The first was to secure the Polish population's maximum exposure to Soviet as well as Russian artistic and cultural production. The second was to ensure the Poles' constant and explicit acknowledgment of the supremacy of Soviet culture. Polish artists were expected to imitate the socialist realist method, while Polish communists were expected to praise and promote it. Finally, Soviet bureaucrats wanted to see recognition of the entire political context that made this new culture possible—not only within a particular work of art but also in the way in which it was delivered to the Polish public. This manifested as quasi-religious celebrations of Stalin, and strident public recognition of Soviet agency in Poland's cultural transformation. Signs of respect for anything Soviet, including explicit expectations of privilege, became the norm. In the words of a Polish historian, this entire process aimed at "cutting Poland off from anything 'Western,' and from vast territories of its national tradition—that is, from anything that linked it to Western Europe and from almost anything of its own."[98]

The implementation of these goals proved complex and frustrating. "Everything in war is very simple," wrote the nineteenth-century Prussian strategist Carl von Clausewitz in his classic *On War*, "but the simplest thing is difficult." This veteran of the Napoleonic Wars coined the term "friction" to account for the chasm between the theory of war and its lived experience. The dangers of combat—the blood, the bullets, and the bombs—and the extreme physical strain impaired the judgments (and the capacities) of the combatants. So did the flood of ambiguous, contradictory information that exposed the generals "to countless impressions, most of them disturbing, few of them encouraging," which Clausewitz called "the fog of war."[99] Friction is the lifeblood of combat. While real blood colored only the backdrop of the Soviet cultural offensive, and hissing bullets made but background noise, the Soviets inhabited a cultural battleground in Poland just as treacherous and disabling as the Prussian war theorist described.

For despite Soviet pressure and effort to bring Poland's culture in conformity with the Soviet model, it was clear that the Poles would have a long way to go to achieve it. During the bombastic celebrations of the Polish-Soviet friendship month in November 1950, most of Stalin's portraits hung higher than those of the deeply revered Polish leaders. Soviet embassy secretary Iurii Safirov wrote approvingly of this after the event; this, he added, marked a departure from preceding years.[100] Still, such evident successes seemed weighed down by the long list of Soviet complaints about the absence of Soviet models and examples in all areas of Polish cultural life ranging from literature, theater, and film to music, plastic arts, and sporting events. Stalin's benevolent face also overlooked the celebrations of Soviet-Polish friendship month the next year, in 1951; but the posters advertising flashy, American gangster novels during a book show and negligee-clad women featured on them surely distracted from the lackluster and asexual Soviet book jackets.[101] Soviet intentions had misfired here. Ostensibly there to illustrate the perversity of rotten American culture, the bold, racy images hijacked the curious gazes of passersby. Public culture reviled nudity, yet no one turned their eyes away. In the minds of the ever-vigilant and insecure Soviet officials, questions about the political intentions of Polish organizers and the counterproductive effects of anti-American propaganda flew like confetti in a gale.

Again and again, the Soviet officials blamed bureaucrats in Moscow for insufficient support of the Polish efforts to Sovietize. Organizations such as Mezhdunarodnaia kniga continued to struggle against insufficient funding and incompetence.[102] Wrong publications went to wrong destinations within the Soviet Bloc, which sometimes produced effects that now seem comic. In 1950, the organization sent books on ice skating to Albania, while Poland and Czechoslovakia received manuals on the grooming of camels.[103] Clearly here, the Soviets missed the needs of the East European readers by a stretch the size of the Sahara Desert. A year earlier, in May 1949, Zofia Lissa, whom Marian Naszkowski described as "a tiny woman but an outstanding musicologist," had petitioned the Union of Soviet Composers for help with materials on Soviet musicology that were, according to her, completely nonexistent in academic musicology departments across the country.[104] Requests for help must have echoed loudly in Moscow, as cultural bureaucrats in other Soviet vassal states also pleaded for more Soviet sup-port.[105] Soviet complaints about the lag between political standards to which they held up all arts and the state of Polish music multiplied through-out the Stalinist period. Most common among them were references to Western influences among Polish musicians and the absence of a contem-porary Soviet repertoire, especially the "mass song." (Not a single Soviet song "devoted to the struggle for peace" had been published, noted Safirov in 1950).[106] Lissa's pro-Soviet credentials were unquestioned; Soviet gov-ernment officials who processed her letter had few reasons to doubt that here, too, the fault was on their side. But most often at fault was the ma-chine, not the cogs; the bureaucratization and fear of initiative was so great in the USSR, that approval for even minor cultural exchanges was re-quested of Stalin himself.[107]

As late as mid-1949, Soviet officials saw themselves as still competing with the West for the hearts and minds of the Poles and other East Euro-peans. In a report commissioned by the Soviet Central Committee's In-ternational Department, the Soviet ambassador Lebedev informed them in June that the direct propaganda of Western organizations was waning. But he also mentioned that Western influence continued to seep through institutions such as embassies and international organizations, notably charitable and relief agencies operating under the auspices of the United Nations—a "tail" left by the United Nations Relief and Rehabilitation Ad-ministration, which by 1949 was shut down. Sectors of Polish society were still vulnerable to foreign influence, argued the notoriously overeager Leb-edev, which mandated even more energetic involvement from Soviet cul-tural institutions.[108] There were good reasons for this. Polish mass culture, often kitschy, had imitated Western models before the war. The country's cultural and intellectual elites had traditionally showed strong Franco-philia, only accentuated in the decades before World War II; after the war, even those artists and designers who trained one eye on Moscow for new aesthetic forms appropriate to modern times, looked to Paris with the other.[109]

Soviets and even other East European Stalinists blamed Poles' personal ill will or negligence for the grinding frictions of Sovietization.[110] Yet in some cases, Soviet officials managed to resist the temptation. This is re-markable, because the institutional pressure to do just that was enormous in these dreadful years. Thus, in his 1951 report, Safirov refrained from blaming Zofia Lissa for theoretical confusion; but he did point out that the musicologist's insistence that Polish composers write separate music for peasants, workers, and so on showed her misreading of the Soviet principle of *narodnost'*, which stipulated one kind of music for everyone.[111] By 1949, Soviet film production and controls on Western imports had pushed Western cinema out of circulation.[112] In the immediate postwar years, Polish cinemas had been dominated by war movies, but by the early 1950s, spy films and increasingly anti-Western themes prevailed, and a touch of light comedy was always present throughout late Stalinism.[113] Until 1949, the dubbing of Soviet films had frequently been done by Soviet citizens with a weak knowledge of Polish. To avoid latent comic effects, the process was shifted to Polish crews in 1949.[114] But Soviet officials recognized that a quick fix was hardly available for every such problem. For instance, more Soviet plays could always be staged in Poland. But their poor quality often turned them into a farce in the eyes of those Soviet observers who had seen the originals back home. "For example," wrote Safirov in 1951:

> What can you expect from an artist in a theater at the House of the Polish Soldier performing in Lavrentev's play *For Those Who Are at Sea* (Za tekh, kto v more) a role of the military commander of the motor torpedo-boat division, and former worker, a tough communist, who had received higher education, if that artist—a typical Polish bourgeois (*meshchanin*)—during the fifteen years of his career played solely roles of cardinals, senators, officers, and so on. Obviously his scenic habits, customs, and stock phrases make our simple, cordial, but strong-willed man seem like some kind of self-important and cheap character, resembling more an officer of the British fleet, whose roles, incidentally, the artist had played over and over again.[115]

Such cases of plain awkwardness made it difficult for Soviet observers to blame the friction between what was asked and what was delivered on Polish obstructionism. Yet in Stalin's Russia, after the war, as in the 1930s, people charged each other with the most outlandish accusations in order to turn suspicion away from themselves. When arrested, desperately wanting to save themselves, they confessed to fantastically improbable crimes. Here, the Soviet officials chose to apologize for the unskilled Polish artists, and to give them the benefit of the doubt. This is remarkable, for they could not have expected similar understanding if accused of lack of vigilance back in the USSR.

HIDDEN TRANSCRIPTS

When the Soviet audience booed the Polish pole vault jumper Władysław Kozakiewicz after his winning jump in the 1980 Moscow Olympics, the athlete showed them a *bras d'honneur*.[116] In Stalin's time, the communists severely punished insulting the Soviets; anyone daring even to joke about Poland's eastern neighbor could have paid for it with a jail sentence.[117] Poland's public, artistic elites, as well as large sectors of society expressed their anti-Soviet passions more obliquely. Often they displayed what James C. Scott has termed "hidden transcripts," or expressions of veiled or concealed defiance by subordinate groups against those who dominate them. A hidden transcript "represents an acting out in fantasy—and occasionally in secretive practice—of the anger and reciprocal aggression, denied by the presence of domination."[118] Poles relied on hidden transcripts to express their frustration with Soviet domination and lack of reciprocity. Without resorting to obscene gestures, the Poles made the Soviets feel frustrated and unwelcome in less direct, but unmistakable ways.

Were the cultural elites of Poland unable or unwilling to imitate Soviet models? The observers from the USSR had to scan that thin line. The Soviets correctly suspected that some members of Poland's established artistic elites, co-opted into the communist cultural project, cared little about pleasing them. Asked to create party-minded material that would treat contemporary themes in a form accessible to the masses, scores of artists escaped into historical themes, something that worried Polish communists as well.[119] While these artists could not or would not flee the country, they could and did flee into Poland's distant past. Embassy officials I. Kuznetsov and Iu. Safirov, in their early 1950 and mid-1951 reports, bemoaned the fact that most of the leading film directors and musicians explored historical themes precisely in order to avoid addressing contemporary life.[120]

Soviet observers routinely noticed that Polish artists continued to flirt with Western forms in their work. In 1950, Tikhonov commented on the performances of *Pan Tadeusz* and *Evgenii Onegin—the* canonical classics in Poland and the USSR, which he saw in Cracow's Rhapsody Theater. He found both to be artistic letdowns. The young artists were "superb," he clarified, but everything had "such a formalist bent, that it missed the target. The characters speak interchangeably in the third or the first person"; in this manner, he explained, "Pushkin's Tatiana speaks herself about herself." In addition, Mickiewicz, who "wrote *Pan Tadeusz* when he was an elderly man, appears on the scene precisely in that way: as a gloomy old man. None of it looked very good."[121] From the orthodox Soviet perspective, such acts were formalistic follies and scenic schizophrenia. Mickiewicz should have been young and dashing, and reflect the official optimism of this revolutionary era; there was no room for sadness in socialist realism. A party-minded Tatiana would speak of herself only in the first person "I."

No form of Polish art seemed immune from Western influence. As late as March 1952, Safirov reported to Moscow that a sizable portion of Polish painters had notoriously failed to conform.[122] In 1950, when Safirov heard musicians such as Władysław Szpilman (recently commemorated by Adrien Brody in Roman Polansky's *The Pianist*), and Jerzy Sokorski (the brother of Włodzimierz, the vice-minister of culture) drawing on American "jazz cacophony," and the "sugary tunes" of German and Austrian operetta, he was understandably miffed.[123] Yes, Soviet officials understood that long-term habits were hard to break, but many artists maintained strong ties with the West, which testified to their ill will.[124] The artists' deliberate resistance to allow the communist party into their own affairs seemed all too obvious.

Poland's radio editors and presenters further tested the patience of officials such as Safirov; like the negligee-clad women on the gaudy American book jackets, the material they broadcast was fraught with potentially subversive ambiguities. "In the programs of the Polish radio," wrote Safirov in 1951, "one can still observe a strong tendency to imitate the West, especially America." In his account, radio presenters followed every three or five minutes of news broadcasts with musical pieces that were "completely irrelevant" to the content of the news.[125] "In radio programs about the Soviet Union," Safirov reported, "every day one can hear jazz cacophony during breaks between serious announcements." He illustrated his point about the subversive intentions of Polish radio editors with a broadcast from February 10, 1951, when the radio host announced the preparations for elections to the USSR's Supreme Soviet and followed up the message by playing a Boston waltz. "Then he talked about the Polish population's care for the tombs of the Soviet soldiers only to follow up this message with the fox-trot."[126] The same was true throughout 1952. Summarizing the year, Safirov claimed that the radio regularly emitted "dubious materials containing philistine (*obyvatel'skie*), petty-bourgeois (*meshchanskie*) gossip about socialist building in Poland." In addition, a number of radio programs were created "on the West European broadcasting model."[127] Jazz had thrived in the USSR for decades, even under Stalin. In the last months of the war, East Europeans welcomed the Red Army as liberators, of course; but the Red Army bands stirred sheer euphoria among thousands of inhabitants of Cracow, Helsinki, Prague, and Tallinn by playing Glenn Miller's lively tunes.[128] By the late 1940s jazz had become an American instrument in the Cold War, and the New York-based radio Voice of America started "to equate the sound of jazz with the sound of freedom."[129] Soviet soldiers' rape and pillage in Eastern Europe certainly muffled the enthusiasm for the USSR, something for which no amount of Red Army jazz tunes could have compensated. Yet one wonders to what extent the 1946 Soviet anathema against Western music, especially jazz, also deprived the Soviet state of a mighty source of soft power.

More spontaneous than radio, film, and even theater, public events such as festivals, sports games, or musical competitions gave Soviet officials a much more reliable barometer of Polish attitudes toward the USSR. If the sacralization of the Soviet presence in Poland was the expected norm, Polish participants notoriously failed to deliver. Polish audiences enjoyed the performance of the dance ensemble Berezka in 1950. But the audience reaction in the city of Białystok expressed seething resentment. "Only one person stood up" after a local party secretary who was introducing the ensemble mentioned Stalin's name, Safirov wrote to Moscow, while "the others dragged their feet and stood up very slowly, gradually, but there were no cheerful hurrahs to comrade Stalin." Having played the Polish anthem flawlessly, the excellent orchestra completely botched the Soviet one.[130] Safirov did not bother to seek extenuating circumstances, and probably none existed. Białystok had been invaded and occupied by the Red Army in 1939–41; in a familiar scenario reflected only in a "hidden transcript," the resentful inhabitants made their resentment known by barely crossing the party line.

International musical competitions became another litmus test for Poles' willingness to conform with Soviet demands. The charged atmosphere of these events cannot be overestimated: Stalinist decorum required an unequivocal Soviet victory, but national honor was on the line for both sides. During the apex of the Cold War, the fourth international Chopin piano contest in September 1949 and the annual international Wieniawski violin competition in December 1952 turned into cold skirmishes. In both cases, the overwhelmingly Polish juries, supported by Włodzimierz Sokorski, insisted on awarding Polish musicians with first place. The one-hundredth anniversary of Chopin's death in 1949, as one Soviet musician overheard, provided Sokorski with an excuse. Dismayed, even after an intervention, the Soviets had to settle for a tie between the Polish artist Halina Czerny-Stefańska and the Soviet representative Bella Davydovich.[131] Memories of this humiliation hung over Soviet officials like a dark cloud during the Wieniawski contest in 1952, held in Poznań. The Poles again tried to secure victory, but after an aggressive Soviet intervention, the grand prix went to the Soviet violinist Igor Oistrakh.

Poznań, December 1952. Minister of Culture Włodzimierz Sokorski awards the Soviet musician Igor Oistrakh first prize in the Henryk Wieniawski International Violin Competition. Courtesy of Polska Agencja Prasowa.

Two Soviet musicians also placed third; Polish success boiled down to Wanda Wilkomirska's second-place tie with Iulian Sitkovetskii from the USSR, a result that Soviet officials still thought unfair.[132] From the Soviet perspective, the audience's reaction also spoiled the sweet taste of formal victory: "composed mainly of the intelligentsia," the public "vigorously applauded" the Polish and French musicians, "but passed over in silence the great success of the Soviet artists."[133]

"Memoirs and anecdotes from the People's Poland," pointed out historian Iwona Kurz, referring to Kozakiewicz's 1980 antic, "underscore the fact that the Polish-Soviet war had its hidden course precisely on the sports fields and in the sports halls."[134] With so few opportunities for Poles to let off anti-Soviet steam, likely intensified by the Soviet insistence on unequivocal victories, sporting events served as relatively safe occasions to vent one's resentments against the otherwise innocent athletes sent from Moscow to do their job. As with music competitions, the Soviet expectation to win constituted another missed opportunity for forging a true Soviet-Polish friendship. As sports fans, the crowds could express themselves directly and viscerally in ways that would be frowned upon in a respectable concert hall. Boxing especially raised the temperature since, through its "plebeian nature [it] tends to express" a certain "tension inherent in modern

Warsaw, 1953. Soviet Union's Boris Stepanov (dark shirt) boxing with Poland's Zenon Stefaniuk in the finals of the European Boxing Championship. Stefaniuk won the gold medal. Courtesy of Polska Agencja Prasowa.

societies: that between violence that is kept in check, and violence that can spill into the street at any moment."[135] With a dose of satisfaction, Maria Dąbrowska related her experience at the European Boxing Championship in June 1953. She noted in her diary that Poland had won the games, while "only two Soviet contestants scored victories, and not a single one of them was Russian." The atmosphere in the sporting hall was electric: "The enthusiasm for the Polish contestants that was being expressed through screaming and applause could only be compared with the roar of the sea during a storm. It was deafening. And when, after the fifth victory, the crowd of thousands of people began singing in a thunderous voice "Poland has not perished yet" [the Polish national anthem]—and sang it as we never sing it, tears started flowing from my eyes. It's funny, but it was a great patriotic manifestation."[136]

Safirov related having undergone a similar ordeal during the 1950 international boxing championship held in Warsaw. Though the Soviet contestants eventually secured gold, they "were received insufficiently sympathetically" by the Polish audience. The diplomat speculated that this was because the crowd consisted mainly of "merchants, shop owners, craftsmen, and so on." As a result, the venue resounded with an "encouraging roar" when a Pole or a Finn struck a Soviet boxer while "a complete silence" ensued after the most stunning success of a Soviet sportsman.[137] Did he really believe that the ideologically alien petty bourgeois status of the spectators could explain "the roar," or was his comment a safe space-filler on the form destined for Moscow? It could have been either, or both. Some have argued that under socialism, the naked, muscled torsos of boxing men were to express the moral perfection of the new socialist man as much as physical prowess of the contestants.[138] If this is true, then the Poles' consistent support for the non-Soviet side aimed to underscore the moral bankruptcy of Stalinism.

Analogous situations took place at soccer games, such as the four played during Polish-Soviet friendship month in 1951. In an uncanny, if somewhat perverse twist of Sovietization, the Polish fans were expected to cheer for the Soviet goals as well as those scored by their national team. They failed to do so during a game in Warsaw. Perhaps anticipating even more serious incidents in Cracow, Polish officials distributed free tickets among workers and gave them a day off, making sure they would see the game. Thanks to these measures, pressures eased, and the last event was the calmest of all.[139] Jakub Berman himself later told Torańska that "it was at those matches that the old anti-Russian sentiments, and the new anti-Soviet ones, came to the fore."[140] Having been annoyed by some Soviet interventions in the past, Berman perhaps even quietly sympathized with the stirred-up public.

BORDER STREET

"A scandal . . . veiled anti-Polish propaganda," wrote Maria Dąbrowska in her diary on January 14, 1949, shortly after seeing Aleksander Ford's new film *Border Street*. Jerzy Borejsza, proponent of "the gentle revolution" in Polish culture, had invited her to the preview screening to predict what audience responses would be in Warsaw. At first, Dąbrowska was puzzled at the invitation. Having viewed the film, she was outraged. Ford's film about the ghetto uprising of 1943 showed "the Jewish tragedy" "superbly" because "the Jewish Marxists have forgotten about Marxism, and were

Aleksander Ford and Władysław Godik during the filming of Border Street *(Ulica Graniczna), director Aleksander Ford (1948). Photograph by Jerzy Gaus. Copyright by Studio Filmowe KADR, Studio Filmowe TOR, Studio Filmowe ZEBRA, Filmoteka Narodowa. Licence: Studio Filmowe KADR.*

inspired by simple human love," Dąbrowska wrote, but that was where her praise ended. She found the "Polish side" to be "strikingly distorted," seething with "barely restrained antipathy."[141]

Dąbrowska's comments must be read in the context of her own ambiguous feelings about Jews. She had a longtime Jewish lover, and publicly fought against anti-Semitism. But privately, she saw Jews as an obstacle to the realization of Poland's messianic mission of moral regeneration among nations. Underlying this vision were the Romantic beliefs in the "chosenness" of the Polish people and the sense of unique, incomparable Polish wartime suffering—a form of nationalist ideology that came into conflict with the Jews' traditional sense of chosenness, and Jewish survivors' demands for recognition of the distinct tragedy of their own.[142] The film was hardly a neutral commentary on Polish-Jewish relations during the war as it purported to be. As a film exploring hotly controversial social issues in an era of fast-changing political demands, *Border Street* spun furious responses on all sides. A quick detour behind the scenes and into the multiple versions of the script reveals battles over meaning that help explain why Soviet outsiders experienced cultural friction. It also sheds light on the complicated position in which Polish communists, particularly those of Jewish background, found themselves after the war, as they tried to implement their own social visions and political agendas while mediating between increasingly orthodox Soviet officials and various sectors of Polish society.

With his thick, black mustache, the forty-year-old director Aleksander Ford resembled "a gruff version of Groucho Marx." The foreign reporter who made the comparison a few years later also found in him "the same stubbornness lit up by sudden flashes of humor or wry disdain at the things going on around him."[143] In making his first postwar film, Ford built on two decades of cinematic experience. His prewar films such as *The Legion of the Street* (1932) about Warsaw's newspaper boys, combined his interests in the artistic avant-garde with concerns for social justice—a fact that won Ford acclaim especially from the Left. A member of the Communist Party of Poland of Jewish origin, Ford entered adulthood in the era of growing anti-Semitic discrimination, which also forced him to explore cinematically the life of Jews in Poland and the dilemmas they faced. Like many in his generation of artists, he rebelled against the kitschy, commercialized cinema of the interwar era.[144] Paradoxically, the political forces that promised to realize Ford's ambitious social and artistic aspirations would easily co-opt him into activities that served primarily the affirmation of communist power.

After the outbreak of the war, Ford fought in the September campaign against Germany. Following the Polish defeat, and together with several other Polish-Jewish filmmakers, he produced Soviet propaganda films in the eastern part of Poland occupied by the Soviets. Having joined the Kościuszko Division in 1943, he came to head the formation's film unit Czołówka ("opening credits," but also "a vanguard," or "an advance guard," depending on the context). He became the visual chronicler of the division and the Polish Army in the USSR; as an artist, communist, and freshly minted officer, he helped craft the myth of Soviet-Polish friendship that would be acceptable to the Soviets, the Polish communists, and highly suspicious soldiers. In so doing, he resorted to frequent window dressing of historical truths in order to mobilize Polish soldiers, but nonetheless ran into occasional roadblocks with the Soviet military censorship.[145] His talent, convictions, and connections propelled him into the top job at Film Polski; he also became an artistic director of two major film units and "the most important figure in the postwar Polish film industry."[146]

Aware of some potential challenges in setting out to shoot *Border Street*, Aleksander Ford could not have known the full extent to which he would trade the treacherous swamps of the Oka River for the expansive mine-fields of postwar politics. The film underwent multiple revisions before being released. But in all versions, it is a story about the war's effect on the relationships between several Polish and Jewish families living in an apartment building on Warsaw's "Border Street." Shot with a narrow lens, the narrative was set against the backdrop of wartime developments cul-minating with the Jewish ghetto uprising of 1943. It was also to be sym-bolic of larger trends: as the voiceover informs the viewer at the beginning of the film, the house and the street were picked at random.[147] At the cen-ter of the story is a family of Polonized Jews, the Białeks. Dr. Białek is a respected member of the local community. His young daughter, Jadzia (in earlier versions: Zosia) regularly plays with other Jewish and Polish kids, some of whom are anti-Semites. The potential ambiguities gain signifi-cance with the onset of the Nazi occupation. When Jadzia fails to invite little Fredek Kuśmirak to her birthday party, he and his father denounce the Białeks to the Nazis. Subsequently, Jadzia goes into hiding, her father moves to the ghetto and dies of illness, whereas the Kuśmiraks take over their apartment. Fredek's older sister Wanda is having a romance with an SS officer. But Jadzia also has good friends who are ethnic Poles: it is they who accompany and defend her both in the house on Border Street and throughout her flight until the outbreak of the Warsaw Ghetto Uprising at the end of the film.

Ford's and other communists' own experiences of racism, the urgency that their Jewish backgrounds lent to the problem of the Holocaust, and genuine concerns with social equality between Poles and Jews may have sustained their personal interest in the film. The members of Czołówka were among the first to film the liberated concentration camps; the enor-mous scale of the tragedy suffered by people in occupied Poland may have inspired the idea for the movie.[148] But only political motives can explain why the project actually moved forward. By 1946, when the first version of the script was created, few Jews remained in Poland. Thousands more would leave shortly thereafter as a result of the wave of anti-Semitic vio-lence, which shrunk the obvious audience of a film about Jews to insignifi-cance.[149] Moreover, the communists were hardly in a position to confront Polish society on its most sensitive social issues such as anti-Semitism—nor was the commemoration of the Holocaust their top priority at the time.[150]

On the contrary, the Polish Worker's Party (PPR) leadership eagerly strove to bolster their patriotic credentials in the eyes of the masses who were deeply suspicious of the Soviet-backed communists. The film was meant to fulfill that purpose in several ways. First, as a number of observers have pointed out, the goal was to "rehabilitate Jews as members of the Polish nation."[151] Circa 1946–48, this was a Herculean task. On the one hand, the extreme version of the widespread myth of Judeo-Bolshevism falsely held Jews responsible for the Sovietization of Poland.[152] On the other hand, as discussed in chapter 2, for many and often contradictory reasons, ethnic Jews became visible and disproportionately present in the institutions of the unpopular regime. Given the history of mistrust between Poles and Jews and wartime complications in their relations, the relatively large numbers of ethnic Jews in communist institutions discredited the communists even further. Second, some scholars have argued that the communists celebrated Jewish heroism to commemorate the heroism of all Poles: "The Warsaw Ghetto uprising of April 1943," suggested Omer Bartov in his discussion of *Border Street*, "served as an ersatz depiction of what most Poles experienced as a far more traumatic, but equally heroic event, the Polish Warsaw uprising of August, 1944."[153] Third, as Michael C. Steinlauf has pointed out, the communists sought to legitimize themselves by ostensibly breaking with the reactionary legacy of anti-Semitism. *Border Street* constituted an element of a larger campaign of which the commemorations of the 1943 Jewish Ghetto Uprising were also part. Such efforts mostly misfired, however, for "all this reaffirmed what many Poles already felt they knew, namely, that Jews were the government and the government was Jewish"—an impression that could hardly have been alleviated by the communist branding of all political opponents as anti-Semites.[154]

Sensitive to the potentially explosive effect of *Border Street*, Ford's bosses in the PPR told the director in 1947 that the film "should be released 'neither first nor second'" that year.[155] In addition, Ford and his collaborators revised the script several times; its successive transformations show his agonizing attempts to address the problem of Polish-Jewish relations in a way that would be acceptable to the various audiences. Two out of four versions of the story preserved in the Library of the National Film Archive in Poland are, unfortunately, undated. But even examined on their own terms, the drafts reveal consistent trends and dilemmas involved in the making of the film.[156] For instance, the number of anti-Semitic Polish characters grows and shrinks, depending on the version of the script. In one version we see Dr. Białek's sympathetic Polish neighbor Cieplikowski helping his Jewish acquaintance transport his property to the ghetto on his own cart; in another version, Cieplikowski is gone. Similarly, the boy Władek, Jadzia's friend in the film's final version, figures as a Judeophobe in an earlier screenplay—"Jews don't play soccer," he tells another boy, Dawid, as he bars him from entering the game. In one version, we see Wanda flirt with Hans (the SS officer), and the story moves on to tell about Zosia's ill-fated birthday party. In another, Ford inserts a conversation between an old Jew, Liberman and his son-in-law (and Dawid's uncle) Natan about the Jewish stance against the Germans. Liberman doubts the possibility of Jewish resistance; Natan believes the Jews should and will fight side by side with the Poles, taking them as examples. In inserting the scene, Ford blunts the sharp edge of Polish-Jewish antagonism by suggesting that Polish Judeophobia is partly an anachronistic belief of the older (and clearly unassimilated) generation of Jews. In one draft of the script Zosia/Jadzia dies in the arms of her Polish friend Bronek. In another, she remains alive. On the one hand, the change minimized the tally of Jewish victims of the film, and consequently minimizes the weight of Polish complicity in the Jewish tragedy. On the other hand, it allowed Ford to end with a depiction of "profound joy" on the young protagonists' faces—thus suggesting that the experiences of wartime oppression would prove stronger than prejudice and unite all Poles and Jews.

The communists understandably feared running this series of films about Poles' anti-Semitism, of which *Border Street* was probably the most frank. The risk they took was either to win over Polish audiences to a more critical view of their past or simply to offend them.[157] Related was the fear that in trying to address the problem of Polish anti-Semitism, Ford really skewed wartime realities in a most inflammatory way. By suggesting at the outset that the eponymous "Border Street" could be any street, as Adam Ważyk pointed out in his 1946 comments on the script, its authors obscured two facts: first, that the street's location made it a contact point between Poles and Jews—and therefore, a unique place in Warsaw; and second, that while the "ghetto" fought on the street's one side in 1943, 1944 saw another uprising in the "Aryan" part.[158] By 1948 Ford's former comrade in arms Włodzimierz Sokorski threatened the director with "a serious affair" in the event of Ford's continued disobedience. Such considerations required Ford's team constantly to edit the film, thus delaying its release.[159] Faithful to his original vision of cinema as a dialogue with the viewer, Ford refused to make more overarching cuts. His recalcitrance, "stubbornness" and apparent "wry disdain" even in relationship with his bosses had already led him into trouble. The director's defiant financial unaccountability as head of Film Polski provoked a public outcry, and in 1947–48, the PPR leaders still had to publicly protest seriously. His resistance to close supervision in the making of *Border Street*, at a time when communist leaders were fighting any and all independent initiative, further alerted them to Ford's untamed will. In early 1947, Ford was replaced as head of Film Polski by Stanisław Albrecht, "the first true technocrat in Polish cinematography."[160]

In early June 1948, the qualifying commission gathered to discuss *Border Street*. Having largely praised the aesthetic and technical aspects of the film, several of its members expressed doubts about the film's content. Tadeusz Kański, the deputy director of Film Polski, pointed out that the character of Wojtan, a bank clerk, was "shown as a coward who endangers a Jew and treats him like a member of the ONR [Poland's National Radical Camp, a pre-World War II extreme right political party] would have," warning that "the viewer will react differently than the authors predict he will."[161] Film Polski's art director Bolesław Lewicki added a nuance to this view, arguing that, "Our sensitivity is heightened at the moment, and reminding the viewer of sins from the times of occupation irritates him."[162] They were right. Those Poles who harmed Jews during the war had few reasons to want to dwell on their own crimes. But many Poles did not harm their Jewish neighbors in any way. In light of the ethnic, cultural, and social divisions in Polish society that were accentuated by the war, and a longstanding image of the Jew as the oppressor of Poles, not their victim, ethnic Poles already had plenty of reasons to focus on Polish tragedies and heroism. As Krystyna Kersten observed, they had very few such reasons to mourn the distinct drama of Poland's "others."[163] The communists finally released the film in June 1949, largely out of fear that gossip around the controversial film might do more harm than the movie itself.[164] Viewings took place only after the Polish media had been instructed to read the film as a universal story about racism, and trial screenings had also been organized for workers and other groups.[165] Maria Dąbrowska felt gratified that her critical remarks about the "strikingly distorted" views of Poles in the film were considered. Her early screening and incensed response to *Border Street* helped adjust the film, and necessary political concessions were made so that "the anti-Polish elements of the plot have been deleted or changed."[166]

In the meantime, the Cold War intervened, further complicating the tasks of Ford's team and their patrons. The onset of Sovietization forced East European leaders throughout the region to repudiate the "national roads to socialism." Israel's overt pro-American stance and the Soviet Union's subsequent support for the Arabs were accompanied by a wave of official anti-Zionism. The widespread "Jewish national awakening" within the USSR, which had followed the initial Soviet support of Israel, now seemed like a danger to Stalin. The Soviet leader's subsequent anti-Semitic agenda created a dark cloud over the heads of Jewish communists and made any Jewish-centered activities suspect by default.[167] In the Soviet leader's view, the communist internationalists in the Polish leadership, many of them Jewish, fulfilled their function in the fight against the nationalist Władysław Gomułka; after Gomułka's fall from grace, these men were no longer indispensable, and became ever more vulnerable to scapegoating.[168] Even before the official change of Soviet policy, Jakub Berman, who liked the director Aleksander Ford and supported the production of *Border Street*, suddenly began worrying about the film's possible "quasi-religious" overtones.[169] He may have heard of the scene in which little Dawid's grandfather, the traditional Jew Liberman, prays. The scene served to contrast such seemingly old-fashioned responses to anti-Semitic danger with the more appropriate stance of Natan, who takes to arms. But Berman, all too aware that the Soviets were looking over his shoulder, understandably needed reassurance.

Within this dark, swirling cloud of unknowing, *Border Street* premiered in cinemas on June 23, 1949. The release, wrote journalist Alina Madej, marked the end of cinema as a dialogue between artists and audiences.[170]

The Soviet embassy official Kuznetsov, who saw the film a few months later, opined in his report that the struggle of Warsaw ghetto Jews was the strong point of the film. But he also criticized the film for its "many nationalist tendencies," chief of which was the emphasis on Polish support of the Jewish ghetto uprising at the expense of "the basic forces struggling for the liberation of Poland," meaning "the complete neglect of the role and significance of the USSR and the Soviet army." Somewhat contradicting himself, Kuznetsov listed among "nationalist tendencies" the weak depiction of the participation of the Polish people in this struggle," thereby implying that the Jews got too much coverage.[171] Jews had rarely been featured in Soviet films, and he no doubt found Jewish presence in a Polish film equally troublesome.[172] These last comments echoed the remarks of Stalin, an avid notorious movie buff who also saw *Border Street*.[173]

One terrible event coincided with *Border Street*'s release. During Dąbrowska's first viewing of *Border Street*, she learned about Jerzy Borejsza's car accident. Borejsza, the most fervent proponent of "the gentle revolution" in Polish culture, suffered injuries that left him alive but impaired—and unable to attend the screening. It was to Dąbrowska's deep disappointment, believing as she did that "those people" would hardly understand the likely counterproductive impact of the film; Borejsza was "perhaps the only person one could still talk to."[174] She was right, in that Borejsza, who was Jewish, shared her concern about the top communists' seeming partiality toward the Jewish cause, which he deemed politically dangerous.[175] But Dąbrowska was also wrong, for even the hard-boiled Stalinists understood her point of view. It was just that, lacking Borejsza's naive mix of self-confidence and optimism—not to mention his natural extroversion—they were less enthusiastic about frank discussions with reluctant fellow travelers like Dąbrowska.

While *Border Street* had dropped a bomb that silenced dialogue between filmmakers and their audiences, it also symbolized a new low standard in the dialogue between Soviet and Polish officials. Ford and his assistants worked hard for three years to reconcile their own artistic visions and social agendas with the political objectives of the communists. They revised the film to make it acceptable to the Polish public. But ultimately, they offended the political sensibilities of the handful of Soviet viewers who, in making their demands on the Poles, increasingly threatened to destroy those few precious spaces in which the Polish communists managed to create a precarious balance between themselves, the elites, and society at large. By this time, Polish communists, particularly the Jewish ones like Berman and Ford, knew that open defiance vis-à-vis Soviet demands would have meant risking their careers and even their lives. So it was only natural that they would try to wrest tactical advantages within the dark nooks of Polish cultural institutions and behind the scenes. Still, the film's influence spread. In 1949, the year of Kuznetsov's critical report about *Border Street*, the film was released in France under the title *La verité n'a pas des frontières* (The truth has no borders). This powerful metaphor may have played well in Western Europe, but as everyone involved in the making of *Border Street* learned, by then "the truth" had to originate in Moscow.

SOKOLOVSKII, HIS SUCCESSORS, AND THE SOVINFORMBIURO

Vladislav Ivanovich Sokolovskii's new appointment defied the odds. Probably sometime in 1949, he replaced K. I. Orlov as the Soviet Information Bureau's (Sovinformbiuro) field representative to Poland. His knowledge of Polish and his Polish descent, his connections with the country's top cultural bureaucrats, and his journalistic know-how certainly made him more qualified for the job. Yet in many ways, Orlov's dismissal and Sokolovskii's appointment constituted a cookie-cutter response by a regime that was able to deal with internal institutional problems only through finding scapegoats by quota. A verification commission appointed by Stalin and led by A. A. Kuznetsov, N. S. Patolichev, and M. A. Suslov deemed the Soviet Information Bureau's work "unsatisfactory" in the summer of 1946.

The resulting purges of staff that took place in 1947–49 became part of a larger wave of renewed terror that Stalin unleashed to reassert his authority after the war. Stalin also used the purges as an instrument of ethnic cleansing. More than one hundred people lost work in the organization's central apparatus. Promotions went largely to ethnic Russians and Party members.[176] Such passive discrimination reflected what Benjamin Pinkus termed the Soviet authorities' "rather complex compromise" on the Jewish question in 1946–47, which combined official tolerance of Jews in Soviet institutions and even struggle against extreme manifestations of anti-Semitism, with simultaneous unwillingness to recruit Jews to responsible posts.[177]

Sokolovskii's new responsibilities also flew in the face of the rich propagandistic experience he had accumulated while working with the Poles in the Soviet-sponsored Polish Army and at *Wolność*. Earlier, Orlov had advised Moscow to "navigate political reefs" carefully in order not to offend Polish sensibilities. Now Sokolovskii served as a mere instrument of a massive, blind propaganda machine spurting out Soviet journalistic triumphs for the world to consume as news. By undertaking various measures, Sovinformbiuro officials secured a quantitative increase in the publication rates of their press materials (see section below). But even in 1950, 1951, and 1952, when all apparent obstacles to publication had been eliminated, the Sovinformbiuro officials continued to face difficulties in getting articles published on agriculture, international questions, religion, the priority of Soviet science, and theories of the Soviet state. For example, editor Irena Grosz was reported to have answered Sovinformbiuro officials that the "success of the collective farms is not applicable (*ne pokazatel'nyi*) to Polish agricultural cooperatives."[178] Grosz was a former political officer in the Polish Corps, and wife of Wiktor Grosz, a journalist and in 1944–45 chief of the Army's Political Department.[179] According to Sokolovskii, the main problem was the questionable hiring practices of the Polish editors, among whom were "unreliable elements."[180] Other institutions that were parallel to Sovinformbiuro faced similar difficulties.[181]

Eager to publish their articles in the Polish press, Sovinformbiuro officials cared even more that Poles take the initiative. On March 26, 1949, Sokolovskii's boss, A. Volozhenin, congratulated him on recent successes. But he added that in the future "we need to get the editorial offices themselves to start ordering articles on the subject of their interest." "Obviously," he noted, "it is up to you to suggest to them which aspects of Soviet life are important and should be publicized (*osveshchat'*) in a given organ of the Polish press."[182] In response to such pressures, and also in an effort to get factual news from the USSR, the Poles began ordering Sovinformbiuro's articles. But to the great dismay of Soviet officials, these requests ignored the usual subjects, and additionally, concentrated on short news reports and not, as the Soviet officials preferred, the feature articles that were both longer and presented more propagandistic value. Sovinformbiuro officials were apparently uncomfortable with exerting pressure directly and tried to train the Polish editors to guess what they themselves should want, just as Polish party leaders had learned to ask Stalin for "advice" on key political issues. It is likely that the Sovinformbiuro officials were bound by some internal statute, which prevented them from telling the journalists directly what to do, much like Soviet advisers and diplomats who, at least on paper, had a very narrow field for maneuver.[183] Soviet officials sometimes imagined they could make their Polish colleagues see that promoting the Soviet agenda was their "patriotic duty," but no successes on that front have been reported.[184] Instead, based on the often poor results of their interventions with the Central Committee members and information from more forthcoming Polish editors, the Soviets became even more suspicious of the Poles' good faith, and reported their doubts to Moscow through their own bureaucratic channels.[185]

The Polish communists, now that they had successfully monopolized all of the country's political power, lost their main argument for defying the Soviets. This meant that when the Poles did beg to differ on the publication of a particular article, Sovinformbiuro officials made no effort to compromise. It is true that earlier in 1948, upon Soviet request, the Poles fired an editor who had refused to publish the institution's articles on the grounds that "the Polish journalists write better than the Soviet ones."[186] But in other cases, the Polish communists tried to hold their ground. Sokolovskii complained about this in his April 21, 1949, report to the Central Committee of the All-Union (Bolshevik) Communist Party (VKP(b)). The Polish leaders, Sokolovskii reported, were afraid to describe the "superiority of Soviet agriculture" in the party press and explicitly prevented the Sovinformbiuro from doing so as well. In consequence, the press published only 37 out of the 127 articles on the subject that the field office received from Moscow in the first quarter of 1949.[187] Another time, Polish leaders refused (without success) to publish the article "Popov, and Not Marconi," dedicated to the alleged Russian inventor of radio.[188] It was such Soviet material that gave rise to jokes circulating around Eastern Europe at the time. "Adamov was the first man," a resident of Budapest heard on the street, and Adamov had been created by "Jehov."[189] The Poles nevertheless continued to have their way in many cases by saying one thing and doing another—they both refused the Sovinformbiuro's articles and failed to propagandize many aspects of the Soviet experience.[190] The Soviets occasionally discovered the Poles' duplicity directly from sympathetic editors, but chose not to confront the top communists; if their informants were compromised, much would be lost, and so consequently they suffered the humiliations in silence.[191]

The differences between the Polish communists and Soviet officials seem to have been more tactical than ideological. After all, most of the top Polish communists were hardcore Stalinists whose devotion to the Soviet leader helped them survive the Comintern purges of the late 1930s. On June 15, 1950, Sokolovskii reported that the previous day the Polish party's Central Committee had agreed "for the first time" to publish material against the Vatican. He must have meant Soviet materials, since Jakub Berman had kicked off a general anticlerical campaign as early as March 21, 1949, during an editors' conference in the Central Committee.[192] Yet a year and a half after Sokolovskii's message, the Sovinformbiuro representative Ivanov complained that during all of 1951 he was unable to publish anything disparaging about the Vatican or Polish Church leaders. Similarly, careful as the Polish communists were about discussing collective farms, they were surreptitiously introducing the Soviet farm model in several areas of the country as early as 1949.[193]

The directors of the Central Committee's Press Department were equally unwilling to publish an article about the world peacemaking mission of the Russian Orthodox Church. One of them, Stefan Staszewski, allegedly explained this refusal with the potential danger it might have posed: namely, that the Poles might take it as an attempt to impose Orthodox Christianity on Poland.[194] In an interview with Teresa Torańska three decades later, Staszewski explained his attitude toward Soviet news functionaries from *Pravda*, *Izvestiia*, and TASS: "For correspondents I was the chief, so even if they'd wanted to make critical comments of any kind I wouldn't have had to take them seriously."[195] The Soviet Information Bureau had a higher status than the other media outlets, but it appears that the Polish authorities refused to make this distinction. In the same interview, Staszewski expounded on his views concerning importing Soviet culture in general:

> True, I did hold the view that the bathetic style of grand-scale building propagated in Russia should be grafted onto Poland and that the Polish society should be infected with it, but the forms that this grafting process was taking didn't seem effective to me. And I assure you that

that's why we were able to reject and get rid of socialist realism with such relative ease: because first of all it was not inscribed in our cultural tradition, and second we were not excessively enthusiastic in implementing it. Wherever it was possible to wriggle out of some act of servility, we wriggled out of it.[196]

Staszewski's account is certainly self-serving and in many ways typical of autobiographical efforts to accentuate and embellish one's role in history. But it does corroborate the story that emerges from the records of the Sovinformbiuro: well-educated, discerning individuals set on maintaining power at home, Staszewski and other top officials worked scrupulously to filter out the carelessly written news materials from Moscow. It appears that working in their own territory and with the eager support of numerous Polish journalists, he and others were, in fact, able to do so.

Polish readers seemed likewise unimpressed with Soviet journalistic fare. Consider one such article, titled "A Distinguished Engineer" (Znakomity maszynista), which appeared in *Życie Warszawy* on August 13, 1951, with a subheading "from our own correspondent." It told of a Stakhanovite feat by a Soviet locomotive operator, Blinov, who was also a deputy to the Supreme Soviet and a hero of socialist labor.[197] In response, the editors received an incredulous letter from a Polish engineer named Kozłowski who was so impressed by the described stunts that he did the math and concluded it was a joke. It appeared that Blinov, at the speed of 150 kilometers per hour, drove a train that was four kilometers long and consisted of four hundred wagons. Kozłowski berated the editors for publishing the article without consulting a specialist and advised that they should quickly publish a commentary explaining that the article was a mistake, in order to save the paper's reputation.[198] Reactions such as this help to explain why Polish editors often dragged their feet in publishing Soviet material.

Andrei Zhdanov's 1947 division of the planet into "the imperialist, undemocratic" and "anti-imperialist, democratic" camps augured a cultural schism as well.[199] Within months, Soviet journalists bent over backward to elaborate the differences between "democratic" and "undemocratic" music, while exasperated Polish readers struggled to understand what this distinction implied.[200] There were readers who felt strongly about some issues, such as religion and the collective farms. "Try to touch our Church, and you'll see what'll happen," warned one, writing to *Wolność*. "We'll slaughter our cows and won't go to the collective farms anyway."[201] Similarly, Sovinformbiuro representative F. Potemkin reported, in 1953, that some articles on the Soviet Union boasted of the great successes of the Soviet collective farms even though their yields were actually lower than those of Polish farms.[202] Far from projecting the power of attraction, the Soviets were actively damaging their own cause.

Sokolovskii and his successors clearly failed to make the Poles want Sovinformbiuro's material. But to what extent did they succeed in formal terms? Quantitatively speaking, between 1945 and 1953 the Soviets made significant progress in getting their materials into the Polish newspapers (see appendix A, table A.1.). Yet despite that fact, the Soviet message reached the Polish reader in a refracted form. Articles on certain subjects, notably agriculture, Soviet science, and often also economy and international news, were consistently filtered out. Others, such as international news and reports on the economy, theories of the Soviet state and other subjects, tended to vacillate depending on the Polish communists' need. Similarly, since the Poles were likely to accept some themes and genres more than others, newspapers could overfulfill their obligation to the Soviet side as measured in general percentages and quantities, while still being selective. This tendency was clearly evident in 1948. The acceptance rate for that year was 81 percent. But this stunningly high percentage rate was for original articles only. In fact, in 1948, Sovinformbiuro experimented with duplicating articles before sending them off to Poland. As a result of this short-lived practice, as many as 5,864 articles were delivered to the Polish editors. When duplicated articles are removed, the publication rate was only 37 percent.[203] Various newspaper editors, in other words, were likely to publish copies of the same articles while at the same time to shun printing others. The nominal Soviet success between 1948 and 1953 seems even less compelling when we realize that these figures tell us only that a given article was published, but not in how many newspapers. Articles often appeared in one paper but not in others, which limited their propagandistic influence. Quite strikingly, the constant Soviet failure to penetrate the Polish provincial press suggests the limited appeal of Sovinformbiuro's articles, and of Soviet soft power—at the time when the USSR's access to the Polish reading public was, formally, the greatest.

SOVIET ENCOUNTERS WITH POLISH SCIENCE

In his autobiographical and largely self-congratulatory *My Encounters with Polish Science*, published in 1997, the high priest of Polish science under Stalin, Adam Schaff, mercilessly drove home one point. Throughout the communist era, he argued, science in Poland was Polish, not Soviet. "Were we rebuilding Polish science, or maybe one that was Chinese? Were we building Poland from its foundations, or maybe the Soviet Union? Gentlemen, let us not give in to madness!"[204] Schaff was the director of the Central Committee's Science Department, editor of the party's philosophical organ *Myśl Współczesna* (Contemporary Thought), and a person who held several other top positions in the communist apparatus. In *My Encounters*, Schaff largely takes credit for the national characteristics of Polish science between 1945 and 1953. Ostensibly, the book was an argument against perceived anticommunist fanatics of the 1990s, who, in Schaff's view, tried to discredit all aspects of the country's communist past. Lurking behind this explicit goal was the octogenarian's desperate desire to set the historical record straight, and to leave his own positive image for future generations. Hardly the lone knight on the quest to save Poland's scientific tradition that he portrayed himself to be, Schaff nonetheless invites legitimate questions about the influence of "Soviet science" on Polish intellectual life and the reasons behind its relatively short lifespan.

In the war's aftermath, scientific cooperation became another opportunity for the Soviets to connect the genuine talents, interests, and passions of East European elites with long-term stability in the new sphere of influence. In both the Soviet Union and Poland, science (*nauka*) was understood to include research and teaching in natural, technical, social, and human sciences. Contacts between the two scientific communities had been sparse and uneven between the wars.[205] While Polish scholars and scientists working in the increasingly authoritarian state pursued traditional Western models of free scientific inquiry, the Soviet state increasingly subjugated its own scientific community to the ideological demands of Stalinism. After World War II, the surviving Polish scholars were eager to establish (or reconstitute) patronage networks and links with foreign peers that would help them carry on in new, difficult conditions. Also eager, the hitherto beleaguered Soviet scientists hoped that, having proved their loyalty to the Stalinist regime through their wartime sacrifices, they would now be rewarded with a modicum of freedom after the victory; the relative autonomy they had enjoyed during the war seemed to substantiate their reasoning.[206] To be sure, most of them had been able to pursue their own research interests even in the ghastly 1930s. But in order to do so, they had to show that their work met three conditions: materialism, Marxism, as well as party-mindedness (*partiinost'*), through participation in ritualized public debates and a skilled courtship of powerful party patrons. To many scientists, a more relaxed political climate after the war would mean an end to these charades. Promoted and mediated by the two states, early postwar contacts between Polish and Soviet scientists exuded the scientists' optimism, and faith that unfettered international cooperation would soon become possible.[207]

Alas, between the fall of 1947 and the fall of 1948, together with all arts, the mass media, and human and social sciences, the Soviet authorities conscripted most natural sciences into the Cold War effort against the "bourgeois West."[208] The process began with the "Michurinist campaign." It started in the fall of 1948 with the political victory of the Soviet pseudo-biologist Trofim Lysenko over his institutional rivals, particularly in the field of genetics. A charismatic charlatan and a skillful courtier, he was able to sway the party bosses to his point of view. Ostensibly building on the theories of an obscure Russian plant breeder, Ivan Michurin, Lysenko argued that when appropriately treated, plants could be made to inherit certain characteristics they had acquired from the environment. Backed by Stalin, Lysenko succeeded in compelling numerous scientists and administrators from other research and educational disciplines to follow suit and assert the supremacy of the "Michurinist" approach in their own fields—often as remote from biology as pedagogy.[209] Most often this boiled down to a public recognition of *external* factors as the driving forces within a particular field. Consequently, officials in every field consecrated an appropriate "father figure" for this discipline, which was chosen from the official Russian and Soviet scientific canon. Everyone recognized that the rhetorical strength of such claims lay in their resonance both with the immediate political climate amid the growing Cold War tensions as well as the grand Soviet project of social transformation. From that point on, the image of a "politically correct" science involved not only materialism, Marxism, and party-mindedness but also the ostensible affirmation of Soviet scientific superiority over the West (frequently laced with official anti-Semitism) and a version of "Michurinism." Advanced physics and mathematics were among the few disciplines that survived such regimentation and subsequent deterioration; this was possible thanks to the tremendous efforts of those Soviet scientists who worked tirelessly to apply their knowledge to the development of the all-important defense industry, especially nuclear weapons.[210] Officially launching peace campaigns, the Soviet authorities hardly showcased such research to the public at large. Ironically, though understandably, they also excluded these most sensitive research areas from their soft-power arsenal deployed to conquer the hearts and minds of East European elites.

Instead, the Sovietization of Polish science, intensified after the fall of 1947, involved largely structural and ideological transformations. While there were no specific directives about the timing, scope, or scale of the transformation from Moscow to the Polish communists, the Soviet Central Committee's International Department and Mikhail Suslov in particular actively supported the initiatives of those scholars in the Soviet Academy of Sciences who wanted to export the new science to the East European satellite states[211] Nikolai Krementsov convincingly argued that the process was as much "an import" as it was "an export," from which members of various interest groups such as bureaucrats, politicians. and scientists on both sides of the border had much to gain.[212] Certainly, some Polish scientists and bureaucrats welcomed these developments as an opportunity to improve their own positions in the establishment. Poland's older intelligentsia supported Polish communists' efforts to streamline, build up, and democratize the country's scientific institutions through their centralization. But as maintaining links with their Soviet peers turned out to be nearly impossible due to increasing postwar restrictions on cross-border traffic, the scientists' hopes evaporated. Like their analogues throughout the region, Polish scientists were leaving the Soviet-Polish Friendship Society as a result.[213] Originally willing interpreters of Soviet soft power, they lost their enthusiasm when pressured to become servants of Soviet pseudoscience.

By 1949, Soviet specialists in various disciplines began arriving in Poland for periods of time ranging from several weeks to several months. Reciprocal visits by Polish scholars to the USSR were rare.[214] These new specialists tended to be more ideologically orthodox than the Soviet professors and scientists who visited Poland in 1945–47.[215] Institutions such as the Committee for Cultural Cooperation with Foreign Countries (KWKZ) and VOKS worked out exchange plans and a host of scientific organizations actively participated; all were supervised by the highest party organs and implemented by the ministries of foreign affairs on both sides.[216] Tentative Polish projects for 1951 stipulated inviting fifty Soviet scientists for two-month periods. Among them were seven economists, eleven historians, two jurists, eight representatives of technical sciences, eight specialists in agricultural sciences, and six mathematicians.[217] Few "hard" scientists such as physicists or chemists were included. The Soviet authorities, on the contrary, emphasized those disciplines that were either the most useful in restructuring Polish industry or the most saturated with ideology. Given that the Soviet side tended to judge the Polish demands for scientific exchange as excessive, and consequently to revise them, it is most likely that the actual number of guests that year was much smaller.[218]

In discussing Michurinist biology, Krementsov distinguished four basic components of this discipline as it emerged in the USSR after 1948. One can easily extend this typology to almost the entire Soviet science system at that time. Its first element was of a repertoire of scientific concepts and experimental practices. In biology, the former included a set of ideas about heredity and evolution; in history—ideas about Marxist periodization; in political economy—about the advantages of centralized planning, and so forth. According to Krementsov, the Soviets most fervently exported to their East European satellite states the second component of their sciences system, namely, "the image of science and scientists." It was a self-consciously politicized image that closely associated Soviet science with objectivity and progress, contrasted with the "unscientific" and "reactionary" endeavors in the West. One could add that official "patriotism" and institutional anti-Semitism formed the obverse side of this image.[219]

Social practices constituted the third element in Soviet science. They included "methods and modes of scientists—patron relations, institutionalization and institutional competition, discipline and career building, all of which were manifested in particular rituals, rhetoric, etiquette, and styles of scientific criticism" that Soviet scientists adopted to communicate with one another and with the powers that be. Finally, the structural and functional characteristics of Stalinist science made up the system's fourth major component. They included centralization, the prominent role of the party and the significance of client-patron relations.[220] The latter constituted informal networks of influence, which gave members of cultural and scientific elites access to highly placed politicians. In such an arrangement, the scientists gained access to power and professional opportunities, while the bureaucrats acquired a solid base of political support that was always useful during times of political uncertainty.

Despite their occasional optimism concerning ideological progress in Poland's sciences, Soviet scientists and professors who visited Poland in 1949, 1950, and 1951 found the Polish science system wanting in all four respects. The Soviets' stridency and striking lack of tolerance for anything short of Stalinist science as they knew it, beg the question about the value and role of their reports. In his discussion of the Soviet domestic context, Nikolai Krementsov argued that numerous scientists developed a range of public rituals meant to affirm their conformity with the official party line. In reality, the ostensive references to the classics of Marxism-Leninism, acts of self-criticism, and vociferous lambasting of other scientists merely on ideological grounds was a skillful charade, which allowed them to "pursue their own intellectual, institutional, and career objectives."[221] At the same time, some Soviet scholars who visited Poland managed to retain their scientific integrity and omitted the political assessments altogether in their reports. This fact, argued historian Zbigniew Romek, suggests that some Soviet scholars sympathized with their Polish colleagues along professional lines.[222] Romek's insight further illuminates the human potential that the Soviet authorities squandered by empowering the more zealous and less competent scientists they sent to Eastern Europe. Self-interest drove many Soviet experts to berate their Polish colleagues for insufficient commitment to the new science.

In the world of closed borders, the opportunity to travel abroad constituted no small reward to those Soviet scientists who offered their services to the regime at home or abroad. Nikolai N. Nekrasov, the accomplished forty-five-year-old specialist in industrial economics, became a party member only in 1950; had he not made this step, one scholar pointed out, "his later career, especially the role of trusted and certified participant in international activities and travel, would certainly have not been possible."[223] Additionally, each foreign trip hinged on a successful performance during the previous one. In Nekrasov's extensive lifelong itinerary, Poland became the first stop, and the scientist knew how to play the game. In the subsequent report to M. Suslov, Nekrasov dwelled on the faulty academic cadres policies of the Polish party, and the erroneous positions held by some university professors. He wrote, with heat, that the chair of the industrial economy and labor organization faculty in Cracow "does not accept Marxism- Leninism, but lectures the students on Taylorism and Fordism. According to some communist students, he is virtually untouchable, since he is a famous citizen of Cracow."[224] Between these lines of critical commentary about Polish professors, Nekrasov was telling Suslov many good things about himself.

He was hardly alone. Z. A. Lebedeva, director of the Institute of Tuberculosis in the Soviet Academy of Medical Sciences, headed a delegation of Soviet doctors who visited Poland in 1950.[225] She found it difficult to distinguish between "scientific concepts," "the image of science," and, for that matter, the other two elements in Krementsov's typology; in her depiction, all of them formed an organic whole in the system of Soviet science, while any "insufficiencies" in one appeared as symptoms of general problems. Lebedeva reported that Polish medical personnel were characterized by "excessive leaning toward the United States." She argued that this approach directly influenced their medical practices, which tended to favor "treatment of a specific organ, and not the human being; attention to symptoms of a disease, and not their underlying causes."[226] Other negative impressions included chronic understaffing, an ideologically unprepared staff, the excessive decentralization of many institutions, and insufficient knowledge of Soviet science. These specific observations found their logic in the broader image of Polish medical science, which seemed insufficiently brought into conformity with the Soviet model. "A significant group of doctors are cosmopolitans, deprived of patriotic feelings and completely oriented to the West," Lebedeva wrote in the recognizable anti-Semitic code of the late Stalin era. "Then there is a significant group of other doctors, who are elderly and who had studied in universities of pre-revolutionary Russia." They were a problem, she observed, because they had "a false impression of the Soviet Union and they exercise a negative influence on the development of medicine in the democratic country."[227] In total, the Soviet delegates visited about 150 medical institutions, gave 26 lectures to medical employees, and attended about 100 meetings with them.[228] Remarks by a group of Soviet laryngologists who arrived the same year basically echoed Lebedeva's conclusions.[229]

Other scientists and officials also validated their Stalinist credentials by criticizing Polish science. Soviet biologists expected their Polish colleagues to imitate Soviet experimental practices. The prominent Lysenkoist Dr. Ivan E. Glushchenko, who visited Poland between the May 14 and 31, 1949, found the Polish Lysenkoists a numerically weak but promising force.[230] Soviet physiologists and psychiatrists generally also found their Polish colleagues to represent a much lower scientific level and have much inferior ideological knowledge.[231] Not every Soviet scientist thought this way, but those who wanted to maintain a scholarly dialogue faced enormous bureaucratic obstacles.[232] Fear also obstructed scientific cooperation: starting in 1947, "all information on scientific discoveries made on Soviet soil was to be treated a priori as secret; if a scientist let his tongue run away with him in this respect, his carelessness would cost him between 10 and 15 years in a forced labor camp."[233] As ideology trumped science, diplomats like the embassy secretary Safirov too became authoritative judges of Poland's scientific revolution. In the summer of 1951, Safirov reported on the First Congress of Polish Science, which had just finished its proceedings, a watershed in the Stalinization of Polish science.[234] Safirov noted that even the leaders of the Congress made grave errors. For instance, in his June 29 lecture, Jan Dembowski, whom Safirov characterized as "one of the most progressive Polish scientists," ignored "the basis of all sciences— dialectical and historical materialism."[235] Another participant, the leader of the Science Department of the Polish Central Committee, Kazimierz Petrusewicz, perturbed the entire Soviet delegation by giving a lecture titled "Struggle for Existence." The Darwinian concept, rooted in Malthusian conjectures about unchecked growth of the human population and its sinister consequences, had been eliminated from the Soviet scientific paradigm in the 1930s because its individualistic and agonistic implications jibed well neither with the collectivist underpinnings of communism nor with Soviet desire to remake humankind.[236] Safirov could have cited many more such cases of "completely insufficient understanding of the Marxist-Leninist theory on the part of the leading employees of Polish science."[237] The Poles made mistakes and deliberate omissions; by pointing out these errors to their superiors in Moscow, the Soviets showed their unwavering vigilance.

Nor did a wave of official Soviet anti-Semitism spare Polish scientific institutions. In 1951, G. Vasetskii set out to scrutinize the work of the Institute for Education of Scientific Cadres (IKKN), led by Adam Schaff. Modeled on the Soviet Institute of Red Professors, the institute was to train politically conscious and committed cadres of professors, particularly in the areas of philosophy, economy, and history. Unlike the old, "bourgeois" academic staff whose members conducted their own research work in order to broaden the empirical basis in their fields, the graduate students at the IKKN were assigned intellectual tasks whose goal was to reinterpret the existing truths from the Marxist point of view.[238] Having recounted a number of ideological errors in the work of the institute's instructors, Vasetskii expressed particular apprehension about the disproportionate Jewish presence among instructors and graduate students. He complained that "Nationalist/racist theories are popular in the institute, according to which the Poles are not fit for theoretical work and the Jews, on the contrary, are naturally predisposed for scientific research." Vasetskii assured Suslov that his experience proved just the contrary.[239] According to the Soviet professor, the institute's leaders Schaff, Adler, and Brus (who were of Jewish origin) were the most responsible for this state of affairs.[240] His comments echoed observations made by Soviet visitors to other educational and scientific institutions.[241] Indeed, just as Polish Jews led the IKKN, Poles of Jewish origin were likewise vastly overrepresented among graduate students, as compared to their small fraction in society.[242] Yet it is quite likely that merit, not ethnicity, constituted the decisive admission criterion.[243] If in 1944 Soviet reports about Jewish overrepresentation appear to have been motivated by concerns over the impact of Polish anti-Semitism on the legitimacy of the communists, Vasetskii's report constituted an unequivocal commentary on the allegedly devious nature of Polish Jews.

The Soviet state was the supreme patron of Polish science; like some visiting artists and bureaucrats, numerous Soviet scientists who visited Poland expected treatment that would reflect their status. Here, the friction they experienced was highly palpable. Lebedeva complained, after her 1950 visit, that after their talks to more than one thousand Polish medical workers, Sztachelski canceled the Q&A session and generally prevented other informal interactions on the excuse that the Soviet guests were tired.[244] Soviet physiologists who visited the same year experienced similar treatment.[245] Philologist F. M. Zhurko, who taught Russian literature to Polish faculty members in 1951, found himself completely ignored by Warsaw University's academic administration. He reported to the Soviet Ministry of Higher Education that the rector or the dean of the university made no effort to see him at all. "A few friendly faces showed up during the first lecture but then disappeared," he complained.[246] Soviet laryngologists who toured Poland in 1950 felt vexed by what they saw as their audiences' artificial interest in their work. They were further dismayed that while "the Polish doctors willingly talk about themselves," they seemed uninterested in asking questions or speaking Russian.[247]

As in the case of Soviet-Polish artistic exchanges and mass media contacts, it is fair to say that the Soviet Stalinist scientists who felt unwelcome were picking up accurate signals. And here, too, the Soviets disturbed the delicate balance between Polish communists and highly regarded Polish scientists. Jerzy Konorski had been a student of the famous Soviet physiologist Ivan Pavlov in the 1930s, back when the science in the USSR still enjoyed relative freedom. Konorski, one of the established scientists eager to resuscitate Poland's scientific institutions after World War II, achieved international prominence with his 1948 publication in England of *Conditioned Reflexes and Neuron Organization*.[248] One year later, the work drew the attention of Soviet observers because in it Konorski had challenged some of the ideas of his former master. Escalating Soviet xenophobia caused L. N. Fedorov, the head of a 1949 delegation of Soviet physiologists, to attempt to elicit self-criticism from the Polish neurophysiologist. Failing that, Fedorov informed Jakub Berman about the publication of the book, presumably on the assumption that the scientist would be punished.[249] Nothing of the sort happened. The Polish communists wanted to avoid a direct confrontation with Konorski, and instead, made some halfhearted attempts to sway him to change his views. In June 1950, the Polish authorities tried to arrange a meeting between Konorski and a group of Soviet physiologists who would be able to convince Konorski "about the erroneousness of his book." Such a meeting would not be possible in Poland, an aide-memoire from the Polish Ministry of Foreign Affairs lamely explained, "since in Poland there are no scientists who would be able to undertake a discussion on this subject."[250] Soviet scientific ambassadors may or may not have come to Poland; it is unclear whether such a meeting eventually took place, but, according to scholars and Konorski's own testimony years later, he was able to continue his scientific practice without interruption.[251]

Negative personal interactions such as this created feedback loops of mutual antipathies that took on lives of their own; ultimately, these interactions reliably reflected the limited appeal of Soviet science even among Poland's most committed Stalinists. Adam Schaff remembered that Soviet visits unfolded according to a recognizable pattern. Upon arrival, the Soviet guests informed the Poles that "they did not come to lecture, but to learn" from them, as apparently they had been told to say. Then they started to lecture their hosts, as they did throughout Eastern Europe, thus "creating upfront a wall of prejudices and resentments," manifest in the Poles' attitude of "condescending politeness." Schaff further pointed out that the Soviet Union's most brilliant professors were classified as *nevyezdnye* (literally: unfit for leaving) and stayed home; the Soviet professors who did show up in Poland evoked a feeling of "pity."[252] The Poles had few opportunities to argue with their guests openly without taking risks. Instead, they resorted to gestures and innuendos to make the Soviets feel unwelcome, a practice that was ultimately difficult to prove.

The Soviet Union's best and brightest rarely went abroad at this time, focusing on careers at home, and the young Polish neophytes who went to the USSR during these years had few chances to rub shoulders with them. In 1950, the Polish Party dispatched the zealous twenty-three-year-old graduate student from the IKKN, Leszek Kołakowski, to Moscow for his first trip abroad. The goal was, as the philosopher put it decades later, that he and several others would "acquire the wisdom of Marxist thought at the very source."[253] Kołakowski, who described himself as "not being especially educated" in 1950, recounted the "stunning" experience of meeting the poster children of Soviet Marxist philosophy. "They didn't know any foreign language, they knew nothing about the so-called bourgeois philosophy, they knew nothing about philosophy, except what they had read in Lenin and Stalin, and sometimes also Marx, or rather Engels."[254] One of Kołakowski's most vivid examples involved the Soviet ideologue Petr Nikolaevich Pospelov, director of the Central Committee's Marx-Engels-Lenin Institute and onetime editor in chief of *Pravda*. Upon the young men's arrival, the august Pospelov was to read out loud to them his own published pamphlet on Marxism-Leninism "without changing a single word." Kołakowski also recalled with amusement a certain Kutasov who bent over backward to explain "qualitative leaps" in Marxist-Leninist dialectic.[255] This was probably a way to account for Stalin's theory of "active superstructure," which Marx and his interpreters had hitherto thought to be passive and unchanging. Kołakowski's colleague Tadeusz Kroński was said to have had his fill after being told that "there is such a bourgeois philosopher Grusel" (the phenomenologist Edmund Husserl, rendered as Guserl in Russian).[256] These utterly dogmatic professors and Soviet pseudoscientists-professors who came to Poland to teach, "nobody took seriously."[257] Besides the comic effect of translation (Kutasov's name, for instance, evokes a vulgar Polish term for male genitalia), one can think of many reasons why Kołakowski would dwell on these incidents with such relish. Emphasizing the limitations of this visit as mere youthful follies, and casting the Soviets in a humorous light, may have helped Kołakowski—who had by old age become a moral authority—distance himself from his early Soviet zeal. Casting himself as a rational agent who was slowly discovering the world around him enabled the elderly philosopher to underscore reason, not opportunism, as the dictating principle for his choices to embrace and break with Stalinism. These potentially self-apologetic elements in Kołakowski's account make it suspect no less than the Stalinist Adam Schaff's claim that he did not Stalinize Polish science. Still, the philosopher's voice, together with that of Schaff, resonates so powerfully with the voices of many Soviet professors and scientists that it is difficult to dismiss them.

Poles ridiculed Stalinist science, outside the ivory towers of the IKKN (later renamed Instytut Nauk Społecznych, or INS), the elite research institute in which Kołakowski and Schaff worked. Polish humor had more power than all the pamphlets in Warsaw. "What's so good about the cross between an apple tree and a dog?" the bolder Polish university students asked each other, referencing Ivan Michurin's notorious if unsuccessful experiments in genetic crossbreeding. "It waters itself," was the answer, "and it barks at anyone who tries to steal apples."[258] This joke, then deemed political, actually made it to the security police file of one of Ryszard Kapuściński's female colleagues. In 1953, she received a two year-and-a-half-year prison sentence for "spreading false information concerning economic and political relations in Poland and friendly relations between Poland and the USSR," and disseminating "information heard on radio broadcasts of imperialist states that are potentially harmful to the interest of the Polish People's Republic."[259]

The Soviets lent little material support for the Poles to Stalinize science, as John Connelly has shown; but the Soviets constantly nudged the Poles to Sovietize. The orthodox ambassadors of Soviet science who observed—or got involved in—Poland's scientific life experienced an intense sense of friction, perhaps even stronger than the kind that their comrades felt in the course of artistic contacts. East European literatures and the arts bore extremely high costs stemming from their conflicted entanglement with Stalinist socialist realism. However, the way in which agents of Stalinist science torpedoed centuries-old, evidence-based efforts to explore the world through objective inquiry constituted an unparalleled assault on culture as the Poles knew it. This attack on the world of meanings and on the bedrock of the Enlightenment seemed both too foolish and too impractical to captivate the hearts and minds of Poles, save perhaps for the most cynical and uneducated sort.

Stalinist science became the butt of jokes punishable by a prison sentence. But even Jakub Berman—the supreme judge of cultural correctness, the ultimate jury of ideological orthodoxy, and Polish society's top jailer in one—could not have taken seriously the preposterous postulates about "bourgeois" science. What exactly did a brilliant man like Berman, with his interwar law degree, think about "kowtowing to the West" as a meaningful category for judging science? Could he have considered it a productive starting point for rebuilding the country from the ruins of war? He must have known that Stalin himself took the sloganeering about bourgeois science with a grain of salt. The Soviet leader's direct involvement in the politics of science notwithstanding, he spared physics from the disastrous denigrations of the anti-Western campaigns in the Soviet nuclear program.[260] And access to fruits of Western science turned out to be a major bonus behind Stalin's new East European empire—if not a major stimulus for Soviet expansion.[261] Terror continued to intimidate skeptics into conformity, and opportunism triumphed in Poland—for a time; but Stalinist science offered little to all those who, at the end of the day, had to get things done. This was the new empire's major flaw.

REFLEX ACTIONS

Half a century before the Cold War, American reformers referred to "reflex actions" in arguing about the dangers and benefits of the U.S. colonial empire. As historian Paul Kramer has shown, in doing so they shared two core assumptions about the workings of their spatial-political order. The first was that "peripheries pushed back"; more than "simply representing the latest place that the metropole had transplanted itself (for better or for worse), empire's edges remade the whole." Second, peripheries presented a potential for progress and metropolitan renewal: borderlands, it was assumed, "could be remade into spaces of exceptional order precisely because they were beyond the pressures and constraints (understood as corruptions and contaminations) of metropolitan politics."[262] This is a useful starting point for thinking about Sovietization, which scholars of Soviet-East European relations have described chiefly as a process that started in Stalin's head and ended with the about-face of East European institutions and societies. But the process was circular; in order to fully understand Sovietization's impact on the lives of its Polish *and Soviet* enforcers, and to comprehend the powers they were up against, we must leave the East European crime scene and return, if only briefly, to the USSR.[263]

First, for the Soviets, empire became an opportunity to negotiate power with the authorities back home. Soviet observers wrote reports to their superiors in Moscow that tended to be critical of cultural developments in the Soviet sphere of influence.[264] Poland's top bureaucrats also became their natural targets. Most often, Soviet functionaries accused Polish officials of dishonesty, "opportunism," hostility toward the USSR, and "nationalism." Save for Jerzy Putrament, one would be hard-pressed to find a prominent Polish cultural administrator who escaped one or more of the charges. Among the culprits singled out by Soviet diplomats were Włodzimierz Sokorski, the deputy minister (then: minister) of culture and art and the most important cultural bureaucrat in the executive branch between 1948 and 1956; Jakub Berman, who, together with Hilary Minc, was accused of "Jewish nationalism"; Ostap Dłuski, the director of the Polish United Workers' Party (PZPR) Central Committee International Department, whose "nationalist" tendencies were allegedly typical of many others; Edward Ochab of the Soviet-Polish Friendship Society, who served as curator of cultural affairs during Berman's temporary though largely formal isolation from top decision making (between March 26, 1950 and December 1, 1952), and was also the man being groomed for Bierut's replacement as president; Jan Karol Wende of the KWKZ—the Polish equivalent of VOKS—an organization that took over cultural exchanges in July 1950; Zygmunt Młynarski of the Polish-Soviet Institute, and the vice-minister of health, Jerzy Sztachelski, a former political officer in the Soviet-backed Polish Army.[265] Some Soviet officials, like Safirov, scrupulously corroborated their information whenever possible.[266] Others, like Lebedev, tirelessly wove intrigues from thin air. The temperaments of Soviet observers certainly mattered in how they dealt with real and perceived "shortcomings" in the cultures of Soviet vassal states. Yet it also mattered that while Eastern Europe was tethered, it was not tamed; those Soviet officials who wanted to prove their Cold War vigilance to their bosses in Moscow, could easily find Polish, Czech, or Hungarian scapegoats.

On rare occasions, even "ordinary" Soviet expats in Poland joined in the attacks on Polish officials. On April 28, 1951, a certain Liubov Chervinskaia penned a letter to Stalin, in which she lambasted the fifth edition of Adam Schaff's *Introduction to the Theory of Marxism* (1950). The self-identified wife of a Soviet military man who had been stationed in Poland since 1946, and the director of a fat-processing plant near the city of Gdańsk, Chervinskaia took issue mostly with some mistakes in the book and the work's "Aesopian language," which prevented her from understanding parts of it.[267] Chervinskaia saw East European–bashing as a valuable tool for improving her standing with the Soviet authorities; her efforts can be seen as a mechanism that Jan T. Gross has termed the "privatization of the public sphere," typical of totalitarian societies.[268] Her letter elicited official criticism of Schaff's book but never made it to the *vozhd'*.[269] Still, in contacting the authorities, Chervinskaia appear to have played a winning gamble: the only small risk she took was being ignored by the addressee of her note.

Second, Soviet officials, artists, and scientists who traveled to Eastern Europe remained inextricably linked to the machine of state terror at home. They "traveled in time," as Ann Gorsuch termed it, often seeing the East European present merely as a stage in the Soviet past.[270] But they also traveled "in spirit," as it were, leaving their bodies, belongings, fates, and families fully within the firm grasp of the Soviet party-state. Sovietization was a Janus-faced beast. The terror did not manifest only westward. It has been difficult for historians to see—due to their traditional and understandable focus on the tragic consequences of Sovietization—the extent to which Soviet empire's peripheries "pushed back" and to which empire made even Soviet participants politically vulnerable at home.

The Soviet vice-consul in Szczecin Iurii Bernov was hardly the only one to be frightened as he crossed the Soviet-Polish border in 1952. Take the Soviet composer Dmitrii Kabalevskii, who visited Poland in January. In 1948, Kabalevskii narrowly escaped Andrei Zhdanov's cultural pogroms; only his connections in high places saved him from Zhdanov's vitriolic attacks against the so-called formalists such as Sergei Prokofiev and Dmitrii Shostakovich.[271] Four years later, during his stay in Poland, the forty-eight-year-old composer attended a meeting at the Club of International

Press and Book in Warsaw, where he discussed recent tendencies in Soviet music with Polish musicians. Kabalevskii must have been terrified upon learning that the Polish journal *Muzyka*, which published his discussion in early 1952, left only the composer's critical remarks about Soviet music and ignored anything good he had to say about it.[272] The Soviet embassy demanded explanations from VOKS. Kabalevskii wrote a letter to the editors of *Muzyka*, in which he praised the "recent achievements of Soviet composers," such as Dmitrii Shostakovich, Iurii Levitin, and Andrei Shtogarenko.[273] But the embassy remained unsatisfied, since the editors of *Muzyka* left it without any commentary.[274] Excessive Sovietizing zeal was no basis for safety either. The Soviet ambassador Viktor Lebedev's meddling in Poland's top cadres policies, efforts fueled partly by the man's clear anti-Semitic agenda, most likely got him transferred to another post in March 1951.[275] Other Soviet guests were so eager to please their bosses from the Soviet Central Committee that in trying to force the Polish scientific establishment into submission, they overreached their competences.[276] Eastern Europe, therefore, meant opportunities to some Soviets, but an even greater opportunity for the Soviet party-state to test and intimidate its own citizens in tried and tested ways.

Safirov's meeting with Poland's prominent socialist-realist painter, Włodzimierz Zakrzewski, in early 1952 illustrates how confusing, circuitous, and risky Sovietization turned out to be for its enforcers on both sides of the border. Uninvited, Zakrzewski visited the Soviet embassy twice that year. The painter complained about the pro-"formalist" bias on the part of the Polish communists throughout 1951, which left him, a faithful follower of socialist realism, ostracized and indignant. At that time, other East European artists also contested the cultural policies of local communists by directly contacting the Soviets.[277] Zakrzewski accused the vice-minister of culture and art, Sokorski, as well as the prime minister, J. Cyrankiewicz, of promoting the "formalists" to the highest administrative posts and awarding them the highest artistic distinctions at the expense of socialist realists. Having given a lecture at Warsaw's Fine Arts Academy, Sokorski was to have told one listener at the Q&A session that while the Soviet experience was important, "we should pay no less attention to contemporary French painting."[278] Rightfully skeptical about the Pole's intentions, Safirov managed to corroborate the information with his Soviet informants. Then he forwarded a memo to VOKS in early March.[279]

Yet by the time Safirov's note reached Moscow in the spring of 1952, a kind of cultural mini-"Thaw" was already under way among the movers and shakers in the Kremlin and in Warsaw. Stalin, in his 1950 work on linguistics, had already argued that language worked independently of the Marxist superstructure.[280] In so doing, he stated the obvious: after all, no international socialist language developed even in the cradle of communism. But even though not everyone dared to say it at the time, the thesis also implied that artistic production need not necessarily reflect the development of the economic base. The insinuation that novels, plays, films, and so on could treat something other than class struggle, for instance, put into question basic axioms of "socialist realism" as it had hitherto been understood. More explicit signals for change in cultural politics followed. In 1951, *Pravda* lashed out at the critics in defense of a book by a Latvian writer Vilis Lacis, *Towards New Shores*, which had apparently broken the rules of socialist realism. Lacis was soon to receive the Stalin Prize of the first degree.[281] In April 1952—one month after Safirov's memo—*Pravda* published an article denouncing the theory of nonconflict in drama.[282] In September came Malenkov's plea for "Soviet Gogols and Shchedrins in literature." This was a call to arms to Soviet writers, encouraging them to imitate the great nineteenth-century Russian classics, and a reaction to the barren cultural landscape at home.[283]

In calling for "Soviet Gogols and Shchedrins," Malenkov also gave a green light for the campaign against "schematism" in the arts (in Stalinist art criticism, "schematism" referred to a socialist realist work's crudely simplified depiction of society; however, it was contrasted with "typicality," or showing characters and their relationships as reflective of larger trends under communism—making both terms notoriously hard to grasp.).[284] After Jakub Berman's conservative exposé on the subject during the Council for Culture and Art in December 1952, a lively discussion broke out among the attending cultural figures. Many now interpreted Stalin's 1950 work on linguistics as a confirmation of their own view that art could serve socialism regardless of form.[285] In the winter of 1952–53, Berman and Hoffman slightly liberalized policies toward the country's Writers' Union.[286] In the midst of the 1952 campaign against "schematism," just when the correlation between the narrowest understanding of the method and the near halt in artistic production became more evident, Sokorski opened up "socialist realism" to a more flexible interpretation.[287] For Safirov and Zakrzewski, and others who had invested their energies in promoting socialist realism, the concept proved to be a moving target. In 1952, such fervent soldiers of the cultural front were fighting a battle that their generals deemed over. The party line was changing again. As with Jerzy Borejsza and other proponents of the "gentle" revolution in Poland in 1948, now, the tables turned on the most radical proponents of Sovietization.

Exporting contemporary "Gogols and Shchedrins" would have boosted Soviet soft power abroad, but, given the terror, their appearance would have been unlikely in the first place. Did Stalin plan to square the ongoing modest liberalization in culture with the next wave of bloody purges? It is most difficult to imagine the results of such policies. Sadly from a historian's perspective, but fortunately for Stalin's contemporaries, exactly one year after Safirov sent off his scathing note against Sokorski, the Soviet dictator took the definitive answer to his grave.

CONCLUSION

Stalin's brutal policies and the ever-present specter of terror struck a fatal blow to Soviet soft-power initiatives. The Soviets tried to transform Polish culture and society radically—by force, certainly, but also by efforts to appeal to the Poles' hearts and minds. Despite Soviet pressure on the Poles to conform to Stalinist standards, Moscow rarely came through with adequate material support. And those Soviet officials and cultural figures who advocated a more sensible soft-power approach notoriously lacked the materials that would help them to impress the Poles, and many East Europeans.

It was a paradox that the USSR embarked on this project of international cultural outreach at the same time its cultural output was hitting an all-time low. The Soviet inability to deliver attractive goods in sufficient amounts, regularly, and on time, combined with insensitive, cookie-cutter, and often aggressive Soviet interventions. These crude propagandistic tactics not only failed to warm up the Polish masses to the idea of "friendship" with the USSR, they alienated even the Stalinist hard-liners and large sectors of the cultural elite who had much to lose from the cultural orthodoxy implemented so fast and on such a large scale. The resulting Polish resentment led to a subversion of Soviet efforts, even by Poland's hard-line Stalinists, and to what could be termed "refraction" of the Soviet message. They also fueled the vehement, visceral backlash against the Soviet Union and its culture that took place after Stalin's death.

The years 1948–53 in Poland witnessed creeping Sovietization. The Soviets impatiently prodded the process. They actively participated in the overhaul of Poland's culture even if they often lacked the wherewithal to support it adequately or enforce it fully and consistently. For their part, driven by fear, Polish communists frequently took the lead in Sovietizing their country's cultural life, although they often lacked the conviction to remake Poland's culture and institutions as quickly or thoroughly as the

Soviets expected them to. As a consequence, when mid-level Polish officials and cultural figures subverted the process of more rapid Sovietization, the top Polish communists often looked the other way.

Sovietization means many things. On one level, it comprises an array of negotiated micro- and macro-processes whereby East European cultures and institutions evolved into Soviet-like instruments of communist party-states. On another plane, "Sovietization" has been turned into something of a heuristic tool, an illusively stable category of analysis. Infused with assumptions about what constitutes "Soviet" and "East European" and inviting active interest in exploring the tragic fate of the culturally Western lands behind the "iron curtain," "Sovietization" exemplifies what Michel Foucault has called "the positive unconscious" operative in the production of knowledge more generally, "a level that eludes the consciousness of the scientist and yet is part of scientific discourse."[288] Until the era of decolonization, historians of modern colonial empires have studied nearly exclusively the imperial centers and the metropolitan experience of colonial expansion.[289] Exactly the opposite has been true of the USSR: until recently we have known far more about the East European than the Soviet side of the Soviet-East European engagement after World War II. Scholars have closely studied the effects of Soviet actions in Eastern Europe; but these same Soviet actions were often expected to speak alone about the expansive nature of the Soviet system.

So what can we learn by examining the Soviet side of Sovietization—not at the very top, but at mid-level, among the people who lived the experience on both sides? A close look at the dramatic years from 1948 to 1953 shows that individual Soviet officials, cultural figures, and activists drawn into the process of remaking Polish culture were hardly a homogeneous mass of villains. Certainly, some—the intransigent ones—wished to expand at all costs. But others reflected on the risks, and calculated the costs and benefits of every Soviet move. Many felt impotent and frustrated. All were vulnerable to criticisms, demotions, and purges—they could be punished for lack of vigilance, underperformance, or for overstepping the vague and ever-shifting boundaries of permissible Soviet interference in Polish affairs. There were those who felt proud, and even perhaps vindicated, to be spreading the revolution in ever-recalcitrant Poland. But there were also those who, like Rokossovskii, felt unhappy to serve in a foreign post that provoked the resentment of the locals and earned the distrust of the vigilantly anti-Western, anticosmopolitan establishment back home. Power surged from East to West, but also the other way around. It connected people who may not have shared a language or an ethnic or ideological background, but who had to observe similar rules in order to survive. In the early 1950s, Sel'tsy and Siedlce shared more in common than any of the former political officers would have dared to point out in public.

Hundreds of thousands of East Europeans suffered persecution from the communists and the Soviets during the upheavals of 1948–53. But hundreds, even thousands of Soviet citizens involved in the international cultural outreach found themselves pressured to succeed in a task that—as in the story of Sisyphus—was bound to fail over and over again. The Soviet soft-power project in Eastern Europe was a revolving stage in one drama; sometimes the actors changed, sometimes the scenery was transformed, but they were all part of the same plot, the same chain of events. And the epic tragedy of Eastern Europe notwithstanding, there was something tragic, too, about the actual birth of the Soviet empire in Eastern Europe. It resembled a growing giant who rose up, ready to run, only to realize that his feet were made of clay.

4

UNLIKELY HEROES

After all, if we put away this book right now, it may take five years before a work will be born that will satisfy all our demands. And that is not right. Because the Soviet reader and especially youths, are interested in what's going on in the countries of People's democracies. And newspaper material alone cannot satisfy that interest.
—*From the 1952 proceedings of the Foreign Commission of the Soviet Writers' Union*

■

Once in the shade of the barely greening lindens, the writers dashed first thing to a brightly painted stand with the sign: "BEER AND SOFT DRINKS."
"Give us seltzer," Berlioz asked.
"There is no seltzer," the woman in the stand said, and for some reason became offended.
"Is there beer?" Homeless inquired in a rasping voice.
"Beer'll be delivered towards evening," the woman replied.
"Then what is there?" asked Berlioz.
"Apricot soda, only warm," said the woman.
"Well, let's have it, let's have it!"
—*Mikhail Bulgakov,* The Master and Margarita

INTRODUCTION: BOUNDARIES ONE MUSTN'T CROSS

In her 1935 novel *Boundary Line* (Granica), Zofia Nałkowska described the transformation of Zenon Ziembiewicz—a landowner turned radical activist, turned city mayor. *Boundary Line* was written as an impassioned social critique of class inequalities in contemporary Poland. It is also a character study of a man who descends a slippery slope of moral compromises in order to build his political career. Ziembiewicz rejects his lover—a poor, young girl—once he learns she is bearing his child; as a city mayor, he orders the police to shoot at demonstrating workers. These and other similar decisions destroy his inner peace, family life, and career, eventually leading to his suicide. Just before Ziembiewicz kills himself, his wife tells him that "there must exist a boundary that one must not cross"; a boundary,

Wrocław, August 1948. Soviet writer Mikhail Sholokhov (left) and Polish writer Jarosław Iwaszkiewicz at the World Congress of Intellectuals in Defense of Peace. Courtesy of Polska Agencja Prasowa.

beyond which one renounces one's self and humanity.[1] Nałkowska could not have known then that by the end of what the poet W. H. Auden, her English contemporary, described as "a low dishonest decade," the Western culture with which she identified would be "driven mad," it would transgress its own moral standards and bow down to a "psychopathic god"—Adolf Hitler.[2] By 1945, Nałkowska knew what Auden knew, when, with the help of Jerzy Borejsza, she was preparing the novel's fifth edition for Czytelnik.[3] It was less clear that within the next decade—no less base and dishonest than the one that has just elapsed—Stalin, another psychopathic god, would turn Eastern Europe into a temple of his own cult.

At the start of the base and mendacious, brutal Stalinist era that was about to begin, "the boundary that one must not cross" would acquire a life and a laughing-through-tears flavor of its own. For despite the hopes of politicians, bureaucrats, and cultural figures throughout the Soviet bloc for more vigorous international cultural cooperation, the border controls had only intensified. International travel to the West signified a moral transgression. Within the Eastern Bloc, as scholars often pointed out, it meant the sure and steady Sovietization of East European cultures and societies. And yet, as this chapter shows, there was more to this story. Agents of Soviet soft power and their Polish interlocutors recognized that they could build a more stable and mutually rewarding relationship if cultures from the new People's Democracies could be simultaneously exported to the USSR. Their failure to export contemporary belles lettres, in particular, was not the result, as some have suggested, of a lack of trying.[4] In fact, Soviet and Polish cultural officials repeatedly tried to cross the rigid boundaries between the two Stalinist party-states as they attempted to publish contemporary Polish fiction in the USSR. Tracing their painstaking efforts and dynamic exchanges through various institutions in Poland and the Soviet Union can help us to better see how the Stalinist system actively suppressed the budding Soviet soft-power initiatives.

MICKIEWICZ STREET, MOSCOW

In mid-April 1947, the Polish ambassador to Moscow, Marian Naszkowski, moved into his new residence on a quiet street named after Alexei Tolstoi. Before the October Revolution, the building belonged to the merchant Tarasov. Outside, it felt "huge and heavy, but harmonious in form." Inside, it featured lavish rooms decorated with Renaissance-style frescoes.[5] The Germans, who had been leasing the building from the Soviet government before 1941 (it is said to have housed the office of the German trade attaché), painted Prussian eagles over some of the frescoes. Fortunately, the artist, Ivan Zholtovskii, was also the building's architect and academician. A Soviet citizen born into a Polish family, Zholtovskii agreed to restore the original artwork.[6] By August 6, 1948, Naszkowski—the former political officer in the Kościuszko Division and one of its founding "apostles"— was on another mission to convert. Ensconced in his posh Moscow home, Naszkowski had one burning cultural task, a rather large one. Convincing the Soviet authorities to publish contemporary Polish fiction at that time posed no less a challenge than had swaying anti-Soviet Polish soldiers to a pro-Soviet cause half a decade before. Stalin and Zhdanov had, for two years, been sowing terror in the artistic community through carefully orchestrated attacks on so-called formalists. The Berlin Blockade had escalated East-West tensions for six weeks. Alarmed by Tito's defiance, Stalin had just expelled Yugoslavia from the Cominform at the end of June. Official xenophobia was on the rise, and Naszkowski's Soviet interlocutors had everything to lose from fulfilling his literary requests.

Naszkowski's meeting with the Soviet vice-minister of foreign affairs, "young, and round-faced" Valerian Zorin on August 6, 1948, was meant to resolve a three-year stalemate by taking the talks to a new diplomatic level.[7] For years, frustrated, lower-ranking Polish officials had been trying to work out an arrangement with the Soviets that would enable Polish writers to publish in the birthplace of communism.

Writing had long been a privileged art form in Russia and East-Central Europe. It was only natural that Polish communists, eager to win over the intelligentsia, would try to lure their best writers with the promise of financial opportunities and prestige. In the USSR, in the Russia of the Romanovs, and in Poland, *literatura* had traditionally been the mightiest of the muses.[8] The great historical stature of this artistic medium in Eastern and Central Europe made it a natural and promising nexus of Soviet-Polish cultural exchange. Writers in these places enjoyed a social status incomparably higher than that of their equivalents in Western countries. Particularly in the nineteenth century, in response to social and political tensions, members of the literary intelligentsia rose in prominence as they assumed the role of the conscience of the people and spokesmen for the oppressed. In Russia, this meant above all advocacy for individual freedoms within the broader agenda of social reform. Many Polish writers, on the other hand, saw their mission as bolstering Polish national identity, which they believed was threatened by extinction as a result of Prussian, Austro-Hungarian, and particularly Russian colonizing policies.

After coming to power, the Bolsheviks saw the opportunity to harness well-known contemporary writers such as Maxim Gorky to their cause. They established a monopoly of literary output and established institutional structures to manage the creative elites, including not only writers but also composers, actors, and so forth. They also established a version of the Russian literary canon that favored the Marxist vision of history. Throughout the Soviet period, writers who were the most talented or the most obliging to their political masters had access to benefits similar to those enjoyed by high-ranking government or party functionaries. In the absence of any meaningful public discussion in Stalinist Russia, literary fiction turned into a forum: read by everyone from party leaders to students and housewives, it became "a sort of town hall, a platform from which the system justified itself."[9] The Polish communists, who enjoyed little support in intellectual circles, were very interested in developing a similar symbiosis. For Polish authors, building their international career must have carried strong impetus to join the nascent town hall.

The sense of reciprocity with which the Polish officials viewed the emerging Soviet-Polish relationship is surprising. In their report to the Polish Ministry of Culture and the Arts dated August 28, 1945, Polish Embassy officials in Moscow credited "the fatal historical tradition" in Polish-Russian relations as having created a mutual prejudice. They claimed that measured by its own merits or "today's urgent cultural and political needs," Soviet culture was undeservedly unknown in Poland. Reciprocally, Polish literature and the arts were largely unknown in the USSR. Soviet citizens had basically no clue about "the transformations in the womb of Polish society," and neither did the USSR's Polish philologists who had been "deprived of contact with Poland for over twenty-seven years."[10] In these early postwar years, Polish officials in Moscow assumed, quite impressively, that Soviet-Polish talks about "cultural exchanges" would carry genuine cultural curiosity and welcome news of the birth of communist Poland.

Exporting Polish contemporary belles lettres eastward was also about putting the culture of the new People's Democracy on the mental maps of Soviet inhabitants. In April 1946, the Polish government asked the Soviet authorities to put up memorial plaques on those buildings in Moscow in which the nineteenth-century Polish Romantic poet Adam Mickiewicz had lived. Throughout the spring, the Poles persistently lobbied the Soviets to rename one of Moscow's streets after the national bard.[11] They aimed high: the central location of Nastasinskii Lane, placed amid numerous party and government buildings, endowed the street with much political and symbolic value. In the east, it joined Gorky street, Moscow's Kremlin-bound main thoroughfare named after Russia's quintessential revolutionary writer who had died a decade before. In the northeast, it linked to the street dedicated to Gorky's contemporary, the late nineteenth-century short story writer and playwright Anton Chekhov. Nastasinskii Lane lay only one block northwest of bustling Pushkin Square, named after the nineteenth-century Russian poet and a one-time friend of Mickiewicz. The company would have pleased the Polish poet who, despite his opposition to the tsarist regime, had cultivated his Russian friendships and frequented many of St. Petersburg salons. Mickiewicz and Pushkin's fell out after the Polish Uprising of 1831 against Russian rule. But even as Pushkin's political enemy, Mickiewicz continued to admire deeply his Russian acquaintance's poetry, as well as his human sincerity, passion and sharp mind.[12]

The location of "Mickiewicz Street" would also have eased the minds of many of Poland's contemporary writers, even those still hesitant about the cultural policies of the Polish communists. The place had an unexpected affinity with the fledgling People's Democracy circa 1946, with its sweet promises of a "gentle revolution" in culture. Though "party-minded" literature had indeed prevailed for decades in the USSR, around Nastasinskii

Lane, historical ghosts and memories continued to fight the incursions of the present. Facing the lane, across Gorky Street, was the Museum of the Revolution of the USSR. Earlier it had been the English Club, an exclusive refuge of the Russian aristocracy frequented by luminaries such as Pushkin, the iconoclastic Petr Chaadaev, and soul-searching Lev Tolstoy. Russian intellectuals gathered there to discuss the pressing issues of their times. A grand gala in honor of Tsar Nicholas II took place in the English Club on the three-hundredth anniversary of the Romanov dynasty in 1913. Located one block to the southeast, on Gorky Street, was the building of the Soviet peasant newspaper *Trud* (Labor). With its round windows and tiled insets, this fine example of Moscow's Art Nouveau had served as the printing house of Ivan Sytin, a man who, by the early twentieth century, had made thousands of inexpensive copies of Russian literary classics available to the masses.[13]

This dramatic setting would have pleased Mickiewicz, but the decision to name the street rested in the hands of Soviet officials. The Members of the Moscow City Council, housed further down on Gorky Street, (a location that, in the eighteenth century, had housed the residence of the governor-general) turned down the proposal. Mickiewicz's ghost would have to wait until 1964 for his own street. Located northwest of the Poles' original desired location, it ultimately replaced the Great Patriarch's Pond.[14] And here the jab of literary justice goes deeper, as the Great Patriarch's Pond lies in the neighborhood of the early Soviet-era writer Mikhail Bulgakov, best known for his witty, laugh-through-tears depictions of the contradictions of the nascent regime. In an ironic twist, Bulgakov's most famous and subversive work, *The Master and Margarita*, dominated the Muscovites' associations with the area after its publication in 1967–68. Gogolesque in its absurdity and nuanced humor, it is a tale about the Devil, who visits Moscow to punish those artists and intellectuals who were cooperating with the authorities. A magical tale of battling supernatural forces of good and evil, talking cats, and flying humans, *The Master and Margarita* resembled the metaphysical world of the Romantic Mickiewicz. Indeed, the novel's protagonist, the literary bureaucrat Mikhail Aleksandrovich Berlioz, encounters the Devil in the Patriarch's Ponds—a park flanked by the future Mickiewicz Street. Bulgakov's veiled if bitter 1940 commentary on the relationships between Soviet writers and state authorities anticipated the tensions between Soviet and Polish officials and writers over the fate of Polish literary exports to the USSR. In the novel, Satan utters a famous line that no doubt expressed the hopes of the beleaguered Bulgakov who was forbidden to publish: "Manuscripts don't burn," meaning "the created word must not, cannot be destroyed." No matter what happens to books, their content will live on in the hearts and minds of those who read them.[15] The Polish writers and politicians faced an altogether different challenge: what to do if manuscripts do not travel.

At least some Polish writers knew about the constraints that Soviet cultural officials and writers were facing after the war; Polish officials who wooed the movers and shakers in Moscow and who had often spent time in the USSR must have been in on this, too. "Socialist realism" had initially been a method of true revolutionary artists, and in the 1920s, this was the subject of many heated debates. In Stalin's last years, socialist realism became mere shorthand for conformity with the party line. Its function, in Evgeny Dobrenko's words, was "to make conscious that which was made known in the language of decrees," as well as "to formalize and systematize disparate ideological acts . . . , translating them to the language of situations, dialogs, speeches."[16] Cast as a conflict between a simple factory worker and a devious bourgeois "wrecker" who sabotaged the production line, "class struggle" suddenly sounded less abstract.

Conforming with the party line certainly narrowed the repertoire of Soviet-bound Western belles lettres, confining them largely to the classics. A quick glance at the bibliographic record from 1946 reveals characteristic features of the Soviet publishing world. In January, Soviet readers were offered imported works such as a comedic play by Carlo Goldoni, Shakespeare's *Othello*, and short stories by authors such as H. G. Wells. In August, Emile Zola's novel *Stranitsa liubvi* (*A Love Affair*) was the only published foreign work.[17] As noted literary scholar Maurice Friedberg points out, with reference to the entire late Stalin era, the publication of Western translations "was confined to reprinting venerable classics, living foreign writers were restricted, by and large, to those whose pro-Soviet sympathies, particularly as reflected in their writings, compensated for their foreign citizenship."[18] Soviet critics vilified American authors en masse, but Theodore Dreiser, Mark Twain, James Fenimore Cooper, and Harriet Beecher Stowe appeared in multiple editions; the Soviets published lesser known (and less talented) writers from the United States in large quantities, as long as their works contributed "to a uniformly negative commentary on American life."[19] Selected Polish nineteenth-century classics by authors such as Henryk Sienkiewicz, Eliza Orzeszkowa, and Stefan Żeromski, traditionally popular in the Soviet Union, were certainly available. They unquestionably dominated contemporary fare.[20] In the official Soviet canon, World War II became the crucible of the Soviet regime and the victory over the Nazis served as the regime's validation. In contrast, Poland's unexpectedly rapid defeat in the first months of the war forced Polish writers into ideological and moral soul-searching. Whereas in the USSR, writers had been forced into docility over the preceding decades, Poland's artists enjoyed relative artistic freedom in dealing with the country's recent, troubled past. In 1948, Party-minded literature barely existed in Poland, and inward-looking fiction departed strongly from the officially accepted Soviet norms.

This disconnect in the Polish and Soviet literary worlds might have stopped timid men. By offering the available Polish fiction for translation into Russian, the Poles threatened to disturb the tenuous balance between Soviet authorities and the USSR's artistic bureaucracy. Still, Polish diplomats hoped that they could talk the Soviets into publishing some recent works. On July 28, 1948—a few days before Marian Naszkowski's meeting with Valerian Zorin—Polish diplomats had suggested to V. V. Mochalov, chair of the Soviet All-Slavic Committee, that the Soviets publish several Polish works, because these works represented both recent and ideologically the most acceptable trends in Polish fiction.[21] The works they offered reflected a range of intellectual interests in the Polish literary milieu after the war. Jerzy Andrzejewski's *Night* (*Noc*), and *Medallions* (*Medaliony*) by Zofia Nałkowska concentrated on the problems, tragedies, and experiences of Poles and Jews in occupied Poland. These were collections of essays, narrated with poignant realism. In *Ashes and Diamonds* (*Popiół i diament*), Andrzejewski covered the territory of postwar transformations. It was a tale of one Maciek, a Home Army soldier, and his moral dilemma set against the background of the rise to power of the Polish Workers' Party (PPR) (Maciek's quandary was whether or not to kill a chief of the local District Committee. While the communists saw much promise in *Ashes and Diamonds*, some critics disliked that Andrzejewski put far more emphasis on the drama of the Polish resistance than on the revolutionary changes in postwar Poland).[22] In his *Reality* (*Rzeczywistość*), Putrament told a story about a 1937 trial of communists in the city of Wilno. In it, he drew a critical picture of the prewar Polish government. Mochalov wavered, in light of the works before him, but assured the Poles that he would connect them with representatives of Goslitizdat (Gosudarstvennoe izdatel'stvo khudozhestvennoi literatury, or Soviet State Publishing House specializing in belles lettres) and the Soviet Writers' Union, who would be more competent to discuss the matter. Based on this conversation with Mochalov, Zambrowicz concluded that "it is not easy to arrange such a meeting or to get the translation work started. Translations are not the problem, since at least several are ready for publication. The decision to publish them seems to be the real difficulty."[23] Zambrowicz's tone of discovery and surprise suggests that he was little aware of the Soviet limitations under which Mochalov was laboring.

In his subsequent meeting with Zorin, Marian Naszkowski complained about the lack of progress in publishing Polish works of contemporary fiction. More significantly, he also pointed out that the Soviets might have been using inadequate criteria for evaluating Polish literary imports, namely, looking for works that were "politically mature." According to Naszkowski, this attitude was detrimental to both sides because such writings did not yet exist. Instead, he argued that it would be useful to introduce the Soviet reader to new works that reflected the early stages of Poland's cultural revolution—that is, "the struggle between the new and old, the struggle between the new social content and the old idealistic concepts." He saw value, given the appropriate introductions, in showcasing the process of becoming politically mature. Zorin agreed, promised to facilitate a meeting between Polish representatives and responsible officials from the All-Union Society for Cultural Relations Abroad (VOKS), and he contacted V. S. Kemenov shortly thereafter.[24]

But the resulting conference on September 9, 1948, organized under the auspices of VOKS, only showed that the impasse over translation had deeper roots. M. V. Urnov, chief of the literary section in Inoizdat's (Izdatel'stvo inostrannoi literatury, the State Publishing House of Foreign Literature), elaborated on the substantial difficulties associated with the publication of contemporary Polish fiction in the USSR, thereby confirming the earlier suspicions of the Polish ambassador. The Soviet reader, Urnov argued in the vaguest of terms, "is looking for the truth about contemporary Poland," which, according to him, many recent works coming out of Poland failed to provide. Urnov listed Andrzejewski's *Ashes and Diamonds* among books that "falsified" or "distorted" the true picture of contemporary Poland. The second such work noted was Kazimierz Brandys's *The Invincible City* (*Miasto niepokonane*), a story about wartime Warsaw, which even recent observers would agree "was devoid of ideology."[25] The third book calling forth Urnov's scrutiny was *The Walls of Jericho* (*Mury Jerycha*) by Tadeusz Breza (1946), a critical analysis of individual mentalities in the increasingly authoritarian Polish state at the end of the 1930s. The Poles in attendance, noticeably frustrated with the Soviet attitude, repeated their opinion about the futility of waiting for the perfect piece of socialist realism. Polish authors had a lot to offer, the embassy officials maintained, adding that the translated works could be published with an appropriate introduction, "which would illuminate a given work from the point of view of Marxist criticism."[26] As was the case with Andrzejewski's *Ashes and Diamonds*, though ideologically imperfect, the works that the Polish communists were offering for publication in the USSR represented Poland's most progressive literary fare at the time. But to Soviet eyes, these often introspective narratives posed a danger, exploring themes only recently pushed outside the boundaries of the acceptable by Soviet censors.

Consider the war theme, which figured so prominently in the literature that the Poles pushed consistently. Following the defeat of the Germans, Stalin "stole" World War II, to use Jeffrey Brooks's term, and turned it into his own personal triumph. As Nina Tumarkin has shown, the Soviet authorities invented a solemn World War II myth that in Stalin's last years downplayed the sacrifices of the Soviet people, while serving as "a stirring, but safely distant, reminder of the success of the socialist system and its Supreme Leader."[27] Jewish suffering in the war gave place to discourse about Soviet heroism. Although in 1945–47 Soviet writers faced no obstacles in considering Jewish themes, from 1948 on, official anti-Semitism created pressure to avoid Jewish characters and themes, or to portray Jews negatively.[28] The 1948 Soviet shift in official attitudes toward Jews significantly undermined Polish efforts to translate more contemporary belles lettres into Russian, because a high portion of works that the Polish communists considered progressive—and therefore worthy of showcasing— prominently featured Jewish themes.

By contrast with the USSR, in the eyes of most Polish intellectuals, the war had shattered the myth of Poland as a great power and discredited the right-wing orientation of the prewar government that had nurtured this heightened sense of nationalist pride. The Polish communists knew that as their native writers attempted to square accounts with the war, they were likely to reject the falsehoods of prewar Poland and accept the postwar regime, if only through negative elimination. That so many writers did so through honest soul-searching only buttressed the writers' genuine conviction about the necessity of the postwar transformation spearheaded by the communists.

From that perspective, Nałkowska's overtly apolitical *Medallions*, which the Polish officials insisted be translated, reflected a progressive trend. The slim book has been considered the most important Polish work on World War II, and a masterpiece of world antifascist literature.[29] Based on the author's grim firsthand experience as vice-chair of the Central Commission for the Investigation of German Crimes, the series of dark vignettes captivate with their contrast between a cold, minimalist style of narration and the heart-wrenching images that minimalism paints. While touring the Nazi murder sites, Nałkowska had discovered vats filled with human cadavers in Gdańsk's Anatomicum; the memory of "Dr. Spanner," a German professor supervising the production of soap from human fat, and the hero of the eponymous first "medallion," haunted the writer in postwar years.[30] As early as September 1946, Nałkowska had felt "terrified" that the topic was passé, "thoroughly digested by the press and known to everyone."[31] This was hardly the case in the USSR; indeed, the fact that Nałkowska addressed Jewish suffering head on and made no direct references to socialism in the making most likely disqualified *Medallions* in the eyes of the increasingly intimidated Soviet officials. *Medallions* did not make it to the USSR until 1974.

Postwar Poland witnessed several anti-Jewish pogroms, and anti-Semitism intensified. As seen in the context of Aleksander Ford's *Border Street*, the Polish communists were torn between two responses. On the one hand, the communists incorporated Jewish themes and figures into a convenient narrative about class struggle.[32] On the other hand, they tried to avoid the Jewish issue altogether. This led to ridiculous measures. In one instance, Adam Bromberg, who worked for the PPR-run Książka (Book) publishing house, remembered having to change the ethnicity of the Jewish merchant in Maria Konopnicka's nineteenth-century short story. In order for the work to be published, the one and only Jew had to go. Bromberg quit his job instead.[33]

But in the immediate postwar years, many Polish works about the war addressed at length—and some even concentrated on—Jewish experiences under the occupation, and the complexities of Polish-Jewish interactions. These works had little chance of getting across the border at a time when Soviet authorities sought to efface the memories of Jewish suffering and their active participation in World War II from the public record. Yet Polish variations on this theme were many. Kazimierz Brandys's *Samson* was the story of a young Jewish man in wartime Warsaw; colored by socialist realism, it also dealt with Polish anti-Semitism before the war. Later Andrzej Wajda turned it into a film. Krystyna Żywulska made Jewish suffering in the death camp Auschwitz-Birkenau central to her autobiographical *I Survived Auschwitz* (*Przeżyłam Oświęcim*). Jerzy Andrzejewski wrote *The Holy Week* (*Wielki tydzień*, 1945), as a dramatic, empathetic tale about the Jewish ghetto uprising in 1943.[34]

What works, ultimately, survived Soviet resistance and appeared in Russian translation? Jerzy Putrament's *Reality*, which takes place before the war, and Poland's first novel devoted to the process of mechanized production, Jerzy Pytlakowski's *Foundations* (*Fundamenty*, 1948). Hot off the presses, *Foundations* featured the reconstruction of the national train car factory. In the novel, the war figures primarily in the context of the postwar challenge of reconstruction. The ending is forward looking: a throng of workers marches to the factory at dawn, thinking about "the day, which, ... would unite them in the labor of creation of the truest, most durable and most difficult greatness—one built on human sweat, human fears, and pain, human misery meant to end all misery."[35] The novel represented a future-oriented Poland that the communists wanted to see, and hardly reflected the country's self-absorbed, morally confused, and defeated present. As such, *Foundations* also failed to convey the actual problems, concerns, and works of Polish writers at the time.

Zofia Nałkowska, whose *Medallions* would not reach the Soviet Union for another three decades, made the trip herself in 1947. She celebrated the thirtieth anniversary of the October Revolution and her own sixty-third birthday in Moscow—a bustling metropolis without a Mickiewicz Street. As she was riding the train toward the USSR, she was carried by a stream of history, though she was not quite certain what it meant. It was early in November, and barely a month had passed since the Cominform conference in Szklarska Poręba sealed the fate of East European societies and cultures. Yet throughout the postwar years, Nałkowska had worked to convince herself—though the surrounding reality made doing so increasingly difficult—that, as she wrote on May 4, 1945, "I live, borne by the enormous current of that transformation, which fortunately suits me, which is my cause."[36] Her trip to the USSR as part of an official delegation of writers was no small victory for the Polish communists, who courted established writers like Nałkowska. To the sick, elderly woman it meant another opportunity to examine her own role in the still ambiguous political arrangement, by confronting the hearsay about the USSR. Accompanied by Ehrenburg and a handful of Soviet writers and bureaucrats returning from Poland whom she found most affable, Nałkowska reflected, in silence, on the barren landscape and poorly clad population that thronged into the cattle cars attached to the train.[37] Sightseeing in Moscow left her with a mixture of awe at its scale, fascination with cultural differences, and disgust with socialist realist paintings—"a style free of France, impressive, but not good."[38] But she was happy to have seen it: "Moscow counts 7 million [inhabitants]," she wrote, "today's tour put some flesh on the heavy volumes" she had read.[39] Following the charmingly shy advances of the Soviet poet Aleksandr Tvardovskii, Nałkowska's junior by more than two decades, the two spent several days exchanging yearning glances, words of admiration for each others' work, and a kiss. "Of all of the most delicate kisses I have known, I give that last one," she wrote, sensing perhaps that with her advanced age and fragile health, future opportunities for romance would be few. Pretense and politics framed the trip, as the Soviet hosts resorted to what Paul Hollander has termed "techniques of hospitality."[40] Yet Nałkowska's intimate encounter, fueled by physical attraction tangled with mutual professional recognition and a craving for more interaction, put into tender relief the genuine undercurrent of Soviet-Polish friendship.

THE TALE OF A WHITE BULL

Poland was certainly not the only frustrated vassal state. Writers and officials from the other People's Democracies likewise tried, but consistently failed, to publish new prose fiction from their countries in the Soviet Union. In working to establish a more reciprocal relationship, the East Europeans enjoyed the support of allies in the USSR.[41] The State Publishing House of Foreign Literature (Inoizdat) issued works of foreign fiction in Russian translation. The political heart of the organization was the Scientific-Editorial Council, chaired by Inoizdat's director and composed of specialists in the hard and social sciences and humanities. The council's vaguely formulated objectives, as described in the organization's (draft) statute of 1946, must have been difficult to meet. Inoizdat was, on the one hand, to express "progressive" social opinion and to publish "indispensable" scholarly books and literature. Yet it was also charged with promoting the party line: nurturing Soviet patriotism, highlighting the superiority of the Soviet system, and "unmasking the reactionary character of bourgeois morality."[42] The council's principal tasks included the recommendation of "the most valuable" literature to other publishers and the critical assessment of Inoizdat's work in the publication and distribution of information. Inoizdat's discretely political mission and its direct responsibility to the highest party organ are most likely what made its employees extremely cautious about moving a given book to the publication stage. Approving the wrong work was risky in the fearful climate of Stalin's last years; even though the Central Committee had the last word on the subject, people at lower levels paid for missteps anyway.[43] Not surprisingly, the editors at Inoizdat who were charged with advising others on publication plans, found themselves seeking counsel to tread the treacherous party line.

In search of sound advice, the Inoizdat editors turned to a panel of experts of the Foreign Commission of the Soviet Writers' Union. A subdivision of the powerful literary organization, the commission was established in December 1935. Its first statute of April 1936 explicitly charged it with the task of coordinating the union's international contacts, including exchanges of delegations, information, and literature as well as with preparing surveys of the foreign press. Soon after the establishment of the Cominform, on November 21, 1947, a new statute was implemented. Its militant language reflected the newfound official hostility toward the West. "Decisive and consistent criticism of reactionary and decadent tendencies in foreign bourgeois literature" became one of the commission's main responsibilities. So did "a systematic rebuff to the slanderous attacks of foreign reactionaries on Soviet literature and culture." More important, the Department of Slavic Literatures was created; its status as one of the three major departments of the commission is revealing of the institution's new priorities. Its tasks included the systematic study of tendencies in contemporary Slavic literatures and specific literary material from the region. It was also to recommend the best works for translation and publication in the Soviet Union, and to regularly advise publishers on future thematic plans.[44]

The Foreign Commission's Polish Section began meeting in 1947, the year in which the Cold War became a full-fledged reality and the USSR stepped up its pressure on Eastern Europe. The Polish section met several times per year to discuss the country's recent works of literature and drama.[45] Most participants—usually from eight to twelve individuals at a time—were literary critics, translators and cultural activists. A representative from Inoizdat was always present, taking scrupulous notes for later consideration. Although the exact makeup of the group varied from one occasion to the next, some people appeared more frequently than others. These included the translator of Polish literature Mark Semenovich Zhivov (1893–1962), another translator and critic of Polish literature Maria Efimovna Abkina (1892–1962), the literary critic Mikhail Iakovlevich Apletin (1885–1981), writer Arnold Il'ich Gessen (1878–1976), the critic and playwright Kh. N. Khersonskii (1897–1968), the literary critic Tamara Lazarevna Motyleva (1910–92), and the translator, critic, and essayist Sofia Aleksandrovna Shmeral' (1893–1971). Zofia Marchlewska, who worked on the Foreign Commission until 1951, also made a few appearances. She was the daughter of the Polish revolutionary Julian Marchlewski, and, immediately after the war, an article consultant in the Soviet Information Bureau. During several meetings, even selected doctoral students from Moscow State University were given the opportunity to participate. While some members of the group belonged to the Party, others did not, as was true of all those involved in the Soviet Writers' Union.[46] The minutes of the commission's proceedings show a consistent diversity of opinions within the group about what to do with a given book and why. This is perhaps not surprising, given the participants' differences in age, professions, and political commitments.

Members of the Foreign Commission's Polish Section found themselves in the crossfire of conflicting expectations. The pressure to print from the eager Polish communists, took aim at the Inoizdat editor, who had the final say but preferred to err on the side of conservatism in such uncertain times. Personally, these literary advisers in the Soviet Writers' Union felt propelled by a strong sense of reciprocity to their Polish colleagues who could already read Soviet works in translation, but who could not get their works out in the USSR. In March 1950, the issue appeared on the agenda of the meeting of the Soviet Writers' Union's Secretariat. Besides representatives from Inoizdat, Goslitizdat, and VOKS, several Soviet writers as well as members of the Foreign Commission were present. The publication of literary works from People's Democracies was "becoming more important every day," commented literary critic A. Palladin, who chaired the meeting—the very same man who had felt slighted by his less-than-welcoming hosts during his 1946 trip to Poland. Palladin pointed out the growing relevance of East European literature in the USSR: "our publishers" issued "very few" such works during the preceding five years. According to Palladin's account, the total number was fifty-two, and as few as twenty-eight came from contemporary East European writers, the rest being classics. Most of the fifty-two books were of Polish origin (nineteen), and Inoizdat was the most energetic publisher of East European fiction works (thirteen).[47] According to Palladin, only two serious works came out in Soviet journals.

Palladin reminded his listeners that it was "the duty" of the Soviet literary organization and the publishers to familiarize the Soviet reader with the best works of contemporary writers from Europe's new socialist states. He admitted that "the complaints of our friends from Poland, Bulgaria, Czechoslovakia, Romania, and Hungary are entirely justified." The Soviet literary organizations, he implied, were bound by a reciprocal relationship with East European authors: "The writers in People's Democracies have done a lot to popularize our writers." He reminded the listeners that up to 90 percent of the literary translations in these countries comprised Soviet literature. The opposite was not the case. So far, he admitted, "we have done too little to publish the literary masters from the People's Democracies."[48] He accused the publishers of employing a double standard with regard to Western and East European works. "If they have a book by an

American author that contains flaws, they simply publish it with an appropriate introduction. But in the case of this kind of work that was written by, let's say, a Czech or Polish author, they tried to avoid publishing it altogether."[49] America, the USSR's arch enemy, took precedence over the new communist regimes that occupied an ambiguous place in Soviet political culture. Palladin encouraged the publishers not to ignore poetry or works of short fiction. It was unacceptable, in his view, that a number of worthy works that had come out in the People's Democracies two to three years before were still waiting to reach the Soviet reader. Speaking in the name of the entire Foreign Commission, Palladin then listed six works from Poland not yet released in the USSR—three collections of poems, a collection of essays by W. Zalewski, a production novel by Jan Wilczek, and an anthology of short stories about the new Poland.[50] All these titles were published soon thereafter, but in such scarce numbers that it seems Palladin's reproachful criticism had largely been ignored.

Members of the Foreign Commission's Polish Section likewise vented their frustration on the cautious publisher. In 1952, Mark Zhivov, a veteran participant of anti-Polish, antibourgeois literary discussions of the interwar era and a committed translator of Polish fiction, framed his argument about the necessity to publish more Polish fiction by linking it to the welfare of Soviet readers.[51] Referring to a book [on collectivization] by Lesław Bartelski, he said:

> We should reproach Inoizdat for such delays, that is, for waiting to receive only the literary works that do not raise any doubts. . . . If we are going to procrastinate like this, we will not be able to publish literature for which the Soviet reader is waiting. . . . If Bartelski's book will be waiting for half a year, and if we are only going to discuss it, then a new book will appear and then we are also going to discuss it—it is going to turn into a tale of a white bull. And the Soviet reader awaits the literature, wants to get to know the works of Polish writers.[52]

By comparing the publication process to "the tale of a white bull," a folksy Russian cumulative tale in the tradition of "The House that Jack Built," Zhivov underscored the seeming endlessness of the process and his own resulting exasperation. The Foreign Commission members' exasperation was aggravated by a widespread sense of their apparent irrelevance. As another member, M. E. Abkina, remarked caustically in 1950—just when the agent of Inoizdat happened to be absent from the room—the publisher treated the Foreign Commission according to the standards of the Eastern proverb: "Ask a woman for advice, and do exactly the opposite."[53]

And yet, Zhivov's and Abkina's carping at the publisher can be only partially justified. The Inoizdat editor who usually sat in on the proceedings of the Polish Section witnessed lively debates about the meaning and acceptability of works considered for translation into Russian. What sometimes turned into surprisingly violent verbal altercations surely made it difficult for the beleaguered representative of Inoizdat to assess the risks involved in the publication of a given work. Such battles nonetheless reveal the persistence with which some members of the Soviet literary community fought for the Polish writers' right to publish in the USSR, sometimes resorting to circuitous strategies to achieve their goals. The lively debates also show the widespread confusion about what constituted politically correct art—thus, in turn, illustrating how the Stalinist system consistently promoted short-term mechanisms of control at the expense of opportunities to sustain a stable empire in Eastern Europe over the long term.

Nominally, all members of the commission agreed about the kind of contemporary Polish literature to which the Soviet reader *should* have access. The stories had to reinforce the official scenario about the People's Democracies' reorientation toward the USSR. The emerging narratives also had to reflect the political, social, economic, and cultural developments that had taken place in the Eastern Bloc since 1947. Different members of the Polish Section used these same arguments to justify the need to give attention to specific books. In 1950 the members of the Foreign Commission chose works for consideration: "because the author is interested in the most current events of the day—the successes of free Poland on the front of strengthening its own economy as the fundamental basis for transition toward socialism"; because this "is a book about the new Poland." One day, a member of the Polish Section remarked that: "apparently the three authors attempted to show . . . how the working masses, which had been demoralized by the years of occupation, began to believe in themselves and their own creative forces," and this was a sufficient reason to discuss them in the meeting of the Polish Section.[54] In the absence of Polish books that could not even meet the above standards, the Soviets could not afford to be too picky. At the same time, a publisher's interest and a decision to print stood a distance apart. Polish and other East European writers, even had they known their work was being considered, would have had no reasons to celebrate.

From that theoretical perspective, the criticisms coming from various members of the Foreign Commission's Polish Section were both consistent and predictable. Speaking at one of the meetings in 1953, the Soviet literary critic I. K. Gorskii accurately captured the Foreign Commission's approach during the preceding several years. The panel was discussing Jerzy Putrament's *September* (*Wrzesień*), a satirical take on Poland's military campaign against the Germans and the Soviets in September 1939. Gorskii identified three types of weaknesses in the novel: "those that have to do with ideas, those concerning composition, and finally those having to do with the treatment of particular images."[55] Most frequently, the Soviets demanded that the authors allot a larger role to the working class, the Communist Party, or the Soviet Union.[56] On other occasions, the issue was the author's lack of an explicit moral stand: "Boguszewska is hiding behind her heroes, she tries to elude direct authorial speech," chided Tamara Lazarevna Motyleva in 1950, with respect to *Iron Curtain* (*Żelazna kurtyna*), a novel about a Polish family torn apart by ideological disagreements after the war.[57] The charge of "naturalism" also appeared consistently. This happened during the discussion of Jan Wilczek's otherwise-lauded production novel *Number 16 Begins Production* (*Numer 16 produkuje*) about the reconstruction of a sugar factory in the city of Wrocław. Some members of the Polish Section accused Wilczek of including in his work a morally questionable Soviet character who is bribed by a cunning Pole with a bottle of vodka.[58] Officially, Soviet people were vulnerable neither to vodka nor to bribery. The shady deal hardly fit into the official canon of Soviet-Polish interactions. Naturally, the scene had to go.

Often, a given work did not fit into the official Soviet canon because the characters were too superficial. M. E. Abkina complained, "Konwicki and Kowalewski cannot combine the typical with the individual. They have either [pure] types or people that they had not been able to construct as typical."[59] "Typicality" was one of the necessary characteristics of a true "socialist realist" character; this could mean a character was clearly defined as either good or bad, contrasted with the superficialities of "schematism," yet the definition was notoriously vague.[60] The members of the commission did not use the term "socialist realism," but the critical terms used to discuss potential imports allowed them to disqualify the Polish works from translation. Swearing had its own disqualifying nomenclature. For instance, in 1951, the Soviet literary critic Staniukovich called the foul language of the positive characters, shock workers Kokot and Migoń in a book by Ścibor-Rylski "atypical."[61] In the socialist realist universe, Soviet laborers worked hard without the use of expletives.

Most members of the Polish section agreed over the years that none of the books they had received for consideration was perfect from the point of view of socialist realist poetics. Yet strikingly, various members of the commission had different ideas for handling these imperfections. Consider, for example, the 1950 discussion of Helena Boguszewska's novel *The Iron Curtain*, which was first published in Poland in 1947. The author belonged to the older generation of Polish writers. Born in 1883, Boguszewska received a higher education and spent the interwar era as a writer and activist for broadly based social justice and equality. Sympathetic to the socialist cause, she nevertheless scorned the flagship tenets of socialist realism. The writer Maria Dąbrowska recalled in her memoirs that when a Polish publisher accused Boguszewska of having failed to produce "typical" characters in her stories, as prescribed by the socialist-realist canon, Boguszewska retorted she "had not made any effort to make the characters typical. 'Typical' is cliché (*sztampa*)."[62] Boguszewska's underlying resistance to meet the criteria of Stalinist literary criticism obstructed the Foreign Commission's efforts to get anything published because it provided more fodder for debate.

Boguszewska's *The Iron Curtain* reflected her interest in the individual human being. In this story of family conflict in postwar Poland, Karol, an officer who survives the defeat of the Polish army in 1939, leaves his family, and wanders around Western Europe during the war. His wife Celina does not hear from him for many years, but finally she is delighted to receive a letter from Karol, who turns out to be alive. Yet her initial joy quickly disappears: Celina does not finish reading the letter, suddenly finding herself, like the rest of Karol's Polish family, indifferent to her husband. The Soviet literary critic Motyleva, who introduced the novel to her colleagues in the Polish Section, summarized what she understood to be the main point: "The iron curtain is hanging between the Poles who remained in Poland and those who decided to leave." This turns Churchill's metaphor, an obvious reference, on its head. Motyleva correctly says, "The man living in the capitalist world, who has renounced his family, his motherland, has also lost the right to the love and respect of his family—this is the key thought of the novel.[63] In general, the participants approved of the book's subject, but they also criticized it for a number of flaws, including the narrow focus on family life, insufficient political commentaries, insufficient condemnation of the prewar Polish government, and the lack of a discussion of the role of the Soviet army in liberating Poland and the Polish working class.

Yet the exchange that followed these introductory comments reveals the underlying disagreements concerning the best course of action with regard to the book. "In order to publish this book," argued Iakovlev, "we are going to have to give it a very serious and qualified foreword, which will help the Soviet reader grasp the processes that are taking place in contemporary Poland." Gorskii vehemently opposed this idea, claiming that the book represented a very low artistic level unworthy of publication. The translator of Polish literature Zhivov proposed a third option for deciding to publish *The Iron Curtain* or not, by taking the larger view of considering the writer and her entire body of work. Zhivov's criteria were in Boguszewska's favor, he pointed out, as her earlier stories constituted sufficient evidence of her literary skills and firmly established her credentials as "a reliable pro-Soviet person." The translator's approach underscored his strictly political criteria for considering the book, unrelated in any way to "socialist realism." Zhivov's perspective provoked a violent reaction from the other participants. "To publish this just because Boguszewska was running to the Red Army is not correct," Shmeral' pointed out, referring to the author's autobiographical account of the joy with which she met her liberators.[64] Finally, Novikov, an editor from Inoizdat, voiced the most pragmatic point of view. "So far we have published only two books about the new Poland because [otherwise] they do not exist," he said. "*The Iron Curtain* is the only novel that talks about Warsaw. If we treat these books so critically we will wait many years before giving our readers something about Poland. The publisher cannot ignore this fact, and I think we should publish it."[65] Not being able to publish anything constituted a major consideration in the literary import process on the Soviet side.

Although later the Foreign Commission received books that came closer to meeting Soviet ideological demands, the anatomy of the discussions remained the same. A politically safer tendency to reject the book battled with the willingness to compromise on its aesthetic or ideological qualities. For example, Lesław Bartelski's novel titled *The People from across the River* (*Ludzie zza rzeki*), was on the agenda of the Foreign Commission in 1952. The book's main subject was Polish collectivization, and this was the most likely reason why the work also won two Polish literary prizes for 1951. Although some members of the Polish Section recognized the book's political value, others were strongly against publishing it. "Personally, I did not like the book from the first to the last page. The work is schematic, not artistic, and the author is awkward in resolving the problems he himself set out to address," argued Janina Krotowska, the Polish-born translator of Polish to Russian. "Judging by its deliberate primitivism, the book is not simply about a village, but also for the village," she added condescendingly. Muranovskii emphasized that the role of the party was not shown clearly enough. The literary critic R. Vikhireva defended the book, while Shtein reproached his colleague for giving "discounts," "and being unwilling to admit that the book is simply not satisfactory."[66] Motyleva, Zhivov, and Ia. Staniukovich, another critic, recognized the imperfections of the novel and the relative inferiority of contemporary Polish fiction in general. But they also repeated the familiar claim that from the perspective of the Soviet reader, who up to that point had had few opportunities to read about contemporary Poland, the book presented considerable value. An appropriate foreword, they argued, would help the reader interpret the text correctly.[67]

Clearly, the tensions present in the Soviet literary milieu at that time affected Moscow's imperial project in Eastern Europe. The seemingly free exchange of opinions about each book was in fact informed by each individual's awareness of calculated risks concerning his or her career, or even life. All Soviet institutions, including the Writers' Union, were subject to extensive purges.[68] Increasingly, many such campaigns were anti-Semitic in character, and several members of the Polish Section, including M. E. Abkina, M. S. Zhivov, and A. I. Gessen, were Jewish.[69] But everyone was at risk for articulating an opinion that could later be used against them; the sense of threat must have been heightened by the fact that a clerk in the room transcribed the discussions.

The question of social values became another bone of contention among the members of the Polish Section. Accepted norms of social behavior, as expressed in fiction, constituted problems distinct from any strictly methodological considerations. In fact, values appeared to be the most divisive issue between the Polish writers and their Soviet judges. The Poles tried to promote works that emulated the Soviet classics of the 1930s. While the Soviets, in making their choices, had to respond to the most current signals from the Stalinist leadership. The 1949 discussion of the first Polish production play *Engineer Saba* (*Inżynier Saba*) is a case in point. The author, Juliusz Wirski, weaves a tale about opening up the first assembly line for synthetic fibers.[70] Polish Section participants spoke mostly about the literary style and quality of the play. But among their comments, two stood out, two quite unrelated remarks of translator Valerian Artsimovich. A Soviet Pole, Artsimovich was a former editorial secretary at *Żołnierz Wolności*, the newspaper of the Kościuszko Division, who had been transferred from the Red Army.[71] In his new role, he pointed out that there were not enough women in the play. Second of all, he felt that the playwright Wirski had given excessive attention to the Jewish problem: "What in Poland is accepted, maybe even understood, our viewer will simply not understand, because the question of Palestine is being touched on a bit broadly; the German occupation, the martyrology (as they call it in Poland) of the Jews during the Hitlerite occupation—I thought it could be shortened; only the principal and most important thing should be shown. So, the role of Shtern should be diminished, but nevertheless kept."[72]

As shown earlier, Polish communists at the time pressured artists to minimize Jewish themes. But they vacillated between incorporating a narrative of class struggle and a story about the wartime drama of the Polish nation. In Soviet fiction, there was no place for Jews. Aware of official anti-Semitism in the USSR, the Polish Section members who wanted to see *Engineer Saba* published in Russian had to square the play with postwar Stalinist value system.

Interestingly, on some occasions even these mandarins of Soviet literary culture appear to have been confused on the question of what was or was not allowed. Vera Dunham has demonstrated that Soviet writers after World War II began to embrace a new set of values that formed a stark contrast with the early Bolshevik period's emphasis on themes such as self-denial, revolutionary struggle, and the primacy of the collective. In contrast, argued Dunham, the 1930s and particularly the post–World War II period witnessed the emergence of a new relationship between Stalinist officialdom and the society at large, which she dubbed the "Big Deal." In an effort to defuse rising tensions between the oppressive Stalinist authorities and an increasingly impatient society, the Soviet leadership relaxed its previously rigid standards of public austerity, allowing members of the Soviet "bourgeoisie" to openly espouse "middle-class values." Popular fiction became the terrain for this new relationship; Soviet writers acquired license to ruminate on previously forbidden issues such as personal happiness, love and romance, material well-being and comfort—the latter characterized by symbolic household props such as a geranium or an orange lampshade.[73]

The sessions of the Polish Section suggest that the members of Soviet literary officialdom did not all endorse or even understand the terms of the "Big Deal." Section members diverged widely in their opinions about what constituted an acceptable departure from the ascetic world of early Bolshevik fiction. The critic Regina Merkina obliquely expressed this dilemma in 1951, during the discussion of Ścibor-Rylski's novel *Coal (Węgiel)*. In this book about coal miners, Ścibor-Rylski appears to have consciously flouted the official rules of the socialist realist canon by including a rather self-indulgent main character, the miner Migoń. Four years later, in an essay published after his suicide, the Polish writer Tadeusz Borowski would issue a sardonic indictment on the "positive hero" of the Stalinist novel. "A wretch," Borowski described him, who "does not drink, does not smoke, does not smile at girls, and walks stiff and straight."[74] In Jerzy Borejsza's terms, he was the perfect starched Stalinist. Migoń appears to have departed from that hallowed model, thereby raising suspicions among some Soviet officials. The Soviet critic Merkina and other members of the Foreign Commission found that Ścibor-Rylski's portrayal of Migoń "created too big a contrast between the character at work and his everyday life." Underscoring Migoń's vices by implication, Merkina was quick to point out: "It never happens that way," that the main character "is somebody who does not smoke, does not drink, and does not like women."[75] Merkina's anticipation of Borowski's quip shows that members of the two literary communities shared common skepticism about the official literary standards. It may be that the impassioned haggling over literary standards brought the two sides closer together than each of them was to their political superiors in the party apparatus.

Ambivalence about themes of romance did not prevail in the Foreign Commission discussions. In 1949, Ziablov criticized the ending of *Engineer Saba*, in which the female character Anna confesses to Saba, "And you know what gives me the most joy? It is the fact that you love me." Ziablov was promptly scolded by his colleagues for reading the Polish version of the work. They informed him that the love scene had been struck out of the Russian translation, thus revealing that differences of opinion were occasionally a consequence of mere disorganization. Yet the fact that the sugary exchange had been filtered out again raises questions about whether anyone on the Foreign Commission of the Soviet Writers' Union grasped the terms of the alleged "Big Deal." If the specific placement of the romantic dialogue in the final scene had posed a difficulty for the commission, giving it too much emphasis, the fragment could simply have been moved to another part of the novel. Can we suppose then, that the commission members consciously reserved the spectrum of "middle-class values" specifically for "middle-class" readers? This does not seem to be the case either. Iakovlev, during the 1950 discussion of Boguszewska's *The Iron Curtain*, specifically reprimanded the author for including noteworthy details of Polish middle-class life. He accused Boguszewska of "being infatuated" with the milieu she was describing, and especially "with the geranium, the moonlight, a dog who folds up on the bed."[76] The objects that so displeased Iakovlev might well be—and in the case of the geranium, exactly are—a showcase for Dunham's "Big Deal." It would probably be too much to accuse Iakovlev of a double standard. After all, what difference did it make whether the geranium (or the dog, or the moon) was Polish or Soviet? He objected to their inclusion regardless of locale, symptoms of how bewildered some mid-level officials were concerning the vision of the new empire, as well as what was supposed to appear under the rubric of socialist realism.

The outcome of the deliberations fails to impress. Out of the ten works that the Polish government urged the Soviets to publish, the Foreign Commission considered only two in 1947–54: Jerzy Andrzejewski's *Night* and Jerzy Putrament's *Reality.* Of the twenty-two works considered by the Polish Section in 1947–54, exactly half came out in the USSR. Of that number, however, only four were published contemporaneously, between 1947 and 1954. They were: Putrament's *Reality* (published in the USSR in 1948); Wilczek's *Number 16 Begins Production* (1950); Zalewski's *Tractors Will Conquer the Spring* (1950); and Marian Brandys's *The Beginning of the Story* (1952), a series of sketches from the construction site of The New Steel Mill, Poland's socialist city rising near Cracow (see appendix A, table A.3.) Jerzy Putrament won the socialist realist jackpot; the former political officer, a mediocre writer, and a formidable general secretary of the Polish Writers' Union with power over literati more talented than himself, enjoyed the support of bureaucrats on all sides. Although we are considering prose, it is worth noting that, astonishingly, even the greatest proponent of literary Stalinization, the young, "pimpled" poet Wiktor Woroszylski never published his militant works in the USSR.[77] Ultimately, the only works that made it to the USSR were uncontroversial, grammatically and ideologically correct texts. Focusing on the evils of interwar Poland and the benefits of collectivization and industrialization, their Polish authors blandly described the world that the Soviets had already known all too well.

While the boon of the "Big Deal" may have indeed touched a number of Soviet writers, for those few Polish authors who tried to get published in the birthplace of communism, the deal proved to be nothing short of "raw." One may speculate that the denizens of the new empire had yet to earn their right to imagine "bourgeois" pleasures in their fiction through undergoing an ideological quarantine of the existing remnants of bourgeois values. But to assume that the Soviet establishment engaged in such elaborate long-term planning would be to give its confused and intimidated members too much credit.

WARM APRICOT SODA

These seemingly insurmountable bureaucratic hurdles compelled the members of the Soviet and Polish literary communities to search for more direct links of communication with one another. To be sure, nothing was possible without party and government involvement on either side, but the very initiative in establishing international contacts did not have to originate with the officials. For example, the more determined Polish writers wrote letters to the responsible representatives of the Soviet Writers' Union to inquire about the status of their works in the USSR. Others took advantage of professional meetings with their Soviet colleagues to seek guidance in writing specifically with the Soviet context in mind. The meager evidence of the late Stalinist era suggests that as a consequence of these Polish efforts, and of professional sympathies on the Soviet side, an informal, nascent system of literary mentorship developed in the womb of the ossified bureaucracy of the new Soviet empire.

The example of Leon Kruczkowski (1900–1962) shows that neither a high position in the communist *nomenklatura* nor literary prestige promised Soviet publication. The writer made his debut in the early 1920s and remained artistically prolific throughout the interwar era. After 1933, he devoted more and more time to leftist political activism by associating himself closely with the Polish Socialist Party and the peasant movement. He spent the war years in a German POW camp. Kruczkowski became a member of the PPR in 1945; in the same year, he was nominated vice-minister of culture and the arts, a post he held until he was replaced by Włodzimierz Sokorski in 1948. During the decade that followed, he fulfilled many important functions in Polish cultural life, the most important of which was chairing the Polish Writers' Union between 1949 and 1956. In his literary work, Kruczkowski addressed difficult social problems and openly expressed his sympathy for communism. Enthusiastically espousing socialist realism, in much of his work he managed to avoid catering to the immediate demands of the party-state. His keen insight and literary talent brought him domestic and international acclaim, and even the post-1989 critical reevaluations of the cultural legacy of Polish communism failed to deprecate the value of Kruczkowski's work.

One of his more interesting plays, titled *The Germans*, landed on the table of the Foreign Commission as early as 1947. The work was first published in Poland in 1949, and by 1953, it had been staged or published in twelve countries of Eastern and Western Europe (East Germany), Asia, Latin America, and the Middle East.[78] In it, Kruczkowski tells the story of Dr. Sonnenbruch, a German university professor who, like other members of the German intelligentsia at that time, took pride in his apoliticism. Sonnenbruch maintained his passive stance even during the war years; his son's membership in the SS challenges that fact, at the same time

making it easier to understand Sonnenbruch's avoidance of all things political. This ambiguity constitutes one of many complexities in the story.
Sonnenbruch increasingly starts to see his conduct more in the context of
a moral dilemma, in order finally to realize the disastrous consequences
of his own passivity—the victory of fascism. Inspired by his discovery, the
professor decides to cross over to Berlin's Soviet Zone of Occupation and
remain there. The obvious political overtones of the story may seem amus-
ing today. Yet Kruczkowski succeeded in creating an image of "Germans"
that was both multidimensional and human before the establishment of
the German Democratic Republic (GDR) created the imperative of doing
so in the official culture.[79] The problems raised in *The Germans* as well as
the author's restraint in moralizing situated the play largely outside the
canon of Soviet "party-minded" literature. Despite this fact, its domestic
(and international) successes surpassed those of any socialist-realist play
produced in Stalinist Poland.[80]

The Foreign Commission found the play too flawed for staging or publication in the USSR. The principal criticism was its narrow focus. The title
The Germans, one person argued, suggests a broad scope, whereas the
reader learns only about the German intelligentsia. Others pointed out that
"only the old professor comes to understand his mistakes [i.e., someone
who] cannot participate in the struggle for Democratic Germany. The
struggle is being fought by the German proletariat. Incidentally, [the play's]
young protagonists either perish (Ruth) or remain fascists (Willi, Liesel)."[81]
The main problem was that Kruczkowski made the German proletariat
seem embarrassingly irrelevant. Nor did this "incompetent" literary perspective help to show the new Poland in a positive light. It is thus not surprising that Kruczkowski had to wait until 1955 to see the Russian edition of *The Germans*.

Yet he was hardly indifferent to the idea of reaching Soviet audiences.
The Polish translator of *The Germans*, Juliusz Gosiewski, sent several letters to responsible Soviet officials asking when the play would be staged
in Soviet theaters. The two letters he sent in 1950 (in April and December) remained unanswered. He had discussed the issue with Kruczkowski
earlier that year, and certainly would not have undertaken such an initiative without his knowledge and consent.[82] In December 1951, Gosiewski
wrote again to Leonid Sergeevich Viv'en, a seasoned theater director and
actor from Leningrad who, based on the destination address in the letter,
must have been spending time in Warsaw at the time.[83] Gosiewski found
Soviet unresponsiveness "curious." After all, he pointed out, Kruczkowski
was Poland's leading socialist-realist writer, and the play received critical

*Prague, 1950. Leon Kruczkowski (left) and Czechoslovak director
Ota Ornest speak before the Prague showing of* The Germans *on December 15
that year. The Soviet translation of the play would not appear until 1955.
Courtesy of Polska Agencja Prasowa.*

acclaim all over the world—from the GDR to South America.[84] The translator repeated his inquiry on January 19, 1954.[85] It seems, though, that the publication of the play a year later and its staging in the USSR were less a result of Gosiewski's efforts than of the general relaxation of artistic constraints in the country.

Meanwhile, Kruczkowski took the relationship with the Soviet critics to another level in 1953. He sent an unfinished manuscript of his new play, titled *Colorado Beetle* (*Żuk z Kolorado*), eventually published in Polish as *A Visit* (*Odwiedziny*), to the Foreign Commission, asking for help in writing the final part. According to Staniukovich, who had spoken to Kruczkowski earlier in the year, the gesture was the Pole's response to being unable to stage or publish *The Germans* in the USSR. Involving the judges in the creative process, he thought, was a way of ensuring that his work would appear in Soviet bookstores. While some members of the literary body hailed Kruczkowski's step as a "very good precedent" (Glebov), others pointed out the practical complications associated with such an arrangement. Zhivov observed, for example, that it was difficult enough to work with a writer when he was present in Moscow, and "this one was not simply somewhere farther in Kiev, but in Warsaw." Another problem, according to the translator, was that everyone involved would have a different idea about how to finish the play. Consequently, it would be nearly impossible to offer any useful suggestions to Kruczkowski.[86] Like the manuscript in question, the meeting remained inconclusive. The entire incident illuminates the discrete process whereby the author sought to synchronize his artistic output with the official vision of empire. Kruczkowski was driven into conformity not so much by pressure from above, but by his own desire to take advantage of what Soviet tutelage had to offer. Ultimately, like Berlioz and Homeless at the end of the "hot, spring day" in Bulgakov's *The Master and Margarita*, Kruczkowski was ready to settle for a warm, apricot soda. But in 1953, even that was unavailable, and a true spring was yet to come.

Kruczkowski was not the only Polish writer to seek guidance from his Soviet peers. Nor were the members of the Polish section always unwilling to oblige with direct feedback. The author of *Engineer Saba*, Juliusz Wirski, when his play was being considered by the foreign commission in 1949, apparently gave the Polish Section "carte blanche" to make the necessary changes to his play. But he also requested that the Foreign Commission "work with him" on such changes. This necessitated the Pole's visit to the USSR—a complicated operation (and a dream for many other East European writers at the time), but one that apparently had the support of the Soviet consul in Cracow.[87] According to one member of the Polish Section, Shmiral', the Soviet translator could simply take care of the necessary corrections: he could "change the minister into the director of a department [and] he can change particular cues." She had no doubt that Wirski would "be deeply thankful for our help" in revising the play, and that the changes would also benefit Polish drama at large.[88] Unlike Kruczkowski's unfinished play, the one by Wirski needed only a few changes. Its imperfections were therefore a manageable obstacle within the administrative constraints on Soviet-Polish interactions.

Rare personal encounters between Polish writers and members of the Polish Section also constituted an opportunity to give or receive feedback. During a meeting in 1950 dedicated to the discussion of Polish postwar fiction, M. Zhivov described his encounter with another young Polish writer Bogdan Hamera. The Pole complained that opportunities for receiving constructive criticism of his work were few in his homeland, even from members of the Polish Writers' Union. Hamera felt that even such a hardboiled Stalinist literary critic as Poland's Melania Kierczyńska "was not able to say everything she wanted to say." This is when he started looking for guidance across the eastern border. He found one of Zhivov's translated articles in the Polish party newspaper *Trybuna Ludu*, and after further research he found the original full version in *Izvestiia*. According to Zhivov, their subsequent meeting turned out to be beneficial to both parties. Hamera received useful advice, and the Soviet critic learned a lot about how to be an effective mentor.[89] Contacting members of the Soviet literary community directly at a time of Bloc-wide isolation required daring and an enormous amount of energy. The sparse evidence for such initiatives suggests that few Polish writers had the wherewithal. But many Polish literati had reasons to wish to see their work published in Russian. The failed efforts of the accommodationists like Kruczkowski showed to all and sundry that such hopes were unrealistic. The "hot, spring day" continued. And the Soviet regime's ultimate inability to capitalize on the affective bonds between Soviet and Polish writers, linking the two literary communities through professional opportunities, failed to transform the Soviet soft-power project into an attainable dream. The modicum of success achieved, if it could be called that at all, was a lukewarm apricot soda.

CONCLUSION

In the popular press, the Soviet authorities encouraged the masses to think of socialist Eastern Europe as a source of pride. But the Soviet reading public was unlikely to learn about the new empire from the East European writers themselves, or from the heroes of their novels. Similarly, the heroic efforts of Soviet soft-power advocates in Poland also went largely unnoticed and unrewarded. Still, the Soviet-Polish efforts to publish new Polish belles lettres in the USSR are historically revealing in three ways.

First, they expose the systemic tethers of Stalinism, which forced the Kremlin to ignore the long-term consequences of depriving East European writers of opportunities to publish their works in the USSR. Like Homeless and Berlioz of *The Master and Margarita* who could only dream of drinking a cold beer, the Polish writers had no choice but to focus on writing for audiences outside of the Soviet Union. It was warm soda for the Polish communists as well. Thanks to them, in Poland, writers' lives shifted away from their art. "A writer became a figure of public life, in which earlier only a most talented few could participate." Writers served as high diplomats and public servants, chaired important institutions, sat on committees, and so on; "on the state scene, [the writer] acted as a representative of public interest and an ideological authority."[90] But ironically, by failing to secure them the opportunities to publish in the USSR, the communists prevented them from being truly respectable writers. That cultural failure cannot be underestimated.

Second, the abortive cultural exchange reveals the severe limitations of the vast Soviet empire in advancing cultural reciprocity. Opportunities were squandered at every turn. Harmonizing the interests of the Soviet center and the Polish periphery proved more challenging than the Soviet takeover. Historically, successful empires have absorbed and transmuted the cultural gifts of their dominated nations. Stalin and his leaders quite simply failed to see the real merits of power in its soft form.

Finally, failed as they were, the attempts to establish reciprocity further underscore the limited utility of "Sovietization" as the dominant analytic category to make sense of Soviet-East European cultural interactions even during the apex of Stalinism. The urge to Sovietize Eastern Europe was firmly in place; indeed, the process defined Soviet-East European interactions in 1948–54. But a closer look at exchanges between Soviet Bloc institutions shows that despite the terror, xenophobia, and isolation, at least some agents of empire on both sides continued to advocate an approach to cultural relations grounded in reciprocity and exchange. Intimidated, confused, and frustrated, they tried to cross the boundary line in order to create cultural relations within Stalin's new empire that worked best for them.

5

SOVIET SOFT POWER
AND THE POLISH THAW

It is too early to close down; Wolność is a good platform of the Soviet people,
and real friendship with the Poles is still far away.
—Soviet journalist Nikolai Bubnov, 1954

■

I will never believe, my dear, that a lion is a little lamb,
I will never believe, my dear, that a little lamb is a lion!
I will never believe, my dear, in a magic spell;
I will never believe in minds kept under glass.
—Polish poet Adam Ważyk, "A Poem for Adults" (1955)

FROM SORCERY TO MAGIC

One month after Stalin's death, a hint of thaw spread like sunlight through the USSR. Soviet writer Ilya Ehrenburg could not contain himself. "But now I am seized with the urge to break off and describe the charm, the magic of April in our part of the country which does not enjoy the warmth of the south," he recalled, describing how he and many of his compatriots felt. Only the language of the supernatural could depict the changing atmosphere. The future intoxicated Ehrenburg. Though in places "the snow still lies in grey patches," he continued, one could "see that the festival of spring is about to start." The writer described "tiny blades of grass and the tender stars of future dandelions" that were "pushing their way up out of the earth, the pussy-willows are beginning to show and birds that have flown in from everywhere are chirping; all is noise, restlessness and gaiety after the trials of the winter."[1]

Only a year and a half later, Boris Pasternak would also rejoice in a letter to a friend at having "found and given names to all this sorcery that has been the cause of suffering, bafflement, amazement and dispute for several decades."[2] Where Ehrenburg delighted in the future, Pasternak

187

Warsaw, April 1954. Soviet Ambassador Nikolai Mikhailov presents his letters of credence to the Polish government. Courtesy of Polska Agencja Prasowa.

seemed enthralled by his intimate encounter with truths about the past. Sorcery under Stalin meant sudden disappearances or guilt by association, all but surreal by the standards of ordinary logic. In April 1953, magic meant a great rupture filled with long-term hope, muddied with a sudden sense of loss and confusion.

Moved by the upsurge of emotion, and perhaps a desire to stay atop current events, Ehrenburg quickly wrote a novel *The Thaw*, to describe the impact of Stalin's passing on ordinary people in a provincial town in the southern Volga. The spring 1954 issue of *Novyi mir* (New World) printed the first work of Soviet fiction to refer to the infamous "Doctors' Plot." In 1952–53, Stalin assaulted hundreds of Jewish doctors for allegedly conspiring to murder him. *The Thaw* dared mention this plot, while painting a less-than-joyful atmosphere in Soviet society.[3] It broke new ground by portraying one character, a committed socialist-realist painter Pukhov, as a cynical party hack. In so doing, the novel consolidated Ehrenburg's reputation as a commentator on events of his day. It also brought him immediate criticism from the Soviet regime and more orthodox Soviet writers. The regime, in December 1954 was, in the words of Ehrenburg's biographer, "unsure of itself, not knowing how to celebrate Soviet literature publicly and still maintain absolute control."[4] This hesitation would continue for years to come, and would make the era seem like a spring festival only by the standards of the ice-cold Stalin years.[5]

More important, Ehrenburg's novel succeeded in naming an epoch in the history of the Soviet Bloc.[6] The chronological boundaries of "The Thaw," as experienced by each communist society, are somewhat blurry. In Poland, as in the USSR, for instance, the authorities made cautious but noticeable steps to halt the most orthodox and destructive cultural trends of the preceding years while Stalin was still alive; these trends accelerated after 1953, each country moving at its own pace, thus forming several conventional caesurae. In one instance, Ehrenburg himself had to explain to Mikhail Suslov why, during his visit to Budapest in late 1955, he talked to Hungarian literati about his novel *The Thaw*. Nobody had forewarned Ehrenburg that in Hungary—unlike the USSR, or even Poland, where Jan Brzechwa's translation of the novel came out in January 1955—only a few Hungarian officials had access to *The Thaw*.[7] While many "Thaws" and de-Stalinizations have been written about by historians, these processes have rarely been considered as mutually interacting phenomena within a single Soviet imperial mechanism. Yet Ehrenburg's metaphor invites a historian to do exactly that. The window from which to view this early thaw begins on March 5, 1953, at Stalin's death and ends in the all-important year 1956, when Khrushchev officially broke with Stalinism and a wave of popular unrest spread throughout the Soviet Bloc.[8]

The real ice that melted in the spring of 1953 poured into rivers that flowed freely between the notoriously harsh political border regimes. Rushing in different directions, the rivers affected the physical geographies of the lands through which they passed in significant and unpredictable ways. The Thaw enthralled many people across the Soviet Bloc, but it also entangled them anew. One month after his April exultation, Ehrenburg's May 1 article in *Pravda* remained upbeat: "Everyone realizes that the days of monologues are past and that the time for a dialogue has come."[9] The writer was crediting the Soviet government with willingness to move beyond bipolar brinkmanship with the West, so characteristic of the earlier stage of the Cold War. But he may well have been expressing the hope that the kind of Soviet-Polish friendship he sought throughout his life—and which many others increasingly felt encouraged to practice—would now carry the day. Not everyone embraced the new vision of friendship grounded in reciprocity, to be sure, and the new circumstances created new tensions. But the very fact that people could discuss their differences without fearing arrest helped to propel the soft-power initiatives in new directions.

Soviet journalist Nikolai Bubnov seized this sudden opportunity to change the terms of the Soviet-Polish relationship. On May 10, 1953, exactly ten days after Ehrenburg's article in *Pravda*, Bubnov embarked on a train from Moscow to Legnica, a small town in southwestern Poland. The journalist had spent the past three years working for *Krasnaia zvezda* (Red Star), a Soviet military newspaper. Now he traveled to Poland charged with "an important task." His commander in the Army Political Department told Bubnov to "mend the editorial office of *Wolność*. There is no boss there and the staff is crawling apart."[10]

Wolność was the mouthpiece of the Northern Group of the Red Army (from 1946, known as the Soviet Army), which was stationed in Poland. The newspaper came out in Polish. The impact of Stalin's death on relations with the West, and the struggles for domestic succession within the country itself, again made cultural ties with Eastern Europe a low-priority issue for the Soviet leaders. Bubnov received vague directives that seemed to reflect lower-level officials' cautious concerns about maintaining the status quo more than any policy shift from above. In the spirit of these uncertain months, Bubnov himself wondered why his superiors had even sent him. "But they said nothing" about other possible reasons, he wrote, "and asking is not my habit—they sent me, which means I must go, which means they trust me."[11]

Personal life narratives are notoriously unreliable sources of factual information. Individuals forget and misinterpret the past in memoirs and autobiographies; as in journals, they often unconsciously play up and embellish their own roles in the events they describe. They may confabulate, deliberately or otherwise, and search for patterns where none existed. Bubnov's account of his work at *Wolność* is no exception to the rule. But the journalist's diary, even when read critically, offers a rare, extensive, and at times intimate Soviet official's account of his work in Eastern Europe— and thus has great historiographic value. When corroborated by the other sources on which the present study relies, Bubnov's diary helps to reconstruct the secretive world of Soviet propaganda outreach. It reveals all the meaningful ways in which Bubnov "wrote himself" into the USSR's "social and political order" at this all-important historical juncture; and, simultaneously, it shows how a willing and able Soviet interpreter of Soviet soft power made his way through "an existential terrain marked by self-reflection and struggle," connecting his official task to a genuine effort of reconciling empire with socialism.[12]

Bubnov's years as editor of *Sovetskoe slovo* (*Soviet Word*), a newspaper published by the Soviet Military Administration of Germany in 1945–49, gave him an advantage over those who had no experience in foreign propaganda. But the journalist also feared that his complete lack of knowledge of the Polish language would be an obstacle to his mission. As with Ehrenburg on his first interwar trips to Poland, Bubnov's anti-Polish prejudice weighed heavily on him, too. "My feelings toward the Poles are perhaps the most awful thing," he confessed to himself in his journal on the train. As he rode west, "memories came alive of Henryk Sienkiewicz's novels, Gogol's novellas, and especially *Taras Bul'ba*," a gory tale about Zaporozhan Cossacks' struggles against the Poles. Literature spoke loudly. Bubnov had never met any Poles in person, he admitted, but these readings produced in him a certain distrust toward them. That sentiment, too, sat uneasily with his anticipated role as editor of *Wolność*, that is, "educating [*vospitaniie*] the Poles in the spirit of friendship with the Soviet people."[13] But the terms of that friendship were about to change again. And in his diary Bubnov cast himself as a man who was willing to evolve.

Legnica, given its troubled history and present-day realities, served as an ironic home base for Bubnov and his mission to reach out to the Soviet Union's new friends. The Northern Group of the Red Army had headquartered in the city since the end of the war. Before the war, Legnica belonged to Germany and housed the largest garrison of the German army in Silesia. To their credit, the Red Army had liberated Poles from Nazi rule, but they were subsequently seen as the country's new occupier. Legnica lay in the territories that Germany ceded to Poland following World War II. The new Polish inhabitants of Legnica, who moved into town following the expulsion of the Germans, had particular reasons to contest the Soviets' purportedly friendly intentions. Usurpation, not support, had ruled their first encounters, and those memories were fresh and fierce.

Following the fateful day of July 11, 1946, the first of only three days given them to evacuate beyond the Kaczawa River, some five thousand Poles rushed to pack all their belongings and property from local institutions. Soviet authorities not only failed to provide the logistical support they had promised. Worse by far, Soviet troops appropriated what they found in the empty private residences and offices of Legnica. They also took property that had been abandoned by the expelled Germans, while Soviet generals and high-ranking officers moved into the spacious villas of the

German elites who had resided there. The beleaguered Poles, upon their return nearly three months later, found that roughly one-third of Legnica had moved over to Soviet hands. Nicknamed "the Little Moscow," that part of town suddenly became off limits to them. Legnica, with its nearly intact communications infrastructure and strong strategic position near Dresden, Germany, had been a natural choice for the Soviets.[14] Set at the crossroads of Europe and crisscrossed by walls and fences, Legnica symbolized the paradoxes of Cold War topography just as divided Berlin would half a decade later.

As Bubnov went for a stroll one June day, he contemplated the city's ancient history. Legnica witnessed, in the mid-thirteenth century, Batu Khan's formidable Mongol armies make a sharp eastward U-turn, thus sparing the rest of Europe the conquest, carnage, and humiliation to which the Russian principalities had been subjected. The journalist must have known, too, though he chose not to record the fact, that the Red Army soldiers were initially seen as latter-day Mongols. Truly, the Soviet presence in Legnica had a bitter historic flavor with which Bubnov would now, nolens volens, have to contend.[15]

The editor's first priority, though, was to set a new rhythm in the newspaper's lethargic editorial office. He immediately addressed the myriad strictly organizational challenges that impeded effective propaganda. Bubnov directly supervised the entire article production process, identifying weak links among journalists, translators, typists, proofreaders, and printers, rebuking and even firing some of them for lack of discipline or for open defiance. He established and enforced a strict chain of procedures that pushed the articles smoothly through successive stages of production. Bubnov could do little directly about the low wages of some technical staff— the typists were leaving for better-paying jobs, he learned, while the translators were paid as little as the janitors.[16] Instead, he tried to boost the staff's morale by attending to their spiritual needs. He assigned one journalist agricultural topics Bubnov knew the writer was passionate about.[17] Battles for humane treatment also stirred Bubnov to action. Appalled to learn that the authorities showed little concern for the needs of some twenty Soviet soldiers who guarded the printing presses, Bubnov stepped in. The food was foul, the men complained, and the radio, their only window on the world, had been broken for a month. Their morale was low in part because none of the guards, he learned, knew much about the newspaper they worked for or indeed, the country in which they lived. He discovered, with rather personal horror, that few on the editorial staff were aware of Poland's history and current affairs, hardly anyone knew the language, and some of them openly stated they could not care less about it. "That is why we cannot put things in order!" Bubnov lamented. Only one week earlier, he had made acquiring the necessary Polish language skills a party task.[18] Setting an example to all, relying solely on his dictionary and "an editor's hunch," he plowed through the draft articles for *Wolność* by late May.[19] After only a few months in his new mission, Bubnov claims to have held a few editorial meetings in Polish, not Russian. Some staff members merely pretended to follow the discussion, but nobody dared to protest.[20]

As many other Soviet officials had realized in previous years, effective foreign propaganda required compromises. Bubnov enjoyed more flexibility than those Soviet editors who preceded him. In his diary, Bubnov described how he emphasized that the Soviets should pay attention to the Poles' reading habits. As one of his editors pointed out during a staff meeting on May 19, 1953, "we are enamored of quotations, but the Poles don't like them."[21] The editor in chief began to hound his coworkers, demanding less empty verbiage, more timely, factual information, and more content to which the Poles could potentially relate. During the same meeting, Bubnov himself underscored that the study of Polish affairs, and "interests of the Polish reader, his tastes and particularities" should be seen by the staff as their "official duty."[22] Likewise, he asked the journalists to avoid sensitive historical subjects, such as General Suvorov (responsible for quelling the 1794 uprising against Russian rule and capturing its leader Tadeusz Kościuszko) and Semen Budennyi (a hero of the Russian Civil War and Soviet-Polish War of 1920).[23] Cultural sensitivity was a two-sided coin, with the Polish past and present on either side. Bubnov's approach marked a change of tone from that of Soviet Information Bureau officers who had insisted, in the early 1950s, that Poles must accept their Soviet-leaning articles as a "patriotic duty" (see chapter 3).

Bubnov fell back on poetry to bring the reluctant Soviet editorial staff closer to Polish affairs, organizing "literary soirees" on Polish themes. A decade earlier, Polish communists had enlisted the nineteenth-century poet Adam Mickiewicz and the contemporary revolutionary bard Władysław Broniewski to rally the suspicious soldiers under Zygmunt Berling's command to their cause. Now, on September 15, 1953, Bubnov was "cramming" Mayakovsky's famous poem, "My Soviet Passport," in order to elicit the interest of his subordinates who could not be bothered to learn Polish.[24] The 1929 poem affirms pride in Soviet citizenship, it is Mayakovsky's ode to the "vermillion booklet." Mayakovsky wrote the poem, ironically, at a time when foreign travel documents were becoming increasingly useless in the USSR. It expressed the author's revulsion at the languid, scoffing western border officials, and sympathy for the Polish passengers who were treated dismissively by them, thus bringing out a rare theme of Soviet-Polish camaraderie from an era of Soviet culture dominated by anti-Polish propaganda.[25] In turning to Mayakovsky, Bubnov brilliantly stressed the aspect of Soviet cultural heritage that would have appealed to much of the Polish intelligentsia.

Bubnov's self-described actions as editor aimed at a greater cultural reciprocity between the Soviet and Polish peoples. The Soviets had to provide better journalism to earn their readers' interest and even trust. In turn, coverage by *Wolność* of Soviet-Polish relations had to reflect the new discursive possibilities of the immediate post-Stalin months. During an emergency staff meeting on June 16, 1953, and just as the temperature among striking East German workers was beginning to rise, Bubnov argued that the journalists "mustn't create the impression among their readers, that the Soviet people are giving everything to the Poles—almost building socialism for them."[26] Stalin and the Soviet officials used to take credit for all of the real and invented successes of East European socialism; now that Stalin was dead, and with official values shifting, editors like Bubnov were in a position to share the credit.

To the extent that Bubnov followed his motto, the editor gained a natural ally in Vladislav Sokolovskii, the veteran of the Soviet-sponsored Polish Army and the Soviet Information Bureau, who now edited the Polish section of *Wolność*. Echoing the editor in chief's earlier comments, Sokolovskii noted in October that friendship (*druzhba*) implied solely the realm of consciousness, and was therefore too narrow a concept to thematize the Soviet-Polish relationship. Instead, he maintained, *Wolność* should reframe these links around the principle of concord, cooperation (*sodruzhestvo*), which could be extended to the economic, political, and ideological domains.[27] Immediately after the war, Sokolovskii was compelled to adopt an ever more rigid approach to foreign propaganda. Now that the political atmosphere had changed, he tried to rescue Soviet soft power from the sidelines by expanding the Soviet-Polish middle ground.

Bubnov, too, showed a spirited commitment to soft power, but he was no iconoclast either. In portraying himself as a lone crusader against bureaucratic indolence, the journalist most certainly overstated the frictions he was facing in the broader context of Soviet cultural politics. Thanks, in part, to Ilya Ehrenburg's *The Thaw*, narrow-minded, obstructive bureaucrats became villains par excellence precisely within the months following Stalin's death. In setting up the contrast between industrious young engineers such as Egorov and cagey old-timers like the factory director

Zhuravlev, Ehrenburg redefined the post-Stalinist value system.[28] Bubnov, who cast himself as the energetic, ingenious force behind the new *Wolność*—a Egorov of Soviet cultural outreach, as it were—identified himself with the political pacesetters.

Bubnov and other Soviet authorities used poetry to rejuvenate the artistic scene and attract young people to the program of reform, because poetry had been the least tainted by socialist realism.[29] The Soviet elites were now debating the merits of Mayakovsky, the revolutionary poet who had been considered a "formalist" under Stalin. Even the hard-line Viacheslav Molotov, although critical of the poet's break with the Bolshevik Party, wrote to Konstantin Simonov that he considered Mayakovsky to be "our most talented poet."[30] Aleksandr Fadeev, chairman of the Soviet Writers' Union and exemplary Stalinist bureaucrat, had in 1948 crashed the Wrocław Congress of Intellectuals in Defense of Peace with his bellicose anti-Western rhetoric. Yet in his letter to Georgii Malenkov and Nikita Khrushchev, in late August 1953, Fadeev asked why the "reactionary tsarist regime" was able to give birth to "dignified" artists "literally each decade," whereas nearly half a century after the founding of Soviet socialism, under "the most progressive" form of rule, "there exists only one single Mayakovsky—and everyone else lags behind?" Somewhat disingenuously, Fadeev went on to blame "bureaucratic distortions" for this state of affairs.[31] So while Nikolai Bubnov, the editor in chief of *Wolność* struggled against the elements here, in Legnica, he had the winds of history blowing forcefully at his back.

Perhaps too forcefully. It was Bubnov's bad luck that just as he poured so much energy into recasting *Wolność* as an outpost of Soviet soft power, the very rationale for the newspaper began to wane. Ironically, Bubnov's analytic mind was partially to blame for shaking his own confidence. The new year, 1954, brought a fresh, if doleful perspective. While reflecting in mid-January on his ultimate impotence with regard to increasing the quality of translations, it dawned on Bubnov that the Poles, not the Soviets, should be publishing the paper, because "what was accepted during the war and, say, in 1945–48, now constitutes an anachronism."[32] Still, he concluded, weighing both the pros and the cons, that it was too early to close the paper, as *Wolność* "made a good platform for the Soviet people, and a real friendship with the Poles is still far away."[33]

While Bubnov may have been right, the decision to close down *Wolność* was hardly up to him. In another prank of history, he learned just six months later that his paper would close, while attending the tenth anniversary of the People's Republic of Poland, in late July 1954. The Soviet prime minister, Nikolai Bulganin, who flew in to Lublin for the celebrations, cracked a few jokes about the Polish press in Bubnov's presence. Bulganin claimed that in the Polish Party newspaper, *Trybuna Ludu*, he looked like Feliks Kon in one photograph, and like Dzierżyński in another; a third image of Bulganin was, in his view, altogether hard to make out. "Does our newspaper, what is it called . . . yes, *Wolność*, is its quality just as bad?" he asked.[34] Some colleagues spoke up and defended the newspaper. Indeed, *Wolność* employees generally took pride that the superior print quality of the newspaper distinguished it from the Polish press.[35] This hardly mattered now—Bulganin had signed the Central Committee decision, and the fate of *Wolność* had been sealed.[36]

But Bubnov fought back: in September he wrote to Mikhail Suslov of the Central Committee, pointing out that one must not close the paper just yet, since more than one hundred thousand people had already paid for this year's subscription. He thus extended the paper's life until January 1955. But Bubnov's take on *Wolność* as "a good Soviet platform," Suslov found "clearly ungrounded." Still Bubnov fought on. For "historical reasons," he perorated in his letter to the top, "anti-Russian and anti-Ukrainian nationalism is alive among Poles as it is in no other country." According to Bubnov, *Wolność* could and would do much more to solidify Soviet-Polish friendship.[37] But the skeptical Suslov thought otherwise. "And what about Poland's sovereignty? Poles themselves should be building socialism, and they should learn how to write about our achievements and experience." Suslov cited as a prime example Bubnov's previous paper, *Sovetskoe slovo*, which had also been closed down. And if Germany, Suslov reasoned, the vanquished country, is beginning to rise up on its feet, then "this independence (*samostoiatel 'nost'*) is all the more necessary for Poland."[38] Bubnov had to make do with this explanation. But the curiosity of this passionate editor who rarely questioned authority took the upper hand. He had to know the real reasons for the closing of *Wolność*. In October 1954, he approached the new Soviet ambassador Nikolai Aleksandrovich Mikhailov about the matter. "This, Bubnov," the diplomat told the editor, "must be explained by reasons of a higher order." "And which reasons?" Bubnov asked. Ambassador Mikhailov "did not say."[39]

Though Bubnov could not know it, his efforts were entangled in paradoxes of political transitions of the post-Stalin era. On the one hand, his efforts to revamp *Wolność* dovetailed with Moscow's attempts to improve socialism at large. Soviet leaders—alarmed by social instability that began to shake up East-Central Europe in May and June—began forcing the communists in their vassal states to adopt the "New Course," a program of economic reforms meant to improve daily living conditions among citizens and thus offload the existing social tensions.[40] The publisher of *Wolność*, the Soviet Army Political Department, had followed the cues from *Pravda* that, particularly after the uprisings in East Germany of mid-June 1953, began publishing materials about "the construction of housing, stores, sanatoriums."[41] Ironically though, as Jakub Berman had recognized shortly after the war, the very existence of *Wolność* constituted an intrusion in Poland's affairs. *Wolność* brought attention to the unwelcome and legally unregulated status of the Soviet Army on Polish soil. As the direct Soviet propaganda platform in Poland, it irked the Polish public. By now, it also represented a policy from which the new Soviet leaders wanted to dissociate themselves. While the fate of *Wolność* was being decided, Khrushchev argued for recognition of Yugoslavia as a socialist state (Stalin had expunged it from the Soviet Bloc in 1948), thus implicitly condoning "national roads to socialism" in the Soviet Bloc; Molotov opposed him on the grounds that this would lead to the disintegration of the empire—and loss of Poland in particular.[42] Khrushchev prevailed and Molotov's voice no longer carried weight. *Wolność*, therefore, symbolized Stalin's footprint in an era of de-Stalinization. Though Bubnov brought nuanced understanding and a flexible approach to the newspaper's mission, in these circumstances, his fight for *Wolność* was a losing one from the start.

Bubnov's self-professed faith in the transformative power of socialism may have spared him much bitterness and many feelings of dejection. It gave the editor of *Wolność* the hope that the kind of friendship he envisioned would eventually be concretized; the sense that his efforts to bring it about had not been entirely in vain saved him. While in Poland, Bubnov met no horse-charging, saber-waving sadists as his teachers had trained him to expect. He was struck, nonetheless, by a rhythm of life, customs, and mentalities that differed starkly from his familiar Soviet ways. He did perceive oddities, such as the "stormy, disorganized, festive enthusiasm" of the crowds during sports events, which the journalist attributed to the "hotheadedness" of the Polish people (*goriachii narod*), resulting, Bubnov claimed, in their disorganization and lack of discipline.[43] Other behaviors, such as the feeding of pigeons "with magnificent, dark-yellow wheat" in Cracow's old town, Bubnov explained with the awesome power of tradition.[44] Repeatedly, this champion of Soviet-Polish friendship found himself annoyed with the Poles' nationalism. Remarkably, he tried to understand its roots: after all, he wrote shortly after arrival, "they suffered much from the Russian tsars and princes; if it had been different, why publish a Soviet newspaper in the Polish language?"[45] Still, he found it exasperating that his hosts "wanted to believe that the Poles themselves had liberated Poland with the help of the Soviet Army, and not the other way around."[46] Poles were quick to point out that the Germans had not destroyed a single building in Cracow. Bubnov found it vexing that "none" of the Poles knew that the advancing Red Army had saved their beloved city. But "with time," Bubnov consoled himself, "the Poles will find out about that too; for now, let them learn about the greatness of Lenin and the noble goals of socialism."[47]

Nothing appalled the editor of *Wolność* more than the Poles' vibrant religious life. Without outright banning it, the Polish Stalinists had harshly persecuted the Catholic Church; the faithful rightfully felt under siege. In fact, since the summer of 1953 the Soviet authorities themselves had curbed the Polish communists' major antireligious campaigns, considering them too strict.[48] Thus, for all his enthusiasm, Bubnov was wrong when he wrote on May 12, 1954, that "not a single pillar of religion is harmed in Poland."[49] For someone coming from a state where churches had been turned into museums of atheism, the "hundreds of bicycles" parked near churches in the Polish countryside seemed like an extraordinary spectacle.[50] A scene he witnessed in St. Mary's Church, in Cracow, must have made even the pigeon-feeding seem ordinary: "some woman threw herself on her knees in front of the 'mother of god,' and pounded her forehead against the cool slabs, and her face bore marks of madness."[51] Bubnov's contempt for the Poles' "religious fanaticism" battled his view that the failure to take into account Poland's "particularities" can "complicate the construction of socialism and Polish-Soviet friendship.[52] A practical and reasonable man, Bubnov was simultaneously a great believer in the ultimate victory of socialism. In his faith, he shared more with the religious Poles than he was willing to admit.

The first week of 1955 marked Bubnov's last days in Poland. During an official ceremony, the Polish government awarded him, Sokolovskii, and several other Soviet military officials the Officer's Cross of the Order of the Rebirth of Poland. Bubnov found the medal "pretty, even very pretty," and the recognition sweetened the bitterness caused by the closing of *Wolność*. "Now," he wrote in his diary, "there's absolutely nothing for us to do in Poland." He knew he would be going home, to study and to find out where "the last third" of his career would take him.[53]

THE SOVIET INFORMATION BUREAU AFTER STALIN

Like Bubnov, the officials at the Soviet Information Bureau (Sovinform-biuro) also landed in a post-Stalinist no-man's-land. In his lengthy memo to the Central Committee's Department for Agitation and Propaganda, dated August 10, 1953, Sovinformbiuro's V. Sorokin outlined the challenges and contradictions of his post. He assured the Central Committee that the new streamlining of Sovinformbiuro's apparatus was a good thing. Sorokin was referring specifically to the recent abolishing of Sovinformbiuro's section responsible solely for producing articles about "the life of the USSR." He also approved the cutting of the central editorial staff. Both had promoted red tape and a "cookie-cutter" approach to the articles sent abroad. Readers disdained the articles' irrelevance to the local contexts and their dull, off-putting tone.[54] But while these chief problems had disappeared, the Soviet state provided no support that would help push the bureau in another, clearly defined direction. Where earlier, the dry articles had at least filled up pages, now Sorokin had nothing to fill the void.[55] Where before, the Central Committee provided Sovinformbiuro with guidance through its Foreign Policy Commission, ever since the newly created Ministry of Culture took control of Sovinformbiuro, such crucial feedback on the institution's monthly production plans became a rarity. This reflected, Sorokin speculated bitterly, the growing "absence of interest" on the part of the Central Committee.[56]

According to Sorokin, the elimination of the central editorial office helped prevent *vkusovshchina*—head editors imposing their tastes on the territorial sections. But the recent decision to create a "Main Editorial Office," Sorokin worried, might simply mean new bottles for old wine.[57] The official argued that only decentralization of control of production could increase the quality of the articles. He suggested that "a creative discussion" between department heads and Sovinformbiuro leadership might work toward the same ends.[58] More than just "remarks," his were familiar old complaints articulated in the new language, which the newly created "collective leadership"—one of several terms introduced "to fill the void" left after "the loss of the almighty *vozhd'* [leader]"—was likely to understand.[59] Sorokin's confusion about the role of his institution could be summed up in one question, which he posed directly: "Where is Sovinformbiuro going?"[60]

Desperately trying to save his organization's impressive momentum, Sorokin sought to bring Sovinformbiuro's decade-long propaganda experience in Eastern Europe into full focus and full force in the service of empire. Sorokin worried about the suggestion made by some of his colleagues to restrict the Soviet Information Bureau's international activities. Unlike Bubnov, Sorokin thought that leaving the promotion of the Soviet Union to foreign journalists lacked justification. He resisted centralization within the Sovinformbiuro because the resulting bureaucracy would prevent the smooth production of articles, but he also feared vesting foreigners with the task of writing about the USSR. "Why should we assume that the local journalists can write better than we can about our country, about our achievements, and about our experience?" he asked.[61] The press in the People's Democracies is likely to place more, not fewer of Sovinformbiuro's articles, he argued, as already the number of orders coming from these countries had grown rapidly. But the vassal states demanded specific kinds of material: original, provided for exclusive use of a given news organization, well-written, and signed by concrete authors.[62] Such articles should then be translated, edited, and tailored by the communist journalists abroad, Sorokin maintained, and while "it is not difficult to find such people," he emphasized, "doing so still requires certain means."[63] He had "no doubt" that "the interests of our state and our party" required a more thorough restructuring, training more qualified cadres and carrying out more robust propaganda work. None of this meant curtailing Sovinformbiuro's activities.[64] Many Soviet bureaucrats and most Polish officials had supported greater flexibility in such work all along. After Stalin's death, Sorokin and his colleagues could advocate for such flexibility with candor and resolve.

The year 1955 confirmed Sorokin's insights concerning the nature of the new possibilities. The People's Democracies continued to order more materials from the Soviet Information Bureau. Teletype connections were established with Warsaw, Prague, Budapest, Berlin, Sophia, and Bucharest, which facilitated the distribution process. The authorities enlisted more Soviet writers to write articles, including A. Fadeev, K. Fedin, B. Polevoi, K. Simonov, M. Shaginian, and others, although, no doubt, amid the excitement of the Polish Thaw the names of these coryphaei of the Stalin era had a stale ring to them. Contrary to the expectations of the organization's leadership, liquidation of the field offices in January brought an increase in orders, since Sovinformbiuro's representatives abroad no longer filtered requests.[65] Local telegraph agencies took over the distribution of materials, which made the process more efficient, more interesting to the target countries, and, one can safely guess, less fraught with tensions. It also complicated life for the Soviets, since the telegraph agencies rarely bothered to track the publication rates. But we do know that in 1955, Poles, who received the most materials of all the People's Democracies (842 articles, including 452 original pieces), accepted 49.6 percent of the total of Soviet articles.[66] This approximated the rates from 1946, but now that 49.6 percent reflected genuine Polish interest in Soviet news.

If Sorokin took courage from these developments, he was soon to be disappointed. In 1955, the authorities slashed Sovinformbiuro's editorial staff by half. So, paradoxically, while the demand for articles increased—Sorokin's dream come true—the beleaguered staff journalists doubled and tripled their efforts, but still found themselves unable to meet the demand. The newspaper's output dropped by half, and in some cases the quality of the articles plummeted noticeably as well.[67] Far from being the result of a renewed, more sophisticated propagandistic offensive, the "liberalization" of Sovinformbiuro's practices reflected a broader Soviet "hands-off" approach to those domestic affairs of its vassal states that posed no immediate threat to the Soviet Bloc. Stripped of many of its already inadequate resources, the Soviet Information Bureau confronted a particular disadvantage in Poland. The press there, since the fall of 1954, had played the leading role in Poland's social, cultural, and eventually political upheavals.[68] The Soviets could have found a bigger niche for Soviet news, and shaped public opinion more assertively. Instead, they backed off. Reversing the interventionist practices of the preceding years, the Soviets ceded more column space to Polish and other international news sources. In so doing, they squandered the potentially useful experience of dozens of people and frustrated the hopes of committed officials like Sorokin. The Soviet Central Committee took the position held by many Polish communists in 1945—namely, that Soviet soft power could be most effective when wielded from a safe distance.

A POEM FOR ADULTS

Nothing prepared the observers of Poland's cultural life for the publication of Adam Ważyk's "A Poem for Adults" in the summer of 1955. The poem's juiciest bits focus on the builders of Nowa Huta, or the New Steel Mill, a massive Stalinist housing project near Cracow. Politically and socially, Cracow was Poland's most conservative city, which Nowa Huta was designed to dominate, in time. Ważyk paints the young Polish men and women as a savage "mob," "thrust out from medieval darkness" and into "barracks," "hostels," and "huts" of the construction site, in which they drink, vomit, swear, and fornicate out of boredom and out of the need to drown out the powerful sense of emptiness in their lives and souls.[69] This description of Poland's working class—the purported makers and beneficiaries of communism—shocked readers. A frontal attack on the canon of socialist realism, the poem—indeed, a *poemat*, a more grandiose form reserved in the immediately preceding years solely for the glorification of communism—delivered a telling commentary on the hypocrisy of the communist authorities. One Czechoslovak translator attempted to publish the poem, as did the elderly East German playwright Bertold Brecht. Brecht died before finishing the translation, and, unsurprisingly, censors in the USSR and other People's Democracies banned the work.[70] In Poland, "A Poem for Adults" came out because a cohort of cultural Stalinists were losing their faith in Stalinist culture. The recalcitrant hard-liners were losing their political clout. The enforcers of orthodoxy were leaving the historical stage or making peace with the post-Stalinist present. The Stalinizers of Polish culture conceived "A Poem for Adults" and made its publication possible; they cowrote the script for the undoing of Stalinism in their country and coproduced the unique drama of the Polish Thaw.

Poles and Soviets knew Ważyk, a former political officer and the official poet of the Kościuszko Division, as the poster boy of Poland's socialist realism. The public about-face of this coryphaeus of communism occurred in the pages of *Nowa Kultura* (New Culture), the debut site even more shocking than the poem itself. Launched in 1950 and supervised by Jerzy Putrament as editor in chief in 1952–53, *Nowa Kultura* had been part of the party's ideological offensive against the old, "bourgeois" forms of culture and mentality.[71] With the publication of Ważyk's poem, the journal's mission demonstratively came undone. In the momentous summer of 1955, the poem opened up a floodgate to literature that aimed to "square the accounts" with the moribund Stalinist regime.[72] No certain explanation exists for Ważyk's sudden epiphany; to the readers of "A Poem for Adults," and even to Ważyk himself, it seemed as uncanny as the magical mendacity of Stalinism that he now disavowed.[73]

Those guardians of cultural orthodoxy who would have criticized Ważyk a few months before would now have to defend themselves; "A Poem for Adults" was a poem about them. For Jakub Berman, the top policeman of Stalinist cultural norms in Poland, Stalin's death brought a tremendous sense of relief. Though he shed tears as he announced the event to his subordinates in the Central Committee, Berman's exaggerated gestures and his "voice modulation that transformed into weeping" struck his listeners as poor histrionics.[74] In fact, they may have been private tears of joy. The frequency and scope of interventions by Soviet officials constantly breathing down his neck had annoyed and frustrated Berman. Far more important, Berman's Jewish ethnicity had made him increasingly fearful for his life. A number of Soviet officials, ambassadors, and Polish communists had woven intrigues against Berman in the preceding years. Their multiple complaints to the Kremlin about his alleged misdeeds, and accusations of "anti-Polishness," "anti-Sovietness," and Zionist sympathies, often went hand in hand with statements of dissatisfaction about the ethnic makeup in the party at large.[75] Official complaints had real consequences. The November 1951 arrest of Rudolf Slánský, the general secretary of the Communist Party of Czechoslovakia, initiated a wave of show trials in Eastern Europe, which, from Berman's perspective, must have looked ominous. Like Slánský, Berman was Jewish, and their remarkably similar biographies led the Polish leader to suspect that he would be next to go.[76] Furthermore, Berman's brother Adolf lived in Israel, while his brother-in-law, Zygmunt Grynberg, was involved in an "affair" uncovered in the Polish Ministry of Health in 1952, which, additionally, made Berman guilty by association.[77] The Doctors' Plot in January 1953 intensified anti-Semitic propaganda. Clearly, Stalin's death spared Berman Slánský's tragic fate. Berman himself credited Bolesław Bierut for shielding him and refusing to yield to Stalin's pressure to turn Berman into a scapegoat.[78] Berman's biographer Anna Sobór has argued convincingly that Berman's overt lack of interest in fighting for the top leadership post, as well as his willingness to imprison Gomułka and Marian Spychalski, were the main reasons that he lasted in his position for so long.[79]

And with release comes downfall. Saved from imminent arrest and possibly even death, Berman's life began its slow but steady decline. Most members of Poland's communist old guard found it difficult to reinvent themselves in the new realities, as the fresh crop of Soviet leaders veered away from Stalin's policies. Jakub Berman, heavily associated with the bygone era, found himself challenged by newcomers who had spent their Stalinist years safely on the sidelines. In fact, hard-line Stalinists became a convenient target for attacks.

These attacks served to distract public opinion from the Stalinist crimes committed by their accusers. Thus, when Khrushchev and Malenkov arrested Lavrentii Beria in June 1953, the two leaders succeeded in destroying their political opposition and securing their own names. Beria's arrest sent shockwaves through "Little Moscow." Just seven days after the event, one of Bubnov's editors openly complained about the local agent of the dreaded military counterintelligence organization who was said to have disparaged the employees of *Wolność*. Moscow sent another agent shortly to carry out an investigation, while the abusive counterintelligence agent was removed from his post. "That's how the times are changing!" commented the paper's editor in chief. "It's the first time in my life that I have heard an open criticism of the representatives of state security organs."[80]

Beria's arrest constituted a blow to Jakub Berman because it thrust the practices of the Polish security apparatus into the spotlight. An event that brought even more attention to the feared Ministry of Public Security was the escape of Józef Światło, first to West Berlin in December 1953, and eventually to the United States. Światło had been vice-director of the Tenth Department of Poland's Ministry of Public Safety, responsible for gathering compromising materials on members of the party. Now eager to speak, Światło made CIA-sponsored broadcasts on Radio Free Europe titled *Behind the Scenes of Security and the Party*, telling thousands of Polish listeners, in often spiced-up language, about the real and purported crimes, sexual dissolution, and moral degeneracy of the country's top officials.[81]

Heavily colored by Soviet and Polish anti-Semitism, a search for scapegoats in the party, cultural institutions, and security apparatus followed. Ironically, Berman supervised the process. These investigations eventually raised questions about Berman's own responsibility for the widespread violence and coercion.[82] Between 1954 and 1956, the Pole found himself strongly criticized and sidelined; in the spring of 1957, he was expelled from the party.[83] Sensitive to the logic behind the new party secretary's actions, former political officer-turned-book publisher Adam Bromberg pointed out bitterly that Władysław Gomułka had picked his favorites. Gomułka "forgave [Zenon] Kliszko, [Marian] Spychalski, and [Ignacy] Loga-Sowiński, who had framed him during the investigations," earlier, and who were all ethnically Polish. But he "[did] not [forgive] Berman, Minc or Zambrowski," the men who "delayed his case and saved him from what happened to Slansky, Rajk, and Kostow."[84] Incidentally, Nikita Khrushchev believed that Roman Zambrowski, former chief of the Political Department in the Soviet-backed Polish Army and then head of the Personnel Section in the United Polish Workers' Party (PZPR) Central Committee, "had a reputation for cold-shouldering the Polish cadres . . . and promoting Jewish cadres," when, in Khrushchev's words, there was no "objective" reason to do so.[85] It may well have been true, but Bromberg's insight brings clearly into relief the anti-Semitic mechanism that shaped the trajectory of Berman's downfall.

And that downfall came fast. Berman's visibly growing weakness emboldened those around him who had wanted to loosen up the party's strict cultural policies for some time. It also empowered those who had despised the Stalinist norms altogether and those, who, like Ważyk, had suddenly had their fill. During 1953–56, Berman assessed some of his earlier cultural policies, particularly "excessive interventions" in the artistic life, quite critically.[86] Yet his continued warnings against "harmful" developments in Polish culture—referring largely to the attempts to promote "abstractionism and other such things," and to negate socialist realism and even the leading role of the party—remained the dominant themes in his public statements.[87] Berman shared his concern about excessive license (*samo-wola*) of the artists with many other party members, urging them to conduct an "ideological offensive" in December 1955. Although he hoped the offensive would reverse unwelcome cultural developments, Berman articulated his anxieties in a language that revealed his inability, or perhaps unwillingness, to adjust to the changing times.[88]

Ważyk's "A Poem for Adults" had been the immediate impulse behind Berman's renewed call to arms. Berman was present when Edward Ochab, a Soviet-sponsored Polish Army veteran, led the session of the Political Bureau on September 22, 1955, which was devoted to the worrisome cultural developments. The participants deemed Ważyk's work "harmful," "anti-Party," and "offensive to the working class." Paweł Hoffman, another former political officer in the Army commanded by Berling, was removed from his position as editor in chief of *Nowa Kultura*.[89] Yet the very fact that Hoffman had authorized the poem's publication, and then avoided arrest, broadcast the news that Stalinist norms and methods no longer defined Poland's cultural politics.

As someone who had been "making the weather" in Polish culture during its most radical transformations, Jerzy Putrament, like Berman, was determined to weather the storm. For the former political officer, troubles also arrived from all directions nearly at once. Previously untouchable, he had been removed from his position as general secretary of the Polish Writers' Union in January 1953. Berman and Hoffman, as part of the modest liberalizing push, sent the notoriously despotic official on "creative holidays.[90] By spring, Putrament had withdrawn from the executive board of the Party Organization of the Writers' Union and had quit as editor in chief of *Nowa Kultura*. Early 1953 saw the simultaneous publication of Czesław Miłosz's *The Captive Mind* in Polish and English. Although the Polish version came out in Paris, and officially did not exist in Miłosz's home country, Poland's writers, critics, and readers found out about it anyway. The chapter "Gamma, the Slave of History" is Miłosz's excoriating and thinly veiled description of Jerzy Putrament. Putrament's gradual semivoluntary stepping out of the limelight at that time, writes his biographer Emil Pasierski, was a deliberate step meant to soften the fall that his tarnished reputation inevitably would have brought.[91] For several decades, Miłosz and Putrament had been entangled in a complicated relationship at first defined by opposing views, then by shared leftist goals, and finally resulting in violent disagreements and increasing distrust. Even though Miłosz's work can be read as a more universal reflection on the vulnerability of intellectuals and the power of ideologies, his critique of Putrament boldly and publicly revealed his view of their relationship. In its form and implications, *The Captive Mind* was not unlike Światło's on-air radio revelations about Berman: an informed yet emotionally charged attack from a former insider of the communist regime.

Putrament, like Berman, remained a committed crusader for cultural orthodoxy in these years. Immediately after Stalin's death, Putrament composed a commemorative poem, "The Ninth of March." In it, he described Stalin not only as the benefactor of the liberated Auschwitz prisoners but also a source of reason that would "illuminate darkness, age-old poverty."[92] Knowing Putrament's frequent ideological transformations over the course of his life, it is tempting to see the poem as a continuation of his opportunism, or perhaps the very weakness of character that is so central to Miłosz's assessment of the writer. It is certainly more difficult to see Putrament's position as opportunistic in June 1955, when cultural figures were challenging the party openly. Building on Berman's statements, Putrament vehemently warned his party comrades and writers against the dangers of "the recidivism of a bourgeois understanding of art."[93] He fulminated against "A Poem for Adults," sharing Berman's outrage against Ważyk's "contemptuous" portrayal of the working class. In particular, and somewhat curiously, he rejected the poet's amoral depictions of the female workers, which he saw as abhorrent, an accusation he is said to have repeated during subsequent decades.[94]

Putrament remained an unflinching supporter of the communist regime until his dying days in 1986. Yet, within two years of Stalin's death, his views on culture began to evolve. Emil Pasierski has observed that Putrament's feuilletons about contemporary Polish life and about the United States, where he stayed in 1955, convey a sudden change of tone. Earlier, Putrament had argued from a clearly ideological perspective deeply colored by contempt for the West, yet he was now willing to engage with his readers on more rational terms.[95] Putrament perceived nonsense and contradiction in Poland's cultural life, making this critic, by the mid-1950s, into "something of an oppositionist" in the eyes of some. Of course, he had helped to create the contradictions he now criticized. Pasierski, therefore, makes great sense in claiming that Putrament had aligned himself with the subcurrents of the "Thaw" primarily because his desire to break with the past now weighed heavily on him.[96] Although in his autobiography, written in the 1960s, Putrament painted a somewhat liberal image of himself, this self-portrayal squares uneasily with the record of his activities or indeed others' opinions about him. While Jakub Berman showed himself as an instrument of history until his dying days, explaining his actions in Marxist terms, Putrament did not. The writer displayed a liberal side when the powers above him required flexibility, but stood for harshness when political winds blew the other way. Miłosz labeled him a "slave of history," thus suggesting Putrament's complete lack of agency vis-à-vis Marxist historical logic. In fact, Putrament appears to have been a bondsman of circumstances.

Wiktor Woroszylski resembles more accurately a "slave of history," Miłosz's moniker for Putrament. Woroszylski was the young and most militant exponent of vigorous Stalinism in literature. And Jerzy Putrament took credit for Woroszylski's breaking with cultural orthodoxy, and his passionate love for the Soviet Union. Recalling his meeting with "the pimpled one" in the editorial office of *Nowa Kultura*, where they both worked in 1952, he described with scorn Woroszylski's stated desire to quit the journal in order to go to study in the USSR. Putrament's contemptuousness of the young writer's uncritical attitude toward the USSR contrasted with his own affirmative writings about the birthplace of socialism. Putrament valued his own firsthand knowledge about "the courage, discipline" of the Soviet people," and their "kindness to others."[97] The general secretary of the Polish Writers' Union at the time, Putrament claims to have let the young writer Woroszylski travel to the USSR to give him a chance to produce more conscious and convincing works.

Later, Woroszylski himself framed his trip to the Soviet Union as his own journey of discovery, not as a gift from Putrament. Writing in 1956, he remembered "the atmosphere of mistrust, suspiciousness, fear." Arriving in the USSR, Woroszylski had thought that Polish socialism was imperfect, crude, and violent, because "little, weak people" were "corrupting" it. He thought that mingling with Soviet people—the true Soviet proletarians—would allow him to experience what socialism should be like, and he was ready to endure physical hardship to see the Soviet Union for himself. He arrived at the height of terror to see the unfolding of the Doctors' Plot, and felt immediately terrified by the accompanying "fascization of atmosphere, the twistedness of human consciousness, and demoralization of youth." The sudden immersion in the reality of "brutal, and not in the least poetic" Moscow hit Woroszylski between the eyes. He once witnessed a fight between two students—war veterans at the Gorky Literary Institute. One of them had been a regular soldier, the other belonged to the *zagraditel'nye otriady*—shooting squads that executed those troops who were retreating from the front. "And that terrible hatred between them survived." Experiences such as this dealt a heavy blow to Woroszylski's image of the perfect Soviet society.[98]

During Woroszylski's first vacation in Poland, in the summer of 1953, the young writer shared his doubts with the director of the Polish Central Committee's Culture Department, the "exceedingly intelligent" Paweł Hoffman, who merely nodded, and said calmly "we were afraid that you would break over there."[99] That same summer Woroszylski read Arthur Koestler's *Darkness at Noon*, which had been smuggled from the West, together with several copies of the Paris-based Polish journal *Kultura*. Deeply disturbed, Woroszylski discussed the book—and his misgivings about the USSR—with his friend Jerzy Andrzejewski. In 1954, still a literature student in Moscow, Woroszylski talked to returnees from the Soviet Gulag. This was a time when the Soviet authorities began to release thousands of victims of Stalin's crimes who had been imprisoned in labor camps in the North and the East of the USSR. At the same time, however, the wave of "rehabilitations" continued to strike him with the "true beauty" of the Soviet system, which seemed capable of self-purification through acknowledgment of its own guilt.[100] Once the most militant apologist for Stalinism, the now-disgusted Woroszylski held on to his dreams by reinvesting his hopes in the new, and allegedly better, Soviet Union—and in an improved version of communism. Woroszylski came back to Poland in the summer of 1956, reformed, shorn of his youthful zeal. "My therapy turned out more effective than expected," Putrament gloated, in his memoirs.[101] But by then, Woroszylski had personally toured the Stalinist camps in Central Asia. Amid the watch towers, barbed wire, and barren landscape, Poland's chief devotee of Stalin and most devoted Stalinizer of Polish literature saw for himself that Stalin had been a murderer and a cynic. Putrament, may have claimed credit for Woroszylski's breaking with Stalinism, but a tour of labor camps was nothing that he had ever planned.

Włodzimierz Sokorski transitioned more smoothly into the new era than any of his peers. He remained relevant after Stalin's death by morphing into an energetic impresario for de-Stalinization in the arts. Sokorski had been at the forefront of a modest cultural liberalization as early as the latter months of 1952. By 1954, the party had chosen him to preside over the correction of "errors and excesses" in the official policy of the preceding years.[102] As Putrament did with Woroszylski, Sokorski claimed credit for Ważyk's 1955 anti-Stalinist metamorphosis. He brought Ważyk and several other artists to the New Steel Mill on purpose, he recalled, after the mill's director, who was also Sokorski's friend and an alleged fan of Gomułka, convinced him that they should see "everything—the real bottom."[103] Was Sokorski's new role and enthusiasm simply political opportunism akin to that of Putrament? Certainly, Sokorski combined his guidance with a much keener sense of foresight. Or could it be that Sokorski's consistently moderate approach, suppressed largely by fear in 1949–52, could at last concretize itself in these more propitious conditions?

I venture that Sokorski genuinely welcomed the gradual retreat from orthodoxy. The former minister of culture's well-known penchant for exaggeration certainly raises red flags; but so do the claims of his detractors, who, by blaming him for all the wrongdoings of cultural Stalinism, sought to minimize their own responsibility for collusion with the system.[104] Clearly, the facts and complaints from contemporary observers support Sokorski's claim that he had been paying a degree of lip service to socialist realism. Unquestionably self-absorbed, the chief cultural official eagerly cultivated his image as a rebel throughout his life. Unlike the biographies of Berman or Putrament, Sokorski's life story reveals a pattern of moderate risk-taking—from the 1943 "theses" controversy in the Kościuszko Division to awarding state prizes to less orthodox artists in the early 1950s. Analyzing his statements in the spring and summer of 1954, Barbara Fijałkowska concluded that even at this stage, Sokorski's relatively liberal stand on culture hardly reflected the official views of the entire party leadership. "Sokorski all too easily disavowed the hitherto mandatory concept of culture and the nature of creative activity in a socialist state," she asserted, adding that "he rejected them earlier than political power was willing to do, or, indeed, a significant portion of the artists themselves were willing to do."[105] During this early Thaw, therefore, Sokorski continued to be an outlier in the communist establishment. No matter the personal weaknesses that enabled him to change skins, no matter any other impulses that drove him to embellish his own role after the years, Sokorski's choices consistently led him into situations that invited collisions with his equals or those more powerful than himself. If anything, this revealed a certain tolerance for danger and independence that few of his friends in high places manifested—and at a time when even the most cynical of opportunists struggled to guess just what kind of stance *right then* would help them stay afloat in the years to come.

By 1955, few artists defended "socialist realism," and most, like Ważyk, began to "see what they didn't see or did not want to see before."[106] The writer Leon Kruczkowski remained a rare, steadfast proponent of the doctrine well into the subsequent decades. But even he used the phrase to capture a broader tradition of progressive humanism, opposing it to the party-led efforts to create a strictly didactic body of literature.[107] During the Sixth Congress of the Polish Writers' Union in June 1954, Kruczkowski said that "the boundaries of realism are the boundaries of truth about life." The writer reminded Polish and foreign deputies to the congress, including Konstantin Simonov, Nazim Hikmet—and also party leader Jakub Berman—that "writers-realists" whose "philosophical and social outlook was far from revolutionary," also "revealed" in their works much "truth about life."[108] Kruczkowski himself, of course, had fallen victim to Stalinist literary orthodoxies, unable to publish his deeply humanistic but not necessarily party-minded play, *The Germans* (or, for that matter, any other work) in the USSR. Now, in expanding the boundaries of socialist realism, he was also forcing the boundaries of Polish-Soviet literary cooperation, boundaries few Polish writers had been able to cross.

In the meantime, the new political tide forced many exponents of any kind of cultural orthodoxy into more moderate positions. Those who, like Berman, failed to succumb to the tidal wave, gradually slipped into political irrelevance. These men had been among the most eager promoters of Poland's cultural Stalinism. Their departures and vacillations turned the Polish Thaw into a uniquely iconoclastic series of events.

IN LIMBO

The completion of Stalin's behemoth Palace of Culture and Science on July 22, 1955, required the work of more than three thousand skilled laborers. By the time the proletariat had delivered this crude towering specimen of Stalinist gothic, the building constituted something of an anachronism. Its generous benefactor had been dead for more than two years, and among its collective recipients—the Polish people—the Palace evoked "magical horror" more than genuine gratitude.[109] Stalin's name, so central to the cultural and moral universe of Poland in 1949–53, was gradually but noticeably receding into the background. As Rafał Kupiecki observed, the new propaganda of "collective leadership" severely limited the possibilities for continued popularization of the Stalin cult.[110] Thus, the aesthetic rationale behind the monumental building had lost ground. The challenge came not only from Polish proponents of Western modernism, who sought to embrace more human-friendly "open forms" in architecture, but also from Khrushchev himself, who one year before had begun promoting technologically simpler, cheaper, and more pragmatic architectural solutions. Ever the pragmatist, Khrushchev sought to further boost the authority of the Soviet party-state by encouraging more modest buildings designed to solve the notorious housing shortage problems in the USSR.[111]

The thousands of youngsters who arrived in Poland's capital during the World Festival of Youth and Students in August 1955 posed yet another

Warsaw, summer 1955. The Fifth International Festival of Youth and Students. The newly completed Palace of Culture and Science appears in the background. Courtesy of Polska Agencja Prasowa.

challenge to the official values of the era that the Palace symbolized. Nearly 200,000 young men and women descended upon Warsaw, among them 30,000 foreigners from a record number of 115 countries. The authorities could not have controlled what the youngsters did, or when, even if they wanted to.[112] These boys and girls, often in their teens, brought color and fashion blazing into the city; they met in small groups, recited poetry, listened to jazz, and discussed art. Authorities in Poland, Hungary, and even East Germany had by then relaxed their policies on Western music. While the Soviet cultural authorities debated changes in the official position on jazz in the pages of *Pravda*, the East European Stalinists only ground their teeth watching the youth from East Berlin, Budapest, and Warsaw indulge in music that had been officially off limits since 1946.[113] At the festival's culmination, abstraction appeared at the Polish art exhibition in Warsaw's "Arsenal." The paintings roared off the walls, not so much imitating Western trends as vividly (if "desperately") "making up for lost time."[114] "Laughter returned from its distant exile" in these days, and wisecrackers could openly accuse their "fellow comrades" of an "insufficient amount of red cells in their blood" without losing a single a drop of their own vital fluid.[115]

Vladimir Mayakovsky returned to Polish theaters by route of post-Stalin Moscow. In late 1953, the Soviet capital's Theater of Satire staged *The Bathhouse*. The comedy had first been presented in the USSR in 1930. The title, according to the play's author, referred to the "scrubbing" and "ironing out" of bureaucrats. The play counterposes innovative "worker-enthusiasts" with indolent bureaucrats. The workers are led by Chudakov, a visionary time-machine inventor. *The Bathhouse* wowed audiences with "unexpected and startling stage effects, buffoonery, magic, pyrotechnical displays," thus marking a departure from the sterility of socialist realism." It was "Meyerhold without Meyerhold," wrote David Caute, noting that critics and audiences received it well.[116] In October 1954, the director of Łódź's *Teatr Nowy*, Kazimierz Dejmek, expressed his gratitude to VOKS for sending the photographs from the play as well as the reviews and articles from the Soviet press. Clearly, he was testing the waters to see how provocative he could make his own upcoming performance: "Especially the reviews are valuable," he wrote, "during our work on the Polish premiere of Mayakovsky's play."[117] In December 1954, the audiences of Łódź saw *The Bathhouse*. Dejmek's "abundant" reliance on the grotesque obliterated the stale atmosphere of past years. Audiences in Łódź flocked eagerly to see this powerhouse performance as had the inhabitants of Moscow.

Yet Mayakovsky meant different things in the two countries. In the USSR, the poet embodied the fresh, bold, spontaneous, and iconoclastic quality of the Revolution. For many Poles, in addition to all that, he served as an icon for the Soviet Union they liked and understood. From the perspective of the Soviet state officials, *The Bathhouse* was the best soft power they could hope for. But the critique of Stalinism implicit in the performance was understandably hard to swallow for those Soviet bureaucrats who were used to lecturing in the East European vassal states and who, far from being "scrubbed" or "ironed out," were still around. A few years down the road one Soviet official would remember the performance as "an excuse to criticize life in the Soviet Union." The Poles used the show, he wrote, "to propagate the view that after Mayakovsky, Soviet writers and playwrights only varnished life," as opposed to inviting a critical reflection on the human condition.[118]

This open artistic dialogue carried on across the "iron curtain" and across time. It showed on the radar of the ossified bureaucracies, but was increasingly out of their reach. For their part, the more conservative bureaucrats seemed increasingly out of touch. The spontaneous festivities stood out amid the pompous, scripted celebrations of the eleventh anniversary of the "rebirth of Poland," and of the Soviet and Polish governments' signing of the "Treaty of Friendship, Cooperation and Mutual Assistance."[119] Taken together in their growing intensity, the unscripted celebrations of post-Stalinist spring also created a ferment, a watershed that the Soviet society would experience only in the months to come.

This sudden, spontaneous, and surprisingly confrontational nature of the Polish "Thaw" caused consternation in some agents of Soviet cultural outreach who had been shaped by the terror, institutions, and values of Stalinism for two decades. Without encouragement, without leadership, Poles rejected its legacy overnight, after only a few years of incomplete Sovietization. But no official "new course" to provide this leadership in Soviet culture was announced. After only a few months of liberalization, which included the publication of Ehrenburg's novel, the Soviet authorities rescinded the mandate for a more open discussion. *The Thaw* was quickly condemned. So was *Novyi mir*, the journal that, in December 1953, had published Vladimir Pomerantsev's article demanding "sincerity in literature."[120] While Stalin's omnipresent name suddenly disappeared from view, no discussion of what it meant followed either.[121]

The terror subsided, to be sure, especially after Beria's arrest. Stalin's death activated young people seeking to reconnect themselves with one another and with a culture they could call their own.[122] Hundreds of thousands of Gulag survivors who returned home after a so-called amnesty destabilized the regime by talking to others about the labor camps. From the perspective of the authorities, the returnees to the Western borderlands of the USSR especially became a liability: they tuned into foreign radio broadcasts and made the region the Soviet Union's subversive "window to the West."[123] The Soviets themselves expanded cultural contacts with Western countries as well—renowned American, British, and French musical and theatrical troupes were traveling to the USSR for the first time since the October Revolution.[124]

But the actual ferment in Soviet society had no support at the top, and, unlike in Poland, the party remained firmly in control of its own cultural institutions. So while in 1954–55, members of Soviet artistic unions set out to broaden the definition of socialist realism, Polish writers began to negate the artistic method openly during their official meetings.[125] A few months after Pomerantsev demanded "sincerity" in literature, Poland's *Nowa Kultura* began referencing George Orwell's *Animal Farm* and *1984*.[126] And at the time when Ważyk published his iconoclastic "A Poem for Adults" in 1955, Soviet humanists sought inspiration from quiet, lyrical verses of another apostate of Stalinism—the twenty-three-year-old poet and future dissident Yevgeny Yevtushenko.[127] Yevtushenko embodied the two key elements of the Soviet Thaw culture: youth and poetry. The Soviet authorities began to support vigorously young poets in order to gain new allies among a new generation of artists, rejuvenate the moribund Soviet cultural scene, and appeal to Soviet youth.[128] If Ważyk's published poem constituted a challenge to the Polish authorities, Yevtushenko's work in 1954–55 was an instrument of the Soviet party-state.

Even among sympathetic Soviet observers of Polish cultural life, a sense of moral repulsion set in as a response to some new trends. In these years, Polish newspapers led the way by pushing the boundaries of acceptable coverage. "Acceptable" lies in the eyes of the beholder. The journalists, eager for expanded readerships, did not always cater to lofty idealism. Nikolai Bubnov enthused, on October 2, 1954, about the Poles having a chance to read "the verses of the young poet Yevtushenko" in the pages of *Wolność*. The newspaper had published his poem about a girl setting off for Siberia as part of the Komsomol compulsory work assignment; not a subversive piece, but without references to Stalin, and with allusions to Sholokhov, the poem was clearly inspired by the characteristic form of Mayakovsky's compositions. And yet Bubnov simultaneously shuddered at what he saw in the Polish mass media. All of Warsaw's newspapers, except *Trybuna Ludu*, he complained, largely imitated the French yellow press. A cursory glance at a women's journal proved a shock: "So much sex, what details from intimate family life! In our country such things are impossible. With this kind of 'free press' it is difficult to build socialism."[129]

Bubnov's media exaltation and despair occurred a little over a year after he had met with the explosive ambassador Popov, and listened to the diplomat's furious diatribe against the ungrateful Poles. Popov's career, like Bubnov's, seemed to end with indignation. The ambassador had called for a new national anthem in Poland. The anthem stayed but Popov was yanked back to Moscow by Khrushchev on charges of misconduct.[130] Besides plotting anti-Semitic intrigues against Berman and others, the diplomat had told Boleslaw Bierut jokingly that for the kind of job the Polish president was doing, he would not make him even a secretary of a district committee.[131] According to Lazar Kaganovich, the "arrogant" ambassador "conducted himself like a governor-general."[132] Clearly, his despotic habits as a longtime apparatchik, as well as his temperament, eventually propelled him out of his ambassadorial post. Both Popov and Bubnov had dedicated their lives to the building of a system that was now being challenged on the peripheries of the Soviet imperial state—a state that had been liberated by the Red Army. In the post-Stalin era the two men resembled bodies without a prime mover, not unlike Warsaw's Palace of Culture and Science, which they had watched rise during the preceding months.

Soviet embassy officials routinely criticized the new trends on strictly political grounds in 1954 and 1955. They pointed to "serious insufficiencies and even direct distortions" in some areas of Polish cultural life, finding particularly offensive some artists' efforts to reject the leading role of the party-state. "Standing up for some kind of supernatural (*sverkhestestvennuiu*) freedom of creative activity," a section of Poland's creative workers was perceived as "rethinking Marxist-Leninist theses about the arts." Jadwiga Siekierska, a literary critic working in the Central Committee's Culture Department, the writer Jerzy Andrzejewski, and critics Jan Błoński and Jan Kott were chief among the exponents of such views. The journals *Przegląd Kulturalny* (Cultural Review), *Nowa Kultura*, and *Życie Literackie* (Literary Life) figured among the main institutional culprits. Soviet embassy officials singled out "errors" in *Trybuna Ludu* as well.[133] Political reports for the second half of 1955, flowing into the Soviet Central Committee, regularly mentioned Adam Ważyk's name as shorthand for the ideological excesses taking place in Poland. Ważyk "obliged the tastes of the Western bourgeois press," detractors claimed in the winter of 1955, watching Western media cast the poem as representative of the ideological foment sown in Poland's artistic establishment.[134] In a rather unexpected turn of history, Jerzy Putrament defended the rights of Poles to express themselves freely. During a talk in the town of Bydgoszcz, on April 17, 1955, Putrament demanded "giving cultural workers full freedom to create only such works as they want to." Hidebound party members were outraged, as the former political officer called party workers "tyrants" (*dzierżymordy*) and "pessimists," who "don't believe that the Polish people can create a socialist culture by themselves, without leadership, without orders from above."[135] As N. Talyzin, the Soviet consul in Gdańsk, learned from the local Polish party secretary shortly after the event, the region's writers welcomed Putrament's remarks, causing the Soviet observers even more concern.[136]

Developments in Polish science came under Soviet scrutiny as well. De-Stalinization enabled Soviet and Polish scientists to reestablish working contacts. The hitherto "insignificant" contacts between the two Academies of Sciences marked a contrast, with twenty to thirty scientists from each country visiting the other in 1954, and twice that in 1955.[137] Visiting Soviet professors as well as government officials became particularly alarmed over the revisionist tendencies in social and human sciences. The above-mentioned Jadwiga Siekierska launched herself into the center of Soviet attention by publishing an article on March 2, 1952, in the *Przegląd Kulturalny*, provocatively titled "Matters of Art Should Be Decided by the People of Art." Inspired by Sokorski's own words, quoted in the title, Siekierska argued forcefully that art was a sphere of human activity autonomous from the party—thus offending orthodox Soviet observers. In the Soviets' eyes, this ideological error was overshadowed by another greater problem—Siekierska, as the chair of the Department (*katedra*) of Dialectical and Historical Materialism of the Institute of Social Sciences (INS; earlier, the Institute for Education of Scientific Cadres, IKKN), was not necessarily qualified to put forth publicly her views on aesthetics. The two Soviet visiting professors noted that the institute's rector, Adam Schaff, was simply too busy to mend the institute's cadres problem.[138] Was Schaff gladly too busy, appreciative of the new freedom not to be at the Soviets' beck and call?

Even Schaff raised red flags that same year. In the spring of 1955, the famous Polish professor Józef Chałasiński published an article arguing that, dominated by dialectical materialism with its concerns for strictly social implications of culture, Polish human sciences had been stagnating in recent years.[139] While the Soviets quickly branded the view as "anti-Marxist," Schaff defended its author. Schaff even furthered Chałasiński's thesis by pointing out that the human sciences suffered not only in Poland, but in the entire socialist camp.[140] Schaff's outlandish comments piqued Panteleimon Ponomarenko, a member of the distrusted Stalinist cadres. Khrushchev had recently sent Ponomarenko off to assume the "honorable but uninfluential" ambassadorial post in Poland.[141] Ponomarenko was a veteran leader of the Soviet occupation of Poland in 1939–41; in his new role, Bernov's new "demanding and severe" boss stayed true to the old cause.[142] By late November the ambassador was forwarding Schaff's two articles to the Soviet Central Committee. The communist philosopher had committed a serious error, Ponomarenko complained, by claiming that true Marxist philosophy failed to develop not only in Poland, but in the entire socialist camp—including the USSR.[143] Schaff amended and softened his thesis by emphasizing the role of the party in his subsequent article.[144] But Ponomarenko, who was forwarding both articles to Moscow, appeared unconvinced by Schaff's sudden change of tone.

Back in the USSR, de-Stalinization affected the realm of science, and charges of "cosmopolitanism" lost their relevance. The influence of the charlatan agrobiologist Trofim Lysenko was waning. The hitherto sidelined proponents of genuine science were gaining ground.[145] The situation of people like Ponomarenko engendered two related paradoxes. Partly because they found sinecures in strategically less important foreign posts, change in the USSR became possible. But Ponomarenko had landed in a place where his Stalinist impulses and habits were by this time least likely to make any difference. Still, the old Stalinist habits died hard. In a familiar scenario, Soviet visitors to the Institute of Social Sciences raised objections concerning ethnic makeup among the school's professors, implicitly linking Polish Jews to the "petty bourgeois" ideologies affecting the professoriate.[146] Yet now the Polish communists took the lead in mobilizing Polish anti-Semitism; Polish anti-Semites, even if they shared the views of their Soviet guests, cared little about what the Soviets had to say.

The linkage between Jews and "petty bourgeois" mentalities was far-fetched. In contrast, when the Soviets perceived the ideological ferment in the arts and sciences as a Soviet Bloc–wide phenomenon, they had it right. The authors of a draft memo dated November 2, 1955, made that point clear, listing "the appearance of bourgeois ideology in literature and the arts," "the struggle against party-mindedness in literature and the arts," artists' flight from contemporary themes into the past, the "intensification of formalism," and the rise of negative attitudes toward Soviet literature and the arts as some of the major transgressions. In sciences, the chief problems included "separation from the tasks of socialist construction," "hostile and enemy scientific cadres," "the intensification of Western bourgeois ideology," and efforts to minimize the achievements of Soviet science.[147] For decades, Soviet diplomats and visiting cultural figures had been duped into believing that they were in the revolutionary vanguard of history. But the dead language they used to describe what they saw suggests that the burgeoning new life stirring Poland, circa 1955, spoke an ineluctably living language: history was now leaving them behind.

THE MIKHAILOV METHOD

Next to army generals, spies, and special forces agents, Soviet ambassadors also did their part in consolidating Moscow's new sphere of influence. Of course, each ambassador's position in the USSR, his intellectual capacities, tastes, and temperament shaped his unique style. The powerful and experienced Viktor Lebedev (January 1945–March 1951) energetically intervened in Poland's domestic affairs with the Kremlin's support. However, his anti-Semitic bias and excessive self-confidence pushed him too far. To punish Lebedev, Stalin sent him to the strategically less significant ambassadorial post in Finland. Lebedev's successor, Arkadii Sobolev (March 1951–June 1953), also a professional diplomat, oversaw the most intensive stage of Poland's Stalinization. His daily functions included careful monitoring of Poland's Sovietization, and especially collectivization. He did not try to test the patience of his Moscow bosses. Even still, Stalin's death resulted in Sobolev's swift departure from Poland. Then there was the notoriously undisciplined Georgii Popov (July 1953–April 1954), former activist and factory manager, who stormed into Poland, stayed there for less than one year, and left with a bang. If Popov and Lebedev pushed their Stalinist inclinations to the extreme, Panteleimon Ponomarenko (1955–57), a Stalinist ambassador to post-Stalinist Poland, was at odds with the spirit of the times. But none of these diplomats cared about winning the hearts and minds of the Poles; rather, they strove to rewire them.

Yet in the narrow interval of time after Popov left and before Ponomarenko arrived, Nikolai A. Mikhailov demonstrated a very different style of leadership. The thirty-eight-year-old diplomat seized the chance to harness soft power to strengthen the foreign outreach of the Soviet state. Mikhailov replaced Georgii Popov as ambassador to Poland on April 22, 1954. As head of the Komsomol, Mikhailov had had contacts with Poland through the country's youth organization, the ZMP. He had served as secretary of the Central Committee and former chief of the Moscow Party Committee (and of the Central Committee's Department of Propaganda and Agitation). For Mikhailov, the new diplomatic post was, observed one historian, "clearly a demotion."[148] But Mikhailov may have enjoyed the change of scenery; only one and a half years before his appointment, Stalin had assigned him a key role in publicizing the recently "uncovered" "Doctors' Plot." Mikhailov resorted to tried and true anti-Semitic scaremongering as he spoke about "hidden enemies of our people."[149] In his new role as ambassador, he could use culture to more constructive ends.

Mikhailov enjoyed the sympathy and respect of his subordinates. Iurii Bernov, now a consul in Cracow, liked Mikhailov for his approachability and genuine interest in helping out the Poles. Unlike his predecessor (and Mikhailov's own domineering wife), the ambassador showed no desire to Sovietize everything at all costs.[150] Meeting with him in October, Nikolai Bubnov found Mikhailov to be a "gentle man who thought a long time before making a decision," someone after his own heart.[151] The journalist and the ambassador were peers in age; now, in 1954, both were to face similar obstacles in their efforts to optimize Soviet soft power in Poland.

The Mikhailov method involved the new ambassador's efforts to recast Soviet-Polish cultural relations via his new approach—his peculiar "style of work," as Bernov put it.[152] Within weeks of taking office, Mikhailov embarked on a minicampaign to convince the authorities in Moscow that Soviet cultural relations with Poland could and should assume a more reciprocal form. "Over the entire course of the thousand-year history of relations between Poland and Russia," he began, somewhat bombastically, in a report of January 1955, "there was not and could not have been as [close] a relationship between our peoples as we have right now." Mikhailov warned that given the continued class struggle in Poland, the country's receptiveness to and family links with the West, the renewed activities of the Catholic Church and Western propaganda outlets, the Soviet state was hardly in a position to rest on its laurels.[153]

Mikhailov took it upon himself to rectify two problems. First, he sought to improve the quality and distribution of Soviet cultural exports in and around the Soviet Bloc. In a letter to the Soviet Central Committee dated September 1, 1954, the diplomat pointed out that despite the enormous demand for Soviet books, and despite the decision of the Council of Ministers of June 29, 1954, to improve the matter, exports of literature from non-Russian republics of the USSR, and especially Ukraine and Belarus, were still sluggish, thus preventing him from fulfilling all the requests from Poland. The amount of literature exported from the USSR to Poland has been declining steadily each year since they peaked in 1950 (see appendix B, figure B. 2). This decline resulted partly out of the shifting structure of Polish demand.[154] Soviet distributors could meet only 50 percent of the Polish requests, while the demand for Soviet scientific and technical literature could be met at only a 25–30 percent rate. Ironically, the situation was even more troubling during the recent "Months of Polish-Soviet Friendship," usually October or November occasions during which communist propaganda intensified. At these times, the Soviet ability to supply literature lingered around 1% (the Poles asked for 185 titles in 1,500–2,000 copies each, the Soviets sent some 5–20 copies). In addition, Poles had very limited access to information about the kinds of books they could potentially order since, unlike other foreign countries that furnished thematic catalogs and rich bibliographic information, the Soviet distributors offered none.[155] Likewise, musical records from France, the United States, and Czechoslovakia arrived in attractive packaging and accompanied by helpful descriptions. "Parts of those coming from the USSR," Mikhailov informed his bosses on the Central Committee, "not so much."[156] There was, of course, nothing new about the Soviet inability to deliver. But Mikhailov's constant emphasis on taking into account Polish needs, echoed by some officials in the Soviet Ministry of Foreign Affairs, constituted a clear departure from the previous era.[157]

Poland became a battleground of the cultural Cold War once again. While Mikhailov worried about missed propaganda opportunities, the United States government, pressured by the fiercely anticommunist senator Joseph McCarthy and his ferociously anticommunist supporters, pulled Henry David Thoreau and Jean-Paul Sartre off the shelves of its foreign libraries.[158] Mikhailov may or may not have known about American's sense of insecurity in Western Europe, but it would have made little difference: with the loss of its monopoly on cultural exports, the Soviet Union also lost its artistic and institutional competitive edge in Poland. For instance, the lax Soviet approach to film exports alarmed Mikhailov. Soveksportfilm's constant violation of international agreements on minimum film quota to be delivered to Poland only facilitated the work of Western film distributors. As a result, Soviet cinema rapidly lost ground.[159] Soviet musical ensembles visiting Poland likewise needed a facelift—literally, as, according to Mikhailov, writing in January 1955, selected members of the Georgian dance ensemble felt so embarrassed about their advanced age that they were hiding behind younger artists during their Polish performances.[160] Polish communists had found the Georgian show somewhat monotonous, reported the ambassador, and requested groups that would both dance and sing instead.[161]

This was all the more important, Mikhailov emphasized, since the USSR had to confront international competition in all areas. Poland eagerly expanded its cultural links with other countries, hosting artistic groups from France, Germany [Dresden], China, and India.[162] "Some of our comrades insufficiently take into account the enormous changes [that] have taken place in Poland in the past decade," exhorted Mikhailov, emphasizing the new conditions of life and rapid developments in Polish culture. Discussing the Mazowsze, Poland's foremost folk ensemble, he wrote what would have been a heresy only two years before: "In some of its dance performances, it approached the level of even such a well-known group as the Moiseev state folk dance ensemble" from the USSR.[163] All this suggested that only the best performers should go on tours to Poland. It also invited the conclusion, Mikhailov continued, that "in artistic affairs we must not only teach the Polish comrades but also sometimes learn from them as well."[164] Poles often heard this phrase from their Soviet visitors; this time around, in trying to convince his compatriots, Mikhailov appears to have really meant it.

New, too, was the more decisive and frank tone of Soviet self-criticism. Clearly, neglect and passivity characterized the Soviet cultural institutions' relationships with all "People's Democracies." In a lengthy report dated September 3, 1955, S. Rumiantsev of the Information Committee listed numerous areas where improvement seemed necessary lest the relations between the Soviet Union and other socialist countries continued to be "harmed": Soviet institutions' notorious failure to reply to correspondence from Eastern Europe; East European scientists' difficulties being published in the USSR and obtaining scientific literature from the Soviet Union; too few exchanges and delegations, and a "cookie-cutter" approach to Soviet cultural exports.[165] As a cause of the above transgressions, Rumiantsev identified the persistent fear of "relations with the abroad" among Soviet individuals and institutions. This fear led to an "excessive covering of one's back" (*perestrakhovka*), which "harmed the development of cultural cooperation with our foreign friends."[166] (Old habits died hard—a few months earlier, Mikhailov had dismayingly noted cases of excessive precautions that led local authorities to warn a Moscow State University expert departing for Poland not to tell anyone about his destination, not even his wife!)[167] In urging "consideration of national peculiarities" of his Polish comrades, Rumiantsev echoed traditional recommendations from agents of Soviet soft power—that fact alone was symptomatic of the new era. Given the twists and turns in recent Soviet history, it was no wonder that to many, fear became second nature. The Stalinist legacy continued to weigh down the soft-power project two years after the Soviet leader's death. Still, a new, more open approach to old methods and habits constituted a mark of change.

Mikhailov's second project involved increasing Poland's visibility in the USSR as a way of bringing the two countries together. Moscow did not have a Mickiewicz Street, but Mikhailov had a method. In diplomatic letters to the Soviet Central Committee, Mikhailov put forth dozens of suggestions concerning Polish authors to be published in the USSR, accelerating the plans for cultural cooperation, and so forth.[168] As a result of these efforts, and the less stifling political climate, Polish culture began to surface in the USSR in the second half of 1954 and throughout 1955. Events propagating a new infusion of Polish culture included: an exhibition in Moscow commemorating the 105th anniversary of Chopin's death (October 1954); a festival of Polish film in Moscow, Leningrad, Minsk, Kiev, Vil'nius, and L'vov (November 1954); an exhibition of Polish plastic arts in

Kiev (March 1955); and another film festival in Moscow (October 1955).[169] During the Soviet Thaw, culture and politics danced closely intertwined. But the Soviet leaders chiefly used literature to reach out to the liberal intelligentsia.[170] The ambassador's pet peeve likewise was insufficient attention to the publishing of Polish belles lettres in his motherland—with as many as "660 people in the Polish Writers' Union," he wrote in September, 1954, and so few Polish books to show to the Soviet readers, the lack of appreciation for such work on the part of Soviet journal editors "is hardly beneficial"[171] in bringing about genuine Soviet-Polish cultural rapprochement. In January 1955, Mikhailov suggested that Kruczkowski's *The Germans* should be staged in the Soviet Union.[172] Further, he pointed out that while Soviet writers collected honoraria for works that had been published in Poland, there was no legal basis for the Poles to do the same. "Even though the quantity of Polish works published in the Soviet Union is quite insignificant," he admitted, the honoraria situation contradicted "the principle of reciprocity" that existed between the two countries.[173]

At the end of December 1954, Mikhailov described an embarrassing situation where an exhibition titled "Polish Books in the Soviet Union" had to be canceled because Soviet organizations were unable to send any such books. In the same letter, he recommended twenty-eight authors who should be published in the USSR in the near future; among them were Kruczkowski, Boguszewska, Broniewski, and Tuwim, writers whom Polish officials had wanted to see in Russian translations for years.[174] Mikhailov's letter coincided with the proceedings of the Congress of Soviet Writers. The Polish writer Jaroslaw Iwaszkiewicz visited the USSR for the first time in eight years; for the first time ever he, or perhaps any writer from Eastern Europe, lectured his Soviet peers on what they should publish. Iwaszkiewicz criticized Nikolai Tikhonov's earlier call for Soviet-Polish dialogue through literature as too abstract. Most of the authors mentioned by the Soviet poet, such as Maria Dąbrowska or Zofia Nałkowska, had not been translated in the USSR; and "works are being translated, the artistic level of which cannot give the Soviet reader the correct idea about our contemporary literature."[175] Probably nothing reflected more starkly the shifting constellation of power in Soviet-Polish cultural relations than these irreverent remarks.

Soviet people wanted news from Poland, Mikhailov observed on another occasion, but the lack of a legal framework made it impossible to satisfy the growing demand for Polish newspapers. "Suffice it to say," the ambassador remarked bitterly, "that the newspaper of the PZPR's Central Committee, *Trybuna Ludu*, is being imported into the USSR in a quantity of only sixteen copies."[176] In the fall of 1954, Mikhailov pointed out that the journalists from the two countries' party newspapers were practically strangers to each other.[177] Later, in his January 29, 1955, report, the ambassador duly acknowledged the Central Committee's efforts to improve the situation in cultural outreach. He also recognized that officials in the Ministry of Culture had their hands full with all kinds of requests. Still, he pleaded, "we also also ask that the position of the embassy be considered, to help prevent the erosion of its authority."[178] Just like the Soviet orthodox keepers of the flame, the accommodationist Mikhailov, too, found himself in limbo.

Limbo did not suit him. Mikhailov churned out endless ideas about how to improve Soviet-Polish cultural relations. Clearly most concerned about Soviet interests abroad, Mikhailov's views and methods, together with the new circumstances, reciprocally thrust the diplomat into the role of Poland's unofficial cultural ambassador to the Soviet Union.

Mikhailov's multiple calls for help landed on the desks of the officials of the Information Committee (Komitet informatsii). Stalin had set up the organization in 1947 both to claim more power in the USSR and to fight the Cold War more effectively. Its chief goal was to coordinate intelligence reports from various Soviet institutions ranging from military intelligence services to the Ministries of Foreign Affairs and Foreign Trade. On the micro level, noted one scholar, the committee's "work was aimed only at providing the Soviet leadership . . . with data that had been cleansed of disinformation."[179] As intermediaries between Mikhailov and Moscow, the members of the Information Committee regularly tempered the ambassador's zeal. In April 1955, for instance, in response to the ambassador's lengthy report from January, the Information Committee officials pointed out that several suggestions had been implemented already, and decisions about others had recently been made. The committee also advised against a number of measures proposed by the diplomat. Thus the idea of creating a new center that would help coordinate the distribution of visual materials to foreign countries was struck down on the grounds that the existing institutions responsible for that could simply do it better. For the same reasons, the members of the committee maintained, there was no need to create a separate publishing house specializing in works originating in People's Democracies, or a separate review of literature from these parts—the publisher (Goslitizdat) and the existing journals, they maintained, could simply improve instead.[180]

The men on the Information Committee held realistic views of the possibilities for Soviet international outreach. "The main reason why we are publishing so few books from Poland (as well as books from other People's Democracies), has to do with the limited capacities of Inoizdat, which is responsible for the task," the Information Committee informed the Soviet Central Committee. Given the funding at the disposal of the publisher, and its allocations of paper, Inoizdat could publish only twenty-five to thirty books of foreign literature per year. Two Polish books made the cut in 1954, while seven were included in the publishing plan for 1955. "Any further expansion of the plan," the authors concluded, "is presently not possible."[181] Their candid appraisal of problems within the Soviet Union demonstrates a new and freer articulation. Similar exchanges before 1953 wove together moderate criticism of Soviet institutions with militant rhetoric against the real and invented Polish sabotage of Soviet initiatives; now Soviet self-criticism dominated. The frank admission that the Soviet Union's cultural outreach was circumscribed by the structure of its funding certainly gives us a window on the priorities of Soviet foreign policy, and especially the economic limitations of Soviet soft power in the world.

In an ironic turn of events, Mikhailov himself endured the lash of such economic constraints. Bernov recalled how the ambassador's energy and multiple initiatives had left Soviet diplomats overwhelmed; Mikhailov's numerous proposals to Moscow, written in haste and "without the necessary consideration of the possibilities of our country," remained largely unanswered.[182] One day, Mikhailov asked a group of diplomats to prepare a critical assessment of the work of the Soviet Ministry of Culture. The ambassador supervised the painstaking work on a document that outlined an array of specific proposals for broadening and deepening cultural relations with Poland. Then, shortly thereafter, Mikhailov himself became minister of culture of the USSR. He continued his energetic "style of work" seeking to revive Soviet cultural life.[183] When embassy officials telephoned him, hoping for a breakthrough in their efforts to improve the self-same document on Polish-Soviet relations—they found themselves unconsoled. Mikhailov, the former Polish ambassador, "having apparently forgotten that he himself had signed the note," told them that the document needed more work and that "currently, the ministry has no means" of satisfying their proposals.[184]

CONCLUSION

Squandered opportunities show up best in a future light. Clearly, Stalin's death, "collective leadership," and Khrushchev's ascendance to power offered new possibilities for reciprocal cultural relations and a more flexible

Soviet approach in Poland. But the cautious de-Stalinization in the USSR together with the rapid Polish Thaw complicated the work of Soviet international outreach institutions. Cold and warm fronts struck like cumulus clouds, producing little rain, revealing the limitations of Soviet soft power and of the Kremlin's capacity to maintain empire via noncoercive means. The new Soviet "hands-off" approach to East European affairs meant that a number of institutions that hitherto had intervened in the cultural affairs of the Soviet Union's East European satellites were suddenly deprived of Moscow's support. Though many Soviet cultural outreach officials toyed with ingenious ideas about how to run these operations more effectively, the state of limbo negated their best efforts—and they were forced to leave.

Those resourceful Soviet officials and cultural figures who remained, had many reasons to be frustrated as well. While the "Thaw" began in the USSR, by early 1955, the liberalizing trends in Poland had outpaced Soviet events. Polish cultural—and even political—elites defended such radical critiques of the bygone era, that even generally sympathetic Soviet observers found their views hard to digest. Soviet officials in charge of cultural contacts with Eastern Europe were equally concerned about their own persistent inability to deliver Soviet propaganda and cultural products of good quality and in sufficient quantities. Despite Soviet oversight, Poles and other East Europeans generally held on to higher prewar standards in areas such as literature and the arts. But the new wave of cultural interventions from Western nations, including Great Britain, France, and the United States, raised the standards to a level with which the Soviets could not compete. Additionally, the general opening of East European countries to more vigorous cultural cooperation with one another and with the world discouraged Soviet cultural initiatives. No longer mere apprentices, Poland and other East European countries developed attractive socialist cultures of their own: in subsequent decades, for instance, the Polish folk and dance ensemble Mazowsze, scored successes all over the world. As the events of 1953–56 thrust the Soviet Union's East European captive audiences onto a world stage, as it were, the Soviets had to work harder to make a cultural case for the new empire. A better, more vigorous Soviet soft power could have lifted up the imperial mission. Instead, old obstacles continued to bog down Soviet-Polish cultural cooperation. Soviet officials blamed Stalinism for the persistent problems of the post-Stalin era. In pointing to its onerous legacy, they were right. But few recognized or dared to point out that the Soviet system itself might have obstructed Soviet efforts to project a positive power of attraction to the broader world.

EPILOGUE

The Old and the New

"It's my third time here over the past three years," said the Polish radio journalist Edmund Osmańczyk into the microphone, nearly a week into his visit to Moscow on June 5, 1956. "And each time I'm struck by the constant growth of the modern, the new, and the simultaneous preservation of many conservative forms of life—forms that should forever remain unchanged." Recorded for broadcast both in the USSR and in Poland in the coming days, Osmańczyk recalled the sight of young pilots "dressed in modern aircraft suits," who disembarked from their shiny, modern jets—which the journalist compared to Picasso's dove. The men entered a restaurant—a new restaurant, Osmańczyk recalled, but built with old-fashioned luxury. The contrast overwhelmed the Pole. The pilots' young, excited faces and the building that evoked "the era of the first engine" caused Osmańczyk to shout: "Here we have the nineteenth and twentieth centuries existing side by side!" To him, this event became "kind of a symbol of contemporary Russia."[1]

Osmańczyk's startling if somewhat condescending comparisons may have offended the Soviet censors; but the real reasons why his remarks never made it onto the airwaves in either country most likely lay elsewhere. The journalist went on to contrast the USSR and Poland in the wake of the Twentieth Congress of the Communist Party of the Soviet Union (KPSS). It was then, in February 1956, that the triumphant Nikita Khrushchev for the first time condemned "the cult of personality" and coercion that he, somewhat disingenuously, linked solely to Stalin. He did so in front of some 1,500 delegates during a so-called secret speech. But it was not so secret, after all. While Osmańczyk's radio talks were being squelched, Khrushchev himself disseminated the content of his "cult of personality" address orally among KPSS members. In late March, the newly elected first secretary of the Polish United Workers' Party (PZPR), Edward Ochab, made the transcript of Khrushchev's four-hour speech broadly available (he was the only East European leader to do so). And shortly thereafter someone—most likely a Polish journalist—leaked the talk to foreign journalists, resulting in a *New York Times* piece in June 1956.[2] Large blocks of the speech also sold on the black market, available to anyone who wished to spare a few hundred złoty.[3] Like the death of Stalin, this speech affected the Polish people palpably and immediately. Attuned to change, the Polish mass media and cultural outlets used this as an opportunity to voice the most radical new demands, often interpreting Khrushchev's statements as Moscow's green light for a political and cultural laissez faire in the Eastern Bloc. A new generation of reform-minded "young secretaries" of the Polish Party rose up to profit from the liberalizing ferment. The young sought to bury old-timers like Berman politically, thus amplifying the momentum of anti-Stalinist and anti-Soviet backlash.

Speaking in the Soviet radio studio on that June day, Osmańczyk granted that the Soviet Union "had gone further and deeper" in implementing decentralization and new methods of economic management, especially in agriculture. But the Poles, he emphasized, led the way in popularizing the ever-growing transparency in political and economic life of their country through the daily press and radio, "[a process] that was a natural consequence of our Polish specificity, and corresponds to our democratic traditions."[4] And who was to blame for the slower changes, the delays in the USSR? Osmańczyk faulted neither the Soviet authorities nor the popular masses; the obvious culprits were the hitherto privileged bureaucrats who were now being sidelined, and the "mentality of some people who are accustomed to thinking in old ways."

In juxtaposing the new democratic trends with the old bureaucratic ways, Osmańczyk tapped into a familiar theme: following Ehrenburg's example in *The Thaw*, now *Pravda* editors published stories about how bureaucratic bosses were stifling the energy and initiative of young engineers and inventors.[5] Osmańczyk saw how "here the nineteenth century is trying to slow down the revolutionary leap into the twenty-first century."[6] Clearly, in the Polish journalist's view, the old and the new in the Soviet Union made a dazzling though disturbing dyad. The birthplace of socialism and the cradle of a new modern civilization seemed too caught up in its own past to lead; instead, it was being outpaced by a "People's Democracy" next door, which, up to that point, had been portrayed (and treated) as a passive beneficiary of Soviet generosity. Osmańczyk's bold "interpretation" of "certain issues concerning Soviet reality" offended the bureaucrats screening his radio speech. They deemed it "arbitrary and incorrect" the very next day—and sealed the fate of the broadcast that never was.[7]

The journalist's speech may have ruffled the feathers of those Soviet deciders who were personally invested in their country's messianic ethos. But for very practical reasons, and despite its underlying Marxist dialectical logic, Soviet censors found Poland's de-Stalinization gone wild an understandably ill-conceived example for millions of Soviet radio listeners to follow.

Yet, despite the abortive radio broadcast and notwithstanding Osmańczyk's debatable claim that events in Poland should be seen as the genuine path to socialist modernity, the journalist's trip to the USSR reflected a different era in Soviet-Polish cultural relations that embodied a synthesis of old and new trends. Yes, he was hushed up, while he and his colleague from the Polish Press Agency occasionally found themselves ignored by the Soviet authorities.[8] But the two journalists made it across the border, which marked an improvement, even by the standards of the previous year. Osmańczyk dared to speak his mind on controversial issues, and both men complained about being snubbed—all this without the fear of reprisal that characterized the past years. Indeed, the sudden loosening of restrictions on cross-border traffic within the Soviet Bloc ushered in new and unpredictable sources of imperial instability.

One stark example of the widespread effects of cultural rapprochement occurred during the "Polish October" of 1956. The political dimension of the story is well known. By early April, after the news of Khrushchev's denunciation of Stalin, popular hopes for concrete transformations rose even higher in Polish society.[9] In late June, workers protested low living wages and unfair promotion practices at a major industrial plant in the city of Poznań. The crisis grew as the communists observed the scale of social discontent, while at the same time realizing that indiscriminate state violence was no longer a possible means of imposing order. Tensions culminated on October 19, 1956. During the Eighth Plenum of the PZPR's Central Committee, Polish communists planned to exclude their most conservative members from leadership positions within the party—the Soviet marshal of Polish origin, Konstantin Rokossovskii, among those barred from service. Furious, Khrushchev flew to Warsaw on the morning before the plenum opened, accompanied by scores of KPSS Politburo members and top Soviet commanders, in order to prevent the Poles from making and implementing decisions of such weight without him. News about Soviet troop movements toward Warsaw spread throughout the country.[10] Khrushchev's appearance and rumored troop movements notwithstanding, the Poles went on with the changes. They nominated Władysław Gomułka, the champion of the Polish road to socialism who had been released from arrest in December 1954, to the post of PZPR first secretary. In his initial act, Władysław Gomułka managed to convince Khrushchev that these political changes presented a safety valve in a period of turmoil, not a threat to Soviet interests. Gomułka's diplomatic skills and his personal charisma saved Poland from Moscow's military intervention.

Meanwhile, the Thaw and its resultant political upheavals brought thousands of inhabitants of the Soviet Bloc together. Nikita Khrushchev had relaxed restrictions on Soviet foreign tourism only one year before, in 1955, as part of his de-Stalinization measures. While, previously, only members of the Soviet elite could afford to travel to the most faraway and exotic places, the financially better off now had the chance to explore the socialist "near abroad."[11] Some of them became part of a colorful tour de force in October 1956; these accidental tourists saw more than their travel agents had expected.

The twenty-eight Soviet tourists who visited Poland between October 18 and 26, 1956, found themselves sucked into the sociopolitical whirlwind that had shaken the entire country before, during, and after the Eighth Plenum of the PZPR.[12] At that juncture in Polish history, wrote Paweł Machcewicz, "the Poles, taking advantage of the unexpected freedom of public expression, tried to shout their lungs out at mass gatherings and demonstrations." They wanted to voice "everything they felt strongly about, say in one breath . . . all the pains that had grown over the years as well as all the demands that occurred to them at the moment."[13] From the perspective of the Soviet authorities, the timing of the tourist trip could not have been less fortuitous.

Having arrived in Gdańsk for sightseeing one late October evening, the tourists witnessed one of many mass demonstrations in support of Władysław Gomułka. They could have seen such throngs in the USSR only on the day that Stalin was buried. Yet, so very unlike their compatriots in mourning, these Polish men and women, often youths, came out into the streets of their own free will, expressly to challenge the status quo. In Gdańsk, and throughout Poland, demonstrators laced anti-Soviet slogans with nationalist sentiments, and they did so loudly. People demanded that Soviet Army bases be closed, and that Soviet interference in Polish affairs be stopped—they called for the firm ending of Stalinism. They wanted "the recovery of the eastern territories, clearing up the Katyń question, changing the names of Stalin and Rokossovsky streets, and an end to the teaching of Marxism-Leninism and of political economy, and the return of the May 3 holiday."[14] May 3 marked Poland's traditional Constitution Day, but, because in the nineteenth century Poles had used the occasion to protest against Russian rule, the communists had stopped celebrating the holiday, and emphasized the significance of the nearby May Day instead.[15] Culture—memories and meanings—was at the heart of the Poles' complaints. Many called for the removal of Marshal Rokosovskii as minister of defense, hoping to replace him with General Michał Rola-Żymierski or General Zygmunt Berling. Soldiers cried out for "the return of former uniforms"—those predating the creation of the Kościuszko Division.[16] As these Poles turned culture into a vehicle for overt confrontation with the vestiges of the Stalinist régime, they came to see 1943—the year that the Kościuszko Division formed—as the year of squandered promise of a "national road to socialism."

Soviet newspapers reported nothing about the Polish October and post-October transformations, but the accidental tourists eagerly engaged with live Polish editorials, directly at the source.[17] On a tramway in Gdańsk, for instance, a young Polish man accosted the group and offered his views on what was transpiring in his home country. "Poles consider these events a revolution (*perevorot*) in politics for which they'd been waiting for a while," he informed his captive audience between the stops. "Your government's meddling" in Poland's internal affairs, the young man claimed, conflicted with Poles' desires to "live independently" (*samostoiatel'no*), but also "to maintain friendly relations with the S.U. as two equal (*ravnopravnykh*) states." To the chagrin of the group's director Khokhlov, some of the other Soviet tourists approved. "You are correct in carrying out democratization," Muscovite V. Lebedev replied, adding that "there was something wrong in the relations with the Polish people." Reprimanded by Khokhlov, Lebedev turned defiant: "Let them know what we think about their events. Why are you lecturing me? I know myself what to say." The same Khokhlov reported that "there had been no direct attacks against the Soviet tourists anywhere."[18]

Thousands of East European, and especially Polish and Hungarian students in the USSR, also spread information about the unrest back home, and Soviet students keenly followed the news. Soviet officials reported local students taking active interest in political events in East-Central Europe. One Moscow party official complained, for example, that influenced by some erroneous materials in the Soviet press, but also "by articles about literature and art published in Polish newspapers, many politically incorrect opinions and statements appeared in the student milieu."[19] According to them, the Soviet students had expressed lively interests in the Polish press, read it, or asked the Polish students for translation of some articles.[20] One communist Soviet student told his party bosses that the foreign students at the State Institute of Cinematography had distributed "harmful information (especially from Poland and Hungary) and the students believe them."[21] Newspapers imported for the East European students from their home countries were exempt from censorship.[22] The Polish embassy in Moscow made consistent efforts to supply the students with the Polish press, lest the young men and women become too isolated from the political and social life of their country.[23] Polish students distributed the Russian-language newspaper *Pol'sha* (Poland) in their dorms, which Soviet authorities, including Khrushchev, saw as anti-Soviet.[24] Soviet students were so "morbidly" interested in news from Poland, said one Soviet official during a closed meeting, that it compelled them "to buy out momentarily" all Yugoslav newspapers. He added that "everyone reads them and wants to be up to date."[25]

The old and the new comingled uneasily in official cultural contacts as well. For the first time since the war, the Soviet and Polish governments developed a concrete, detailed legal framework for cultural relations between the two countries. "The Agreement on Cultural Cooperation between Poland and the USSR," signed on June 30, 1956, in Warsaw, stipulated robust development of cooperation in the fields of science, education, literature, fine arts, music, theater, film, press, radio, television, sport, and tourism. Both parties pledged to exchange mutual experiences in the popularization of culture. Plans for such cooperation were to be worked out on an annual basis by a mixed Soviet-Polish commission (three members from each country), and with the help of experts. The commission was to gather alternatively in Warsaw and in Moscow, and the host country would pay for the proceedings each time. The very formalization of cultural relations symbolized a significant departure from the ad hoc initiatives of the preceding years. The agreement emphasized reciprocity of cultural relations between the two countries. It was perhaps appropriate, then, that Nikolai Mikhailov, who had so recently and ardently advocated a cultural dialogue, as ambassador to Poland, now cosigned the document as Soviet minister of culture.[26]

Still, such formal recognition of reciprocity, undoubtedly backed up by considerable good faith on both sides, was too little too late for many Poles. Officials from the USSR reported ongoing personal discrimination against themselves and their work.[27] Under the chairmanship of Antoni Słonimski, a former Skamandrite poet who had found a reluctant modus vivendi with the communist regime, the leaders of the Polish Writers' Union boycotted their Soviet counterparts for several years before they were brought to heel by the exasperated Władysław Gomułka.[28] One Soviet official took

heart in that a handful of Polish writers such as Kruczkowski and Putrament continued to see "the past and the future of Polish culture correctly,
in a party-minded fashion."[29] But that was a small consolation in the face
of worrisome dominant trends. The stalwarts of Soviet Stalinist literature
Alexei Surkov (the secretary general of the Soviet Writers' Union) and Konstantin Simonov were ostentatiously denied an invitation to the proceedings of the November 1956 Congress of the Polish Writers' Union. During
this congress, the Polish participants struck out from the organization's
statute all references to socialist realism as their guiding principle.
Słonimski called the previous authorities of the union "an execution squad
of literature."[30]

Shortly afterward, Słonimski happily answered the journalists who
asked him what the union would do from now on. The most important
thing Słonimski could report was what the union would *not* do: "it will
not lecture, organize, instruct, expose, oblige, censure, mobilize, activate,
praise, coerce."[31] Słonimski had been to the USSR in 1932, but, upon return, he found it difficult to discuss his mixed impressions with those in
Poland who uncategorically believed in the Soviet Union. The writer lived
in exile in London until 1951. He hardly spoke against cultural Stalinism
after his return to Poland that same year, and even wrote a eulogy of
Bolesław Bierut; in December 1954, the intransigent Kruczkowski reminded Słonimski of what he perceived as the writer's conformity of con-
venience.[32] Now, in his new role, Słonimski minced no words. He saw little
soft power in the Soviet Union; what was left of it, like so many of his
peers then, he was no longer willing to interpret.

In speaking out against socialist realism in 1956, Słonimski must have
been rekindling the memories of his youth. His words echoed the manifesto of the Skamander group, poets known for their apoliticism and love
of sonic harmony, which stated "we are not tempted by sermonizing, we
do not want to convert anybody, but we want to conquer, to enrapture, to
influence the hearts of men."[33] Most Polish writers agreed with Słonimski's
assault on the critical terminology of Stalinism, as part of their war against
using literature to engineer the souls of others. Dogmatic art now rankled
not only those who had opposed it, but who tolerated and even promoted
it as well. But for the Soviet officials, who had been immersed in such literature for two and a half decades, the "new winds" in Polish literary life
created "confusion in the development of ideological thought."[34] As such,
they represented an assault on sacred principles of the Soviet system.

And what about the "willing receivers" of Soviet soft power? East European audiences voted with their feet against Soviet cultural offerings in

the 1950s and 1960s, overwhelmingly choosing Western films and live theater instead.[35] These choices were assuredly part of a massive backlash against unwelcome Stalinist intrusions and also Soviet failure to create a culture attractive enough to mobilize the masses at home and abroad. In 1957, taking full advantage of the soft-power vacuum left by the Soviets, the Eisenhower administration moved—aggressively using loans and Radio Free Europe to lure Poles away from Soviet influence. The American president's advisers reported with well-documented glee that their efforts in Poland were more successful than anywhere else in Eastern Europe.[36]

New opportunities clashed with old mentalities and long-standing Soviet limitations in other ways. Stanisław Jung was editor in chief of *Przyjaźń* (Friendship), an illustrated journal of the Polish-Soviet Friendship Society. In early November 1957, he met with Soviet embassy official I. Lukovnikov in order to request more visual materials for his periodical. Circulation figures had been dropping rapidly. Jung needed more pictures to boost sales. In the absence of materials from the USSR, he explained, he had to rely heavily on photographs from Britain and France. Pictures of attractive Soviet women would make the most welcome contribution from Moscow, Jung told Lukovnikov. The diplomat was incredulous. Jung then pulled out a chart, explaining that "the content of the journal also plays an important role. But the facts show, that no matter what content, the issues with a 'girly cover' return from the newspaper kiosks in the smallest quantities. Such is the nature of the Polish reader." Jung's statistics proved that those issues of the journal featuring the décolleté Soviet artist Tatiana Piletskaia, the ballerina Galina Ulanova, and other Polish and foreign women on their covers, were most successful by far.[37] Clearly, Polish mass audiences wanted to see cleavage, not collective farms, on the cover of the journal about the USSR. But in a country loathe to admit that sex still existed, using feminine charms to sell newspapers astonished the Soviet bureaucrat.[38]

The new Soviet leaders may have abandoned Stalinist methods of rule, but they did not relinquish empire. When Soviet soft power had an inadequate effect, due to its lack of cultural appeal, ongoing Soviet rule ultimately became dependent on force. The fruit had not fallen far from Stalin's tree. The Soviet government issued a declaration on October 30, 1956, affirming "absolute equality of rights" with "other socialist countries," and "respect" of the latter's "territorial integrity, state independence, and sovereignty" just days after its brutal military invasion of Hungary (October 23–24), and on the eve of a second brutal invasion (November 4) involving a total of more than 90,000 Soviet troops.[39]

In the Polish city of Poznań, a workers' uprising in late June of that year had been pacified by Polish Army troops. The workers demanded "more bread" and higher wages; common criminals also joined the protest, and the demonstrations spun out of control. The authorities responded with brute force, branding all protesters as counterrevolutionaries. "Anyone who will raise his hand against the People's Power," chided Prime Minister Józef Cyrankiewicz on June 29, "can be sure that his hand shall be chopped off."[40]

City residents were still burying dozens of workers who had perished during the violent clashes, as the Polish Army withdrew. During their retreat, Soviet Minister of Culture Mikhailov and his Polish counterpart signed the cultural cooperation agreement on June 30. This famous Polish rebellion did not involve Soviet tanks, serving as a direct statement against the oppressive Polish regime. But the reaction of the Soviet-backed Polish communists and their internationalist rhetoric put this domestic conflict clearly in the context of the international empire. A decade-long *danse macabre* between cruelty and culture continued. As Poles and especially Hungarians found out a few months later, unresolved domestic conflicts in the bloc would be subject to violent Soviet arbitration. The specter of Soviet interventions in Eastern Europe soon belied the official rhetoric of reciprocity. Soviet force against the protesting crowds in East Germany in 1953, Hungary in 1956, and Czechoslovakia in 1968, would tarnish the Soviet image in the West until the present day. The shattering violence of the Soviet invasion of Hungary turned the Polish Stalinist writer Wiktor Woroszylski into a "revisionist." With the full powers of his pen and his lifelong zeal, Woroszylski now accused the Soviet authorities of genocide, point blank.[41] The quelling of Hungarian revolutionaries embarrassed and outraged even the most pro-Soviet activists across the Third World, the leaders of nationalist movements took note of the parallels between the Soviet suppression of East European independence movements and the simultaneous French imperialist interventions in Algeria.[42] The hellish images sent round the world revealed that in the Soviet Bloc, the USSR raged and ruled like a repulsive dragon, to which the Polish writer Stanisław Lem once compared the Soviet Union. And unlike the devil, who bought and sold souls, this dragon had nothing to offer the population it terrorized.

CONCLUSION

Trapped in History

"The Honorable Louis Sears, American Ambassador to Sarkhan, was angry." Thus starts *The Ugly American*, a novel about U.S. effort to win over the hearts and minds of the masses in Southeast Asia during the early Cold War. The work is replete with revealing analogies and connections to our story. Self-righteous and ignorant with regard to the conditions, culture, and customs of the people in his host country, Sears closely resembles Georgii M. Popov. Just like the Soviet ambassador to Poland, Sears explodes with fiery indignation over an image—a caricature of himself that appears in a local newspaper. "A short, fat American, his face perspiring," leads a local man by a tether around his neck toward a sign reading "Coca Cola," two of the few words, we learn, that the ambassador recognizes in Sarkhanese.[1]

This scathing critique of U.S. foreign policy pits characters like Sears against those who spread American power through a mix of flexibility, sensitivity, and genuine efforts to help the locals improve their lives. The eponymous Homer Atkins—a physically unattractive engineer with great ideas and skills—actually moves to the countryside and designs a bicycle-powered water pump that would enable the Sarkhanese to irrigate their fields more efficiently. The pump, Atkins insists, must be constructed out of something that the natives can use and understand, for if it "is going to work at all, it has to be their pump, not mine."[2]

The Ugly American tracks the more ingenious agents of American soft power as their work is overwhelmed by the policies of clueless top embassy officials. Though the people of Cambodia need chickens and eggs, the generals send them contracts for the construction of modern highways.[3] The "chair-borne generals" impose a string of useless ideas and military equipment on American soldiers who know from experience that it takes something else to defeat the guerillas in the Viet Cong. Thus, the Americans forfeit their opportunity to engage with the natives on a genuine basis, and American efforts simply prepare the stage for communist victory.

This influential bestseller mirrors the realities of Soviet soft-power politics during the Cold War. Against the received knowledge of a lockstep oppressive Soviet regime, I hope to have shown that not every Soviet bureaucrat, or cultural figure, resembled Popov or Sears. There were Atkinses as well, who tried to improve Stalin's new empire by forging sensitive and reciprocal cultural relations with their East European allies. The Orlovs, the Safirovs, the Panferovs, the Palladins, and the Ehrenburgs tried to project genuine soft power—the power of attraction—to the extent that they could. Yet, time after time, their efforts were stifled by the system that Stalin had hammered brutally in place. The "bourgeois" Hungarian writer Sándor Márai captured well the crucial distinction in his reminiscences of the last months of World War II. Freezing and fearful, trapped in a Hungarian village without water or electricity during Christmas of 1944, Márai watched the Red Army soldiers approach. Were they liberators from Nazi oppression, or were they another conquering army? One Soviet soldier asked Márai, "Who are you?" Weighed down by age-old prejudice against communism and the USSR, and overwhelmed by the momentousness of this clash of civilizations, Márai longed to ask that soldier the same question. Márai knew that "to many, to those persecuted by the Nazis, this young Russian brought along a kind of liberation," and yet, as the writer reflected later on, the soldier "couldn't bring freedom with him because he didn't have any."[4] Likewise, the numerous Soviet writers, intellectuals, bureaucrats, and officials charged with cultural outreach to the People's Democracies did not simply "fear freedom."[5] They themselves had none. They were not liberals, democrats, or early forerunners of perestroika. They were often the Soviet Union's "best available men," people whom empires traditionally mobilized to "renovate themselves" and extend their political lifespans.[6] They wanted to project soft power abroad, but they were unable to, because there was nothing soft about Stalinism in the Soviet Union.

Culturally, Soviet citizens faced too many constraints to produce their own version of *The Ugly American*. Indeed, the mechanism that prevented the appearance of such a work reflected the major structural flaws of Soviet institutions: the notorious lack of incentives to generate constructive criticism, the refusal to entertain or absorb such criticism, and very few means to improve ineffective practices. In some ways, the Soviet propagandists shared the problems and dilemmas with their East European analogues. As Jan Behrends found, the Polish and East German communists found themselves stuck between the pragmatic and utopian approaches to cultural politics.[7] But in other ways, the Soviet constraints reflected much less the revolutionary drama. The "totalitarian system" doomed Soviet efforts to influence countries in the West, wrote historian Vladimir Pechatnov. Soviet propagandistic outreach in the early postwar years employed "primitive ideologism, formalism, sluggishness (caused by endless 'checking it with the authorities') and extreme stereotyping."[8] The same was true of Soviet attempts to woo its new vassal states in Eastern Europe, and Poland in particular. As we have seen, the Kremlin's efforts to maintain its new sphere of influence became an awkward dance: one step forward, many crushed toes, and seven steps back. As in *The Ugly American*, the resulting Soviet failure to project soft power in its new empire meant squandered alliances with the crucial and influential strata of East European societies. This unflagging Soviet rigidity proved doubly problematic in the zero-sum game of the Cold War, since the United States projected its own soft power in Eastern Europe much more effectively than people like Sears did in the imaginary country of Sarkhan.

Coercion is costly. Soviet soft-power initiatives arose out of the need to supplement force with the power of attraction. Instead, much of the cultural outreach to Eastern Europe during the last years of Stalin's rule came to depend on terror, which added to the cost of imperial expansion. Terror complicated the work of Polish communists who considered themselves Stalin's most loyal allies, alienating their fellow travelers, the curious but uncommitted. In many ways, Sovietization was consistent with other aspects of Stalin's postwar policy, which favored the assertion of immediate control over finding a long-term modus vivendi between the rulers and the ruled. Yet it would be inaccurate to see the counterproductive Soviet cultural outreach simply as a net loss. It was not mere collateral damage. It was not even the heavy price of Stalin's wager to win the present. On the other hand, it would be naive to think that the impulse to transform East European mentalities actually propelled the propagandistic efforts. While some communists may have believed in the building of the "new man," the aging Soviet leader knew that the painstaking effort to transform East European societies and the mentalities of the region's people would be even more difficult without his own authority and charisma. Stalin once compared imposing communism on Poland to saddling a cow. Stalin needed his vassal states to behave, but held out little hope for their actual transformation into horses.

Though ineffective and often counterproductive, the wide-ranging cultural outreach initiatives nevertheless played a distinctly positive role within the framework of Stalin's system and policy. Not for their host countries, to be sure, but for Stalin. The soft-power initiatives helped to institutionalize, on an international scale, the key sphere of human activity that caters to the mind and soul; they sustained a network of organizations with few means and unattainable goals, linked by a chain of command flanked by the Soviet leader himself, thus providing Stalin with yet another well-tuned instrument of terror. To the people involved in cultural initiatives, international outreach meant various things—ranging from genuine efforts to appeal, to moral compromises in exchange for opportunities to travel and other perks. Outreach sometimes gave them pride about participation in the great project of social engineering, or the nationalistic sense of satisfaction that Czesław Miłosz once described. Ultimately, despite the genuine efforts and abilities of Soviet functionaries, cultural figures, and their East European interlocutors, the cultural outreach initiatives generated no more actual soft power than the web of Stalinist labor camps had boosted the Soviet economy.[9] Indeed, like the Gulag, they constituted only an instrument of top-down control.

Soviet functionaries on all levels instrumentalized ethnicity in a way that reflected their two impulses: to appeal to Polish society and transform it. Numerous Soviet officials served in Polish institutions largely because of their remote Polish ancestry, which the official propaganda heavily emphasized. These "cultural insiders," to use Paul Gilroy's term, were to make the Soviet presence in Poland more efficient and acceptable.[10] At the same time, they were agents of the Soviet regime, fully responsible to their bosses in Moscow. In Poland, nobody doubted the true allegiances of these hybrids, the most famous of whom was Konstantin Rokossovskii. At the same time, their international backgrounds and duties, during the era of omnipresent, manic suspicion, xenophobia, and isolation, made them more vulnerable to potential accusations back home and therefore even more loyal to Stalin's party-state.

The demoted Marshal Rokossovskii summed up his own position accurately as he waited for a Moscow-bound aircraft in November 1956. He stood at the airport in plain, civilian clothes, and not a single Polish official came to wish him farewell. "Such is life," he allegedly told Iurii Bernov, first secretary of the Soviet embassy, who alone accompanied him. Rokossovskii is said to have glanced toward Warsaw one more time, and added bitterly: "In Russia I have always been a Pole; and in Poland—I have been a Russian."[11]

The period of gestation, the years from 1943 to 1957, show the rough-and-tumble beginnings when the Soviet system itself wrecked the efforts of the few people who knew how to take advantage of the empire's potential. When new types and scales of diversity confronted the Kremlin, Stalin reverted to terror and isolation. This created large, resentful, captive audiences, which the Soviets did not win over by delivering better goods.

A key process in the Soviet expansion, "Sovietization" became a major concern for East Europeans and Western observers after World War II. Yet it captures neither the nuances of contemporary solutions nor the full range of processes involved in the cultural formation of the Soviet Bloc. Full and rapid Sovietization, which began in earnest in the spring of 1948, was inconvenient to the Polish hard-liners, who followed through with the process largely out of fear. Many Soviet officials who were au courant in Polish affairs thought Sovietization inexpedient, but could do little to prevent it. Although many on both sides benefited from Stalinist policies in cultural affairs, some Soviet cultural figures and scientists suffered as much from Stalin's repressive measures as their Polish peers or more; it is hardly surprising that a good number of them sympathized with their colleagues in Eastern Europe along professional lines. Efforts to publish contemporary East European fiction in the USSR reflect their deep sympathy and sense of commitment to fellow writers and translators in the "People's Democracies." The value of the term "Sovietization" is only limited in making sense of what really transpired. These multivectored postwar transformations, with their tangled fault lines, can better be described in terms of "imperial consolidation." Contemporaries waded into the cultural transformation of the Soviet Bloc filled with hope. Many agents of Soviet soft power and their Polish interlocutors wanted to create a new sphere that, outside the *kto kogo* (the "who will get whom") of politics, could support elements of authentic exchange. The project was ultimately doomed. By the late 1940s, the Soviet propagandists and Polish intermediaries found themselves in a shrinking no-man's-land. They failed to change the course of history, if only to a small degree, but that failure must not constitute a mandate for reducing the complex Soviet-East European cultural negotiations to questions of whether, why, and to what extent Eastern Europe became Soviet-like.

The Soviet failures to engage through culture were hardly unique to Poland; on the contrary, as has been shown, to some extent, they affected the entire Soviet Bloc. Yet, against the broader background of Soviet-East European cultural contacts, this study has focused on understanding the idiosyncrasies of Soviet-Polish interactions, comparatively heavily weighed down by the history and memories of past conflicts. Czesław Miłosz once remarked that "the history of Polish-Russian relations can largely be reduced to the collision of two different concepts of freedom," concepts "maintained by writers" in each country, each group in their own way.[12] In his view, Poles have embraced the Western, liberal, individualistic freedom from constraints. Russians, in contrast, have emphasized the freedom that absolves the individual of responsibility for his actions. In the tradition of early nineteenth-century German philosophical tradition, Russians placed the heavy burden on the independent forces of history. Miłosz's overarching comparison is compelling, but his vision of Polish-Russian relations precludes the possibility of a dialogue. In contrast, this work challenges the long-standing tradition of thinking about Polish-Russian relations as largely and inevitably antagonistic. There was plenty of conflict, to be sure. And yet, Soviets and Poles often shared ideas, approaches to soft power, and tastes in literature and the arts. In some cases, the staunch Sovietizers from the USSR had as much to fear as those East Europeans who covertly sabotaged some Soviet initiatives. Soviets and East Europeans, including many Poles, wanted well-written daily news but also more Russian classics and some Soviet avant-garde. Many shared a commitment to flexibility in propaganda and to a degree of reciprocity in cultural relations. Stalin squandered the chance to build solid foundations of exchange, ignoring the tremendous human potential and rich cultural heritage that the Soviets had at their disposal. In so doing, he opened up the gate for an anti-Soviet backlash that would destabilize the empire for decades to come.

Surely, "squandered potential" implies alternatives, but could Soviet-Polish and Soviet-East European cultural relations have taken a different route? And could tinkering with culture have attenuated the tremendous tensions in the Soviet Bloc, thus changing the course of the Cold War? In his authoritative study of the cultural Cold War, David Caute posed a similar question: "How would the West have coped if postwar Soviet culture had paraded under the banners of Mayakovsky, Meyerhold, Tatlin, Rodchenko, Malevich, Zoshchenko, and Stravinsky?" Caute replies, "It could not happen, because a political dictatorship cannot tolerate genuinely free and innovative artistic activity."[13] The inevitable conclusion that Mayakovsky could not have sweetened the sour taste of empire to East Europeans goes hand in hand with the deeper structural and ideological features of Stalinism that prevented the staging, publishing, and distributing of Mayakovsky—or Dostoevsky, or contemporary East European fiction in the USSR. These same mechanisms propelled the Soviets to intervene in the crudest of ways in East European cultures, bringing down the likes of the proponent of a "gentle revolution" in Polish culture, Jerzy Borejsza, and, later, a frustrated editor in chief of *Wolność* Nikolai Bubnov. Writing about the "irresistible" power of America's consumer culture in twentieth-century

Europe, Victoria de Grazia points out that "all empires rely for their power on the means that are historically available to them."[14] America relied on glitz and promise, the USSR relied on overweening force. De Grazia's insights suggest that the hard-working Borejszas and Bubnovs together also fell into a historical trap. They were doomed neither because their philosophical differences disrupted a common dialogue nor because any of them surrendered in the face of greater forces of history. Rather, they were trapped because Soviet soft power, something they were so well-equipped to interpret and project, was not a real option in the postwar decade. They could not have single-handedly altered the Soviet system, or changed the course of history. But their efforts and failures help us to understand Soviet weaknesses in the formative stages of the Cold War.

By underscoring the failures of Soviet soft power, I do not wish to deny genuine Soviet cultural influence in Eastern Europe. Indisputably, the influence of Soviet-sponsored political, economic, and cultural integration has been enormous. The communists profoundly transformed the East European landscapes, languages, fashions, rhythms of industrial production, identities, and values. By the 1970s, the inhabitants of the Soviet Bloc or, more broadly, the "socialist second world," came to share a distinct culture that eventually outlived socialist political systems.[15] This culture was born partly out of the new possibilities for travel and exchange that arose during de-Stalinization and détente. This culture certainly would not have developed had the Soviets not expanded territorially after World War II, and then intervened in the affairs of other states to a greater or lesser degree throughout the Cold War. This book does not negate the vast influence of Soviet transformative energies; it merely suggests that particularly in the postwar decade, all those changes had little to do with the Soviet Union's authentic power of attraction.

Those Soviet officials who would try to maintain the empire through more effective instances of soft power after 1956 would have to do more than mend Stalin-era flaws. Terror subsided in this new climate, while international cultural cooperation flourished under the double aegis of détente and a new policy labeled "socialist internationalism." And those very circumstances made the Soviet system vulnerable. Thousands of foreign tourists and students from the Eastern Bloc entered the USSR. They suffered only mild consequences for violating official Soviet norms. They undermined Soviet soft-power efforts upon returning home, because through personal testimonies, they contradicted the rosy picture of the USSR that Moscow had worked so arduously to project. Several East European regimes—more liberal, economically more prosperous, and more open to the West—became attractive to Soviet citizens from all social groups. Poland, in particular, became a source of cultural and intellectual radiation to the USSR, it generated reverse soft power within the imperial framework. In the words of dissident Soviet turned Russian writer Viktor Erofeev, he and his wife liked to spend summers in Poland, a country that became his only "window to the West" in the 1970s. "Among the wonderful people of Russia roughly three out of a hundred were ready to share my ideas," he wrote, adding that "in Poland exactly the opposite was the case."[16] Many other Soviet dissidents, intellectuals, and ordinary travelers experienced a similar sense of connection beyond fiercely held political borders. The story of how this true "friendship of the peoples" impacted the Soviet empire in its final decades has yet to be written.

Appendix A

TABLES

Table A.1. Articles from the Soviet Information Bureau in Polish Press, 1944–1958 (Data incomplete)

Year	Articles received from Moscow	Articles published in at least one newspaper	Total number of publications	% of original articles published— Soviet duplicates included	% of original articles published
1944	495[a]				
1945	2,531[a]	In April: 60[b]			43
	In April: 138[b]				(April only)
1946					50[c]
1947					
1948	2,703 (5,864)[d]		2,190[d]	37	81
1949	2,839[e]	2,232[e]	4,738[e]		79[e]
1950					84[f]
1951					92[f]
1952	1,243[g]	1,024[g]			82
1953	1,279[h]	1,106[h]			86.5
1954	In July: 144[i]	In July: 57[i]			In July: 40
	Whole year: 1,410[j]				
1955	842[k]	418[l]			50
1958		304[m]			

[a] GARF, f. R-8581, op. 2, d. 154, l. 34.
[b] GARF, f. R-8581, op. 1, d. 146, l. 23.
[c] RGASPI, f. 17, op. 125, d. 385, l. 21.
[d] GARF, f. R-8581, op. 1, d. 264, ll. 553–54. During 1948–49 some articles were being duplicated in Poland. The data in parentheses refer to the duplicates.
[e] GARF, f. R-8581, op. 2, d. 277, l. 2. In 1949 the duplicates were made in Poland.
[f] GARF, f. R-8581, op. 2, d. 342, l. 16.
[g] GARF, f. R-8581, op. 2, d. 373, l. 8. The figures in the first column take into account 122 articles from the year before.
[h] GARF, f. R-8581, op. 2, d. 398, l. 25.
[i] GARF, f. R-8581, op. 2, d. 398, l. 130.
[j] GARF, f. R-8581, op. 2, d. 402, l. 118.
[k] GARF, f. R-8581, op. 2, d. 402, l. 125. (Includes cutouts from the Soviet press to be reprinted.)
[l] GARF, f. R-8581, op. 2, d. 402, l. 121.
[m] GARF, f. R-8581, op. 2, d. 402, l. 125; GARF, f. R-8581, op. 2, d. 497, l. 90.

Table A.2. Soviet/Russian Plays in Poland, 1945–1957

Year	Authors	Plays	Premieres	Performances	Viewers
1945	4	4	4		
1946	3	3	3		
1947	9	11 (5)	19	47	31,000
1948	14	17 (30)	36	521	314,000
1949	28	49 (63)	82	10,000	3,500,000
1950	28	37	71		
1951	32	44	69		
1952	30	41 (46)	71	2,712	1,103,000
1953	24	33 (76)	54	5,405	1,983,000
1954	34	37	58		
1955	27	34	40		
1956	13	17	26		
1957	6	8	9		

Sources: In bold, Olejniczak, *Polsko-radzieckie kontakty*, 186; in roman, RGANI, f. 5, op. 28, d. 162, k. 63.

Table A.3. Contemporary Polish Fiction Considered by the Foreign Commission, 1947–1954, by year (titles of works cited in the chapter given in English translations)

Year	Works considered by IK SSP (original year of publication of 1st ed.)	Author's birthdate	Published in USSR? / year
1947	Putrament, *Reality* (*Rzeczywistość*) (1947)	1910	1948
	Andrzejewski, *Noc* (1945)	1909	—
	Kruczkowski, *The Germans* (*Niemcy*) [1949]* (1950)	1900	1955
1948	[No titles considered]		
1949	Wirski, *Engineer Saba* (*Inżynier Saba*) [1948]* (1949)	1893	-
1950	Wilczek, *Number 16 Begins Production* (*Nr. 16 produkuje*) (1949)	1916	1950
	Boguszewska, *The Iron Curtain* (*Żelazna kurtyna*) [1948]† (1949)	1883	—
	Dróżdż-Satanowska, *Topiela* (1949)	1910	—
	Zalewski, *Tractors Will Conquer the Spring* (*Traktory zdobędą wiosnę*) (1950)	1921	1950
	Gałaj, *Rodzina Lebiodów* [1947–48]† (1950)	1908	—
	Olcha, *Most nad urwiskiem* (1948–49)	1914	—
	Hamera, *Na przykład Plewa* (1950)	1911	1964
	Kowalewski, M., *Kampania znaczy walka* (1950)	1919	—
	Konwicki, *Przy budowie* (1950)	1926	—
	Lutowski, *Próba sił* [(1950)]	1918	—
1951	Ścibor-Rylski, *Coal* (*Węgiel*) (1950)	1928	1959
1952	Bartelski, *Ludzie zza rzeki* (1951)	1920	—
	Brandys, M., *Początek opowieści* (1951)	1912	1952
	Brandys, K. *Człowiek nie umiera* (1951)	1916	1958
1953	Kruczkowski, *A Visit* (earlier title: *Colorado Beetle*) [(1955)]*	1900	1956
	Putrament, *September* (*Wrzesień*) 1951	1910	1961
	Braun, A. *Lewanty* (1952)	1923	—
1954	Brandys, K. *Obywatele* (1953–1954)	1916	1955

Dates in parentheses refer to publication in print and those in brackets refer to the premier of the work either in the theater (*) or on the radio (†).

Sources: RGALI, f. 631, op. 14; RGALI, f. 631, op. 26; Czachowska and Szałagan, *Współcześni polscy pisarze i badacze literatury*; Artsimovich and Morshchiner, *Khudozhestvennaia literatura stran narodnoi demokratii v perevodakh na russkii iazyk*; *Khudozhestvennaia literatura Pol'shi*; Stefanovich and Mentsendorf, *Khudozhestvennaia literatura Pol'shi*; Mentsendorf, *Khudozhestvennaia literatura Pol'shi*.

Appendix B

FIGURES

Figure B.1. Soviet Literary Exports to Poland, 1947–1953 (in Russian, via Mezhdunarodnaia Kniga; data incomplete)

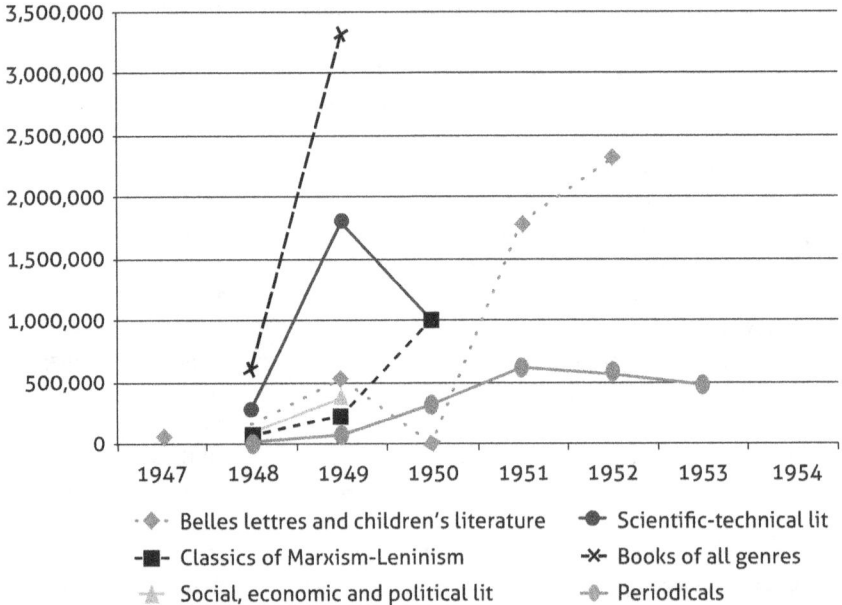

Sources: GARF, f. R-8581, op. 22, d. 128, l. 10; ibid, d. 307, l. 123; RGASPi, f. 17, op. 137, d. 172, l. 145; RGANI, f. 5, op. 28, d. 162, l. 61.

Figure B.2. Soviet Literary Exports of Books and Brochures (excluding Periodicals) to Poland, 1950–1953 (in Russian)

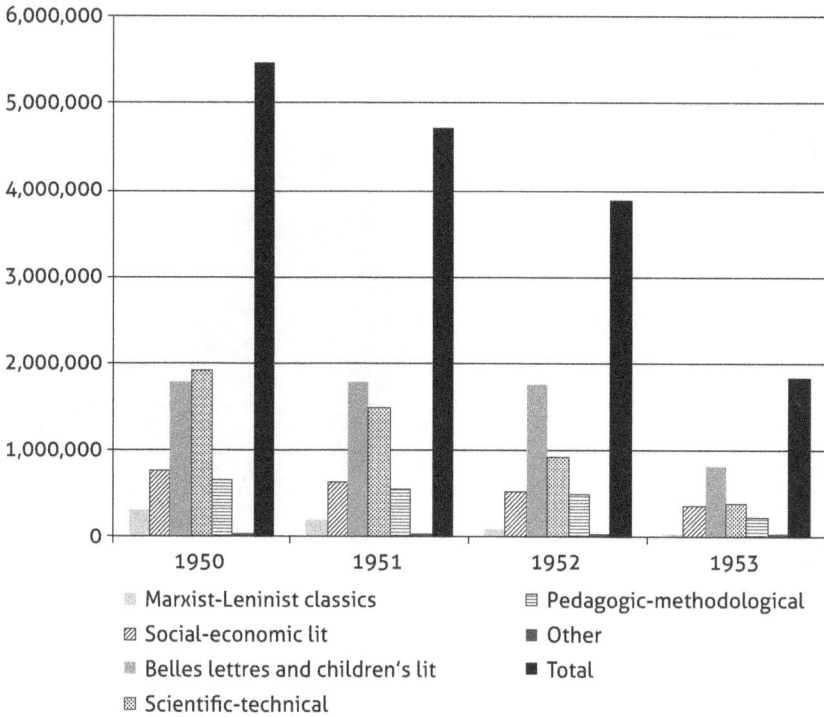

Marxist-Leninist classics
Social-economic lit
Belles lettres and children's lit
Scientific-technical

Pedagogic-methodological
Other
Total

Source: RGANI, f. 5, op. 28, d. 162, l. 60.

Figure B.3. Soviet Subjects on Polish Radio, June–December 1948

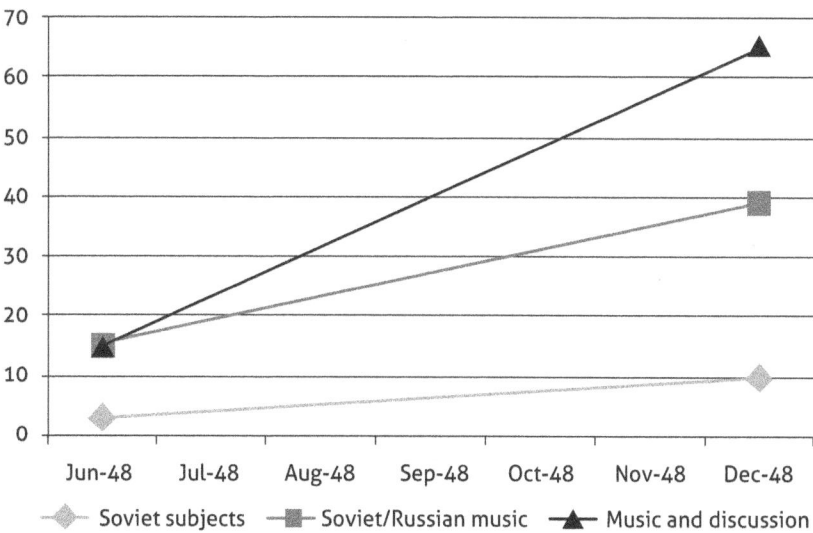

Soviet subjects   Soviet/Russian music   Music and discussion

Sources: GARF, f. R-5283, op. 22, d. 183, l. 21

Figure B.4. Polish Radio Broadcasts on Russian Topics, 1950

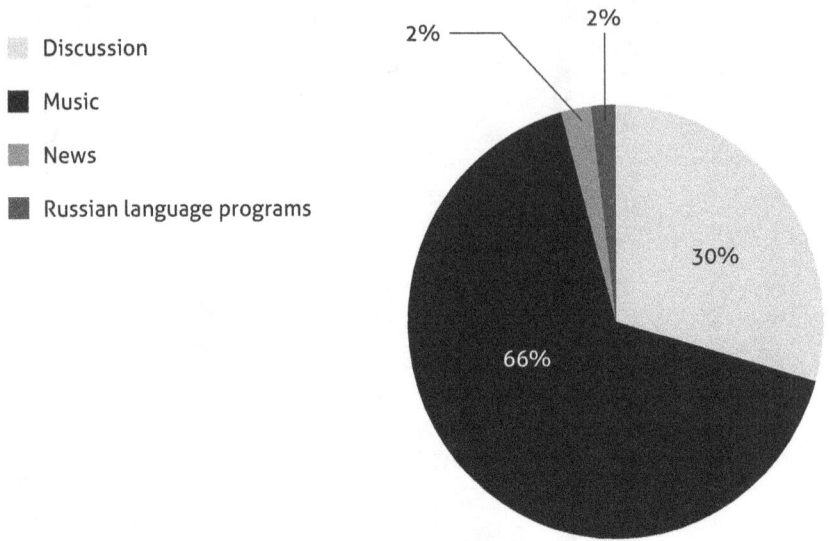

Discussion
Music
News
Russian language programs

2%
2%
30%
66%

Source: GARF, f. R-5283, op. 22, d. 307, l. 126.

Figure B.5. Soviet Films in Poland, 1945–1956

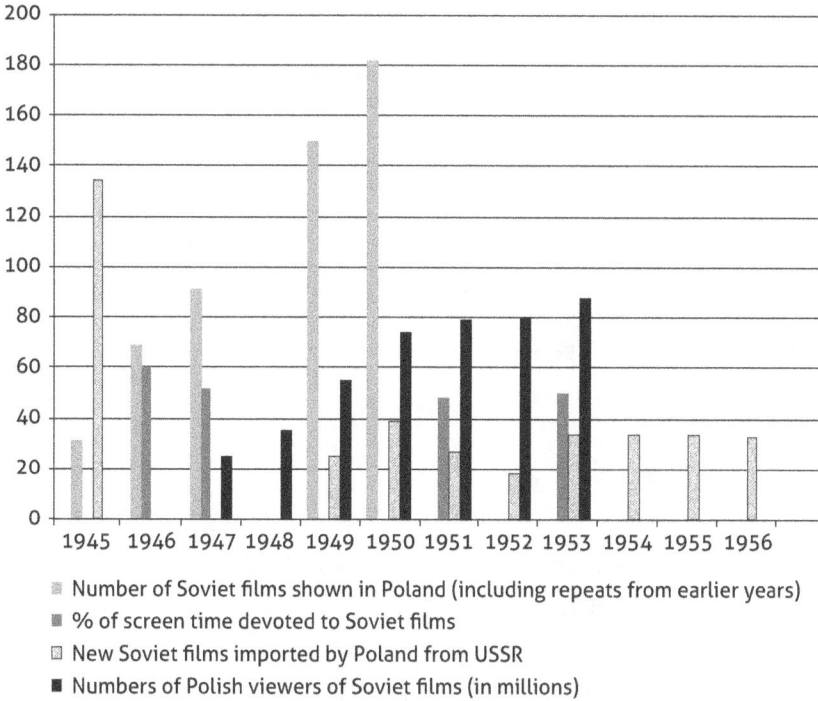

- Number of Soviet films shown in Poland (including repeats from earlier years)
- % of screen time devoted to Soviet films
- New Soviet films imported by Poland from USSR
- Numbers of Polish viewers of Soviet films (in millions)

Sources: GARF, f. R-5283, op. 22, d. 64, ll. 71–72; GARF, f. R-5283, op. 22, d. 373, l. 55; GARF, f. R-5283, op. 22, d. 373, l. 54 (data for screen time in 1951—compare with: Polish and East European films—38 percent; Western, especially French and Italian—14 percent); Olejniczak, *Polsko-radzieckie kontakty*, 187; RGANI, f. 5, op. 28, d. 162, l. 62.

Figure B.6. Soviet Periodicals in Poland, 1948–1953

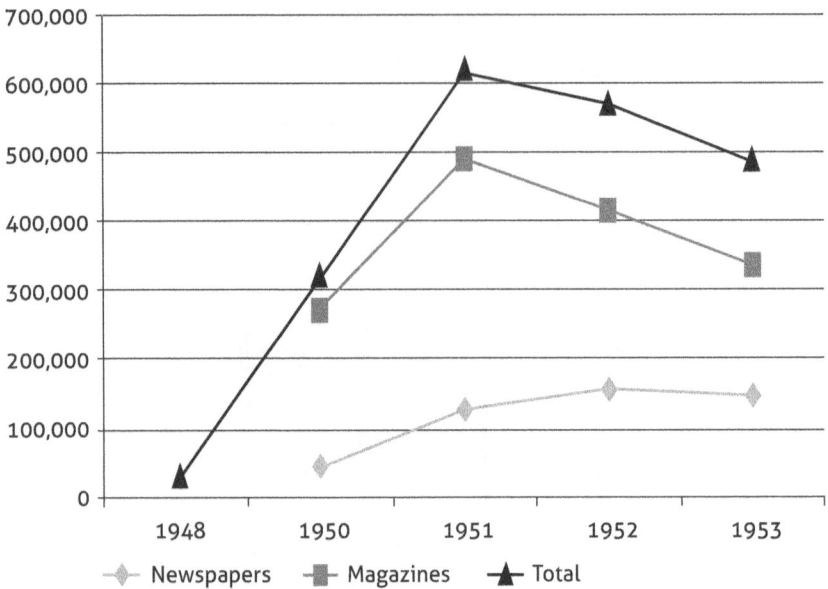

Source: RGASPI, f. 17, op. 132, d. 140, l. 55.

Figure B.7. Russian/Soviet Books Translated into Polish, 1947–1953 (number of titles)

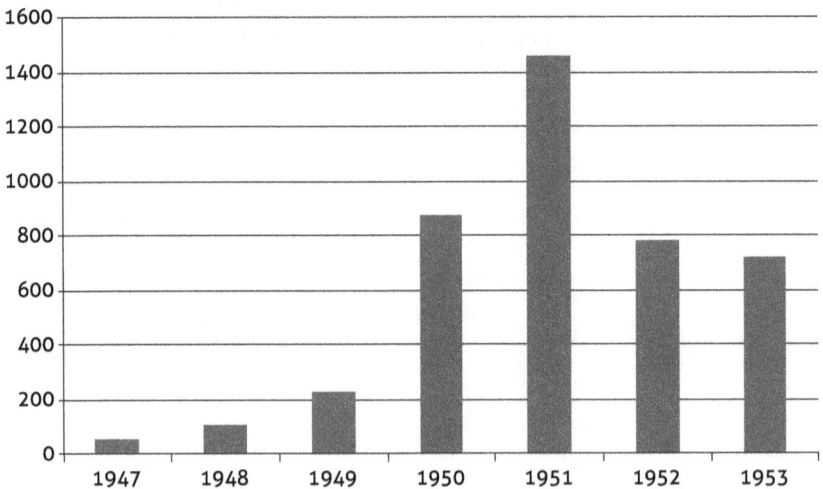

Sources: RGASPI, f. 17, op. 137, d. 172, l. 145; 1950–51: GARF, f. 5283, op. 22, d. 373, l. 52; for 1952: GARF, f. R-5283, op. 22, d. 431, ll. 48–49. RGANI, f. 5, op. 28, d. 162, l. 60.

Figure B.8. Russian/Soviet Translations into Polish, 1948–1952 (circulation)

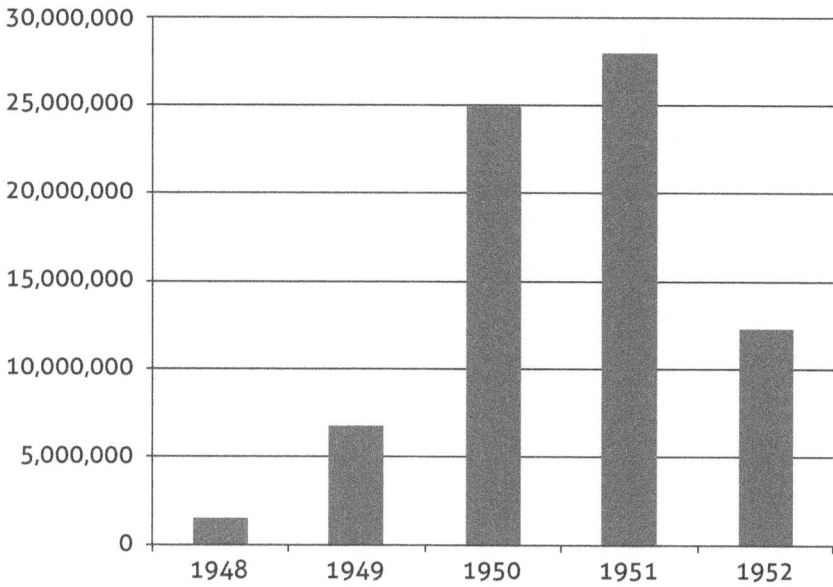

Sources: RGASPI, f. 17, op. 137, d. 172, l. 145; 1950–51: GARF, f. 5283, op. 22, d. 373, l. 52; for 1952: GARF, f. R-5283, op. 22, d. 431, ll. 48–49. RGANI, f. 5, op. 28, d. 162, l. 60.

Figure B.9. Russian/Soviet Books Translated into Polish, 1951

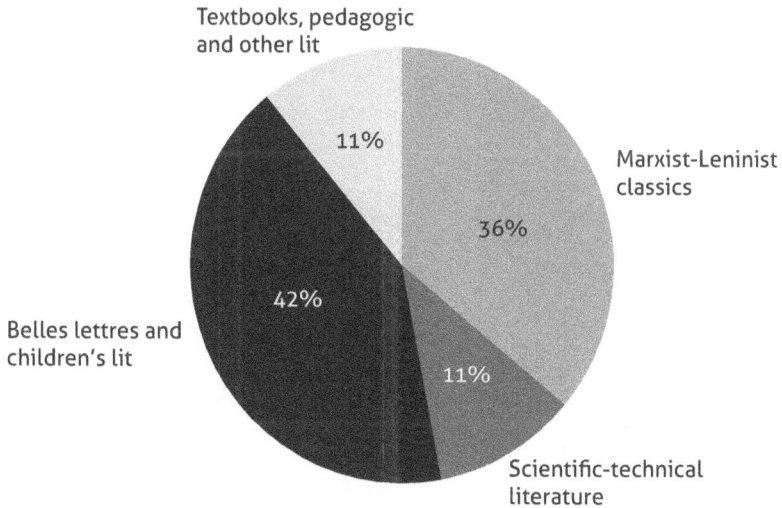

Source: GARF, f. 5283, op. 22, d. 373, l. 52.

Notes

CBKP   Central Bureau of Polish Communists (Centralne Biuro Komunistów Polskich)

IKKN   [Polish] Institute for Education of Scientific Cadres (Instytut Kształcenia Kadr Naukowych)

INS   [Polish] Institute of Social Sciences (Instytut Nauk Społecznych), successor to IKKN

JAFC   Jewish Anti-Fascist Committee

KGB   [Soviet] Commissariat of State Security, a successor of NKVD

KPP   Communist Party of Poland (Komunistyczna Partia Polski), a predecessor of PZPR

KPSS   Communist Party of the Soviet Union (Kommunisticheskaia Partiia Sovetskogo Soiuza, former VKP (b))

KWKZ   [Polish] Committee for Cultural Cooperation with Foreign Countries, an equivalent of Soviet VOKS

MID   [Soviet] Ministry of Foreign Affairs (Ministerstvo Inostrannykh Del)

MK   International Book (Mezhdunarodnaia kniga), Soviet state book distribution organization

MBP   [Polish] Ministry of Public Security (Ministerstwo Bezpieczeństwa Publicznego)

NKVD   [Soviet] National Commissariat of Internal Affairs (Narodnyi Kommissariat Vnutrennykh Del], predecessor of KGB

OVP   [Soviet Central Committee's] Foreign Policy Department (Otdel Vneshnei Politiki]

PKWN   Polish Committee of National Liberation (Polski Komitet Wyzwolenia Narodowego)

PPR   Polish Workers' Party (Polska Partia Robotnicza), a reactivated KPP

PPS   Polish Socialist Party (Polska Partia Socjalistyczna)

PSL   Polish Peasant Party

PZPR   Polish United Workers' Party (Polska Zjednoczona Partia Robotnicza), a merger of PPS and PPR

TRJN   [Polish] Provisional Government of National Unity (Tymczasowy Rząd Jedności Narodowej)

SIB   Soviet Information Bureau

TPPR   Polish-Soviet Friendship Society (Towarzystwo Przyjaźni Polsko-Radzieckiej)

VKP(b)   All-Union (Bolshevik) Communist Party, a predecessor of KPSS
VOKS   (Soviet) All-Union Society for Cultural Relations Abroad
ZMP   Polish Youth Association (Związek Młodzieży Polskiej)
ZPP   Union of Polish Patriots (Związek Patriotów Polskich)

INTRODUCTION

1. N. A. Bubnov, "Dnevnik voennogo redaktora, 1942–1970," GARF, f. R-8127, op. 1, d. 33, ll. 410–11. All translations are the author's unless otherwise indicated.

2. Bernov, *Zapiski diplomata*, 12, 11–18; on circumstances of Popov's transfer see Sobór, *Jakub Berman*, 409–10; Bernov, *Zapiski diplomata*, 17. In the winter of 1949, Popov lost his post as secretary of the Moscow Party Committee for his self-righteous, neglectful, and "un-Bolshevik" behavior, thus freeing the spot for N. S. Khrushchev. See Khlevniuk, *Politbiuro*, 319–24.

3. The grain shipments constituted a means of stabilizing Poland's domestic situation and making the country economically dependent on the USSR. See Skrzypek, *Mechanizmy uzależnienia*, 146–49, 196–206. The Soviet advantages included: widespread looting and devastation of industrial equipment on Poland's new territories annexed from Germany after World War II (calculated at four billion postwar dollars); the violation of international agreements and bilateral treaties with the USSR that guaranteed Poland 15 percent of German war reparations to the Soviet Union (Poland received 6.1 percent); compulsory coal shipments to the USSR at eleven times below the international prices; an artificial ruble to złoty exchange rate (as a result of which Poland lost some four hundred million dollars); vastly reduced Soviet communications operations in Poland; and Poland's full financial responsibility for building and maintaining the huge infrastructure of the stationing Soviet Army (which in no way benefited the national economy). See Korzon, "Niektóre problemy." For a view stressing the indeterminate nature of grounds for some of these Polish claims, Poles' failure to take into account certain forms of Soviet assistance and open-endedness of selected disputes concerning Soviet-Polish economic relations in 1944–56, see Parsadanowa, "Polityka i jej skutki." On postwar Soviet looting in Eastern Europe, see also Jersild, "The Soviet Union."

4. Visiting Soviet officials also complained about the painting; they were the likely source of Popov's information. See RGANI, f. 5, op. 28, d. 163, l. 24.

5. Bubnov, "Dnevnik voennogo redaktora," 411; Hanna Małachowicz from the Fine Arts Center in Warsaw's Royal Castle (where *Bathory at Pskov* is currently on display) confirmed the unlikeliness of the painterly edits. E-mail message to author, March 12, 2013.

6. Paczkowski, *The Spring Will Be Ours*, 266.

7. Crowley, "Paris or Moscow," 772; Crowley, *Warsaw*, 38–47; also, Paperny, *Architecture*, 116–17.

8. Bubnov, "Dnevnik voennogo redaktora," 410.

9. On the leftward shift in Eastern Europe, see esp. Volokitina, Murashko, Noskova, eds., *Narodnaia demokratiia*, 9. Jan T. Gross has argued that World War II had

prepared East Europeans mentally and structurally for left-wing totalitarianisms. See "Social Consequences of War."

10. Werblan, "Conversation," 138. On Stalin's similar warnings to the Polish communists in the fall of 1944, see Polonsky and Drukier, *Beginnings of Communist Rule*, 300; Kochański, *Protokoły*, 23.

11. On Czechoslovakia, see Abrams, *Struggle*; on Hungary, see Kenez, *Hungary*; on Germany, see Naimark, *Russians in Germany*.

12. "O budynku Ambasady Rosji w Polsce," www.rusemb.pl/index.php?option=com _content&view=article&id=442&Itemid=79&lang=pl (accessed December 15, 2011).

13. For the references to Stalin as a "god," see Khrushchev, "Speech by N. S. Khrushchev," 207; and in Russian: Khrushchev, "O kul'te lichnosti," 51.

14. Works that examine the Soviet side include Zubok and Pleshakov, *Inside the Kremlin's Cold War*; Zubok, *A Failed Empire*; Naimark, *Russians*. Andrzej Korzon's important but in many ways outdated work covered only 1945–50; see Korzon, *Polsko-radzieckie kontakty*. The literature dealing with all aspects of Stalinist culture in Poland is enormous and shall be cited when relevant; important and exemplary is Kupiecki, *Natchnienie milionów*. Several comparative accounts also exist: perhaps the most important is Behrends, *Die erfundene Freundschaft*, which examines the role of Polish and German institutions in Stalinist propaganda campaigns; also, Connelly, *Captive University*; Jirásek and Małkiewicz, *Polska i Czechosłowacja*.

15. Of the classic works, the most thorough study of Soviet-East European cultural linkages can be found in Brzezinski, *The Soviet Bloc*; recent scholarship that stresses the successes of Sovietization includes Andrzej Skrzypek, *Mechanizmy uzależnienia*; Applebaum, *The Iron Curtain*; Soviet shortcomings are a key theme of Naimark's *Russians*; and, in a broader international context, of Jersild's *The Sino-Soviet Alliance*; in his *Captive University*, Connelly explains the East Europeans' various responses to the planned Sovietization of higher education; Behrends underscores multiple discursive and structural contradictions, which prevented the Polish and East German communist party-states from producing effective pro-Soviet propaganda in *Die erfundene Freundschaft*, esp. 168–69, 281. See also Apor, Apor, and Rees, *The Sovietization of Eastern Europe*; for historiographical overviews, see Naimark and Gibianskii, "Introduction" in Naimark and Gibianskii, *Establishment of Communist Regimes*, 1–16; Naimark, "Post-Soviet Russian Historiography;" Naimark, "Stalin and Europe."

16. Brzezinski wrote that "having viewed international affairs in terms of a hostile external world ranged against the Soviet Union, they could not think of the new Communist camp in any other way except as slightly more expanded Soviet system" (*The Soviet Bloc*, ix). Emphasizing factors other than ideology, Norman Naimark similarly found that "The Soviets also went to Germany with commonly shared historical experiences and social instincts that influenced the development of occupation policy as much if not more than articulated principles of ideology. Soviet officers bolshevized the zone not because there was a plan to do so, but because that was the only way they knew to organize society" (*Russians in Germany*, 467). Commenting on failed Soviet efforts to form alliances in Central Europe, A. S. Stykalin spoke of "extreme shortsightedness of those in charge of popularization (*propagandoi*) of 'the

land of the Soviets' abroad, through their intolerance pushed away quite a few potential allies." See "Politika SSSR," 60. David Caute interrogates Sheila Fitzpatrick's argument about the 1930s in the postwar context, and suggests the primacy of ideological orthodoxies over professional ones among Soviet literary elites, an implication that bears on any attempt to explain Soviet-East European interactions. See Caute, *The Dancer Defects*, 9–10.

17. Applebaum, *The Iron Curtain*, xxxvii.

18. In his discussion of the Soviet Information Bureau's western outreach, Vladimir Pechatnov aptly observed that a major obstacle for the Soviet foreign propaganda was the Soviet system itself. The "totalitarian system," he writes, "doomed propaganda to primitive ideologism, formalism, sluggishness (caused by endless 'checking it with the authorities') and extreme stereotyping." See "Exercise in Frustration," 16.

19. Connelly, *Captive University*, 45–46. Most accounts of the cultural Sovietization of Eastern Europe that do discuss the Soviet role emphasize the broad structural influences and top policymaking: in the context of the mass media, see, for instance, Goban-Klas and Kolstø, "East European Mass Media."

20. A rare example emphasizing Soviet cultural officials' attentiveness to local conditions and the systemic constraints to which they were subjected is Anne Hartmann's work on the Soviet zone of German occupation. See, for example, "Sowjetische 'Leitkultur'"; or, in Russian, Khartmenn (Hartmann), "Rukovodstvo kul'turoi."

21. Sviatoslav Igorevich Kaspe develops such a functional definition of empire in "Imperii," 34–36. In her inquiry into the longevity of empires, with a focus on the Ottoman case, Karen Barkey works from the same premise about flexibility of imperial formations, citing the Roman, Byzantine, Habsburg and Russian empires as other examples of enduring imperial polities—see Barkey, *Empire of Difference*. On the Cold War empires, see Gaddis, *We Now Know*, ch. 2. Timothy Snyder has pointed out that the failure to accommodate the Cossack hetmanate within the structure of the Polish-Lithuanian Commonwealth in mid-seventeenth century contributed to the commonwealth's decline. See *The Reconstruction of Nations*, 112–17. Discussing modern western colonialism, Ann Laura Stoler and Frederic Cooper pointed to the tension between the universal basis of the bourgeois imperial projects and their insistence on a particularistic "grammar of difference" that structured the limits of inclusion and exclusion in different colonies—see "Between Metropole and Colony." See also the introduction by Stoler et al. in *Imperial Formations*, 3–32. Stoler's approach influenced the "new imperial history" of prerevolutionary Russia and critical historiography of the United States. See Gerasimov et al."New Imperial History," and Kramer, "Power and Connection." Challenges arising from cultural diversity of Eurasian empires are a major theme in Alfred J. Rieber's recent work *The Struggle for the Eurasian Borderlands*.

22. Babiracki, "Interfacing the Soviet Bloc." In adopting a functionalist approach, I also join others in going beyond the "tragic" narrative of Polish history and of "filling the blank spots" in the Polish past. For a thoughtful discussion, see Kenney, "After the Blank Spots Are Filled."

23. Brzezinski, *The Soviet Bloc*, 155–56, 184.

24. Paczkowski, "Polish-Soviet Relations."

25. Behrends, *Die erfundene Freundschaft*, 167.

26. The comparative dimensions of the leader cult have been explored in Apor et al., *Leader Cult*.

27. Stykalin, "Politika SSSR," 52.

28. Mizerski, "Idzie Olchowik po słupkach," 116.

29. Zubok, *Zhivago's Children*, 21.

30. See Stokłosa, "La vie à la frontière," 447.

31. For different angles and interpretations, see Chandler, *Institutions of Isolation*; Hollander, *Political Pilgrims*; Kenney, *A Carnival of Revolution*; Mazuy, *Croire plutôt que voir?*; Coeuré and Dullin, *Frontières du communisme*; Gorsuch and Koenker, *Turizm*; Péteri, *Imagining the West*; Stola, *Kraj bez wyjścia?*; David-Fox, *Showcasing the Great Experiment*; Gorsuch, *All This Is Your World*; Babiracki and Zimmer, *Cold War Crossings*; strictly on the Polish case, see Rokicki and Stępień, *W objęciach wielkiego brata*.

32. More than four thousand of them were shot in the Katyn Forest, near Smolensk. See Lukowski and Zawadzki, *A Concise History of Poland*, 256. For exact figures and locations see Cienciala, Lebedeva and Materski, *Katyn*, esp. 332–33.

33. For a discussion of Russian stereotypes of Poles, see Babiracki, "Enemy to Friend."

34. Dobbs, *Six Months in 1945*, 66.

35. Nye, *Soft Power*, 16.

36. Siefert, *"Meeting at a Far Meridian,"* 169.

37. Barkey, *Empire of Difference*, 33.

38. Power is understood to be legitimate here "when it is judged positively in moral categories as just, right (*słuszna*) and deserving recognition" and is not, for instance, based on material interests. See Zaremba, *Komunizm, legitymizacja, nacjonalizm*, 14–23.

39. For more on this element of the imperial practice, see Filippov, "Nabliudatel' imperii," 105.

40. Geertz, *The Interpretation of Cultures*.

41. Kolakowski, *Main Currents of Marxism*, vol. 3, 95.

42. Crowley and Reid, "Socialist Spaces," 7.

43. Erofeev, *Khoroshyi Stalin*, 14.

44. Matsuda, *Soft Power and Its Perils*, 6.

45. Pomianowski, "Torowanie drogi," 515.

46. See Brooks and Zhuk, "Soviet Culture, 1932–1992."

47. Guilbaut, *How New York Stole the Idea of Modern Art*.

CHAPTER 1

1. Naszkowski, *Lata próby*, 273–74. The passengers included: Marian Naszkowski, Jerzy Putrament, Bolesław Dróźdź, Zygmunt Modzelewski, and Jan Karaśkiewicz as well as Lieutenant Colonel Leon Bukojemski. Zbiniewicz, *Armia Polska*, 44.

2. Pasierski, *Miłosz i Putrament*, 16.

3. Ibid., 18; the English translation is Jane Zielonko's as it appears in Milosz, *The Captive Mind*, 138.

4. Pasierski points out that Miłosz's sensibility was probably the result of a trauma he had undergone at the age of twelve, when a teacher at his gymnasium reprimanded him after his own anti-Semitic incident. Pasierski, *Miłosz i Putrament*, 37.

5. Ibid., 27.

6. Ibid., 33.

7. Ibid., 35.

8. Urbanek, *Broniewski*, 169.

9. Grosz was a political officer in the Red Army in 1941-43. *Polski słownik biograficzny*, 9:13-14; Wasilewska, "Wspomnienia Wandy Wasilewskiej," 348n17; Borejsza served in the same capacity between April 1942 and May 1943. See Krasucki, *Międzynarodowy komunista*, 89-91.

10. Cf. Sobór, *Jakub Berman*, 63. The Soviet state apparatus was evacuated from Moscow to Kuibyshev in September–October 1941. The Comintern and the Kościuszko Radio Station (directed by Wiktor Grosz) were relocated to Ufa. In addition, a Polish section of the Ukrainian Radio Station existed in Saratov.

11. The Organizational Committee of the ZPP consisted of Wanda Wasilewska, Alfred Lampe, Hilary Minc, and Wiktor Grosz. Wasilewska and Stefan Jędrychowski, Stefan Skrzeszewski, Władysław Sokorski, and Zygmunt Berling were on the Main Board. See also "1943 czerwiec 10, Moskwa—Deklaracja ideowa uchwalona na I Zjeździe Związku Patriotów Polskich w ZSRR," in Basiński and Cieślak, *Stosunki polsko-radzieckie w latach 1917-1945*, 361-65; Kersten, *The Establishment of Communist Rule*, 16.

12. Several contemporaries point to this symbolic value of the Polish units: Wasilewska, "Wspomnienia Wandy Wasilewskiej," 428; Sokorski, *Polacy pod Lenino*, 72.

13. Zbiniewicz provides a detailed taxonomy of the new recruits in *Armia Polska*, 50-51. See also Sokorski, *Polacy pod Lenino*, 12; Honkisz, *W pierwszym szeregu*, 45; Wasilewska's anecdote about a soldier who ran away from the Kościuszko Division because the nationalist symbolism convinced him it was a "reactionary formation" strikes as exceptional, as compared with other evidence. Wasilewska, "Wspomnienia Wandy Wasilewskiej," 431.

14. Kołodziejczyk, "Postawy Polaków," 109.

15. On the myth of the "apostles," see essays by Broniewska and Putrament in *Ludzie Pierwszej Armii*, 11-19, 25-28.

16. Naszkowski, *Lata próby*, 273-74; Sokorski, *Polacy pod Lenino*, 12.

17. Naszkowski, *Lata próby*, 287.

18. Ibid., 289. On Grosz, see also Szczurkowski, *Słownik biograficzny*, 39-40, and *Polski słownik biograficzny* (1935). The title of the officers and the name of the apparatus changed three times, from *kulturalno-oświatowy* (in some accounts: *oświatowy*), to *polityczno-wychowawczy* (October 9, 1943), to *polityczny*; for narrative purposes, and since their basic tasks remained the same, I shall refer to political officers and political apparatus throughout the study.

19. Grynberg, *Memorbuch*, 150.

20. Broniewska, *Z notatnika*, 144.

21. See Zawiśliński, *Wyznania zdrajcy*, 19–21; Putrament, *Pół wieku*, 2:143. On Sokorski, see also *Polski słownik biograficzny* (2005).

22. Zawiśliński, *Wyznania zdrajcy*, 19.

23. Naszkowski, *Lata próby*, 295, Putrament, *Pół wieku*, 2: 180. For the English version of the novel, see Dmitrii Furmanov, *Chapaev: A Novel* (Moscow: Progress Publishers, 1974).

24. Naszkowski, *Lata próby*, 289.

25. Paweł Ettinger (1886–1948) was an art historian, a bibliophile, and a collector of book plates. Having gone for a research trip to Moscow in 1889, he settled there permanently, becoming Poland's unofficial cultural ambassador to Russia/USSR and a popularizer of Russian culture in Poland. See a useful biographical note in Nałkowska, *Dzienniki*, 1:518–19.

26. Broniewska, *Z notatnika*, 138–41.

27. Quoted in Zbiniewicz, *Armia Polska*, 71.

28. See, for example, Anusiewicz "Wytyczne idowe polskiej jednostki wojskowej," 49–51; "Instrukcja tymczasowa o służbie kulturalno-oświatowej 1 Dywizji Piechoty im. Tadeusza Kościuszki," *Organizacja i działania bojowe*, 53–54; for a new statute of political officers issued in November 1944, see Centralne Archiwum Wojskowe (Central Military Archive, henceforth CAW), syg. III-5-197, k. 40.

29. Naszkowski, *Lata próby*, 293; CAW, syg. III-4-347, k. 125.

30. Naszkowski, *Lata próby*, 293.

31. On religion and Kubsz, see Naszkowski, *Lata próby* 306–7, 340; and Sokorski, *Polacy pod Lenino*, 13.

32. For Naszkowski's biography, see Nałkowska, *Dzienniki* 1:523–24 n. 1.

33. Naszkowski, *Lata próby*, 303–4; Honkisz, *W pierwszym szeregu*, 43.

34. Sokorski, *Tamte lata*, 60; Pasternak, *W marszu*, 184–85. On Pasternak, see *Polski słownik biograficzny*.

35. Sokorski, *Tamte lata,* 51–52.

36. Naszkowski, *Lata próby*, 310.

37. With their humanistic embrace of ordinary topics and the harmony of rhyme and rhythm members of Skamander are considered to have "played the paradoxical role of the traditional wing of the avant-garde." Shore, *Caviar and Ashes*, 23.

38. Sokorski, *Tamte lata*, 52–53.

39. Naszkowski, *Lata próby*, 311; on Ważyk, see Bikont and Szczęsna, *Lawina i kamienie*, 17–28.

40. Wende, *Ta ziemia*, 128.

41. Member of VKP (b) since 1931; in early July, 1944 he was deputy commander for political affairs of the second infantry division. See Bordiugow, *Polska-ZSRR*, 74, fn. 4.

42. Wende, *Ta ziemia*, 128. On Antoni Alster, see *Słownik biograficzny działaczy polskiego ruchu robotniczego*, vol. 1.

43. Bikont and Szczęsna, *Lawina i kamienie*, 19; Shore, *Caviar and Ashes*, 165–69.

44. Urbanek, *Broniewski*, 132–33.

45. See Pryzwan, *Wspomnienia*, 129.

46. Urbanek, *Broniewski*, 154, 171.

47. Ibid., 213–17.

48. Wende, *Ta ziemia*, 129.

49. Werth, *Russia at War*, 594.

50. Ibid.

51. Ibid., 595.

52. Naszkowski, *Lata próby*, 321–23.

53. Grzelak, Stańczyk, and Zwoliński, *Armia Berlinga*, 95.

54. Nalepa, *Oficerowie Armii Radzieckiej*, 16–17. The figure 330,000 refers to the date May 1, 1945—see Grzelak, Stańczyk, and Zwoliński, *Armia Berlinga*, 120.

55. Soviet Poles made up 65 percent of Red Army officers serving in the Polish units in May–July 1943 and 53 percent in March 1944, though overall, between May 1943 and May 1945 they made up 17.84 percent or 3,510 men—see Nalepa, *Oficerowie Armii Radzieckiej*, 16–18.

56. Różański, *Śladami wspomnień*, 72.

57. Naszkowski, *Lata próby*, 278–79. Communist historiography often classified Red Army officers with Polish names as Poles to emphasize the national character of the army. Of all "Polish" officers in the First Army understood in this way, 22.5 percent were in fact Soviet citizens. Their proportion was greater on higher levels of command (66 percent among army commanders), and much lower on the level of platoons (10.4 percent). See Kusiak, *Oficerowie 1 Armii*, 26–27. On the purges of ethnic Poles in the USSR during the 1930s, see Snyder, *Bloodlands*, ch. 3.

58. Sokorski admitted to having been aware of the crime during a meeting with scholars in Poland's Military Historical Institute in 1989—see Grzelak, Stańczyk, and Zwoliński, *Armia Berlinga*, 333n14; Jaroszewicz and Roliński, *Przerywam milczenie*, 47. In *Lata próby* Naszkowski mentions that "we did not know the truth about Stalin," 293.

59. Naszkowski, *Lata próby*, 293.

60. Gilroy, *The Black Atlantic*, 3.

61. Putrament, *Pół wieku*, 2:179; Naszkowski, *Lata próby*, 293.

62. Nalepa, *Oficerowie Armii Radzieckiej*, 24.

63. Naszkowski, *Lata próby*, 327–29; Nalepa, *Oficerowie Armii Radzieckiej*, 24; Honkisz, *W pierwszym szeregu*, 33.

64. Sokorski, *Polacy pod Lenino*, 14–15.

65. "Deklaracja ideowa," 361–65.

66. Berling would enter the Polish United Workers' Party only in 1963. See Szczurowski, *Dowódcy Wojska Polskiego*.

67. Grzelak, Stańczyk, and Zwoliński, *Armia Berlinga*, 34–35; "1943 r., wrzesień—październik [rejon Wiaźmy i Smoleńska]—Tezy programowe pt.: "O co walczymy", opracowane dla aktywu 1 Dywizji 1 Korpusu (Materiały do dyskusji)," *Organizacja*, 4:98–100. See also Kersten, *The Establishment of Communist Rule*, 36, who points out that Sokorski and Prawin's references to "our camp" evoked associations with the pre-war, nationalist Camp of National Unity. Prawin served in this function between August 1943 and September 1944—see *Polski słownik biograficzny* (1935).

68. Różański, *Śladem wspomnień*, 114.

69. Bordiugow, *Polska-ZSRR*, 34n5; Wasilewska, "Wspomnienia Wandy Wasilew-skiej," 393. The Political Department of the division was the executive organ of the division's deputy commander for political affairs, and had its own chief and deputy chief. Zbiniewicz, *Armia Polska*, 54.

70. Sokorski, *Polacy pod Lenino*, 23.

71. Behrends, "Nation and Empire," 447.

72. Grzelak, Stańczyk, and Zwoliński, *Armia Berlinga*, 37.

73. "Wstęp do zarysu programu (tak zwane tezy nr. 2)," in Syzdek, *Dyskusje ideologiczno-polityczne*, 124–49. At roughly the same time in Poland, the first secretary of the newly created Polish Workers' Party (a reactivated KPP, which had been dissolved by the Comintern in 1938) Władysław Gomułka published the party's manifesto, "What We Are Fighting For,"outlining similar proposals. The two groups of communists had no contact with each other.

74. Jaczyński, *Zygmunt Berling*, 315–16.

75. Jaroszewicz and Roliński, *Przerywam milczenie*, 59; Mołdawa, *Ludzie władzy*, 423.

76. Sobór, *Jakub Berman*, 103; on Zawadzki, see the entry in Szczurowski, *Dowódcy wojska polskiego*.

77. Zhukov's name has been a source of mistakes in both primary documents and secondary sources. Various documents refer to him as Iurii G. Zhukov, Georgii S. Zhukov, I. V. Zhukov, or simply Zhukov (Jaroszewicz's usage). Most likely this is one and the same person, and part of the confusion arises from the existence of a famous Soviet marshal of the same name, Georgii K. Zhukov as well as Georgii Aleksandrovich Zhukov, deputy editor of *Pravda* in 1952–57 and then chairman of the State Committee for Cultural Relations with Foreign Countries, the successor of VOKS, in 1957–60 (on him, see Goriachev, *Tsentral'nyi komitet*). On Iurii K. Zhukov, the NKVD functionary and Soviet plenipotentiary see: Honkisz, *W pierwszym szeregu*, 34; Nalepa, *Oficerowie Armii Radzieckiej*, 13; Grzelak, Stańczyk, and Zwoliński, *Armia Berlinga*, 30; for the mistaken references to Georgii S. Zhukov, see Wasilewska, "Wspomnienia Wandy Wasilewskiej," 389n131; Bordiugow, *Polska-ZSRR*, 34–35 and Kersten, *The Establishment of Communist Rule*, 93; Georgii Sergeevich Zhukov figures in Różański's memoirs *Śladem wspomnień*, 133; finally, for I. W. Zhukov, see Bordiugow, *Polska-ZSRR*, 74–75. In an unauthorized interview with Teresa Torańska, Jakub Berman suggested that Sokorski's inspiration to draft "Theses number 1" was Aleksandr Shcherbakov. See Torańska, *Oni*, 249.

78. Jaroszewicz and Roliński, *Przerywam milczenie*, 56–60; see also Zhukov's report to Shcherbakov, in which he lays the entire blame on Sokorski, in Bordiugow, *Polska-ZSRR*, 34–35.

79. Dańko, *Nie zdążyli do Andersa*, 296.

80. Ibid., 20.

81. See, for example, Skurnowicz, "Soviet Polonia."

82. Grzelak, Stańczyk, and Zwoliński, *Armia Berlinga*, 213.

83. Putrament, *Pół wieku*, 2:190–91.

84. Honkisz, *W pierwszym szeregu*, 62–64, 69, 73; Grzelak, Stańczyk, and Zwoliński, *Armia Berlinga*, 43.

85. Grzelak, Stańczyk, and Zwoliński, *Armia Berlinga*, 101; Honkisz, *W pierwszym szeregu*, 61, 104.

86. Grosz, *Gdy rodziło się Wojsko Polskie*, 7.

87. Honkisz, *W pierwszym szeregu*, 58–63.

88. Naszkowski, *Lata próby*, 338; Sokorski, *Polacy pod Lenino*, 33.

89. Naszkowski, *Lata próby*, 370–73. Bromberg was also the Third Division's senior instructor for the department of "special propaganda" among enemy soldiers. See Śnieć, "Działalność aparatu propagandy," 64.

90. CAW, syg. III/4/231, k. 158.

91. Ibid., kk. 143, 154.

92. Ibid., k. 157.

93. Ibid., k. 158.

94. Ibid., k. 166.

95. Ibid., k. 167.

96. Nalepa, *Oficerowie Armii Radzieckiej*, 25.

97. See Thompson, "The Katyń Massacre."

98. CAW, syg. III/4/231, k. 151.

99. Jaczyński, *Zygmunt Berling*, 217–27. Włodzimierz Sokorski claims to have participated in a delegation to Katyn in late fall 1943, but he is likely making a mistake. See Zawiśliński, *Wyznania zdrajcy*, 78.

100. CAW, syg. III/4/231, kk. 144–45.

101. Kersten, *The Establishment of Communist Rule*, 39–40, 69, 106–7.

102. CAW, syg. III/4/231, k. 155.

103. Ibid.

104. Ibid., k. 156.

105. Ibid., kk. 143, 156, 166.

106. Ibid., k. 156.

107. Ibid., kk. 151, 157.

108. Zaloga, *Bagration*, 38.

109. Kersten, *The Establishment of Communist Rule*, 63.

110. Grzelak, Stańczyk, and Zwoliński, *Armia Berlinga* 216–17; for numbers, 106.

111. Grynberg, *Memorbuch*, 158; Różański, *Śladem wspomnień*, 130.

112. Grynberg, *Memorbuch*, 158.

113. Grzelak, Stańczyk, and Zwoliński, *Armia Berlinga*, 216, 218; in early November 1944, the First Belorussian Front was given to Zhukov and Rokossovsky was moved to command the Second Belorussian Front—see Richard Wolff, "Rokossovskii," 191.

114. For good, critical overviews of Rokossovskii's career, see Wolff, "Rokossovskii"; and Noskova, "K. K. Rokossovskii v Pol'she."

115. Grzelak, Stańczyk, and Zwoliński, *Armia Berlinga*, 85.

116. Kersten, *The Establishment of Communist Rule*, 33–34.

117. The consolidation took place on July 27, 1944. See Grzelak, Stańczyk, and Zwoliński, *Armia Berlinga*, 106 and n. 9.

118. For example, CAW, syg. III/4/276, k. 7.

119. Jaroszewicz and Roliński, *Przerywam milczenie*, 364; Mołdawa, *Ludzie władzy*, 365.

120. CAW, syg. III/5/197, k. 249; CAW, syg. III/4/276, kk. 26–27.

121. Grzelak, Stańczyk, and Zwoliński, *Armia Berlinga*, 100.

122. Ibid., 72. Żymierski thus replaced General Berling, who, together with General Aleksander Zawadzki, became his deputy commander.

123. Ibid.

124. CAW, syg. III/4/231, k. 57.

125. *Organizacja i działania bojowe*, 4:386 (reproduced in Baliszewski and Kunert, *Ilustrowany przewodnik*, 90.

126. CAW, syg. III/5/197, kk. 249–50.

127. Grynberg, *Memorbuch*, 150.

128. Lower-estimate figures (based on the army's official statistics that reflect pressure to Polonize) reveal the following numbers of ethnic Jews in the political apparatus of the army: October 1, 1943—23 out of 195 (11 percent); November 15, 1943—49 out of 261 (18 percent); January 1, 1944—58 out of 333 (17.4 percent). See Honkisz, *W pierwszym szeregu*, 58. His data appear to be based on Zbiniewicz, *Armia Polska*, 190. Klemens Nussbaum states that nearly 49 out of 210 (25 percent) of political officers were Jewish on January 31, 1944; see Nussbaum, "Jews in the Polish Army," 100. But that appears to be an error of reading the table in Zbiniewicz, *Armia Polska*, 190 (the figure 210 refers to the number of Polish political officers, not the total). On December 10, 1944, they made up 10.1 percent of staff in the political apparatus and 15.8 percent in the structures of jurisprudence of the First Army, as compared, for example, with infantry (4.5 percent) or artillery (1.6 percent)—see Kusiak, *Oficerowie 1 Armii*, 26, 186–87.

129. Henryk Werner was the editor in chief of the expanding press apparatus of the army. See Surgiewicz, "Z dziejów prasy frontowej." See also Szulzycer, "Żydzi w 1 Dywizji," 19–21. See also Haltof, *Polish Film and the Holocaust*, 13.

130. Grynberg, *Memorbuch*, 150. When approached by the NKVD recruiting agent, Bromberg himself at first protested, citing his own "incorrect looks" and the fact that there were already too many Jews among the officers.

131. During his first night in the Sel'tsy camp, Bromberg learned from fellow soldiers that Jews stood behind the war, the Polish defeat, and the occupation by the USSR and Germany, "because Jews rule everywhere. Even in Germany." Grynberg, *Memorbuch*, 149. Krystyna Kersten noted the reverse psychological mechanism whereby the popular perception of linkages between Jews and communism only complemented older Polish stereotypes about Jews; they only helped rationalize aggression and feelings of enmity against Poland's traditional "others." Kersten, *Polacy. Żydzi. Komunizm*, 133. Likewise, Bolesław Bierut was often thought to be Jewish because he was a communist. See Ibid., 79.

132. He was born into a family of Polish peasants, but although on the VKP(b) questionnaire he listed Polish as his native language, he was fluent only in Russian and Belarusian. Sokolovskii participated in the political life of the Polish units on several

levels, at first, as deputy commander for political affairs of the Third Infantry Regiment, then as an instructor in courses for political officers. From April 1944, he served as inspector of the Political Department's Organizational-Instructional Department, and then, from June 1944, Sokolovskii was on again as deputy commander for political affairs of the Armored Brigade. For age and other biographical data, see of the uncatalogued Party information cards for member number 04789821, available at RGASPI; see also Putrament, *Pół wieku*, 2:176; Naszkowski, *Lata próby*, 288; Honkisz, *W pierwszym szeregu*, 35; on Sokolovskii's involvement in instructional activities, see CAW, syg. III-3-88, k. 11; on his duties as an inspector and political officer, see Bordiugow, *Polska-ZSRR*, 74n3.

133. For another photograph of the same moment, see Naszkowski, *Lata próby*, 305, verso.

134. Bordiugow, *Polska-ZSRR*, 74–81.

135. Kersten, *Polacy. Żydzi. Komunizm*, 134.

136. After the war, some Poles openly joked that the Berling Army was Jewish—see Trznadel's conversation with Marian Brandys in Trznadel, *Hańba domowa*, 228. Putrament brings up a similar but much grimmer story, also highlighting the contrast between the girl's beauty and her anti-Semitic comments in *Pół wieku*, 2:267–68.

137. Grynberg, *Memorbuch*, 162.

138. CAW, syg. III-4-231, k. 39. Report from September 18, 1944.

139. CAW, syg. III-4-231, k. 30. Report from September 21, 1944. In Polish: "Marzą o otrzymaniu miana 'Warszawskich.'"

140. CAW, syg. III-4-231, k. 36. Report from September 20, 1944.

141. On the discrediting of the West, see Paczkowski, *Spring Will Be Ours*, 126.

142. Nalepa, *Oficerowie Armii Radzieckiej*, 17.

143. CAW, syg. II-5-197, k. 250.

144. Nalepa, *Oficerowie Armii Radzieckiej*, 25; on the poor Polish-language proficiency of Soviet officers, see CAW, syg. III-4-231.

145. CAW, syg. III-4-276, k. 7; the author's first name is missing from the document. In his memoirs, Naszkowski refers to an Oskar Okręt, but this is probably an error. See Naszkowski, *Lata próby*, 398. The man was most likely Zygmunt Okręt, who was the chief of the "special propaganda" department working with enemy combatants in July–August 1944 in the rank of captain—see Śnieć, "Działalność aparatu propagandy," 64. For much of the postwar decade, Zygmunt Okręt worked as director of the archives department of the Ministry of Public Security. See Piotrowski, *Poland's Holocaust*, 60. Okręt's public profile as security officer can also be accessed via the Institute of National Remembrance: http://katalog.bip.ipn.gov.pl/showDetails.do?lastName=Okr%C4%99t&idx=&katalogId=2&subpageKatalogId=2&pageNo=1&osobaId=22856& (accessed September 12, 2012).

146. Nalepa, *Oficerowie Armii Radzieckiej*, 24–25; CAW, syg. III-4-292, k. 64; CAW, syg. III-5-201, kk. 155–56.

147. CAW, syg. III-4-231, kk. 30, 37.

148. Mołdawa, *Ludzie władzy*, 364.

149. CAW, syg. III-4-290, k. 567.

150. CAW, syg. III-4-231, k. 38

151. Ibid., k. 57.

152. Behrends, "Nation and Empire," 446.

153. Różański, *Śladem wspomnień*, 142–43.

154. CAW, syg. III-4-290, k. 541. Maskalan's brief but informative biography can be found in his obituary in *Wojskowy Przegląd Historyczny* 93, no. 3 (July–September 1980): 324–25; see also Kusiak, *Oficerowie 1 Armii*, 177.

155. Żenczykowski, *Polska Lubelska*, 97, 107; Grzelak, Stańczyk, and Zwoliński, *Armia Berlinga*, 286.

156. Aleksander Zawadzki was deputy commander for political affairs and then Politbiuro member in 1944–54; Roman Zambrowski, chief of the Political Department in the army in 1944 was a member of the Politbiuro in 1945–63; Piotr Jaroszewicz has been discussed in the text. Mieczysław Mietkowski became vice-minister of Public Security but was removed in 1954, see Paczkowski, "Jews in the Polish Security Apparatus," 464.

157. Krawczyk, *Pierwsza próba indoktrynacji*, 5–24; on Matuszewski, see Nałkowska, *Dzienniki*, part 1, 2:558–59.

158. Krasucki, *Międzynarodowy komunista*, 102.

159. Madej, *Kino, władza, publiczność*, 57.

160. Minc was chief of the Political Department until July 7, 1943, when he became prosecutor in the Kościuszko Division. See Zbiniewicz, *Armia Polska*, 44, 54; "Minc, Hilary" in Dubiel and Kozak, *Polacy w II Wojnie Światowej*, 108.

161. On July 21, 1944, V. V. Mochalov of the All-Slavic Committee reported that the ZPP activists who were preparing the celebrations of the anniversary of the Battle of Grunwald, in which Polish and Lithuanian and Russian armies defeated the Teutons, were excessively nationalist. The Pole Andrzej Nowicki is said to have objected to the Russian prop and set design by arguing that "the helmet on the painting is slightly too Russian, it might be too offensive to the Poles." The Poles also insisted on changes to the program of the celebration as well. For example, they preferred that a Pole, and not a Russian, give an opening address. They succeeded in striking out from the speech of the Soviet representative Paletskis references to Vilnius (a Polish city before the war) as an ancient Lithuanian city, arguing that "there is no need to irritate a wounded bull [i.e., the Poles] with a red rag." Furthermore, Nowicki demanded the enumeration of ethnic groups that defeated the Teutonic Knights in such a way that "the Poles were listed before the Russians." The Poles also protested about the drafts of speeches of the Soviet representatives, in which the latter described the Russian people as an older brother of the Slavic peoples. After the standoff, the Poles made a phone call to Jakub Berman who supported them and demanded from the Soviet officials that the changes be made. The Soviet officials complied despite protests. In criticizing the ZPP, Mochalov especially singled out Nowicki, "who always instigates *nationalist* demands, and tries to spread dissatisfaction in the Polish community." Emphasis mine. See GARF, f. 8581, op. 2, d. 122, ll. 44–47.

162. On Modzelewski, see *Polski słownik biograficzny* (2005).

163. Mołdawa, *Ludzie władzy*, 437.

164. On Hoffman, see Mielczarek, *Od "Nowej Kultury"*, 84, and Sobór, *Jakub Berman*, 373.

165. Olejniczak, *Polsko-radzieckie kontakty*, 20n33. On Ochab, see "General Edward Ochab" in Szczurowski, *Słownik biograficzny*, 98.

166. Bikont and Szczęsna, *Lawina i kamienie*, 17.

167. Putrament, *Pół wieku*, 2:91; Wasilewska, "Wspomnienia Wandy Wasilewskiej," 341–42; Schatz, *The Generation*, 155, 160.

168. Grynberg, *Memorbuch*, 151; Colonel Petr Kozhushko was chief of the Polish military counterintelligence force, staffed nearly entirely with Red Army officers, and Sokorski's shadow agent. His name comes up regularly in Sokorski's memoirs. On one occasion, Kozhushko was portrayed as almost vulnerable, anxious about Sokorski's upcoming attempt to explain the significance of the Soviet-Polish war of 1920 to the soldiers. Another time, he authored a menacing report accusing Sokorski of excessive tolerance of the Division Theater's risqué piece of satire (Sokorski claims to have found this out from Berling). Nalepa, *Oficerowie Armii Radzieckiej*, 22; Sokorski, *Polacy pod Lenino*, 24; Sokorski, *Tamte lata*, 54.

169. For the song "Oka," see Pasternak, *W marszu*, 190–91.

170. Putrament, *Pół wieku*, 4:11.

CHAPTER 2

1. Różański, *Śladem wspomnień*, 139–40.

2. On the relevant aspects of Berman's background, see Shore, "Children of the Revolution," 29–35. The quotation comes from Shore's *Caviar and Ashes*, 149, where she also writes that "Jakub Berman's name appeared on a Comintern list of suspected spies and provocateurs."

3. "Beseda ministra pol'skogo pravitel'stva Bermana s korrespondentom gazety 'Vol'nost.'" GARF f. R-8581, op. 2, d.172, ll. 12–14. Sokolovskii co-conducted the interview with major Vladimir Shirkin.

4. For further discussion of the term, see Naimark, "Post-Soviet Russian Historiography," esp. 567–75; Brzezinski, *The Soviet Bloc*.

5. Archiwum Ruchu Robotniczego, vol. 7 (Warsaw, 1981), cited in Krystyna Kersten, *Narodziny systemu władzy*, 38. In January 1946, Gomułka likewise complained to the commander in chief of the Red Army forces stationed in Poland, Konstantin Rokossovskii, and the Soviet ambassador Viktor Lebedev about the violence and robberies of Red Army units in Poland's western "Recovered Territories," see Behrends, *Die erfundene Freundschaft*, 107.

6. Borodziej, "Dekada powojenna," 565.

7. On June 30, 1956, the population of Poland was 23,767. See *Rocznik Demograficzny 2012 / The Demographic Yearbook of Poland 2012*, 28.

8. According to lower-end estimates, in 1944–48, the Polish security organs arrested some 156,000 people. Also, "during 1945–1948 (Red Army and NKVD victims not included) the number of people killed in combat, pursuit, and ambushes reached 8,668."

See Dudek and Paczkowski, "Poland," 272–75; and Paczkowski, "Polska droga przez stalinizm," 12.

9. Dudek and Paczkowski, "Poland," 240.

10. Checinski suggests that throughout Eastern Europe "Jews—and especially those with Jewish names or striking Semitic features—could be placed in the most controversial posts (for example, those dealing with Church affairs or the campaign against the political underground) and thus deflect antiregime feelings into anti-Semitism." See *Poland*, 63. Adam Bromberg pointed out a similar logic—asking himself why he was requested to summon General Jerzy Kirchmayer to his office and remain present during his arrest in 1950, he reasoned that "when a Pole arrested another Pole, he wanted to have a Jew in the background." See Grynberg, *Memorbuch*, 207–8.

11. Scholars and contemporaries have remarked that the Soviets courted ethnic Jews to bring them into the repressive security apparatus hoping that, as traditional pariahs in Polish society, they would be more loyal allies in the communists' crackdown against the opposition. See Miłosz, "Anti-Semitism in Poland," 37; Schatz, *The Generation*, 212–13, 225–26; Werblan, *Stalinizm w Polsce*, 23; Smolar, "Jews as a Polish Problem," 50, 59–60; Korboński, *The Jews and the Poles*, 78–79. On this, see also Checinski, *Poland*, 11. In addition, in regard to the Polish case, L. W. Gluchowski pointed out, "Stalin's wartime and postwar nationalities and cadres policy . . . tended to prefer those who had taken Soviet citizenship and Soviet party membership as well as 'comrades of Jewish origins' to many important posts." See Gluchowski, "The Defection of Jozef Swiatlo."

12. Charles Gati claims that "among Jews who joined the [communist] movement after World War II many did so because of recent experiences in concentration camps and labor battalions. They sought to avenge the recent past, believing that the Soviet Union and the Hungarian Communist party, having distinguished themselves in the struggle against Fascism in general and Nazi Germany in particular, would support their claim for retribution." See Gati, *Hungary and the Soviet Bloc*, 101. Jaff Schatz suggests that for some Jews who joined the security services, "equal to or more important than their sense of personal duty was a desire for revenge and a personal rage. Their families had been murdered and the anti-Communist underground was, in their perception, a continuation of essentially the same anti-Semitic and anti-Communist tradition. They hated those who had collaborated with the Nazis and those who opposed the new order with almost the same intensity and knew that as Communists, or as both Communists and Jews, they were hated at least in the same way." See Schatz, *The Generation*, 226.

13. For instance, those Soviet officials who were actively following Polish affairs on the ground were worried that the large proportions of Jews in the security apparatus would undermine the Soviet goals by channeling anti-Semitism into anticommunism and anti-Sovietism—see, for example, a report by N. N. Selivanovskii (an adviser to, but a de facto chief of the Polish security) to Lavrentii Beria dated October 20, 1945 in Volokitina et al., *Vostochnaia Evropa*, 1:267–70.

14. Thus according to Andrzej Werblan, a historian, biographer of Gomułka, and member of the communist elite, the secrecy of the security services also made the presence of Jews more tolerable—see Werblan, *Stalinizm w Polsce*, 79. On the Jewish role in the security services, see Paczkowski "Jews in the Polish Security Apparatus." Paczkowski examines carefully the available statistical data for 1944–56, and concludes that "Jews were over-represented, occupied higher rather than lower positions, and that the higher level, the greater their proportion" (p. 458). For example, in the Head Office of the Ministry of Public Security (MBP) officials of Jewish nationality made up 24.7 percent of the total, and "wavered around" in subsequent years, until 1956 (p. 457). Dudek and Paczkowski write elsewhere: "Out of 450 people holding executive post between 1944–1956 at the MBP headquarters, 21 per cent were prewar Communist Party members or of its youth organisation, with nearly 30 per cent of Jewish descent. Virtually all of the latter category were saved from the Holocaust only because they had been deported to the interior of the Soviet Union in 1940 or fled before the advancing front in 1941. The local offices had far fewer security executives of Jewish descent, but there were significant regional differences. . . . This situation was conducive to latent anti-Semitic tendencies within the apparatus itself, while in society it confirmed the 'Jewish-communist' stereotype." See Dudek and Paczkowski, "Poland," 241. The proportion of Jews in communist institutions increased gradually in the immediate postwar years as a result of growing anti-Semitism and subsequent Jewish emigration. In 1947, 14 percent of the remaining Jewish population was employed in state administration, while some 10,000 out of 70–80,000 Jews belonged to the PZPR. See Schatz, *The Generation*, 208–9, 218–9 and 369n5. The party and state hierarchies overlapped, and many apparatchiks juggled multiple functions. Schatz also writes that although there were "few" seasoned communists among the party's paid political employees after World War II, "they constituted the trusted core of the party cadres, occupying key positions on the central and regional levels" (ibid., 218); on Jewish visibility in top party, state, and diplomatic cadres after World War II see also 206, 229. Hugh Seton-Watson, a contemporary scholar and observer, wrote that "the leadership of the Communist parties of Poland and Hungary is very largely of Jewish origin," *East European Revolution*, 317; Aleksander Wat wrote that "Many of the wives of today's ministers, many of the egerias of the communist poets, today's high-ranking women officials in the UB [Polish equivalent of the KGB] were either from the needleworkers' union or the Jewish nurses' union." Wat, *My Century*, 3. Both contemporary observers and later scholars suggested that the large proportion of Jews in communist institutions and their relative prominence was bound to and did exacerbate Poles' anti-Semitic feelings after the war—see Schatz, *The Generation*, 206; Kersten, *The Establishment of Communist Rule*; Werblan, *Stalinizm w Polsce*, 23; Schaff, *Pora na spowiedź*, 139; Lukowski and Zawadzki, *A Concise History of Poland*, 284; On the Hungarian case, see also Gati, *Hungary and the Soviet Bloc*, 107. Padraic Kenney noted that as late as 1945, Polish workers drew on prewar stereotypes to voice anti-Semitic sentiments, without linking Jews to communism. See Kenney, *Rebuilding Poland*, 111. Michael Steinlauf also points out that the hostility against Jews in postwar Poland "was also rooted in the Polish experience of the Holocaust, in the new accusatory death-tainted image of the

Jew that infused the traditional stereotype." Steinlauf, *Bondage to the Dead*, 60. For an alternative view, see Gross, *Fear*.

15. In the Hungarian context, where Jews were even more overrepresented than in Poland, Peter Kenez wrote that "Anti-Semitism among the Hungarian people continued to be a handicap to the Communist Party in its struggle for power, and therefore it had considerable political significance." See Kenez, *Hungary*, 46, 292.

16. Kersten, *Polacy. Żydzi. Komunizm*, 79.

17. Behrends, "Nation and Empire," 450–51; Behrends, *Die erfundene Freundschaft*, 108–10.

18. Paczkowski, "Polish-Soviet Relations," 8; also Werblan, "Conversation," 138.

19. GARF, f. R-8581, op. 1, d. 148, l. 13.

20. GARF, f. R-8581, op. 2, d. 172, l. 44. Lebedev was ambassador to Poland in 1945–51; see Gromyko, *Diplomaticheskii slovar'*, vol. 2.

21. Sobór, *Jakub Berman*, 146–47; Korboński, *W imieniu Rzeczypospolitej*, 320.

22. GARF, f. R-8581, op. 2, d. 172, l. 45.

23. At the turn of 1945/46 there were forty-three of them. They were completely dismantled in mid-1946, which means that the Soviets could not use them for distribution after that. Krogulski, *Okupacja w imię sojuszu*, 11–21.

24. "Pismo Miejskiej Rady Narodowej w Otwocku do MIP w Warszawie," dated June 28, 1945. AAN MIP 168/II-688, kk. 1–6. MIP sent a letter to the Polish Ministry of Foreign Affairs asking for intervention in this matter. AAN MIP 168/II-688, k. 7.

25. For symbolic implications of iron and steel in the Cold War context, see David-Fox, "The Iron Curtain," 16.

26. Władyka, "W prasie zapisane," 54.

27. Vladimir Pechatnov has mostly treated the bureau's western operations in the two postwar years: see "Exercise in Frustration." Nina Petrova focused largely on the World War II period in *Antifashistskie komitety v SSSR*.

28. Gosudarstvennyi arkhiv Rossiiskoi Federatsii (State Archive of the Russian Federation), henceforth: GARF, fond R-8581, opis' 2, delo 154, list 25–26.

29. Ibid., d. 154, l. 27.

30. Ibid., d. 133, ll. 4, 6.

31. The contemporary Michael Voslensky said in an interview: "The *Sovinformburo* was [in fact] an agency of the party Central committee, of the international department. In the beginning it was even located in the same building as the CPSU Central Committee. Then it moved to the former German embassy. . . . *Sovinformburo* was not officially tied to the Ministry of Foreign affairs, except inasmuch as there was a 'personal union' with Lozovsky." See Ra'anan and Lukes, *Inside the Apparat*, 130–31.

32. Draft decision of the Central Committee of the VKP(b) titled "On the Work of SIB," signed by A. Vyshinskii and G. Aleksandrov and sent to V. M. Molotov and G. M. Malenkov on June 29, 1945, RGASPI, f. 17, op. 125, d. 316, l. 18.

33. Ibid.

34. "Otchet otdela pechati Pol'shi i Chekhoslovakii." June 27, 1946. RGASPI, f. 17, op. 125, d. 387, l. 135. Beginning in June 1948, it also began servicing Hungary, and the department was renamed accordingly. "Otchet otdela pechati Pol'shi, Chekhoslovakii

i Vengrii za 1948 god i pervyi kvartal 1949 goda." April 1949. GARF, f. R-8581, op. 2, d. 245, l. 216. Later still—at least in 1954–55—it was called the Department of "European People's Democracies."

35. Based on Lozovskii's own testimony to the Party's Verification Commission in 1946, during an interrogation by A. A. Kuznetsov. "Stenogramma soveshchaniia komissii tsk vkpb ot 28 iunia–8 iulia '46 po voprosu o rabote SIB." RGASPI, f. 17, op. 125, d. 385, l. 41.

36. "Otchet o rabote predst. SIB v Pol'she za 1946 g." December 1946. GARF, f. R-8581, op. 1, d. 207, l. 9. On Lozovskii, see Gromyko, *Diplomaticheskii slovar'*, vol. 2.

37. The head of the Department of Poland, Czechoslovakia, and Hungary, Volozhenin, confirmed these goals in 1949, adding that in the general work of the department, he was guided by the decisions of the Central Committee VKP(b) from October 9, 1946 and June 25, 1947. GARF, f. R-8581, op. 2, d. 245, ll. 216–17.

38. "Dokladnaia zapiska," March 15, 1945. GARF, f. 8581, op. 2., d.158, l. 39. The Home Army was loyal to the Polish government in London and actively battled both the Germans and the Soviets.

39. Orlov's report to S. A. Lozovskii titled "O rabote predstavitel'stva SIB v Pol'she za 1946 g.," December 1946. GARF, f. R-8581, op. 1, d. 207, l. 29.

40. Paczkowski, "Polish-Soviet Relations," 8; Brzezinski, *The Soviet Bloc*, 97–100.

41. GARF, f. R-8581, op. 1, d. 207, l. 10–11.

42. Ibid., l. 13.

43. "Dokladnaia zapiska,"' March 15, 1945. GARF, f. R-8581, op. 2., d. 158, l. 36.

44. Ibid., l. 38.

45. "O rabote predstavitel'stva SIB v iiune, 1946," July 12, 1946. GARF, f. R-8581, op. 1, d. 207, l. 28.

46. For example, a letter from V. Sokolovskii to Volozhenin. Ibid., d. 264, l. 563. See also the discussion below.

47. Stykalin, "Politika SSSR," 56.

48. In 1947, Orlov observed the "curious fact" that nobody in the PPR's Central Committee "was even thinking about centralizing the press." See GARF, f. R-8581, op. 1, d. 207, l. 15; for more extreme views, even from 1945, see GARF, f. R-8581, op. 1, d. 148, ll. 16–17.

49. Naimark, *The Russians in Germany*, 467.

50. On other institutions, see Stykalin, "Politika SSSR," 50–62.

51. Pechatnov, "Exercise in Frustration," 3–8.

52. Untitled document dated March 2, 1945, GARF, f. 8581, op. 2, d. 158, l. 51; "O rabote predstavitel'stva SIB v iiune 1946." July 12, 1946. Ibid., op. 1, d. 207, ll. 5, 6, 27.

53. Curry, *Poland's Journalists*, 39.

54. The PSL press dominated the populist/peasant press in Poland, which, even when taken as a whole, composed a fraction of the total press market: 7.1 percent in 1944, 2.7 percent in 1945, and only 1.9 percent in 1949. Kubicka, "Charakterystyka statystyczna," 40. On restrictions on PSL's press, see Kersten, *The Establishment of Communist Rule*, 193, 195.

55. Słomkowska, *Prasa w PRL*, 223.

56. GARF, f. R-8581, op. 1, d. 207, l. 16.

57. Ibid.

58. Krasucki, *Międzynarodowy komunista*, 100; Bikont and Szczęsna, *Lawina i kamienie*, 22.

59. Cited in Krasucki, *Międzynarodowy komunista*, 103.

60. Grynberg, *Memorbuch*, 202.

61. Krasucki, *Międzynarodowy komunista*, 106–7.

62. Bikont and Szczęsna, *Lawina i kamienie*, 25.

63. Fik, "Kultura polska," 223; Krasucki, *Międzynarodowy komunista*, 102; Krawczyk, *Pierwsza próba indoktrynacji*, 5–24.

64. Krasucki, *Międzynarodowy komunista*, 110.

65. Grynberg, *Memorbuch*, 201.

66. "Dokladnaia zapiska ob osveshchenii v pol'skoi presse vnutrennoi zhizni SSSR," June 9, 1945. GARF, f. R-8581, op.1., d. 146, ll. 24–25.

67. "Ob antisovetskikh tendentsiakh pol'skoi legal'noi pechati," February 21, 1946. GARF, f. R-8581, op. 2, d. 172, l. 28.

68. P. Galdin, an employee of Glavlit, made similar remarks about Borejsza; GARF, f. R-9425, op. 1, d. 308, l. 9.

69. GARF, f. R-8581, op. 1, d. 207, l. 17.

70. Ibid.

71. As Andrzej Paczkowski observed, Lebedev "enjoyed limited opportunities for making decision on Polish questions, and for all practical purposes was entrusted with the task of merely informing Moscow and passing on letters or oral information which he received from the Soviet capital." Moscow remained largely unresponsive to Lebedev's independent initiatives and left the passing on of suggestions to Soviet advisers, and personal meetings between the top leaders. See Paczkowski, "Polish-Soviet Relations," 11. On Lebedev's intrigues, see "Wstęp" in Kochański, *Polska w dokumentach*, 13.

72. GARF, f. R-8581, op. 2, d. 172, ll. 17–18.

73. GARF, f. R-8581, op. 1, d. 207, ll. 18–19.

74. Ibid., l. 15.

75. Lozovskii tells this to A. A. Kuznetsov, in RGASPI, f. 17, op. 125, d. 385, l. 21.

76. GARF, f. R-8581, op. 1, d. 207, l. 16.

77. Letter from Jerzy Putrament to the Propaganda Department of the Central Committee of the PPR, July 12, 1945. From Warsaw's Archiwum Akt Nowych (henceforth: AAN), sygnatura 295/X-24, karta 25.

78. RGASPI, f. 17, op. 125, d. 385, l. 71.

79. Stykalin, "Politika SSSR," 60.

80. See Gorlizki and Khlevniuk, *Cold Peace*.

81. Jarosiński, *Nadwiślański socrealizm*, 13.

82. See Hartmann, "Sowjetische 'Leitkultur,'" for example, 532.

83. Miłosz, *The Captive Mind*, xi.

84. Ibid., 169.

85. Ibid.

86. Shore, *Caviar and Ashes*, 263–64.

87. Fijałkowska, *Polityka i twórcy*, 33.

88. Wende, *Ta ziemia*, 221, 230.

89. Stykalin, "Politika SSSR," 51–52; Stykalin, "Ideologicheskaia i kul'turnaia ekspansiia," 17.

90. Maria Hirszowicz reflects on the complexities of the Polish intellectuals' choices in *Pułapki zaangażowania*, esp. 84–92.

91. Fik, "Kultura polska," 236.

92. Davies, *Rising '44*, 466–70.

93. Fik, "Kultura polska," 236.

94. Sobór, *Jakub Berman*, 55.

95. Miłosz, *The Captive Mind*, 146.

96. See Hollander, *Political Pilgrims*.

97. Shore, *Caviar and Ashes*, 58.

98. Ibid., 58–62, 79–81.

99. On the Western context, see Hollander, *Political Pilgrims*, 110; Mazuy, *Croire plutôt que voir?* The Polish writer Antoni Słonimski found himself ostracized after publishing his ambivalent account from a 1932 trip to the USSR titled *My Trip to Russia*. As Marci Shore observed, "Though Słonimski never parted with his skepticism, it was in this book that he revealed most poignantly how much he would have liked to believe, how much his heart was with socialism. He wished for the great experiment to succeed, and yet he saw that the two eggs fed to all schoolchildren each day were imaginary and suspected that the emperor could be naked." Shore, *Caviar and Ashes*, 113. On different reactions to Soviet Russia by Słonimski and Władysław Broniewski, see Urbanek, *Broniewski*, 132–34, and Shore, *Caviar and Ashes*, 118.

100. Pomianowski, "Torowanie drogi do wolności," 521.

101. Golon, "Dyplomaci Stalina," 556.

102. Ibid., 556–57.

103. GARF, f. R-5283, op. 22, d. 120, l. 43.

104. In the fall of 1945, the Soviet embassy employed fifteen individuals with diplomatic status, including the ambassador, two advisers, four secretaries, seven attachés, and one military attaché. Golon, "Ambasadorowie Stalina," 151, 154. After his return to Moscow, Iakovlev became the deputy director of VOKS, an important function, which he performed until 1957.

105. Wende, *Ta ziemia*, 207; Shore, *Caviar and Ashes*, 210–11, 250–51.

106. Trznadel, *Hańba Domowa*, 20–21.

107. GARF, f. R-5283, op. 22, d. 12, l. 139.

108. Agapkina, "Russkie kontakty Iaroslava Ivashkevicha," 29. A volume of Iwaszkiewicz's stories appeared in Moscow only in 1958.

109. GARF, f. R-5283, op. 22, d. 12, l. 93.

110. Ibid., l. 44.

111. Teresa Chylińska, "Fitelberg, Grzegorz" in Grove Music Online, www.oxford musiconline.com (accessed December 10, 2012).

112. GARF, f. R-5283, op. 22., d. 119, ll. 30–33.

113. Sir Frank Roberts cited in Vaksberg, *Stalin's Prosecutor*, 253.

114. AMSZ, z-6, w. 31, t. 475, k. 6. The same film (*Victory Parade*) praised Suvorov.

115. Caute, *The Dancer Defects*, 116.

116. GARF, f. R-5283, op. 22, d. 12, ll. 15–16.

117. Ibid., l. 141.

118. Olejniczak, *Polsko-radzieckie kontakty*, 15–16.

119. Panferova, *Fedor Panferov*, 35; Vsevolod Surganov mentions Emile Zola and Władysław Reymont in "Zhivaia sila," in *Fedor Panferov. Vospominaniia druzei*, 39.

120. Brooks, *Thank You, Comrade Stalin!* 207.

121. Caute, *The Dancer Defects*, 251.

122. Cited in Agapkina, "Russkie kontakty Iaroslava Ivashkevicha," 30.

123. Ibid.

124. Ibid.

125. Panferova, *Fedor Panferov*, 44–46.

126. Kozieł, "Koncepcje dotyczące prasy," 45–59.

127. Ciborska, *Dziennikarze z władzą*, 52, 124; Kozieł, "Koncepcje dotyczące prasy," 51.

128. Curry, *Poland's Journalists*, 39.

129. Bartoszewicz, *Polityka Związku Sowieckiego*, 269.

130. Volokitina and Murashko, "*Kholodnaia voina*," 42–68.

131. See Kramer, "Stalin, Soviet Policy."

132. Gomułka was arrested on August 2, 1951. See Paczkowski, *Spring Will Be Ours*, 240; on the circumstances surrounding Gomułka's fall, see Taras, "Gomulka's 'Rightist-Nationalist Deviation.'"

133. Grynberg, *Memorbuch*, 202.

134. See Fijałkowska, *Borejsza i Różański*, 115–24.

135. Grynberg, *Memorbuch*, 202.

136. GARF, f. R-5283, op. 22, d. 120, l. 23.

137. Korzon, *Polsko-radzieckie kontakty*, 54–55.

138. GARF, f. R-5283, op. 22, d. 120, ll. 24–25.

139. GARF, f. R-5283, op. 22, d. 12, ll. 129 /ob/-130.

140. Hixson, *Parting the Curtain*, 1–55; Lucas, "Mobilizing Culture." On the British case, see Aldrich, "Putting Culture into the Cold War" (Aldrich focuses on Britain's Cultural Relations Department's involvement with youth contacts).

141. See "Spravka ob anglo-amerikanskoi propaganda v Pol'she," GARF, f. R-5283, op. 22, d. 64, ll. 33–44, esp. l. 43; on the United States Information Service (USIS), see Tobia, *Advertising America*.

142. GARF, f. R-8581, op. 2, d. 133, k. 5. The official referred to an "Office of International Information" but probably meant the USIS.

143. The French operated through the French Institute—see GARF, f. R-5283, op. 22, d. 12, ll. 129–29 (ob); on Anglo-American propaganda, see GARF, f. R-5283, op. 22, d. 120, ll. 31–32.

144. RGASPI, f. 17, op. 125, d. 355, ll. 63–64. For some reason, MK's exports of Soviet books and periodicals to Poland were much lower than those to any other "People's Democracy" or Finland; see RGASPI, f. 17, op. 125, d. 608, k.52; RGASPI, f. 17, op. 125, d. 355, ll. 1–2.

145. See, for example, a July 3, 1947, memo from VOKS chairman V. Kemenov to I. G. Bol'shakov, Minister of Soviet Cinematography, GARF, f. R-5283, op. 22, d. 64, l. 90. On Bol'shakov, see Zalesskii, *Imperiia Stalina*.

146. Iakovlev's letter to the Department of Propaganda and Agitation (G. F. Aleksandrov); with copies sent to OVP (M. A. Suslov), MID SSSR (A. M. Aleksandrov); and VOKS (Kemenov). GARF, f. R-5283, op. 22, d. 64, l. 62.

147. Ibid., l. 63.

148. GARF, f. R-5283, op. 22, d. 12, l. 92.

149. Naimark, *The Russians in Germany*, 413.

150. AMSZ, z-6/w-31/t-473, kk. 3–4.

151. GARF, f. R-5283, op. 22, d. 64, l. 27; Naszkowski, *Paryż-Moskwa*, 196–97.

152. AMSZ, z-6/w-31/t-481, kk. 10–11; AMSZ, z-6/w-33/t-521, k. 49.

153. Brzezinski, *The Soviet Bloc*, 68.

154. A. S. Stykalin found that in the Soviet Zone of German Occupation, the greatest demand was for the Russian belles lettres. However, 80 percent of the Soviet Military Administration's publishing output consisted of political pamphlets produced in excessively high circulation. See Stykalin, "Politika SSSR," 56.

155. AMSZ, z-6, w. 31, t. 475, k. 7.

156. Stykalin, "Politika SSSR," 61.

157. GARF, f. R-5283, op. 22, d. 64, l. 90.

158. Ibid., l. 72.

159. Kenez, *Cinema and Soviet Society*, 188.

160. Zezina, *Sovetskaia khudozhestvennaia intelligentsiia*, 69–70.

161. GARF, f. R-5283, op. 22, d. 64, l. 115.

162. Caute, *The Dancer Defects*, 118; On the famine, see Zima, *Golod v SSSR*.

163. Zubok, *A Failed Empire*; Wettig, *Stalin and the Cold War*; Wettig, "Stalins Deutschland-Politik;" Donal O'Sullivan, "'Wer immer ein Gebiet besetzt; . . .'" Gibianskii, "Forsirovanie sovetskoi blokovoi politiki"; Mastny, *Russia's Road*.

164. The predecessor of the Otdel Vneshnei Politiki (The Foreign Policy Department, or OVP), the Department of International Information (OMI) was officially created in July 1944. But technically it had existed for one year since the dissolution of the Third International (Comintern), from which it inherited both the range of responsibilities and personnel. The OMI was transformed into the OVP on December 29, 1945, when most of the posts previously occupied by foreign communists were taken over by Soviet citizens. The OVP had acquired a controlling function over the MID (and other state institutions working on foreign propaganda including the Sovinformbiuro, TASS, VOKS, and MK)—"mostly on the staffing issues." In December 1948, the department was restructured into Otdel vneshnikh snoshenii (OVS). In March 1949, it was again restructured into the Foreign Policy Commission (Vneshnepoliticheskaia kommissia Politburo TsK). Molotov became the "curator" of the commission (as Polit-

buro member, since he had just lost the MID appointment) and Vagan G. Grigor'ian became the commission's director. In 1952 it was renamed as Kommissiia po sviazi s inostrannymi kompartiiami. Soon after Stalin's death, it became a "department" again and lasted as such until February 1957. See the editor's introduction to Bordiugow, *Polska-ZSRR*, 7–9. Unless otherwise noted, I refer to these various institutional transmutations as the "International Department."

165. Ibid. Some VOKS reports are addressed both to the MID and the CC's International Department. See, for example, Denisov's report to V. A. Zorin and V. G. Grigor'ian: GARF, f. R-5283, op. 22, d. 182, ll. 41–59.

166. GARF, f. R-5283, op. 22, d. 64, l. 62.

167. Behrends, *Die erfundene Freundschaft*, 117.

168. Korzon, *Polsko-radzieckie kontakty*, 40; Basiński and Walichnowski, *Stosunki polsko-radzieckie*, 134–135.

169. GARF, f. R-5283, op. 22, d. 120, l. 34. It was issued on October 27, 1947. See Korzon, *Polsko-radzieckie kontakty*, 40.

170. GARF, f. R-5283, op. 22, d. 12, l. 141.

171. Rubenstein, *Tangled Loyalties*, 110, 221.

172. Ibid., 110.

173. Ehrenburg, *Post-War Years*, 117–23.

174. Rubenstein, *Tangled Loyalties*, 204.

175. GARF, f. R-5283, op. 22, d. 120, l. 37.

176. GARF, f. R-5283, op. 22, d. 183, ll. 46–47.

177. Ibid., ll. 27–28.

178. Ibid., l. 27.

179. Ibid., l. 28–29.

180. GARF, f. R-5283, op. 22, d. 120, l. 43.

181. Behrends, "Agitation, Organization, Mobilization," 190.

182. AMSZ, z-6/w-35/t-553, kk. 8–10; AMSZ, z-7/w-14/t-120, k. 53; AMSZ, z-6/w-35/t-553, kk. 102–11, 124, 127, 158.

183. Naszkowski, *Paryż-Moskwa*, 215.

184. AMSZ, z-6/w-35/t-553, k. 158.

185. Stykalin, "Politika SSSR," 56; Kenez, *Hungary*, 197; Naimark, *The Russians in Germany*, 412–13.

186. AMSZ, z-6/w-35/t-553, k. 165.

187. Ibid., kk. 94–101.

188. Ibid., k. 124.

189. Bikont and Szczęsna, *Lawina i kamienie*, 103.

190. Ibid., 107.

191. See Sobór, *Jakub Berman*, 248–49; Shore, *Caviar and Ashes*, 270–73; Bikont and Szczęsna, *Lawina i kamienie*, 106–7; Dąbrowska, *Dzienniki*, 1:272–74; Torańska, *Oni*, 447–49.

192. Sobór, *Jakub Berman*, 224.

193. See Hołuj, *Dom pod Oświęcimiem*, 49.

194. Eustachiewicz, *Dramaturgia współczesna*, 204.

195. Hołuj, *Ciąg dalszy*, 65, 67.

196. Ibid., 75–77.

197. Hołuj joined the PPR shortly after the war—see "Hołuj, Tadeusz" in *Współcześni polscy pisarze i badacze literatury*.

198. Shore, "Children of the Revolution," 27, citing Jacek Leociak, "Powstanie w Getcie Warszawskim: W zwierciadle prasy," *Polska Izrael* 2 (March–April 1993): 9–12; on co-opting the Holocaust into the narrative of class struggle, see Grynberg, "The Holocaust in Polish Literature," 127, also cited in Kremer, "Introduction," xxxii.

199. Hołuj, *Ciąg dalszy*, 70, 74.

200. Sobór, *Jakub Berman*, 224.

201. Borejsza, "Krochmalizm czy realizm?" 2.

202. Brzezinski, *The Soviet Bloc*, 32.

203. Rieber, "Popular Democracy," esp. 127.

204. Wettig, "Stalins Deutschland-Politik."

205. For the two extreme poles in this controversy, see Volokitina, Murashko and Noskova, *Narodnaia demokratiia*; Gibianskii, "Forsirovanie sovetskoi blokovoi politiki."

206. Mar'ina and Miliakova, "Vvedenie" in *Totalitarizm*, 10.

CHAPTER 3

1. Bernov, *Zapiski diplomata*, 6.

2. See "Bernov, Iurii Vladimirovich" in Gromyko, *Diplomaticheskii slovar'* vol. 1.

3. Lustiger, *Stalin and the Jews*, 222. On the JAFC, see the introductory essays and documents in Rubenstein and Naumov, *Stalin's Secret Pogrom*.

4. On Abakumov and purges in the MGB, see Gorlizki and Khlevniuk, *Cold Peace*, 154, and Lustiger, *Stalin and the Jews*, 215.

5. Gorlizki and Khlevniuk, *Cold Peace*, 87; Pinkus, *The Soviet Government and the Jews*, 161, 195, 199.

6. On the details of the "anticosmopolitan" campaign, see Pinkus, *The Soviet Government and the Jews*, 151–64.

7. Kramer, "Stalin, Soviet Policy," 100.

8. Bernov, *Zapiski diplomata*, 6.

9. Ibid., 7.

10. On such pressuring, see Kramer, "Stalin, Soviet Policy," 73.

11. Zubok and Pleshakov, *Inside the Kremlin's Cold War*, 4.

12. Pikhoia, *Sovetskii Soiuz*, 15; Brooks, *Thank You, Comrade Stalin!* 206–7; Zubok, *A Failed Empire*, 9–10.

13. Bernov, *Zapiski diplomata*, 8.

14. Throughout the postwar period, the Polish leaders tended to consult Stalin directly on the all-important military, economic, and foreign-policy issues, and probably some domestic ones as well. In the breakthrough years of 1949–50 such personal meetings remained frequent. See Paczkowski, "Polish-Soviet Relations," 8–10.

15. Paczkowski, interview in "Communist Poland," 8; and Paczkowski, "Polska droga przez stalinizm,"12; on the comparative aspects of Stalinist terror, see McDermott and Stibbe, *Stalinist Terror in Eastern Europe*.

16. Persak, "Stalin as Editor."

17. For instance, unlike in Hungary and Czechoslovakia, religious orders continued to operate freely. See Rothschild and Wingfield, *Return to Diversity*, 102; Ramet, *Cross and Commissar*, 11–40.

18. Behrends, *Die erfundene Freundschaft*.

19. Bernov, *Zapiski diplomata*, 8.

20. Jarosiński, *Nadwiślański socrealizm*, 5.

21. Sobór, *Jakub Berman*, 351.

22. Urbanek, *Broniewski*, 276.

23. Torańska, *"Them"*, 113–14; Sobór, *Jakub Berman*, 375.

24. Andrzej Paczkowski makes this important point, citing Bierut's letter to his boss that begins with "Beloved and dear comrade Stalin." As the Polish historian observes, "obviously, respect was no longer enough and had to be accompanied by love." See "Polish-Soviet Relations," 11; See also Zawiśliński, *Wyznania zdrajcy*, 70–71.

25. Sobór, *Jakub Berman*, 236.

26. Ibid., 398; Torańska, *Oni*, 486.

27. Hodos, *Show Trials*, 148–49; see also Sobór, *Jakub Berman*, 397.

28. Djilas, "Antisemitizam" (Anti-Semitism), *Borba*, December 14, 1952, published in Pinkus, *The Soviet Government and the Jews*, 104; Kenez, *Hungary*, 292.

29. Szaynok, *Poland-Israel*, 243, 259; see also Jirásek and Małkiewicz, *Polska i Czechosłowacja*, 147, 149; Kichelewski, "Imagining 'the Jews.'"

30. Jerzy Putrament mentioned the strained relationship between the Berman brothers—see Volokitina, *Sovetskii faktor*, 2:198. According to anecdotal evidence, in May 1945, Berman condemned open anti-Zionist rhetoric—see Szaynok, *Poland-Israel*, 41.

31. Szaynok, *Poland-Israel*, 164–76, 241–43.

32. RGASPI, f. 17, op. 137, d. 78, ll. 320–21.

33. Fateev, *Obraz vraga*, 140–42. Published in 50,000 copies.

34. Parker, *Zagovor protiv mira*, 85–86.

35. Shore, *Caviar and Ashes*, 268; see also Fijałkowska, *Borejsza i Różański*.

36. Crowley, "Paris or Moscow," 777–79; the description comes from an extended passage from Leopold Tyrmand's *Dziennik 1954* (Warsaw: TenTen, 1995), 204, translated into English by Crowley.

37. Zawiśliński, *Wyznania zdrajcy*, 59.

38. In this latter capacity, he related meetings with representatives of Western governments to the adviser to the Soviet embassy in France on the Polish position concerning the Marshall Plan on July 4, 1947. See Volokitina, *Vostochnaia Evropa*, 1:665–67. Shortly after the Rajk show trial two years later, and with "evident satisfaction," Putrament told the Soviet ambassador to France, A. E. Bogomolov, about the unfolding class struggle in Poland. Volokitina, *Sovetskii faktor*, 2:198.

39. Sobór, *Jakub Berman*, 351, 360; Fijałkowska, *Polityka i twórcy*, 136. On Sokorski's "newspeak," see Nałkowska, *Dzienniki*, 2:149; Putrament threatened Aleksander Wat by quoting a Russian saying in Russian during one of the Writers' Union meetings in 1952—see Shore, *Caviar and Ashes*, 282.

40. Mackiewicz quoted in Pasierski, *Miłosz i Putrament*, 233.

41. Putrament, *Pół wieku*, 4: 91–95, 113–14.

42. Zawiśliński, *Wyznania zdrajcy*, 19.

43. Ibid., 49.

44. For a full list of state prize recipients in 1950–52, see Fijałkowska, *Polityka i twórcy*, 251–55.

45. Tompkins, "Composing for and with the Party," esp. 274–77.

46. See the discussion of the classical music competitions below.

47. Pasierski, *Miłosz i Putrament*, 233.

48. Ibid., 233.

49. On this stage in Wat's life, see Shore, *Caviar and Ashes*, 273–76, 280–83.

50. Urbanek, *Broniewski*, 255.

51. Shore, *Caviar and Ashes*, 192.

52. Urbanek, *Broniewski*, 171.

53. Ibid., 226, 228.

54. Ibid., 278, 284.

55. Bikont and Szczęsna, *Ławina i kamienie*, 128.

56. For translations, see http://kapuscinski.info/ksiazki (accessed January 30, 2013).

57. Kapuściński, *Imperium*.

58. The quotation comes from Domosławski, *Ryszard Kapuściński: A Life*, 42. Subsequently, I will be referring to the Polish edition, Domosławski, *Kapuściński. Non-fiction*, 65, 83.

59. Bocheński speaking to Trznadel in *Hańba domowa*, 257.

60. Domosławski, *Kapuściński. Non-fiction*, 86.

61. Cited in ibid., 96.

62. Ibid.

63. On Woroszylski, see Nałkowska, *Dzienniki*, 2:290.

64. Noskova, "K. K. Rokossovskii v Pol'she," 83.

65. Paczkowski, "Polish-Soviet Relations," 9.

66. On his looks, see Grynberg, *Memorbuch*, 206; Wolff, "Rokossovsky," 179.

67. Grynberg, *Memorbuch*, 206.

68. Ibid. In order to popularize Rokossovskii, Berman suggested to Lebedev that some Poles' petitions to repatriate their family members from the USSR (some of whom were under arrest) to Poland should be considered favorably. See Volokitina, *Sovetskii faktor*, 2:247.

69. Grynberg, *Memorbuch*, 206.

70. Behrends, *Die erfundene Freundschaft*, 142; on propaganda about Rokossovskii, see 141–46.

71. Skrzypek, *Mechanizmy uzależnienia*, 248; also, Volokitina, *Vostochnoia Evropa*, 2:278n4, and 276–77; Noskova, "K. K. Rokossovskii v Pol'she," 82; Behrends, *Die erfundene Freundschaft*, 146–49.

72. GARF, f. R-5283, op. 22, d. 183, l. 21.

73. Ibid., d. 307, l. 126.

74. Radio subscribers tripled between 1948 and 1955, from 974,000 to 3,057,000. Fijałkowska, *Polityka i twórcy*, 142.

75. Kochański, *Polska w dokumentach*, 31; GARF, f. R-5283, op. 22, d. 128, kk. 34–35.

76. GARF, f. R-5283, op. 22, d. 307, l. 139.

77. Kochański, *Polska w dokumentach*, 31–34. On Kirsanov, see Gromyko, *Diplomaticheskii slovar' v trekh tomakh*, vol. 2.

78. Kirsanov also mentions Czechoslovakia. For the other countries, see a memo from K. D. Levychkin to V. A. Zorin also from March 21, 1949 in Volokitina, *Vostochnaia Evropa*, 2:41–43.

79. On Stalin's control after World War II, see Gorlizki and Khlevniuk, *Cold Peace*; on Suslov, see Adibekov, *Kominform i poslevnoennaia Evropa*, 16.

80. For figures for 1948 and 1949, see GARF, f. R-8581, op. 128, l. 10; for 1950, see GARF, f. R-5283, op. 307, l. 123. Also, the share of translated Polish titles increased: in 1947, Soviet/Russian books made up only 17 percent of translated belles lettres, and by 1949 their share rose to 40 percent). Korzon, *Polsko-radzieckie kontakty*, 54–55. Maciej Olejniczak writes that between 1949 and 1955, 6,338 Soviet titles of all genres came out in Poland in the total circulation of over 100 million copies. See *Polsko-radzieckie kontakty*, 119. The discrepancies between Soviet and Polish figures may result from the fact that Soviet books came from two channels: (1) books translated in Poland after an agreement with Mezhdunarodnaia kniga, and (2) books translated and published in the USSR by Izdatel'stvo literatury na inostrannykh iazykakh (Inoizdat) and then exported to Poland through Mezhdunarodnaia kniga. Soviet officials probably took into account the latter, whereas later researchers—both. See Stykalin, "Propaganda SSSR," 58.

81. RGASPI, f. 17, op. 132, d. 140, l. 55.

82. Ibid., op. 137, d. 172, l. 113. It was the highest figure for all European "People's Democracies," the next one on the list being Bulgaria with 1.8 million copies for 1949. The figures include 363,000 for visual materials in Poland and 710,000 for Bulgaria.

83. RGASPI, f. 17, op. 132, d. 140, l. 55.

84. Ibid., op. 137, d. 172, l. 145.

85. Another report from 1952 mentions 65 million Polish viewers of Soviet films, but references to 79 million were most common. See GARF, f. R-5283, op. 22, d. 373, l. 55.

86. RGALI, f. 962, op. 10, d. 144, k. 52 (l). Olejniczak gives different data, listing 82 premieres of 41 plays by Soviet and Russian authors for 1949. He adds that, between 1949 and 1955, 445 premieres of Russian and Soviet plays took place on Polish stages. Korzon, *Polsko-radzieckie kontakty*, 124.

87. According to Olejniczak's vague statistics based on materials of the Polish Ministry of Culture and Art, in the years 1949–55, 101 exhibitions were organized "dedicated to the Soviet Union," including 71 exhibitions of Russian and Soviet art and 30 devoted to life in the USSR—mostly thematic shows about Soviet achievements in industry and agriculture. Korzon, *Polsko-radzieckie kontakty*, 130.

88. On January 1, 1948, the number of cells was 2,336, individual members—487,496, and institutional members—610. One year later, the respective numbers were: 7,500; 1,100,000; and 700. GARF, f. R-5283, op. 22, d. 183, l. 49.

89. Fijałkowska, *Polityka i twórcy*, 173–74. Specifically, the Polish Ministry of Foreign Affairs began to supervise the KWKZ. On the KWKZ, see Anna Lisiecka, "Działalność Komitetu," 203–60; on its composition, see Olejniczak, *Polsko-radzieckie kontakty*, 20n33; also Fijałkowska, *Polityka i twórcy*, 173–74.

90. Miłosz, *The Captive Mind*, 21.

91. RGALI, f. 631, op. 14, d. 664, l. 6.

92. RGASPI, f. 17, op. 137, d. 617, ll. 19–20.

93. Ibid., l. 23. Earlier, Panferov had written that in Polish literature there dominated "symbolist and formalist . . . currents, . . . briefly, almost everything just like in our country in 1919–1924." On Zak's 1949 visit, see GARF, f. R-5283, op. 22, d. 181, l. 164.

94. RGALI, f. 631, op. 14, d. 664, l. 3.

95. Karavaeva, *Po dorogam zhizni*, 7–8, 384–459.

96. RGALI, f. 631, op. 26, d. 2179, ll. 1–4.

97. Ibid., l. 5.

98. Fik, "Kultura polska," 243.

99. Clausewitz, *On War*, 101, 113–15, 119–21, 193.

100. RGASPI, f. 17, op. 137, d. 284, l. 163.

101. GARF, f. R-5283, op. 22, d. 373, l. 9.

102. GARF, f. R-5283, op. 22, d. 307, l. 123.

103. RGASPI, f. 17, op. 137, d. 284, l. 105; On more offenses of MK, see RGASPI, f. 17, op. 137, d. 284, ll. 119–28; on similar problems in Romania in the mid-1950, see Volokitina, *Vostochnaia Evropa*, 2:372–79.

104. GARF, f. R-5283, op. 22, d. 182, l. 86; Naszkowski, *Paryż-Moskwa*, 197.

105. See the Soviet embassy adviser A. V. Zotov's report on his meeting with an official from the Romanian Association for Cultural Contacts with the USSR in Volokitina, *Vostochnaia Evropa*, 2:30; and the Romanian ambassador's similar request on behalf of the country's Gorky Institute of Russian Language and Literature, in ibid., 294–95. The Czechoslovak Minister of Education delivered a similar request to the Soviet government on February 4, 1949—see Volokitina, *Sovetskii faktor*, 2:31–35.

106. On Zak's impressions, see GARF, f. R-5283, op. 22, d. 181, l. 164; for Safirov's complaints, GARF, f. R-5283, op. 22, d. 307, l. 132.

107. See, for example, Vagan Grigor'ian's letter to Stalin dated April 18, 1950, forwarding the Poles' request that permission be granted to invite a group of Polish cultural bureaucrats to visit the USSR in order to get acquainted with Soviet cultural institutions. The document was ultimately sent only to Molotov, which made the process

an ordeal. See Volokitina, *Sovetskii faktor*, 2:299. See also Rosenfeldt, *The "Special" World*, 531.

108. "Anglo-amerikanskaia propaganda v Pol'she i bor'ba protiv nee pol'skikh progressivnykh organizatsii," June 1949, RGASPI, f. 17, op. 137, d. 79, ll. 145–81. On page 32 of the report (l. 179), Lebedev mentions the following charitable organizations still operating in Poland as fronts for Anglo-Saxon intelligence agencies: the Council of American Polonia (he probably meant the American Relief for Poland (ARP) or the Polish-American Immigration and Relief Committee—see Gatrell and Baron, *Warlands*, 12), Caritas and the Quaker Mission. On concerns about Anglo-American propaganda in Bulgaria at the same time, see Volokitina, *Vostochnaia Evropa*, 2:129–30, 164–67.

109. Crowley wonderfully describes the dilemmas of Polish architects in "Paris or Moscow?"

110. In 1948, Romanian diplomats in Warsaw complained to M. Suslov that the Poles failed to observe the Stalinist decorum. See Kochański, *Polska w dokumentach*, 100.

111. GARF, f. R-5283, op. 22, d. 307, l. 133.

112. For example, GARF, f. R-5283, op. 22, d. 128, l. 19.

113. Korzon, *Polsko-radzieckie kontakty*, 178–92.

114. Stykalin, "Propaganda SSSR," 69; GARF, f. R-5283, op. 22, d. 128, l. 19; dubbing of Soviet films was also a problem in the Soviet Zone of Occupation—see Naimark, *The Russians in Germany*, 421.

115. GARF, f. R-5283, op. 22, d. 307, l. 135.

116. Kurz, "Sport to zdrowie," 321.

117. Domosławski, *Kapuściński. Non-fiction*, 71; the concept of "znieważanie" (insult) in the Polish legal code in many ways conflated crimes against the state, the socialist system in general, and the Allied states—a euphemistic reference to the USSR. See Kładoczny, *Prawo jako narzędzie represji*, 332–44.

118. Scott, *Domination*, 38–39.

119. Fijałkowska, *Polityka i twórcy*, 110, 242–46. In June 1949, vice-minister of art and culture, Włodzimierz Sokorski, announced that among 236 postwar premieres of Polish plays, only about a dozen treated contemporary subjects, and only six addressed pressing issues such as agricultural reform, struggle with the [anticommunist] underground, nationalization of industry, or the struggle for a new style of work.

120. GARF, f. R-5283, op. 22, d. 128, l. 22; ibid., d. 307, l. 133.

121. RGALI, f. 631, op. 14, d. 664, l. 1.

122. GARF, f. R-5283, op. 22, d. 373, l. 40.

123. Ibid., d. 307, l. 133.

124. Ibid., l. 132.

125. Ibid., l. 130.

126. Ibid., l. 131.

127. Ibid., d. 431, l. 28.

128. On jazz in the USSR, see Starr, *Red and Hot*; the author describes the Red Army jazz concerts on pages 204–5.

129. Caute, *The Dancer Defects*, 445.

130. RGASPI, f. 17, op. 137, d. 284, l. 174.

131. Ibid., d. 78, l. 314. On Czerny-Stefańska, see Nałkowska, *Dzienniki*, 3: 120–21n1.

132. GARF, f. R-5283, op. 22, d. 431, ll. 58–60.

133. Ibid.

134. Kurz, "Sport to zdrowie," 321.

135. Ibid.

136. Dąbrowska, *Dzienniki*, entry for June 7, 1953, 4:139–40.

137. GARF, f. R-5283, op. 22, d. 307, l. 141.

138. Kurz, "Sport to zdrowie," 323.

139. GARF, f. R-5283, op. 22, d. 373, ll. 11–12.

140. Torańska, *"Them"*, 304–05.

141. Dąbrowska, *Dzienniki*, 3:199–200.

142. Brenner, "Ideology and Ethics."

143. Moskowitz, "The Uneasy East," 137.

144. Madej, *Kino, władza, publiczność*, 14.

145. Ibid., 38–41.

146. Haltof, *Polish Film and the Holocaust*, 55.

147. See the actual film *Border Street*.

148. Madej, *Kino, władza, publiczność*, 48.

149. Ibid., 185.

150. Haltof, *Polish Film and the Holocaust*, 65.

151. Stuart Liebman, "Les premières constellations," 204–5.

152. Behrends, "Nation and Empire," 450–51.

153. Bartov, *The "Jew" in Cinema*, 180.

154. Steinlauf, "Poland," 111. The most famous memorial was Nathan Rapoport's 1948 monument, erected on the fifth anniversary of the event. A lesser known memorial designed by Polish architect Leon Marek Suzin was unveiled as early as 1946. See Haltof, *Polish Film and the Holocaust*, 56. In one notorious (and oft-cited) instance, after the Warsaw Uprising, they plastered posters deprecating the heroic Home Army side by side with those praising the "heroes of the Ghetto Uprising" of 1943. Putrament criticized such tactics of the Ministry of Propaganda and Information, since in his view, the juxtaposition could not have any result but "to inflame anti-Semitism, anti-Sovietism, antisocialism." See Putrament, *Pół wieku*, 2:329; Kersten, *The Establishment of Communist Rule*, 220; Kersten, "Polacy. Żydzi. Komunizm," 137.

155. Haltof, *Polish Film and the Holocaust*, 55.

156. The four versions of the scenario to *Border Street* that exist in the Biblioteka Filmoteki Narodowej are as follows: (1) an abridged, undated scenario of the film (S-2397); (2) the first version of the scenario (much more expanded), written by A. Ford in Karpacz in 1946/47 (S-2397); (3) a scene-by-scene script (*scenopis*) by Jan Fethke and Ludwik Starski, labeled Łódź, 1946 (S-4558); and (4) an undated scene-by-scene script written by Starski, Ford, and Jean Forge (S-878).

157. Liebman writes that the period 1945–50 was the richest in terms of Poles' and Jews' engagement with the themes of war and Polish-Jewish relations, and that the

Jewish and Polish communists involved risked perpetuating the myth of Judeocommunism. Liebman, "Réflexions sur les Polonais," 176–77n7.

158. Ibid., 195.

159. Ibid., 192.

160. Ibid., 140–41, and for the preceding discussion, 191.

161. "Protokół z posiedzenia komisji kwalifikacyjnej w dniach 1 i 2 czerwca 1948 r.," Filmoteka Narodowa, A-329, k. 1.

162. Ibid., k. 4; half of this quotation is also cited in Haltof, *Polish Film and the Holocaust*, 59.

163. Kersten, *Polacy, Żydzi, komunizm*, 130–31.

164. Madej, *Kino, władza, publiczność*, 192.

165. Haltof, *Polish Film and the Holocaust*, 60.

166. Dąbrowska, *Dzienniki*, 3:203. A note from 1956 written underneath the entry for January 28, 1949.

167. Checinski, *Poland*, 39. Pinkus, "Change and continuity." Stuart Liebman usefully situates *Border Street* in the Cold War context in "Les premières constellations," 214–15.

168. Checinski, *Poland*, 75–76. For an extended account of the Soviet instrumentalization of Polish-Jewish communists in the fight against the Polish nationalist faction, see Taras, "Gomulka's 'Rightist-Nationalist Deviation.'"

169. Haltof, *Polish Film and the Holocaust*, 55; Maria Pijanowska, who played the role of Jadzia, also informed me that Ford faced pressures to limit the scenes with prayers. Personal communication (e-mail), June 11, 2012.

170. Madej, *Kino, władza, publiczność*, 198.

171. GARF, f. R-5283, op. 22, d. 128, l. 21.

172. Kenez, "Jewish Themes in Stalinist Films."

173. Moskowitz, "The Uneasy East," 137.

174. Dąbrowska, *Dzienniki*, entry for January 14, 1949, 4:200.

175. During a meeting with the Soviet official E. I. Dluzhinskii on October 4, 1949, Borejsza remarked on R. Zambrowski's allegedly pro-Jewish cadres policies. While "praising Berman's mind," he also accused him of "indulgence (*miagkoserdechnost'*) toward Jews and Jewish organizations, for which he will experience unpleasantness (*nepriatnosti*) in due time." See Volokitina, *Vostochnaia Evropa*, 2:242–43.

176. "Otchet o rabote s kadrami v SIB s 1. 7. 1947–1. 4. 1949." April 1949. GARF, f. R-8581, op. 2, d. 231, ll. 2, 4. "Central apparatus" consisted of the following categories: top leadership, department directors and deputy directors, main editors, editors, correspondents, reviewers, translators, and international network (*zagranset'*). For more on the purges, see Babiracki, "Between Compromise and Distrust"; on Lozovskii, Kuznetsov, Suslov, and Patolichev, see Zalesskii, *Imperiia Stalina*.

177. Pinkus, *The Soviet Government and the Jews*, 86.

178. GARF, f. R-8581, op. 2, d. 305, l. 78; ibid., d. 342, ll. 18, 21–22; ibid., d. 277, l. 173. On editors' reluctance to publish about the theory of the Soviet state, see the yearly report for 1950: GARF, f. R-8581, op. 2, d. 305, l. 78; on the Church and the Vatican, in 1951, see "Sluzhebnaia informatsiia," January 14, 1952, GARF, f. 8581, op. 2, d. 342, l.

18; The main peasant newspaper *Rolnik Polski* (Polish Farmer) published only four of the bureau articles in 1951, and none on the collective farms. On Groszowa, see GARF, f. R-8581, op. 2, d. 342, l. 21. The editor of *Żołnierz Wolności* (Soldier of Freedom) refused bureau articles altogether, GARF, f. R-8581, op. 2, d. 342, l. 22. On "insufficient" publication rates for articles about international questions and economy, see Sokolovskii's report for the first quarter of 1950, GARF, f. R-8581, op. 2, d. 277, l. 173. He also admits though, that the reason for international news items not to be published might be their lateness.

179. On Irena Grosz's nomination, see CAW, syg. III/3/88, k. 14.

180. GARF, f. R-8581, op. 2, d. 305, l. 80.

181. Letter from V. Kuz'menko to Iu. G. Safirov, November 21, 1950, GARF, f. R-5283, op. 22, d. 244, k. 206; letter from A. Volozhenin to V. Sokolovskii, March 18, 1949, ibid., d. 245, l. 49.

182. Letter from A. Volozhenin to V. Sokolovskii, March 26, 1949, GARF, f. R-5283, op. 22, d. 245, l. 55.

183. Golon, "Ambasadorowie Stalina," 132; Noskova, "Sovetskie sovetniki," 107; Paczkowski, "Wstęp," in Kochański, *Polska w dokumentach*, 12–13.

184. "Otchet predstavitel'stva SIB v Pol'she v 1950 godu," January 10, 1951, GARF, f. 8581, op. 2, d. 305, l. 81.

185. Ibid., d. 245, l. 52.

186. Ibid., d. 217, l. 51.

187. The document reprinted in Polish can be found in Bordiugow, *Polska-ZSRR*, 241–50.

188. GARF, f. R-8581, op. 2., d. 217, l. 53. AAN, syg. 295/X-27, k. 42.

189. Caute, *The Dancer Defects*, 36.

190. In their letter to Grigor'ian of November 3, 1950, Sokolovskii and *Izvestiia* correspondent M. Iarovoi focused on Poles' reluctance to popularize the experience of Soviet Stakhanovites. See Volokitina, *Sovetskii faktor*, 2:395–96.

191. GARF, f. R-8581, op. 2, d. 245, ll. 51–52.

192. Kozieł, "Koncepcje dotyczące prasy," 53; in January 1949, Berman coauthored "a decisively confrontational" policy against the Catholic Church. See Sobór, *Jakub Berman*, 279.

193. In 1949 there were 243 cooperatives that totaled 42,000 hectares; in 1953, after the official collectivization campaign that began in 1951, there were 7,700 cooperatives that together totaled 1.2 million hectares of land. Roszkowski, *Historia Polski*, 215.

194. GARF, f. 8581, op. 2, d. 342, l. 18.

195. Torańska, "*Them*," 144.

196. Ibid., 141.

197. *Życie Warszawy*, August 13, 1951, 4.

198. GARF, f. R-8581, op. 2., d. 305, l. 23.

199. Adibekov, *Soveshchaniia kominforma*.

200. GARF, f. R-8581, op. 2, d. 245, l. 86.

201. Ibid., l. 87.

202. GARF, f. R-8581, op. 2, d. 373, ll. 51–52.

203. GARF, f. R-8581, op. 1, d. 264, ll. 553–54. The practice of duplication lasted briefly.

204. Schaff, *Moje spotkania*, 32.

205. Scientific cooperation during the interwar era was especially vibrant between 1927 and 1936. On this subject, see Róziewicz, *Polsko-radzieckie stosunki*; Fałkowicz and Czernych, "Polsko-radziecka współpraca."

206. Vucinich, *Empire of Knowledge*, 205–10.

207. Diplomatic documents from late 1946 reflect this optimism—see AMSZ, z-6/w-31/t-487/kk. 76–79.

208. Krementsov, *Stalinist Science*, 210–47.

209. On Stalin's role in the scientific debates after World War II, see Pollock, *Stalin and the Soviet Science Wars*.

210. On this, see Holloway, *Stalin and the Bomb*.

211. Krementsov, "Lysenkoism in Europe," 191; Skrzypek, *Mechanizmy uzależnienia*, 290; Gorizontov, "Metodologicheskii perevorot," 59–63.

212. Krementsov, "Lysenkoism in Europe," 180–202.

213. Stykalin, "Nauchnaia intelligentsiia," 98.

214. Connelly, *Captive University*, 54.

215. This was true, for example, with regard to M. M. and B. M. Zavadovskii, one of whom had visited Poland earlier. Vucinich, *Empire of Knowledge*, 234.

216. On the role of the KWKZ and on VOKS, see Wyszomirska-Kuźmińska, *Współpraca Polski z ZSRR*, 39, 49, 155.

217. Skrzypek, *Mechanizmy uzależnienia*, 291.

218. Connelly reports that during the entire period from 1946 to 1955 "some sixty-one Soviet professors gave instruction at Polish higher schools." *Captive University*, 50.

219. For example, Kostyrchenko, *Tainaia politika Stalina*, 555–610.

220. Krementsov, "Lysenkoism in Europe," 184–86.

221. Krementsov, *Stalinist Science*, 6.

222. Romek, "Nauka przeciw ideologii," 101. Connelly also describes a positive report by the historian B. D. Grekov, explaining the latter's sympathy for Polish academics (Grekov had been trained in Russian Poland before World War I), *Captive University*, 51. Scholars of other disciplines who visited Poland also occasionally sent upbeat reports to Moscow. See a report by the Soviet jurist S. S. Kravchuk from 1951, RGASPI, f. 17, op. 137, d. 621, ll. 99–100.

223. Campbell, "Nekrasov," 290–91. See also "Nekrasov, N. N." in *Akademiki-ekonomisty Rossii*.

224. RGASPI, f. 17, op. 137, d. 621, l. 136.

225. It is unclear whether she was related to Vera Pavlovna Lebedeva (b. 1881) whom the Great Soviet Encyclopedia, 2nd ed., describes as a famous health-care activist.

226. RGASPI, f. 17, op. 137, d. 284, l. 29.

227. Ibid., l. 30.

228. Ibid., l. 6.

229. GARF, f. R-5283, op. 22, d. 307, l. 148.

230. The Great Soviet Encyclopedia (2nd ed.), describes Ivan Evdokimovich Glushchenko (b. 1907) as a Michurinist and a close coworker of Lysenko. He was director of the laboratory of plant genetics of the Soviet Academy of Sciences and a scientific secretary of the academy's Presidium; GARF, f. R-5283, op. 22, d. 128, l. 41.

231. On physiologists, see GARF, f. R-5283, op. 22, d. 244, l. 184. The fifty-one-year-old psychiatrist Evgenii Alekseevich Popov from Kharkov who visited Poland in April 1950 made a similar observation: RGASPI, f. 17, op. 137, d. 284, l. 39. Popov specialized in applications of Pavlovian theory to psychiatry. See "Popov, Evgenii Alekseevich (1899–1961)," in *Bol'shaia meditsinskaia entsiklopediia*.

232. For instance, when Professor Ignacy Abramowicz from Gdańsk wanted to send his optometry textbook to his colleague, Professor V. I. Spasskii from Ufa in the spring of 1949, he first turned to the Soviet Consulate. The consulate sent the book to the Ministry of Foreign Affairs (MID), which then forwarded it to Glavlit. Upon receiving the green light from the censors, the MID forwarded the book to VOKS, which was then requested to send it to Spaskii. See Volokitina, *Sovetskii faktor*, 2:79.

233. Rosenfeldt, *The "Special" World*, 533.

234. Hübner, *I Kongres Nauki Polskiej*, 79.

235. GARF, f. R-5283, op. 22, d. 307, l. 208.

236. Todes, *Darwin without Malthus*, 171.

237. GARF, f. R-5283, op. 22, d. 307, ll. 208–9.

238. Bińko, "Instytut," 203.

239. RGASPI, f. 17, op. 137, d. 621, ll. 28–29.

240. Ibid., l. 29.

241. Nekrasov made a similar point in his report, and Romanchenko extended such observations to other higher schools of economics that he had visited. RGASPI, f. 17, op. 137, d. 621, ll. 41, 49–51.

242. During the 1950–51 academic year, Jews made up 29 percent of the institute's graduate students (twenty-three out of seventy-eight)—see Bińko, "Instytut," 205.

243. Schaff noted of the interwar era that "it was not unusual, even in state schools, that most of the students were Jewish." Rejecting any essentialist explanations, Schaff maintained that "the Jewish student had to be the best in order to make a life for himself and overcome various official and factually existing *numerus nullus*." Schaff, *Pora na spowiedź*, 26–27.

244. RGASPI, f. 17, op. 137, d. 284, l. 29.

245. GARF, f. R-5283, op. 22, d. 244, l. 185.

246. RGASPI, f. 17, op. 137, d. 621, l. 18.

247. GARF, f. R-5283, op. 22, d. 307, l. 148. GARF, f. R-5283, op. 22, d. 244, l. 42. See also: RGASPI, f. 17, op. 137, d. 189, ll. 2–9 and RGASPI, f. 17, op. 137, d. 5, ll. 254–68; on the frustrated voices of Soviet linguists, see RGASPI, f. 17, op. 137, d. 180, l. 150.

248. Konorski, *Conditioned Reflexes*.

249. GARF, f. R-5283, op. 22, d. 244, l. 37.

250. AMSZ, z-7/w-13/t-105/k. 111.

251. Jerzy Konorski discussed this in his autobiography, published in *A History of Psychology*, 205; Kuźnicki, *Instytut Biologii*, 1:105.

252. Schaff, *Moje spotkania*, 96; on the German case, see Naimark, *The Russians in Germany*, 418.

253. Mentzel, *Czas ciekawy*, 106.

254. Ibid., 107.

255. Ibid., 108.

256. Ibid.

257. Ibid.

258. Domosławski, *Kapuściński. Non-fiction*, 95.

259. Ibid.

260. See Holloway, *Stalin and the Bomb*.

261. Jersild, "The Soviet Union"; Zubok, *A Failed Empire*.

262. Kramer, "Reflex Actions," 18–19.

263. In his discussion of Soviet cultural diplomacy with the West in the pre–World War II era, Michael David-Fox pointed out recently that in the "internal-external nexus," "the external also affected the internal: international agendas and practices boomeranged back to influence internal Soviet affairs." See *Showcasing the Great Experiment*, 314.

264. The Soviets charged Hungarian cultural figures and officials with "nationalism" as well—see, for example, a report by the Soviet embassy in Budapest dated July 1, 1952, in Volokitina et al. *Vostochnaia Evropa*, 2:753–67.

265. On Sokorski, see GARF, f. R-5283, op. 22, d. 373, ll. 43–46. The document has also been published in Volokitina, *Sovetskii faktor*, 2:569–72. Safirov found confirmation of the Polish painter's statements in Soviet sources, and eventually forwarded his suspicions to V. Grigor'ian in the Foreign Policy Commission; on Berman and Minc, see a letter from the ambassador of the USSR to Warsaw, Viktor Lebedev, to the minister of foreign affairs of the USSR, Andrei Vyshinskii, about the situation in the PZPR leadership," dated July 10, 1949, in Kochański, *Polska w dokumentach*, 41–47. On Dłuski, see "Pis'mo A. I. Lavrent'eva V. Z. Lebedevu o proiavleniiakh 'pol'skogo natsionalizma' i neobkhodimosti otpravki v Moskvu politicheskoi kharakteristiki zaveduiushchego inostrannym otdelom TsK PORP O. Dluskogo," in Volokitina, *Sovetskii faktor*, 2:441 as well as 1:444–45. The International Department was the highest decision-making body below the level of the Politbiuro that dealt with the country's international contacts and, in fact, controlled the official representative of the Polish state and abroad, the Ministry of Foreign Affairs. See Borodziej, "Wydział Zagraniczny." Between 1951 and 1953, the Soviet officials consistently blamed the TPPR leaders for negligence of the organization they headed. This was especially true of the PZPR secretary Edward Ochab, whom they accused of stifling the initiatives of his subordinate Matuszewski. See GARF, f. R-5283, op. 22, d. 308, l. 41; d. 431, ll. 68–69, and 106. On Ochab's roles and his temporary "curatorship" of Berman's affairs, see Sobór, *Jakub Berman*, 269, 273–74. Similar criticisms were made against J. K. Wende of the KWKZ and his subordinates: GARF, f. R-5283, op. 22, d. 307, ll. 95–97; as well as the director of the Polish-Soviet Institute (PSI), Zygmunt Młynarski, who once failed to

emphasize the role of the Red Army in liberating Poland. In addition, during the opening lecture of the PSI, Młynarski underappreciated "the links between some Polish intellectuals and the Russian Decembrists." In the fragments of Polish émigré intellectuals' letters he quoted "absolutely all of the Russian officers who were in Poland at that time were characterized as thieves, drunks, and violators (*nasil'niki*)" GARF, f. R-5283, op. 22, d. 373, ll. 112–13. The Polish-Soviet Institute was created as a result of the First Congress of Polish Science on the initiative of the Company of Slavic and Russian studies in December 1951. It was a new research institute, devoted to researching Russian-oriented historical, social-scientific, and philological subjects. See Wyszomirska-Kuźmińska, *Współpraca Polski z ZSRR*, 73. On Młynarski, see *Polski słownik biograficzny* (1935). On Sztachelski, see RGASPI, f. 17, op. 137, d. 284, l. 6. Sztachelski was the minister of health between 1951 and 1956.

266. This was the case when Safirov received Zakrzewski. Afterward, he felt compelled to verify the Pole's story with Soviet accounts and included both in his report (journal entry), GARF, f. R-5283, op. 22, d. 373, l. 4. Mid-level officials in Moscow were equally skeptical. See, for example, comments of the chair of VOKS, Andrei I. Denisov, who questioned Matuszewski's complaints about Ochab by pointing to the Pole's likely personal motives in his letter to Molotov of April 23, 1951. GARF, f. R-5283, op. 22, d. 307, l. 73.

267. RGASPI, f. 17, op. 137, d. 615, l. 10.

268. Gross, *Revolution from Abroad*, 117–18.

269. RGASPI, f. 17, op. 137, d. 615, ll. 22–26. On June 10, Grigor'ian forwarded the letter to Suslov and requested that a critical review article be written by a specialist in the field. On October 4, the Institute of Philosophy of the Soviet Academy of Sciences sent such an article written by I. Narskii to the technical secretariat of the Central Committee.

270. Gorsuch, "Time Travelers."

271. Maes, *A History of Russian Music*, 310.

272. See "Spotkanie z Dymitrem Kabalewskim," *Muzyka*, no. 1–2 (January–February 1952): 59–63.

273. See *Muzyka*, no. 9–10 (September-October 1952): 110. The report mistakenly lists the letter as having appeared in no. 8–9.

274. GARF, f. R-5283, op. 22, d. 373, ll. 159–64; and d. 431, l. 61.

275. Editor's introduction to Kochański, *Polska w dokumentach*, 13. Citing memoirs of Bierut's son, Jan Chyliński, titled *Jaki był Bolesław Bierut*, 171; Golon, "Ambasadorowie Stalina," 157–58.

276. That was the case with Vasetskii, who, in 1951, single-handedly criticized Polish scientists' feedback on the Soviet chapter of a textbook on the history of philosophy instead of mediating between the Poles and their Soviet colleagues. Vasetskii exceeded his competence, delayed the publication of the volume, and was criticized by his bosses. See RGASPI, f. 17, op. 137, d. 621, l. 31; and d. 613, l. 113.

277. Compare Zakrzewski's case with the Hungarian writer Sándor Gergely's visit to the Soviet embassy in Budapest only two days later in Volokitina et al., *Sovetskii faktor*, vol. 2, 575–76.

278. GARF, f. R-5283, op. 22, d. 373, ll. 43–44. As an example, he gave the prizes awarded at the second art exhibition. Also, Volokitina et al., *Sovetskii faktor*, vol. 2, 569–71.

279. GARF, f. R-5283, op. 22, d. 373, ll. 40, 45–46.

280. See "Marxism and the Problems of Liguistics," published in *Pravda* on July 4, and August 2, 1950, also available at www.marxists.org/reference/archive/stalin/works /1950/jun/20.htm. See also Kupiecki, *Natchnienie milionów*, 124–25.

281. "Schematyzm," in Łapiński and Tomasik, *Słownik realizmu socjalistycznego*.

282. Zezina, *Sovetskaia khudozhestvennaia intelligentsia*, 71.

283. Fik, "Kultura polska," 229; Jarmułowicz, *Sezony błędów i wypaczeń*, 68. According to Zezina, it took place in October; the original quotation is given in *Sovetskaia khudozhestvennaia intelligentsia*, 72. On the mild cultural liberalization under Stalin, see also Bittner, *The Many Lives of Khrushchev's Thaw*, 46–47.

284. Fijałkowska, *Polityka i twórcy*, 78–79, 131; Fik, "Kultura polska," 243.

285. Fik, "Kultura polska," 257, citing Sokorski, *Xawery Dunikowski*, 47–48; Jarmułowicz, *Sezony błędów i wypaczeń*, 70.

286. Sobór, *Jakub Berman*, 401, cites Woźniakowski, *Między ubezwłasnowolnieniem*, 16.

287. Some communist critics had pointed it out in 1949. But by 1952, the communists officially broadened the socrealist canon in a campaign against "schematism" in the arts. See Fijałkowska, *Polityka i twórcy*, 117, 159.

288. Foucault, *The Order of Things*, xi.

289. On developments in the historiography of Western colonial empires, see, for instance, Wolfe, "History and Imperialism." One may add, along similar lines, that few historians of Russia paid attention to non-Russian nationalities of the empire until the breakup of the USSR in 1991. See Gerasimov et al., "New Imperial History."

CHAPTER 4

1. Nałkowska, *Granica*, 301–2.

2. Auden, "September 1, 1939."

3. Nałkowska, *Dzienniki*, part 1 (1945–54), 6:40, 47.

4. Andrzej Korzon explained why there were few Polish translations into Russian as due to the indolence of Polish government officials. See Korzon, "Literatura radziecka." In his study of Stalin-era censorship, A. V. Blium devotes less than three pages to foreign translations and ends its consideration in 1946. Marurice Friedberg's work of Western literary imports in the USSR, suggestively titled *A Decade of Euphoria*, begins only in 1954. Andrzej Korzon's examination of the problem stops with the final caesura of his entire work on Polish-Soviet cultural relations, in 1950. See Blium, *Sovetskaia tsenzura*; Maurice Friedberg, *A Decade of Euphoria*; Korzon, *Polsko-radzieckie kontakty*.

5. Naszkowski, *Paryż-Moskwa*, 195.

6. Ibid., 216.

7. The physical description is Naszkowski's. See *Paryż-Moskwa*, 198, 221. On Zorin's career, see the entry in Gromyko, *Diplomaticheskii slovar'*.

8. In February 1951 Jan Wilczek was to receive 9,153 rubles for the Russian translation of *Number 16 Begins Production*—some eighteen times the average monthly Polish salary at the time. RGASPI, f. 17, op. 137, d. 617, l. 11. The per-sheet renumeration was below the Soviet range (1,500 to 4,000 rubles per sheet). See Zezina, *Sovetskaia khudozhestvennaia intelligentsia*, 60–61. Yet, after the 1950 currency reforms, the 1:1 ruble to złoty exchange rate would have given Wilczek much purchase on his payment, either in złoty, in special shops for the elites, or during trips abroad, since the dollar had an artificially low rate to the złoty—4:1. See Jezierski and Leszczyńska, *Historia gospodarcza Polski*, 542–48. On the importance of literature in Russia and the USSR, see Garrard and Garrard, *Inside the Soviet Writers' Union*, 15–43; on Poland, see Tighe, *The Politics of Literature*, 3–64.

9. Dunham, *In Stalin's Time*, 25.

10. AMSZ, z-27/w-13/t-224/kk. 1–2.

11. AMSZ, z-21/w-114/t-1508/k. 5; AMSZ, z-6/w-31/t-482, k. 6.

12. On a personal level, this respect and appreciation and was reciprocal. For a recent account of this tangled and contradictory relationship, see Koropeckyj, *Adam Mickiewicz*, 77–78, 113–14.

13. Semler, *Discovering Moscow*, 100–103.

14. On the history of this street and Nastasinskii Lane, see A. M. Pegov, *Imena moskovskikh ulits*, 24, 300.

15. Ginsburg, "Translator's Introduction," xii.

16. Dobrenko, "The Literature of the Zhdanov Era," 348.

17. *Knizhnaia letopis'*, January–August, 1946.

18. Friedberg, *A Decade of Euphoria*, 5.

19. Brown, *Soviet Attitudes*, 171.

20. Korzon, *Polsko-radzieckie kontakty*, 99–101.

21. On Mochalov, see Petrova, *Antifashistkie komitety v SSSR*, 254.

22. Bikont and Szczęsna, *Lawina i kamienie*, 37.

23. AMSZ, z-6/w-35/t-554/kk. 14–15.

24. AMSZ, z-26/w-35/t-554, kk. 33–34; GARF, f. R-5283, op. 22, d. 118, l. 157.

25. Bikont and Szczęsna "Towarzysze nieudanej podróży."

26. AMSZ, z-21/w-114/t-1508/k. 20.

27. Brooks, *Thank You, Comrade Stalin!* 195–232; Tumarkin, *The Living and the Dead*, 101.

28. Pinkus, *The Soviet Government and the Jews*, 387–483.

29. Hanna Kirschner's introduction to Nałkowska, *Dzienniki*, part 1, 6:8.

30. Nałkowska, *Dzienniki*, part 1, 6:287.

31. Ibid., entry for September 20, 1946, 286.

32. Grynberg, "The Holocaust in Polish Literature," 127.

33. Bromberg also wanted to publish Adolf Rudnicki; Kasman reluctantly agreed, but in small circulation and without reprints: "There's too much about Jews. . . . One hundred and fifty thousand Jews descended upon poor Poland, and each wants back

his shop, his flat. And someone is there already, where is he going to go, on the street? Perhaps he should hand everything back to the Jew? But he didn't take it from them, the Germans did. Murders, unrest have taken place. Writing about Jews makes things worse, provokes, fuels anti-Semitism. Enough has been written, people don't want this. If he must describe shocking events, there are natural disasters, floods, fires, after all." Grynberg, *Memorbuch*, 203; the story by Konopnicka was "Nasza szkapa." On Rudnicki, Poland's "chronicler of the destroyed Jewish world," see Monika Adamczyk-Garbowska, "Adolf Rudnicki," in Kremer, *Holocaust Literature*, 2:1050–62.

34. For Żywulska's biography, see Nałkowska, *Dzienniki*, part 2, 6:290, 537n3. On Andrzejewski, Brandys, and Nałkowska, see the entries in Kremer, *Holocaust Literature*, 1:43–45, 181–83 and 2:877–79.

35. Pytlakowski, *Fundamenty*, 458.

36. Nałkowska, *Dzienniki*, part 1, 6:48.

37. Ibid., 503.

38. Ibid., 509.

39. Ibid.

40. Hollander, *Political Pilgrims*, esp. 347–99.

41. Consider a letter from a VOKS official to the first secretary at the Soviet embassy to Hungary, dated February 20, 1950, in which he argued that depriving the Hungarian-Soviet Society of the function to propagate Hungarian culture in the USSR may "essentially mean . . . turning the Hungarian-Soviet Society into a single-channel (*odnostoronnuiu*) organization for propaganda of the Soviet Union in Hungary, which in no way corresponds to our objectives and can be used by the reactionary circles for their purposes." Volokitina, *Sovetskii faktor*, 2:273–74.

42. Undated draft statute, RGASPI, f. 17, op. 125, d. 539, l. 136.

43. It was difficult to rectify an error and prove one's innocence even after the Soviet leader's death, as the ten-page letter from Inoizdat's director P. Chuvikov to V. S. Kruzhkov testifies. "In choosing the book for translation into Russian, the publisher relied on the positive opinion of the Hungarian and Soviet literary community," wrote the author in March 1954, in response to accusations for having approved Ferenc Karinthy's book *Kamenshchiki*, and following up his claim with dozens of examples from the Hungarian and Soviet press. See RGANI, f. 5, op. 16, d. 659, ll. 7–16.

44. For the respective statutes, see RGALI, f. 631, op. 14, d. 4, ll. 1–4; and RGALI, f. 631, op. 14, d. 64, ll. 1–4.

45. It met twice in 1947, but no records are available for 1948. Its work picked up speed when it gathered twice in 1949 (i.e., soon after insistence from the Poles and the intervention of the Soviet Ministry of Foreign Affairs); subsequently, it met seven times in 1950, three times in 1951, as many as ten times in 1952, and five times in 1953, discussing one or multiple literary works during each session.

46. The biographical information is based on the *uchetnye kartochki* located in today's Union of Russian Writers at 52 Povarskaia Street, in Moscow. On Marchlewska, see Agapkina, "Russkie kontakty Iaroslava Ivashkevicha," 31. While in Poland, Marchlewska worked for the Soviet Information Bureau and in her self-assumed role as a Stalinist watch dog, informed on various party officials, including Jakub Berman—

see her meeting with the MID official in February 1952, in Volokitina et al., *Vostoch-naia Evropa*, 2:696–701.

47. Out of the 52, the other national literatures included: Czech and Slovak—12; Bulgarian—11; Hungarian—7; Romanian—2. The other publishers were: Goslitizdat—3; Ogonek—11; Voenizdat—2; Molodaia gvardiia—1; Detizdat—6; the journal *Krokodil*—1. RGALI, f. 631, op. 15, d. 1060, ll. 43–50.

48. Ibid., l. 50.

49. Ibid., l. 53.

50. Ibid., l. 53.

51. On Zhivov in the late 1920s, see Shore, *Caviar and Ashes*, 93.

52. RGALI, f. 631, op. 14, d. 2178, l. 50.

53. Ibid., d. 669, l. 1.

54. Ibid., d. 663, l. 2; RGALI, f. 631, op. 14, d. 665, l. 1; RGALI, f. 631, op. 14, d. 669, ll. 1–2a.

55. RGALI, f. 631, op. 26, d. 2204, l. 8.

56. RGALI, f. 631, op. 14, d. 663, l. 15; RGALI, f. 631, op. 14, d. 665, ll. 23, 43; RGALI, f. 631, op. 14, d. 667, ll. 14, 19; RGALI, f. 631, op. 14, d. 668, l. 33; RGALI, f. 631, op. 26, d. 2219, l. 52.

57. RGALI, f. 631, op. 14, d. 665, l. 8.

58. Ibid., d. 663, l. 11.

59. Ibid., d. 669, ll. 1–2a.

60. Fijałkowska, *Polityka i twórcy*, 78–79, 131; Fik, "Kultura polska," 243.

61. RGALI, f. 631, op. 26, d. 2162, ll. 16 ob, 22–23.

62. Dąbrowska, *Dzienniki,* entry for Sunday, June 10, 1951, 4:45.

63. RGALI, f. 631, op. 14, d. 665, ll. 1–3.

64. Ibid., l. 60.

65. For the entire discussion, see ibid., ll. 1–69.

66. RGALI, f. 631, op. 26, d. 2178, ll. 21–44.

67. Ibid., ll. 46, 49, 51–52.

68. Zezina, *Sovetskaia khudozhestvennaia intelligentsia*, 88.

69. *Uchetnye kartochki* in the Union of Russian Writers. My data are incomplete.

70. Jarmułowicz, *Sezony błędów i wypaczeń*, 104, 126.

71. Surgiewicz, "Z dziejów prasy frontowej," 61; Zbiniewicz, *Armia Polska w ZSRR*, 76.

72. RGALI, 631, op. 14, d. 650, ll. 7, 9.

73. Dunham, *In Stalin's Time*, 3–23; the geranium references are on pp. 49, 98; love—65, 99.

74. Borowski, "Praca młodego pisarza," 260. Quoted in Jarosiński, *Nadwiślański socrealizm*, 78.

75. RGALI, f. 631, op. 26, d. 2162, l. 3.

76. Ibid., op. 14, d. 665, l. 23.

77. See "Woroszylski Wiktor" in *Współcześni polscy pisarze i badacze literatury.*

78. "Kruczkowski Leon" in *Współcześni polscy pisarze i badacze literatury*, vol. 4. According to this source, in 1949 the play was staged by Berlin's Max Reinhardt Theater,

but according to *Britannica Online*, the theater had been rechristened National Theater of East Berlin in 1946. One of these reference works therefore contains an error. The play was also published in (East) Berlin in 1949 and in Berlin and Leipzig in 1951, suggesting that the content was perhaps too inflammatory for West German audiences.

79. Bates, "Cenzura wobec problemu niemieckiego."

80. Jarmułowicz, *Sezony błędów i wypaczeń*, 126. Up until 1962, the play received thirty domestic premieres and seventy-one international premieres.

81. RGALI, f. 631, op. 14, d. 640, l. 14.

82. Muzeum Literatury im. A. Mickiewicza, syg. 1067, k. 50.

83. See "Viv'en, Leonid Sergeevich (b. April 29, 1887)" in Mokul'skii and Markov, *Teatral'naia entsiklopediia*.

84. Muzeum Literatury, syg. 1067, kk. 53–54.

85. Ibid., k. 52.

86. RGALI, f. 631, op. 26, d. 2203, ll. 6–10.

87. Ibid., op. 14, d. 650, l. 30. Bulgarian writers likewise complained that their requests to visit the USSR went unanswered. See Volokitina et al., *Sovetskii faktor*, 2:584–86.

88. RGALI, f. 631, op. 14, d. 650, ll. 30–32.

89. Ibid., d. 669, ll. 49–51.

90. Jarosiński, *Nadwiślański socrealizm*, 27.

CHAPTER 5

1. Ehrenburg, *Post-War Years*, 322.

2. Cited in Zubok, *Zhivago's Children*, 1.

3. On the "Doctors' Plot," see Brent and Naumov, *Stalin's Last Crime*; Pinkus, *The Soviet Government and the Jews*, 198–201.

4. Rubenstein, *Tangled Loyalties*, 285.

5. On the various meanings and incarnations of "the Thaw," as well as contradictions and uncertainty associated with the cultural landscape of the post-Stalin years in the USSR, see, for example, Bittner, *The Many Lives of Khrushchev's Thaw*, esp. 1–18, 40–74.

6. Each society behind the "Iron Curtain" experienced the Thaw differently, of course, with the most "liberal" and bottom-up thrusts manifest in Poland in Hungary. But "the Thaw" became a reference point and an "ideal type" of heuristic device for considering developments in the Soviet Bloc and even beyond. See Pavlyshyn, *Glasnost' in Context*.

7. See "Pis'mo I. G. Erenburga M. A. Suslovu o poezdke v Vengriiu i vstreche s vengerskimi pisateliami," in Afanas'eva, *Apparat TsK KPSS*, 452–53. That Ehrenburg also felt compelled to clarify that when he had stated his dislike of his "editor's red pencil" he did not attach to the word "red" "that meaning which . . . American journalists could attribute to it," illustrates the relative nature of Soviet cultural liberalization. On the timing of the publication of Ehrenburg's *The Thaw* in Poland, see Fijałkowska, *Polityka i twórcy*, 286.

8. As Polly Jones points out, "de-Stalinization" refers primarily to "the process of historical revisionism which deconstructed the Stalin cult." Here, I follow the second, broader meaning, which emphasizes "liberalization of the authoritarian political culture of Stalinism . . . 'Thaw(s)' of the Stalinist freeze on freedom of expression and modifications to the autarkic chauvinism especially characteristic of Cold War Stalinism." See "Introduction" in Polly Jones, *The Dilemmas of De-Stalinization*, 3.

9. Quoted in Ehrenburg, *Post-War Years*, 323.

10. Bubnov, "Dnevnik," 387.

11. Ibid.

12. Quotations are from Hellbeck, *Revolution on My Mind*, 4, 8. As Hellbeck shows, numerous diary writers actively "fashioned" their individual "selves" even within the constraints of the totalitarian Stalinist state—a fact, which lends them a degree of authenticity. Bubnov himself held on to his diaries until turning them over to GARF in the late 1980s. He appears to have revisited them twice: in 1970 and in 1985. In his 1970 commentary, he expressed doubts about whether the "details of an editor's life, their 'fleas and bites,'" would be of significance to "the history of Soviet journalism." In 1985 Bubnov was more hopeful, writing that "future generations will certainly be interested in reading an editor's diary." See Bubnov, "Dnevnik," 494–95.

13. Bubnov, "Dnevnik," 388.

14. See Kondusza, "'Mała Moskwa,'" esp. 151–54.

15. Bubnov, "Dnevnik," 399.

16. Ibid., 391.

17. Ibid.

18. Ibid., 400–401.

19. Ibid., 393.

20. Ibid., 434.

21. Ibid., 390.

22. Ibid., 391.

23. Ibid., 426.

24. Bubnov, "Dnevnik," 414.

25. Mayakovsky, "My Soviet Passport."

26. Bubnov, "Dnevnik," 397.

27. Ibid., 417.

28. Schattenberg, "'Democracy' or 'Despotism?'" 64.

29. Lygo, "The Need for New Voices."

30. "Pis'mo V. M. Molotova K. M. Simonovu ob oshibochnosti ego pozitsii v diskussii o tvorchestve V. V. Maiakovskogo," August 3, 1953, in Afanas'eva, *Apparat TsK KPSS*, 129.

31. "Zapiska A. A. Fadeeva v TsK KPSS 'O zastarelykh biurokraticheskikh izvrashcheniakh v dele rukovodstva sovetskim iskusstvom i literaturoi i sposobakh ispravleniia etikh nedostatkov,'" in ibid., 133–34.

32. Bubnov, "Dnevnik," 423.

33. Ibid.

34. Ibid., 446.

35. On June 9, 1953, Bubnov recorded: "What saves us is that the Poles are publishing their own newspapers so carelessly and sloppily, that our *Wolność*, when compared with *Życie Warszawy*, looks picture perfect (*kak kartinka*)." Ibid., 395.

36. Ibid., 446.

37. The actual letter can be found in RGANI, f. 5, op. 28, d. 162, l. 27, reel 41. See ibid. f. 5, op. 28, d. 162, ll. 97–103 for a collection of greetings to *Wolność* from Polish organizations on the newspaper's tenth anniversary (August 24, 1954), which Bubnov also sent along to back up his case.

38. Bubnov, "Dnevnik," 450.

39. Ibid. On Mikhailov, see Gromyko, *Diplomaticheskii slovar'*.

40. Kramer, "The Early Post-Stalin Succession Struggle," 31–34, 40–55. The Poles officially adopted the "new course" during the Second Congress of the PZPR in March 1954, but modest price decreases were implemented earlier, on October 29–30, 1953. See Paczkowski, *Spring Will Be Ours*.

41. Bubnov, "Dnevnik," 402–3.

42. Zubok, *A Failed Empire*, 100, 105.

43. Bubnov, "Dnevnik," 435.

44. Ibid., 424.

45. Ibid., 388.

46. Ibid., 444.

47. Ibid., 424.

48. Skrzypek, *Mechanizmy uzależnienia*, 314.

49. Bubnov, "Dnevnik," 438.

50. Ibid., 437.

51. Ibid.

52. Ibid.

53. Ibid., 459.

54. "Nekotorye zamechaniia o rabote SIB," August 10, 1953, RGANI, f. 5, op. 16, r. 5575, d. 646, ll. 115–33.

55. Ibid., 117.

56. Ibid., 133.

57. Ibid., 121.

58. Ibid., 122–23.

59. Schattenberg, "'Democracy' or 'Despotism?'" 66.

60. RGANI, f. 5, op. 16, r. 5575, d. 646, l. 124.

61. Ibid., 126.

62. Ibid., 126, 132.

63. Ibid., 132.

64. Ibid., 127–28.

65. GARF, f. 8581, op. 2, d. 402, k. 118.

66. Ibid., k. 125.

67. Ibid., 119. In 1954, SIB sent 8,247 articles to all People's Democracies, whereas in 1955 the figure was 4,190.

68. For a good overview, see Persak, *Sprawa Henryka Hollanda*, 26–67.

69. Ważyk, "A Poem for Adults," 42–43.

70. Bikont and Szczęsna, *Lawina i kamienie*, 264. According to the authoritative compendium, Czachowska and Szałagan, *Współcześni polscy pisarze i badacze literatury* (entry for "Ważyk Adam"), referencing another Polish source, Czech and Serbian translations also exist. No dates are provided, however, and it is unlikely that they would have appeared before 1956. Communist officials in the USSR (and presumably in other Bloc countries) did have access to the translation. In the winter of 1955, the translated "A Poem for Adults" landed on the desk of the Central Committee Secretary, Petr N. Pospelov. See RGANI, f. 5, op. 28, d. 296, reel 70, ll. 194–212; on Pospelov, see Zalesskii, *Imperiia Stalina*. On comparison of Polish and Czech de-Stalinizations, see Jirásek and Małkiewicz, *Polska i Czechosłowacja*, 364–84, 389.

71. "Nowa Kultura" in Łapiński and Tomasik, *Słownik realizmu socjalistycznego*, 144–46.

72. Other such groundbreaking publications included the revived Warsaw weekly *Po Prostu* and Jerzy Lutowski's play *Ostry dyżur*. See Jarosiński, *Nadwiślański socrealizm*, 155–56.

73. Bikont and Szczęsna, *Lawina i kamienie*, 266.

74. J. Rasiński, "Bez białych rękawiczek," 8, cited in Sobór, *Jakub Berman*, 402–3.

75. On Lebedev's complaints against Berman, see Kochański, *Polska w dokumentach*, 41–47. On Popov, see Sobór, *Jakub Berman*, 409; see Popov's complaints against ethnic policies in Polish party in Volokotina, *Sovetskii faktor*, 2:859–81, 863–67.

76. Sobór, *Jakub Berman*, 398; Torańska, *Oni*, 486.

77. Sobór, *Jakub Berman*, 400.

78. Szaynok, *Poland-Israel*, 167.

79. Sobór, *Jakub Berman*, 400.

80. Bubnov, "Dnevnik," 401. Bubnov referred to SMERSH (Smert' Shpionam, or "Death to Spies," an organization set up in April 1943 to monitor the loyalties of the Red Army soldiers and commanders), though this actual organization no longer existed. See Parrish, *The Lesser Terror*, 114.

81. On this see Błażyński, *Mówi Józef Światło*.

82. On anti-Semitism see Gluchowski, "The Defection of Jozef Swiatlo," and Sobór, *Jakub Berman*, 397–466. On the firing of Leon Kasman from the post of editor in chief of *Trybuna Ludów*, see his interview by Torańska in *Oni*, 631–32.

83. Sobór, *Jakub Berman*, 465–66.

84. Grynberg, *Memorbuch*.

85. See Khrushchev, *Khruschchev Remembers*, 179–82.

86. Sobór, *Jakub Berman*, 427.

87. Ibid., 428, 438.

88. Ibid., 433.

89. Ibid., 432; Fijałkowska, *Polityka i twórcy*, 362; Shore, *Caviar and Ashes*, 308.

90. Sobór, *Jakub Berman*, 401.

91. Pasierski, *Miłosz i Putrament*, 236.

92. Ibid., 237.

93. Ibid., 431.

94. Jarosiński, *Nadwiślański socrealizm*, 156.

95. Pasierski, *Miłosz i Putrament*, 239.

96. Ibid.

97. Putrament, *Pół wieku*, 4:120.

98. Bikont and Szczęsna, *Lawina i kamienie*, 286–87.

99. Ibid.

100. Ibid., 288.

101. Putrament, *Pół wieku*, 4:114.

102. Sobór, *Jakub Berman*, 416; Woźniakowski, *Między ubezwłasnowolnieniem*, 55–60.

103. Zawiśliński, *Wyznania zdrajcy*, 75.

104. Tompkins, "Composing for and with the Party," 274–77.

105. Fijałkowska, *Polityka i twórcy*, 274–75.

106. Domosławski, *Kapuściński. Non-fiction*, 108.

107. Fijałkowska, *Polityka i twórcy*, 272.

108. Ibid., 356.

109. Not even the Polish communists were thrilled about the "gift;" see Crowley, *Warsaw*, 40. The author cites Polish writer Tadeusz Konwicki, who as an antiestablishment writer recalled the "fear, hatred and magical horror" that the building inspired among the inhabitants of Warsaw (44).

110. Kupiecki, *Natchnienie*, 211.

111. Crowley, "Paris or Moscow?" 789–98.

112. See Koivunen, "Overcoming Cold War Boundaries."

113. See Ryback, *Rock around the Bloc*, 14–18.

114. Fik, "Kultura Polska," 266.

115. Ibid; Domosławski, *Kapuściński. Non-fiction*, 108–9.

116. Caute, *The Dancer Defects*, 76–77.

117. See Gąsiorowska-Grabowska, *Dokumenty i materialy*, 10:357.

118. Fik, "Kultura Polska," 260; "Politicheskaia informatsiia o polozhenii v Soiuze pol'skikh Pisatelei i pol'skoi literature," February 28, 1958, GARF, f. 8581, op. 2, d. 470, l. 68.

119. On these official celebrations taking place in Poland and the USSR see Basiński and Walichnowski, *Stosunki polsko-radzieckie*, 293–94; Gąsiorowska-Grabowska, *Dokumenty i materialy*, 10:467–68.

120. Zubok, *Zhivago's Children*, 53–56.

121. Ibid., 46–47.

122. Ibid.

123. See Amir Weiner, "The Empires Pay a Visit."

124. See Caute, *The Dancer Defects*, 78–79, 452–53. On cultural exchanges with the United States, see Richmond, *Cultural Exchange*.

125. Gilburd, "Picasso in Thaw Culture," 70–71; Woźniakowski, *Między ubezwłasnowolnieniem*, 65–57.

126. Fik, "Kultura Polska," 265.

127. Zubok, *Zhivago's Children*, 59.

128. Lygo, "The Need for New Voices," 194–95.

129. Bubnov, "Dnevnik," 450; Yevtushenko's poem was published as "Skierowanie Komsomołu" in *Wolność*, September 1, 1954, no. 201 (2930), 5. For more on Yevtushenko, see Zubok, *Zhivago's Children*, 58–59.

130. Volokitina, *Sovetskii faktor*, 2:806–8.

131. Popov was then sent off to manage an aviation factory. See Bernov, *Zapiski diplomata*, 17; Sobór, *Jakub Berman*, 406–10; Skrzypek, *Mechanizmy uzależnienia*, 330–31; Golon, "Ambasadorowie Stalina," 162; Zalesskii, *Imperiia Stalina*.

132. Kaganovich made this comparison discussing Popov's case with other members of the Presidium on February 13, 1954. The document is available at the Miller Center's Kremlin Decision Making Project Web site, http://web1.millercenter.org/kremlin/54_02_13.pdf (accessed September 4, 2012).

133. Orekhov, *Sovetskii Soiuz i Pol'sha*, 47–48; on Siekierska, see Sobór, *Jakub Berman*, 337, and also her memoirs, "Niezapomniane lata"; Torańska, *Oni*, 27–40.

134. RGANI, f. 5, op. 28, d. 296, reel 70, l. 147.

135. Ibid., l. 215.

136. "Zapis besedy s I sekretarem Voevodskogo Komiteta PORP v Bydgoshche tov. Vl. Kruchekom," April 29, 1955, RGANI, f. 5, op. 28, d. 297, l. 76.

137. "Informacja o kontaktach naukowych Akademii Nauk ZSRR z PAN w latach 1954–1955," in Gąsiorowska-Grabowska, *Dokumenty i materialy*, 506–7.

138. See reports by two Soviet specialists working at the INS: historian V. S. Aleksandrov (May 20–July 28, 1954), and M. A. Naumova (November 15, 1954–July 25, 1955) at RGANI, f. 5, op. 28, d. 296, reel 70, ll. 127–28.

139. Chałasiński, "Zagadnienia kultury." For his biography, see Nałkowska, *Dzienniki*, part 2, 6:66–67.

140. RGANI, f. 5, op. 28, d. 296, ll. 148–49. Schaff's first article in question was "O pozytywny program badań społecznych, *Przegląd kulturalny*, no. 45, November 16, 1955.

141. Zalesskii, *Imperiia Stalina*.

142. Bernov, *Zapiski diplomata*, 37.

143. RGANI, f. 5, op. 28, d. 296, l. 152.

144. Schaff, "O roli Partii."

145. Vucinich, *Empire of Knowledge*, 257–74.

146. RGANI, f. 5, op. 28, d. 163, reel 41, l. 6

147. "Soobrazheniia k planu informatsionnoi zapiski 'O neblagopoluchnom polozhenii na nekotorykh uchastkakh ideologicheskogo fronta v evropeiskikh stranakh narodnoi demokratii,'" RGANI, f. 5, op. 28, d. 287, ll. 14–15.

148. Golon, "Dyplomaci Stalina," 562–63. See also Zalesskii, *Imperiia Stalina*. On Mikhailov's role during the 1951 Berlin Youth Festival, see Rutter, "The Western Wall, 97–98. On Mikhailov's role in postwar Stalinist purges, see Gorlitzki and Khlevniuk, *Cold Peace*, 152, 157–58.

149. Gorlitzki and Khlevniuk, *Cold Peace*, 158.

150. Bernov, *Zapiski diplomata*, 29, 33.

151. Entry for October 8, 1954, in Bubnov, "Dnevnik," 454.

152. Bernov, *Zapiski diplomata*, 31.

153. RGANI, f. 5, op. 28, d. 296, reel 70, ll. 38–40.

154. One Soviet report explained the decline in literature exports with three factors. First, the Polish government earmarked less hard currency for the purchase of Soviet books, due to Poland's negative trade balance with USSR. Second, the decline had to do with an increase in orders of much more expensive publications such as the *Bol'shaia sovetskaia entsiklopediia*, multi-volume works, as well as medical and technical publications. But the chief cause had to do with the increase in Polish publications of Soviet titles. See Ibid., d. 162, l. 59.

155. Ibid., ll. 69–75.

156. Ibid., d. 296, l. 48.

157. See, for example, ibid., d. 162, l. 66.

158. Caute, *The Dancer Defects*, 27.

159. RGANI, f. 5, op. 28, d. 296, ll. 51–53.

160. Ibid., l. 67.

161. Ibid., l. 66.

162. Ibid.

163. Ibid.

164. Ibid., l. 67.

165. "O nekotorykh nedostatkakh v organizatsii kul'turnykh i nauchnykh sviazei mezhdu SSSR i stranami narodnoi demokraii," RGANI, f. 5, op. 28, d. 286, ll. 175–87.

166. Ibid., l. 189.

167. RGANI, f. 5, op. 28, d. 296, l. 68.

168. See his letter to Suslov of May 3, 1954, at RGANI, f. 5, op. 28, d. 162, reel 41, l. 23.

169. See Gąsiorowska-Grabowska, *Dokumenty i materialy*, 10:368–69, 420–21, 456–57, 475–76.

170. Condee, "Cultural Codes of the Thaw," 161.

171. Mikhailov to Suslov, September 1954, at RGANI, f. 5, op. 28, d. 162, reel 41, l. 90–91.

172. RGANI, f. 5, op. 28, d. 296, l. 59.

173. RGANI, f. 5, op. 28, d. 162, reel 41, l. 26.

174. Mikhailov to Pospelov, RGANI, f. 5, op. 28, d. 162, reel 41, ll. 120–24.

175. Cited in Agapkina, "Russkiie kontakty Iaroslava Ivashkevicha," 33.

176. RGANI, f. 5, op. 28, d. 162, reel 41, l. 25.

177. Ibid., l. 85.

178. RGANI, f. 5, op. 28, d. 296, l. 62.

179. Rosenfeldt, *The "Special" World*, vol. 1, 539, 578–79. According to Rosenfeldt, the Information Committee initially functioned as an independent organ under the Council of Ministers, and later, in a reduced form, under the Ministry of Foreign Affairs. It was informally supervised by the Central Committee. On page 539, Rosenfeldt refers to the "Committee's gradual dissolution in the early 1950s," by which he is probably indicating the beginning, not the conclusion, of the termination process.

180. B. Ponomarev, A. Rumiantsev, and P. Kovanov to the Central Committee, April 16, 1955—see RGANI, f. 5, op. 28, d. 296, ll. 70–75.

181. Ibid., l. 72.

182. Bernov, *Zapiski diplomata*, 31.

183. Mikhailov channeled his energy into reinvigorating the Soviet cultural scene but also into guarding Soviet culture against political and ideological ferment: see documents 100, 102, 157, and 164 in Afanas'eva, *Apparat TsK KPSS i kul'tura*.

184. Bernov, *Zapiski diplomata*, 31–32.

EPILOGUE

1. RGANI, f. 5, op. 28, d. 398, l. 77.

2. Machcewicz, *Rebellious Satellite*, 18–19.

3. Kupiecki, *Natchnienie milionów*, 223–24.

4. RGANI, f. 5, op. 28, d. 398, l. 78.

5. Schattenberg, "'Democracy' or 'Despotism?'" 67.

6. RGANI, f. 5, op. 28, d. 398, l. 79.

7. Ibid., l. 80.

8. Ibid., d. 387, ll. 172–73, 175–76. Soviet officials dismissed the journalists' complaints as untrue.

9. It happened on the initiative of the Secretariat of the PZPR Central Committee, whose members agreed on sending copies of the "secret speech" to local party organs. Friszke, "Rok 1956," 174.

10. Paczkowski, *Spring Will Be Ours*, 275.

11. Gorsuch, "Time Travelers," 205–6.

12. On popular unrest during the "Polish October," see Machcewicz, *Rebellious Satellite*, 170–213.

13. Ibid., 189.

14. Ibid., 177.

15. Behrends, *Die erfundene Freundschaft*, 110–11.

16. Machcewicz, *Rebellious Satellite*, 177.

17. Korzon, "Polska 1957 i 1958 r.," 185–90.

18. RGANI, f. 5, op. 28, d. 397, ll. 419–23.

19. Burtin, "Studencheskoe brozhenie," 17.

20. AAN, syg. 237/XXII-877, k. 117.

21. Burtin, "Studencheskoe brozhenie," 4.

22. Information based on a letter from V. Grigorian, L. Slepov, and K. Omel'chenko to the secretary of the Central Committee of the VKP(b) M. A. Suslov, dated March 29, 1951. RGASPI, f. 17, op. 137, d. 477, l. 5.

23. For example, the party secretary at the Polish embassy in Moscow, Jan Chyliński requested in October 1949 that in connection with tripling of the amount of incoming students, the International Department of the Central Committee proportionately increase the quantity of newspapers and journals being sent for the students in the Soviet Union. AAN, syg. 237/XXII-637, k. 51. Some students received Polish newspa-

pers by individual subscriptions, although this method was not always effective, which caused great dismay among some Polish Communists. AAN, syg. 237/XXII-881, kk. 11–12.

24. RGASPI, f. M-1, op. 46, d. 208, l. 73.

25. Taranov, "'Raskachaem Leninskie Gory!'" 102.

26. "Umowa o współpracy kulturalnej między Polską i ZSRR," in Basiński and Walichnowski, *Stosunki polsko-radzieckie*, 311–13. A year and a half later it was followed by another detailed "Agreement On Scientific Co-operation between the Polish Academy of Sciences and the Academy of Sciences of the USSR" (358–63).

27. The TASS correspondent in Poland N. R. Pantiukhin related his tale of woe to his boss on the occasion of the Tenth European Cup in boxing in May 1953. Already during the preparations for the championship, recounted the journalist, "We, the Soviet correspondents felt the unfriendly atmosphere on our own skins." The organizing committee, he wrote, invited correspondents from all countries to the opening press conference, except for the Soviet ones. The referees' verdicts, the enthusiastic reactions of the public and even public figures upon the failures of the Soviet boxers confirmed Pantiukhin's experience of anti-Soviet discrimination. GARF, f. R-4459, op. 38, d. 446, ll. 59–62. Anti-Soviet sentiments touched even those who had nothing to do with the Sovietization of Poland. The conductor of the Poznań Opera, Russian-born Valeriian Berdiaev requested permission of the Soviet authorities to return to the USSR. As related by an embassy official, he explained that was his wish because "some leading employees of the Polish Ministry of Culture and Art had treated Berdiaev unfairly on account of his Russian background and the fact that he had arrived in Poland from the USSR." The conductor's wish to go to Russia remained unfulfilled—he died in the capital of his adopted country in 1956. GARF, f. R-5283, op. 22, d. 431, l. 75; Waldorff, *Diabły i anioły*, 302–3; "Bierdiajew Walerian" in Lissa and Dziębowska, *Encyklopedia Muzyczna PWM*. See also a memoir by the Polish pianist Grażyna Bacewicz, *Znak szczególny*, 12–13.

28. Woźniakowski, *Między ubezwłasnowolnieniem*, 101–15. An author of a Soviet report noted that from June 1956 to September 1957, contacts were basically broken" between the two writers' unions. See "Politicheskaia informatsiia o polozhenii v soiuze pol'skikh pisatelei i pol'skoi literatury,'" GARF, f. R-8581, op. 2, d. 470, l. 67.

29. "Politicheskaia informatsiia," GARF, f. R-8581, op. 2, d. 470, l. 61.

30. Bikont and Szczęsna, *Lawina i kamienie*, 295.

31. "Politicheskaia informatsiia," GARF, f. R-8581, op. 2, d. 470, l. 38. On Słonimski's attack on socialist realism, see also Shore, *Caviar and Ashes*, 309.

32. Shore, *Caviar and Ashes*, 319.

33. Cited in ibid., 23.

34. See "Politicheskaia informatsiia," GARF, f. R-8581, op. 2, d. 470, l. 37.

35. In early 1958, seventeen Western plays were being staged in Poland, and not a single one from the USSR. See Caute, *The Dancer Defects*, 367. For an interesting argument about the expansion of Soviet cultural infrastructure and simultaneous erosion of Soviet culture's domestic mobilizing force, see Roth-Ey, *Moscow Prime Time*. On page 66, the author reports that the East European distribution agencies were turning

down more than half of Soviet movies. And in the summer of 1962 a Soviet delegation counted only five Soviet (but twenty-five capitalist) films on Cracow's screens.

36. Hixson, *Parting the Curtain*, 112.

37. GARF, f. 8581, op. 2, d. 454, ll. 119–23.

38. Bubnov, who earlier lamented excessive discussions of sexuality in the Polish press, was not alone; on the Soviet view of Polish literature, see "Politicheskaia informatsiia," GARF, f. R-8581, op. 2, d. 470, l. 54. On official Stalinist "prudishness," see Caute, *The Dancer Defects*, 129, 456.

39. "Deklaracja rządu ZSRR o podstawach rozwoju i dalszego umocnienia przyjaźni i współpracy między Związkiem Radzieckim a innymi państwami socjalistycznymi," Basiński and Walichnowski, *Stosunki polsko-radzieckie*, 318–21. On numbers of Soviet troops, see Granville, *The First Domino*, 75, 95.

40. Paczkowski, *Spring Will Be Ours*, 273; see also www.czerwiec56.ipn.gov.pl /portal/c56/1401/Ofiary_i_represje.html (accessed February 15, 2013).

41. Bikont and Szczęsna, *Ławina i kamienie*, 292.

42. Katsakioris, "The Soviet-South Encounter," 143–44.

CONCLUSION

1. Lederer and Burdic, *The Ugly American*, 11–13.

2. Ibid., 216.

3. Ibid., 162.

4. Márai, *Memoir of Hungary*, 28–37.

5. David Caute refers to "fear of freedom" in *The Dancer Defects*, 32.

6. Barkey, *Empire of Difference*, 18.

7. Behrends, *Die erfundene Freundschaft*, 281.

8. Pechatnov, "Exercise in Frustration," 16; on structural problems of Stalinist bureaucracy, see also Rosenfeldt, *The "Special World,"* vol. 1, 536.

9. On the Stalinist authorities efforts to make the camp system economically viable, see Gorlizki and Khlevniuk, *Cold Peace*, 127–33.

10. Gilroy, *The Black Atlantic*, 3.

11. Bernov, *Zapiski diplomata*, 55.

12. Miłosz, introduction to Tertz, *On Socialist Realism*, 11.

13. Caute, *The Dancer Defects*, 13.

14. De Grazia, *Irresistible Empire*, 6.

15. Verdery, *What Was Socialism*; Kotkin, "Mongol Commonwealth?" Babiracki, "Interfacing the Soviet Bloc."

16. Erofeev, *Khoroshii Stalin*, 319.

Bibliography

ARCHIVAL SOURCES

Poland

AAN—Archiwum Akt Nowych (Archive of New Documents), Warsaw
AMSZ—Archiwum Ministerstwa Spraw Zagranicznych (Archive of the Polish
    Ministry of Foreign Affairs), Warsaw
  Zespół (collection) no. 6, Departament Polityczny (Political Department),
    1945–1948
  Zespół 7: Departament I (Department I), 1949–1960
  Zespół 15: Gabinet Ministra (Cabinet of the Minister), 1945–1951
  Zespół 21: Departament Prasy i Informacji (Department of Press and
    Information)
  Zespół 23: Gabinet Ministra (Cabinet of the Minister), 1952–1960
  Zespół 27: Ambasada RP w Moskwie (Polish Embassy in Moscow),
    1944–1947
CAW—Centralne Archiwum Wojskowe (Central Military Archive), Warsaw
  Department III, Archives of the Polish Armed Forces, 1943–45
  Zespół 3: The First Corps
  Zespół 4: The Command of the First Army
  Zespół 5: The Command of the Second Army
Filmoteka Narodowa (National Film Archive), Warsaw
  Selected Documents
KC PPR (Central Committee of the Polish Workers' Party)
  Wydział Propagandy (Department of Propaganda)
  Wydział Zagraniczny (International Department)
KC PZPR (Central Commitee of the Polish United Workers' Party)
  Wydział Prasy i Wydawnictw (Departament of Press and Publishing)
  Sekretariat KC (Secretariat of the Central Committee)
  Biuro Polityczne KC (Political Bureau of the Central Commitee)
  Wydział Zagraniczny (International Departament)
Muzeum Literatury im. Adama Mickiewicza (Adam Mickiewicz Museum of
    Literature), Warsaw
  Papers of Leon Kruczkowski

Russia

Archive of the Union of Russian Writers
  Miscellaneous unedited documents

GARF—Gosudarstvennyi arkhiv Rossiiskoi Federatsii (State Archive of the Russian Federation), Moscow

    f. R-5283, VOKS—Vsesoiuznoe obshchestvo kul'turnoi sviazi s zagranitsei (All-Union Soviet Society for Cultural Relations Abroad)

    f. R-8581, Soviet Information Bureau

    f. R-4851, Ob"edinennyi fond uchrezhdeniia po rukovodstvu izdatel'stvami poligraficheskoi promyshlennost'iu i knizhnoi torgovlei.

    f. R-4459, TASS (Telegraph Agency of the Soviet Union)

    f. 8127, Papers of N. A. Bubnov

RGALI—Rossiiskii gosudarstvennyi arkhiv literatury i iskusstva (Russian State Archive of Literature and the Arts), Moscow

    f. 631, Union of Soviet Writers

        op. 14, 26: Inostrannaia Komissiia SSP (Foreign Commission of the Union of Soviet Writers)

        op. 15, Sekretariat SSP (Secretariat of the Union of Soviet Writers)

    f. 962, Komitet po delam isskustv pri Sovete Ministrov SSSR (Committee for Artistic Affairs of the Council of Ministers USSR), 1935–53

    f. 2845, Papers of M. S. Zhivov

RGANI—Rossiiskii gosudarstvennyi arkhiv noveishei istorii (Russian State Archive of Contemporary History), Moscow

    f. 5, Apparatus of the Communist Party of the Soviet Union

        op. 28: Department for Relations with Foreign Communist Parties (International Department), 1953–57.

RGASPI—Rossiiskii gosudarstvennyi arkhiv sotsial'no-politicheskoi istorii (Russian State Archive of Social-Political History), Moscow

    f. M-1, Central Committee of the Komsomol

        op. 46, Department of Student Youth (1941–65)

    f. 17, Central Committee of the CPSU

        op. 125, Administration of Propaganda and Agitation (1938–48)

        op. 132, Department of Propaganda and Agitation (1948–53)

        op. 137, International Commission / Commission for Relations with Foreign Communist Parties (1949–52)

PUBLISHED DOCUMENT COLLECTIONS

Adibekov, Grant Mkrtychevich, ed. *Soveshchaniia kominforma: 1947, 1948, 1949. Dokumenty i materialy.* Moscow: ROSSPEN, 1998.

Afanas'eva, E. S. *Apparat TsK KPSS i kul'tura 1953–1957. Dokumenty.* Moscow: ROSSPEN, 2001.

Basiński, Euzebuisz, and Tadeusz Cieślak, eds. *Stosunki polsko-radzieckie w latach 1917–1945.* Warsaw: KiW, 1967.

Basiński, Euzebiusz, and Tadeusz Walichnowski, eds. *Stosunki polsko-radzieckie w latach 1945–1972. Dokumenty i materiały.* Warsaw: Książka i Wiedza, 1974.

Bordiugow, G. A., ed. *Polska-ZSRR. Struktury podległości. Dokumenty WKP(b), 1944–1949.* Warsaw: Instytut Studiów Politycznych PAN, 1995.

Cariewskaja, Tatiana, and Ewa Rosowska. *Teczka specjalna J. W. Stalina. Raporty NKWD z Polski 1944–1946.* Warsaw: Rytm, 1998.

Clark, Katerina, E. A. Dobrenko, Andrei Artizov, and Oleg V. Naumov, eds. *Soviet Culture and Power: A History in Documents, 1917–1953.* Annals of Communism. New Haven, Conn.: Yale University Press, 2007.

Gąsiorowska-Grabowska, Natalia, ed. *Dokumenty i materialy po istorii sovetsko-pol'skikh otnoshenii. Uniform Title: Dokumenty i materiały do historii stosunków polsko-radzieckich. Russian.* Moscow: Izdatel'stvo Akademii nauk SSSR, 1963.

Khlevniuk, Oleg V., ed. *Politbiuro TsK VKP(b) i Sovet Ministrov SSSR 1945–1953.* Moscow: ROSSPEN, 2002.

Kochański, Aleksander, ed. *Polska w dokumentach z archiwów rosyjskich, 1949–1953.* Dokumenty do dziejów PRL no. 12. Warsaw: ISP PAN, 2000.

———, ed. *Protokoły posiedzeń Biura Politycznego KC PPR 1944–1945.* Warsaw: ISP PAN, 1992.

Kozlov, V. A., ed. *Kramola: inakomyslie v SSSR pri Khrushcheve i Brezhneve, 1953–1982 gg.: rassekrechennye dokumenty Verkhovnogo Suda i Prokuratury SSSR.* Moscow: Materik, 2005.

Naumov, Oleg V., ed. *Vlast' i khudozhestvennaia intelligentsiia: dokumenty TSK RKP(b)-VKP(b), VChK-OGPU-NKVD o kul'turnoi politike, 1917–1953 gg.* Rossiia, XX Vek. Moscow: Demokratiia, 1999.

Organizacja i działania bojowe Ludowego Wojska Polskiego 1943–1945. Vol. 4. Warsaw: MON, 1963.

Polonsky, Antony, and Bolesław Drukier, eds. *The Beginnings of Communist Rule in Poland.* London: Routledge, 1980.

Syzdek, Eleonora, ed. *Dyskusje ideologiczno-polityczne wśród lewicy polskiej w ZSRR na przełomie 1943/1944 r. (wybór dokumentów).* Warsaw: Wojskowa Akademia Polityczna im. F. Dzierżyńskiego, 1985.

Volokitina, T. V., ed., *Vostochnaia Evropa v dokumentakh rossiiskikh arkhivov: 1944–1953 gg.* 2 vols. Moscow and Novosibirsk: Sibirskii khronograf, 1997–1998.

———. *Sovetskii faktor v Vostochnoi Evrope: 1944–1953. Dokumenty.* 2 vols. Moscow: ROSSPEN, 1999.

BOOKS AND ARTICLES

Abrams, Bradley F. *The Struggle for the Soul of the Nation: Czech Culture and the Rise of Communism.* Lanham, Md.: Rowman and Littlefield, 2004.

Adamczyk, Mieczysław. *Prasa regionalna w 40-Leciu Polski Ludowej. Materiały z Ogólnopolskiego Sympozjum Historyków Prasy, Kielce-Cedzyna, 9–11 Listopada 1984 r.* Kielce: 1987.

Adamczyk-Garbowska, Monika. "Adolf Rudnicki." In *Holocaust Literature: An Encyclopedia of Writers and Their Work,* edited by S. Lillian Kremer, 2:1050–62. New York: Routledge, 2003.

Adibekov, Grant Mkrtychevich. *Kominform i poslevoennaia Evropa, 1947–1956 gg.* Moscow: Rossiia Molodaia, 1994.

Afanas'ev, Iurii N., ed. *Sud'by rossiiskogo krest'ianstva.* Moscow: RGU, 1996.

Agapkina, Tamara Petrovna. "Russkie kontakty Iaroslava Ivashkevicha. 1945–1950-e gody (po materialam arkhivnykh razyskanii)." *Sovetskoe slavianovedenie,* no. 1 (2001): 28–38.

Akademiki-ekonomisty Rossii, 2nd ed. Moscow: RAN, Institut ekonomiki, 1999.

Aldrich, Richard J. "Putting Culture into the Cold War: The Cultural Relations Department (CRD) and British Covert Information Warfare." *Intelligence and National Security* 18, no. 2 (Summer 2003): 109–33.

Anusiewicz, Marian. "Wytyczne idowe polskiej jednostki wojskowej." In *Organizacja i działania bojowe Ludowego Wojska Polskiego 1943–1945,* vol. 4. Warsaw: MON, 1963.

Applebaum, Anne. *The Iron Curtain: The Crushing of Eastern Europe.* New York: Doubleday, 2012.

Apor, Balázs, Péter Apor, E. A. Rees, eds. *The Sovietization of Eastern Europe: New Perspectives on the Postwar Period.* Washington, D.C.: New Academia, 2008.

Apor, Balázs, Jan C. Behrends, Polly Jones, and E. A. Rees, eds. *The Leader Cult in Communist Dictatorships: Stalin and the Eastern Bloc.* New York: Palgrave, 2004.

Artsimovich, V., and M. Morshchiner, eds. *Khudozhestvennaia literatura stran narodnoi demokratki v perevodakh na russkii iazyk. Bibliograficheskii ukazatel'. Pol'sha (konets XVIII v.–1950 g.).* Moscow: Izdatel'stvo inostrannoi literatury, 1951.

Auden, W. H. "September 1, 1939." In *Selected Poems: W. H. Auden,* 2nd ed., edited by Edward Mendelson, 95–97. New York: Vintage, 2007.

Babichenko, D. L. *Pisateli i tsenzory: Sovetskaia literatura 1940-kh godov pod politicheskim kontrolem TsK.* Moscow: Rossiia molodaia, 1994.

Babiracki, Patryk. "Between Compromise and Distrust: The Soviet Information Bureau's Operations in Poland, 1945–1953." *Cultural and Social History* 6, no. 3 (September 2009): 345–67.

———. "Enemy to Friend: Soviet Union, Poland and the Refashioning of the Imperial Identity in *Pravda,* 1943–1947." In *Bridging Disciplines, Spanning the World: Approaches to Inequality, Identity and Institutions,* edited by Rachel Beatty Riedl et al., 132–54. Princeton Institute for International Regional Studies Monograph Series #4. Princeton, N.J.: World Politics Press, 2006.

———. "Interfacing the Soviet Bloc: Recent Literature and New Paradigms." *Ab Imperio,* no. 4 (2011): 376–407.

Babiracki, Patryk, and Kenyon Zimmer, eds. *Cold War Crossings: International Travel and Exchange across the Soviet Bloc, 1940s–1960s.* College Station: Texas A&M University Press, 2014.

Bacewicz, Grażyna. *Znak szczególny.* Warsaw: Czytelnik, 1970.

Balcerzak, Janina, ed. *Słownik biograficzny działaczy polskiego ruchu robotniczego* (3 vols.), 2nd ed. Warsaw: Książka i Wiedza, 1978–1992.

Baliszewski, Dariusz, and Andrzej K. Kunert, eds., *Ilustrowany przewodnik po Polsce Stalinowskiej, 1944–1956*. Vol. 1: 1944. Warsaw: PWN, 1999.

Barkey, Karen. *Empire of Difference: The Ottomans in Comparative Perspective*. New York: Cambridge University Press, 2008.

Bartoszewicz, Henryk. *Polityka Związku Sowieckiego wobec państw Europy Środkowo-Wschodniej w latach 1944–1948*. Warsaw: Książka i Wiedza, 1999.

Bartov, Omer. *The "Jew" in Cinema: From The Golem to Don't Touch My Holocaust*. Bloomington: Indiana University Press, 2005.

Bates, John."Cenzura wobec problem niemieckiego w literaturze polskiej." In *Presja i ekspresja. Zjazd szczeciński i socrealizm*, edited by Danuta Dąbrowska and Piotr Michałowski, 79–92. Szczecin: Wyd. Uniwersytetu Szczecińskiego, 2002.

Behrends, Jan C. "Agitation, Organization, Mobilization. The League for Polish-Soviet Friendship in Stalinist Poland." In Apor, Apor, and Rees, *The Sovietization of Eastern Europe*, 181–98.

———. *Die erfundene Freundschaft. Propaganda für die Sowjetunion in Polen und in der DDR (1944–1957)*. Zeithistorische Studien 32. Cologne: Böhlau Verlag Köln, 2005.

———. "Nation and Empire: Dilemmas of Legitimacy during Stalinism in Poland (1941–1956)." *Nationalities Papers* 37, no. 4 (July 2009): 443–66.

Behrends, Jan C., Malte Rolf, and Gabor Rittersporn, eds. *Sphären von Öffentlichkeit in Gesselschaften sowjetischen Typs*. Frankfurt am Main: Lang, 2003.

Beissinger, Mark. "The Persisting Ambiguity of Empire." *Post-Soviet Affairs*, no. 2 (1995): 149–84.

Berling, Władysław. *Wspomnienia*. Vol. 2: *Przeciw 17 republice*. Warsaw: Polski Dom Wydawniczy, 1991.

Bernov, Iu. V. *Zapiski diplomata*. Moscow: Parusa, 1995.

Bikont, Anna, and Joanna Szczęsna. *Lawina i kamienie: Pisarze wobec komunizmu*. Warsaw: Prószynski i S-ka, 2006.

———. "Towarzysze nieudanej podróży." *Gazeta Wyborcza*, January 22, 2000 http:// niniwa2.cba.pl/towarzysze_nieudanej_podrozy_02.htm (accessed February 10, 2009).

Bińko, Beata. "Instytut Kształcenia Kadr Naukowych przy KC PZPR—narzędzie ofensywy ideologicznej w nauce i szkolnictwie wyższym." *Kultura i społeczeństwo* 2 (1996): 199–214.

Bittner, Stephen V. *The Many Lives of Khrushchev's Thaw: Experience and Memory in Moscow's Arbat*. Ithaca, N.Y.: Cornell University Press, 2008.

Błażyński, Zbigniew. *Mówi Józef Światło*. London: Polska Fundacja Kulturalna, 1986.

Blium, A. V. *Sovetskaia tsenzura v epokhu total'nogo terrora, 1929–1953*. St. Petersburg: Akademicheskii proekt, 2000.

Bobryk, Roman, and Jerzy Faryno. *Polacy w oczach Rosjan—Rosjanie w oczach Polaków. Zbiór studiów*. Warsaw: Slawistyczny Ośrodek Wydawniczy, 2000.

Bol'shaia meditsinskaia entsiklopediia. Moscow: Sovetskaia entsiklopediia, 1962.

Bol'shakova, K. V. "Sovetsko-Pol'skie kontakty v oblasti vysshego obrazovaniia v 1946–1949 godakh (po materialam VOKS i OPSD)." *Sovetskoe slavianovedenie*, no. 6 (1989): 26–37.

———. "Sovetsko-Pol'skie literaturnye sviazi v 1946–1949 gg." *Sovetskoe slavianovedenie*, no. 6 (1981): 37–54.

———. "Sovetsko-Pol'skie teatral'nye kontakty v 1946–1949 gg. (po materialam VOKS i OPSD)." *Sovetskoe slavianovedenie*, no. 2 (1984): 77–86.

———. "Sviazi i sotrudnichestvo mezhdu profsoiuzami SSSR i Pol'shi (1946–1949)." *Sovetskoe slavianovedenie*, no. 4 (1980): 11–26.

———. "U istokov sotrudnichestva istorikov SSSR i Narodnoi Pol'shi (1946–1951)." *Sovetskoe slavianovedenie*, no. 1 (1987): 79–85.

Bonecki, Henryk, Józef Barbag, and Państwowe Wydawnictwo Naukowe. *Encyklopedia Powszechna PWN*. Warsaw: PWN, 1973–1976.

Border Street (film). Directed by Aleksander Ford. Sarasota, Fla.: Polart, 2005.

Borejsza, Jerzy. "Krochmalizm czy realizm?" *Odrodzenie*, no. 20 (1948): 2.

Borodziej, Włodzimierz. "Dekada powojenna (1945–1955). Zwycięstwo i zniewolenie." In *Białe Plamy-czarne plamy. Sprawy trudne w polsko-rosyjskich stosunkach, 1918–2008*, edited by Adam D. Rotfeld and Anatolij W. Torkunow, 555–78. Warsaw: PISM, 2010.

———. "Wydział Zagraniczny KC PZPR." In *Centrum władzy w Polsce: 1948–1970*, edited by Andrzej Paczkowski, 51–80. Warsaw: Instytut Studiów Politycznych PAN, 2003.

Borowski, Tadeusz. "Praca młodego pisarza." In Tadeusz Borowski, *Utwory zebrane*, vol. 3, 250–62. Warsaw: PIW, 1954.

Brandenberger, David. *National Bolshevism: Stalinist Mass Culture and the Formation of Modern Russian National Identity*. Cambridge, Mass.: Harvard University Press, 2002.

Brenner, Rachel Feldhay. "Ideology and Ethics: Maria Dąbrowska's Jewish (and Polish) Problem." *Slavic Review* 70, no. 2 (Summer 2011): 399–421.

Brent, Jonathan, and Vladimir Naumov. *Stalin's Last Crime: The Plot against the Jewish Doctors, 1948–1953*. New York: Harper Collins, 2003.

Broniewska, Janina. *Z notatnika korespondenta wojennego*. Warsaw: MON, 1953.

Broniewska, Janina, and Jerzy Putrament. *Ludzie Pierwszej Armii*. Warsaw: GZPW Wojska Polskiego, 1946.

Brooks, Jeffrey. *Thank You, Comrade Stalin! Soviet Public Culture from Revolution to Cold War*. Princeton, N.J.: Princeton University Press, 1999.

Brooks, Jeffrey, and Sergei Zhuk, "Soviet Culture, 1932–1992." In *Oxford Handbook of Modern Russian History*, edited by Simon Dixon. New York: Oxford University Press, forthcoming.

Brown, Deming. *Soviet Attitudes toward American Writing*. Princeton, N.J.: Princeton University Press, 1962.

Brzezinski, Zbigniew. *The Soviet Bloc: Unity and Conflict*. Russian Research Center Studies 37. Rev. and enl. ed. Cambridge, Mass.: Harvard University Press, 1967.

Bulgakov, Mikhail. *The Master and Margarita*. Translated by Richard Pevear and Larissa Volokhonsky. New York: Penguin, 1997.

Burtin, Iurii. "Studencheskoe brozhenie v SSSR (konets 1956 g.)." *Voprosy istorii*, no. 1 (1997): 3–23.

Campbell, Robert W. "Nekrasov, Nikolai Nikolaevich." In *A Biographical Dictionary of Russian and Soviet Economists*, 290–92. New York: Routledge, 2012.

Caute, David. *The Dancer Defects: The Struggle for Cultural Supremacy during the Cold War*. Oxford: Oxford University Press, 2003.

Chałasiński, Józef. "Zagadnienia kultury współczesnej w humanistyce polskiej szkoły w nauce—instytuty naukowe." *Nauka Polska*, no. 2 (1955): 125–46.

Chandler, Andrea. *Institutions of Isolation: Border Controls in the Soviet Union and Its Successor States*. Montreal and Buffalo, N.Y.: McGill-Queen's University Press, 1993.

Checinski, Michael. *Poland: Communism, Nationalism, Anti-Semitism*. Translated in part by Tadeusz Szafar. New York: Karz-Cohl, 1982.

Choldin, Marianna Tax. "The New Censorship: Censorship by Translation in the Soviet Union." *Journal of Library Studies* 21, no. 2 (1986): 334–49.

Chyliński, Tadeusz. *Jaki był Bolesław Bierut: wspomnienia syna*. Warsaw: Oficyna Drukarska, 1999.

Ciborska, Elżbieta. *Dziennikarze z władzą (nie zawsze) w parze*. Warsaw: Elipsa, 1998.

Cienciala, Anna, Natalia Lebedeva, and Wojciech Materski, eds. *Katyn: A Crime without Punishment*. New Haven, Conn.: Yale University Press, 2007.

Ciesielski, Stanisław et. al., eds. *Represje sowieckie wobec Polaków i obywateli polskich*. 2nd rev. ed. Warsaw: Karta, 2002.

Clausewitz, Carl Von. *On War*. Translated and edited by Michael Howard and Peter Paret. Princeton, N.J.: Princeton University Press, 1976.

Coeuré, Sophie, and Sabine Dullin, eds. *Frontières du communisme. Mythologies et réalités de la division de l'Europe, de la révolution d'Octobre au mur de Berlin*. Paris: Découverte, 2007.

Condee, Nancy. "Cultural Codes of the Thaw." In *Nikita Khrushchev*, edited by WilliamTaubman, Sergei Khrushchev, and Abbott Gleason, 160–76. New Haven, Conn.: Yale University Press, 2000.

Connelly, John. *Captive University: The Sovietization of East German, Czech and Polish Higher Education, 1945–1956*. Chapel Hill: University of North Carolina Press, 2000.

Crowley, David. "Paris or Moscow? Warsaw Architects and the Image of the Modern City in the 1950s." *Kritika* 9, no. 4 (Fall 2008): 769–98.

———. *Warsaw*. London: Reaktion, 2003.

Crowley, David and Susan Reid, "Socialist Spaces: Sites of Everyday Life in the Eastern Bloc." In *Socialist Spaces: Sites of Everyday Life in the Eastern Bloc*, 1–22. Edited by David Crowley and Susan Reid, New York: Bloombsbury Academic, 2002.

Curry, Jane Leftwich. *Poland's Journalists: Professionalism and Politics*. New York: Cambridge University Press, 1990.

Czachowska, Jadwiga, and Alicja Szałagan, eds. *Współcześni polscy pisarze i badacze literatury. Słownik biobibliograficzny.* 9 vols. Warsaw: Wydawnictwa Szkolne i Pedagogiczne, 1994–2007.

Dąbrowska, Maria. *Dzienniki powojenne.* Vol. 3 (1945–1950). Warsaw: Czytelnik, 1996.

Danilov, A. A., and A. V. Pyzhikov. *Rozhdenie sverkhderzhavy: SSSR v pervye poslevoennye gody.* Moscow: ROSSPEN, 2001.

Dańko, Bolesław. *Nie zdążyli do Andersa (Berlingowcy).* London: Unicorn, 1992.

Datner, Szymon. "Na polu chwały. Żydzi żołnierze 1 i 2 Amii Wojska Polskiego Polegli w II Wojnie Światowej. Cz. I: Na Szlaku Bojowym: Lenino—Przyczółki Warszawskie—Jabłonna." *Biuletyn Żydowskiego Instytutu Historycznego* 4, no. 128 (1983): 25–56.

David-Fox, Michael. "The Fellow Travelers Revisited: The 'Cultured West' through Soviet Eyes." *Journal of Modern History* 75, no. 2 (2003): 300–335.

———. "The Iron Curtain as Semipermeable Membrane: Origins and Demise of the Stalinist Superiority Complex." In Babiracki and Zimmer, *Cold War Crossings*, 14–39.

———. *Showcasing the Great Experiment: Cultural Diplomacy and Western Visitors to the Soviet Union, 1921–1941.* New York: Oxford University Press, 2012.

Davies, Norman. *Rising '44: The Battle for Warsaw.* London: Macmillan, 2003.

De Grazia, Victoria. *Irresistible Empire: America's Advance through Twentieth-Century Europe.* Cambridge, Mass: Belknap Press of Harvard University Press, 2005.

Dobbs, Michael. *Six Months in 1945: Stalin, Churchill, and Truman—from World War to Cold War.* New York: Knopf, 2012.

Dobrenko, Evgeny. "The Literature of the Zhdanov Era: Mentality, Mythology, Lexicon." *South Atlantic Quarterly* 90, no. 2 (1991): 323–55.

Domosławski, Artur. *Kapuściński. Non-fiction.* Warsaw: Świat Książki, 2010.

———. *Ryszard Kapuściński: A Life.* Translated by Antonia Lloyd-Jones. New York: Verso, 2012.

Drewnowski, Jan. *Próba ogólnej teorii gospodarki planowej.* Biblioteka Szkoły Głównej Handlowej w Warszawie. Seria 1; Nr 3. Wyd. 2 ed. Warsaw: Trzaska, Evert i Michalski, 1947.

Dubiel, Paweł, and Józef Kozak. *Polacy w II Wojnie Światowej. Kim byli, co robili.* Warsaw: RYTM, 2003.

Dudek, Antoni, and Andrzej Paczkowski. "Poland." In *A Handbook of the Communist Security Apparatus in East Central Europe 1944–1989*, edited by Krzysztof Persak and Łukasz Kamiński, 221–84. Warsaw: Institute of National Remembrance, 2005.

Dunham, Vera Sandomirsky. *In Stalin's Time: Middleclass Values in Soviet Fiction.* Durham, N.C. and London: Duke University Press, 1990.

Ehrenburg, Ilya. *Post-War Years: 1945–54.* Translated by Tatiana Shebunina. Cleveland and New York: World Publishing, 1967.

Eliot, T. S. *The Waste Land and Other Writings.* New York: Modern Library, 2001.

Erofeev, Victor. *Khoroshii Stalin*. Moscow: Zebra E, 2004.

Eustachiewicz, Lesław. *Dramaturgia współczesna 1945–1980*. Warsaw: Wydawn. Szkolne i Pedagogiczne, 1985.

Evtushenko, Evgenii. "Skierowanie Komsomołu." *Wolność*, no. 201, September 1, 1954.

Fałkowicz, Swietłana, and Maria Czernych. "Polsko-radziecka współpraca kulturalna i naukowa w okresie międzywojennym." *Dzieje Najnowsze* 2 (1970): 105–23.

Fateev, A. V. *Obraz vraga v sovetskoi propagande: 1945–1954 gg*. Moscow: Rossiiskaia Akademiia Nauk, Institut Rossiiskoi Istorii, 1999.

Fijałkowska, Barbara. *Borejsza i Różański. Przyczynek do dziejów Stalinizmu w Polsce*. Studia i Materiały. Olsztyn: Wyższa Szkoła Pedagogiczna, 1995.

———. *Polityka i twórcy (1948–1959)*. Warsaw: PWN, 1985.

Fik, Marta. "Kultura polska, 1945–1956." In *Polacy wobec przemocy 1944–1956*, edited by Barbara Otwinowska and Jan Żaryn, 220–75. Warsaw: Spotkania, 1996.

Filippov, A. F. "Nabliudatel' imperii (imperiia kak sotsiologicheskoe poniatie i politicheskaia problema)." *Voprosy sotsiologii* 1, no. 1 (1992): 89–120.

Foucault, Michel. *The Order of Things: An Archaeology of the Human Sciences*. New York: Vintage Books, 1994.

Friedberg, Maurice. *A Decade of Euphoria: Western Literature in Post-Stalin Russia, 1954–64*. Bloomington: Indiana University Press, 1977.

———. *Russian Classics in Soviet Jackets*. New York: Columbia University Press, 1962.

Friedrich, Carl J., and Zbigniew Brzezinski. *Totalitarian Dictatorship and Autocracy*. 2d ed., revised by Carl J. Friedrich. Cambridge, Mass.: Harvard University Press, 1965.

Friszke, Andrzej. "Rok 1956." In *Centrum władzy w Polsce, 1948–1970*, edited by Andrzej Paczkowski, 160–214. Warsaw: ISP PAN, 2003.

Gaddis, John Lewis. *We Now Know: Rethinking Cold War History*. New York: Oxford University Press, 1997.

Garrard, John Gordon, and Carol Garrard. *Inside the Soviet Writers' Union*. New York: Free Press and Collier Macmillan, 1990.

Gati, Charles. *Hungary and the Soviet Bloc*. Durham, N.C.: Duke University Press, 1986.

Gatrell, Peter, and Nick Baron, eds. *Warlands: Population Resettlement and State Reconstruction in the Soviet-East European Borderlands, 1945–50*. New York: Palgrave, 2009.

Geertz, Clifford. *The Interpretation of Cultures: Selected Essays*. London: Hutchinson, 1975.

Gerasimov, Ilya, et al. "New Imperial History and the Challenges of Empire." In *Empire Speaks Out: Languages of Rationalization and Self-Description in the Russian Empire*, edited by Ilya Gerasimov, Jan Kusber, and Alexander Semyonov, *3–32* Boston: Brill, 2009.

———. "Vpered: Nazad, v budushchee." *Ab Imperio* 4 (2007): 9–16.

Gibianskii, L. Ia. "Forsirovanie sovetskoi blokovoi politiki." In *Kholodnaia voina, 1945-1963 gg.: Istoricheskaia retrospektiva. Sbornik statei*, edited by N. I. Egorova and A. O. Chubar'ian, 137–86. Moscow: OLMA-PRESS, 2003.

———. *U istokov "Sotsialisticheskogo Sodruzhestva." SSSR i vostochnoevropeiskie strany v 1944-1949 gg.* Moscow: Nauka, 1995.

Gilburd, Eleonory. "Picasso in Thaw Culture." *Cahiers du monde russe* 47, no. 1–2 (January–June 2006): 65–108.

Gilroy, Paul. *The Black Atlantic: Modernity and Double Consciousness.* Cambridge, Mass.: Harvard University Press, 1993.

Ginsburg, Mirra. "Translator's Introduction." In Mikhail Bulgakov, *The Master and Margarita*, translated by Mirra Ginsburg. New York: Grove Press, 1987.

Gluchowski, L. W. "The Defection of Jozef Swiatlo and the Search for Jewish Scapegoats in the Polish United Workers' Party, 1953-1954," http://ece .columbia.edu/files/ece/images/gluchowski-1.pdf (accessed September 4, 2012).

Goban-Klas, Tomasz, and Pål Kolstø. "East European Mass Media: The Soviet Role." In *The Soviet Union in Eastern Europe, 1945-89*, edited by Odd Arne Westad, Sven G. Holtsmark and Iver B. Neumann, 110–25. New York: St. Martin's Press, 1994.

———. *Niepokorna orkiestra medialna: dyrygenci i wykonawcy polityki informacyjnej w Polsce po 1944 roku.* Warsaw: Oficyna Wydawnicza ASPRA-JR, 2004.

Golon, Mirosław. "Ambasadorowie Stalina—radzieccy dyplomaci w Europie Środkowo-Wschodniej i na Bałkanach w latach 1944-1953." *Czasy Nowożytne* 18-19 (2005): 129–78.

———. "Dyplomaci Stalina—radzieccy ambasadorowie w Polsce i Czechosłowacji w okresie stalinowskim (1945-1955)." In *Nad Bałtykiem. W kręgu polityki, gospodarki problemów narodowościowych i społecznych w XIX i XX wieku*, edited by Zbigniew Karpus, Jarosław Kłaczkow and Mariusz Wołos, 541–64. Toruń: Wydawn. Uniwersytatu Mikołaja Kopernika, 2005.

Golubev, A. V., and V. A. Nevezhin. "VOKS v 1930-1940-e gody." *Minuvshee* 14 (1993): 313–64.

Goriachev, Iurii. *Tsentral'nyi Komitet KPSS, VKP(b), RKP(b), RSDRP(b): 1917-1991: Istoriko-biograficheskii spravochnik.* Moscow: Parad, 2005.

Goriaeva, T. M. *Politicheskaia tsenzura v SSSR: 1917-1991.* Moscow: ROSSPEN, 2002.

Gorizontov, Leonid Efremovich. "'Metodologicheskii perevorot' v pol'skoi istoriografii na rubezhe 1940-1950-kh godov i sovetskie istoriki." *Sovetskoe slavianovedenie*, no. 6 (1993): 50–66.

———. "Pervye gody (po novym istochnikam)." *Sovetskoe slavianovedenie*, no. 2 (2007): 36–57.

———. "'Pol'skaia tsivilizovannost'' i 'russkoe varvarstvo': osnovaniia dlia stereotipov i avtostereotipov." *Sovetskoe slavianovedenie*, no. 1 (2004): 39–48.

Gorlizki, Yoram, and Oleg Khlevniuk. *Cold Peace: Stalin and the Soviet Ruling Circle, 1945-1953.* New York: Oxford University Press, 2005.

Górski, Jan. *Pamięć warszawskiej odbudowy, 1945-1949. Antologia.* Warsaw: PIW, 1972.

Gorsuch, Anne. *All This Is Your World: Soviet Tourism at Home and Abroad after Stalin.* New York: Oxford University Press, 2011.

———. "Time Travelers: Soviet Tourists to Eastern Europe." In Gorsuch and Koenker, *Turizm,* 205–26.

Gorsuch, Anne, and Diane P. Koenker, eds. *Turizm: The Russian and East European Tourist under Capitalism and Socialism.* Ithaca, N.Y.: Cornell University Press, 2006.

Goussef, Catherine. "Wilno, Vilné, Vilnius, capitale de Lituanie." In *A l'Est, la mémoire retrouvée,* edited by Alain Brossat et al., 489–520. Paris: Editions la Découverte, 1990.

Granville, Johanna. *The First Domino: International Decision Making during the Hungarian Crisis of 1956.* College Station: Texas A&M University Press, 2004.

Gromyko, A.A., ed. *Diplomaticheskii slovar' v trekh tomakh.* 4th ed. Moscow: Nauka, 1985.

Gross, Jan T. *Fear: Anti-Semitism in Poland after Auschwitz.* New York: Random House, 2006.

———. *Revolution from Abroad: The Soviet Conquest of Poland's Western Ukraine and Western Belorussia.* Princeton, N.J.: Princeton University Press, 1988.

———. "The Social Consequences of War: Preliminaries to the Study of Imposition of Communist Regimes in East Central Europe." *East European Politics and Societies* 3 (March 1989): 198–214.

Grosz, Wiktor. *Gdy rodziło się Wojsko Polskie.* Warsaw: MON, 1954.

Grynberg, Henryk. "The Holocaust in Polish Literature." *Notre Dame English Journal* 11, no. 2 (April 1979): 115–39.

———. *Memorbuch.* Warsaw: WAB, 2000.

Grzelak, Czesław, Henryk Stańczyk, and Stefan Zwoliński. *Armia Berlinga i Żymierskiego.* Warsaw: Neriton, 2002.

Guilbaut, Serge. *How New York Stole the Idea of Modern Art: Abstract Expressionism, Freedom, and the Cold War.* Chicago: University of Chicago Press, 1983.

Haltof, Marek. *Polish Film and the Holocaust: Politics and Memory.* New York: Berghahn Books, 2012.

Hartmann, Anne. "Sowjetische 'Leitkultur' in der SBZ und frühen DDR." In *Russen und Deutche im 20. Jahrhundert.* Vol. 3: *Tauwetter, Eiszeit, und gelenkte Dialoge. Russen und Deutsche nach 1945,* edited by Karl Eimermacher, Astrid Volpert and Gennadij Bordjugow, 529-60. Munich: Wilhelm Fink Verlag, 2006.

Hass, Ludwik. "Inteligencja polska 1945-1980 (Postawy i zachowania). *Dzieje najnowsze* 34, no. 1 (2002): 73–94.

Hellbeck, Jochen. *Revolution on My Mind: Writing a Diary under Stalin.* Cambridge, Mass.: Harvard University Press, 2006.

Hirszowicz, Maria. *Pułapki zaangażowania. Intelektualiści w służbie komunizmu.* Warsaw: SCHOLAR, 2001.

Hixson, Walter L. *Parting the Curtain: Propaganda, Culture and the Cold War, 1943-1961*. New York: St. Martin's Press, 1997.

Hodos, George. *Show Trials: Communist Purges in Eastern Europe*. New York: Praeger, 1987.

Hollander, Paul. *Political Pilgrims: Western Intellectuals in Search of the Good Society*. 4th ed. New Brunswick, N.J.: Transaction, 1998.

Holloway, David. *Stalin and the Bomb: The Soviet Union and Atomic Energy, 1939-1956*. New Haven, Conn.: Yale University Press, 1996.

Hołuj, Tadeusz. *Ciąg dalszy. Szkice o przygodach utworów*. Cracow: Wydawnictwo Literackie, 1980.

———. *Dom pod Oświęcimiem. Sztuka w czterech aktach*. Warsaw: Wydawn. Literackie, 1979.

Honkisz, Władysław. *W pierwszym szeregu. Formowanie, kształcenie i działanie korpusu oficerów polityczno-wychowawczych, maj 1943-1945*. Warsaw: MON, 1984.

Hübner, Piotr. *I Kongres Nauki Polskiej jako forma realizacji założeń polityki naukowej Państwa Ludowego*. Wrocław: Zakład Narodowy im. Ossolińskich, 1983.

———. *Polityka naukowa w Polsce w latach 1944-1953: Geneza systemu*. Problemy Naukowe Współczesności. Wrocław: Zakład Narodowy im. Ossolińskich, 1992.

Iazhborovskaia, I. S. *Katynskii sindrom v sovetsko-pol'skikh i rossiisko-pol'skikh otnosheniiakh*. Moscow: ROSSPEN, 2001.

Jaczyński, Zbigniew. *Zygmunt Berling. Między sławą a potępieniem*. Warsaw: KiW, 1993.

Jarmułowicz, Małgorzata. *Sezony błędów i wypaczeń. Socrealizm w dramacie i teatrze polskim*. Gdańsk: Wydawn. Uniwersytetu Gdańskiego, 2003.

Jarosiński, Zbigniew. *Nadwiślański socrealizm*. Warsaw: Instytut Badań Literackich, 1999.

Jarosz, Dariusz. *Polacy a stalinizm, 1948-1956*. Warsaw: Instytut Historii PAN, 2000.

Jaroszewicz, Piotr, and Bohdan Roliński. *Przerywam milczenie, 1939-1989*. Warsaw: Fakt, 1991.

Jastrun, Mieczysław, Seweryn Pollak, and Leon Gomolicki. *Dwa wieki poezji rosyjskiej. Antologia*. Warsaw: Czytelnik, 1947.

Jersild, Austin. *The Sino-Soviet Alliance: An International History*. Chapel Hill: University of North Carolina Press, 2014.

———. "The Soviet Union as an Imperial Scavenger." *American Historical Review* 116, no. 1 (2011): 109–32.

Jezierski, Andrzej, and Cecylia Leszczyńska. *Historia gospodarcza Polski*, 3rd ed. Warsaw: Key Text, 2003.

Jirásek, Zdeněk, and Andrzej Małkiewicz. *Polska i Czechosłowacja w dobie stalinizmu (1948-1956)*. Warsaw: ISP PAN, 2005.

Jones, Polly, ed. *The Dilemmas of De-Stalinization: Negotiating Cultural and Social Change in the Khrushchev Era*. New York: Routledge, 2006.

Kapuściński, Ryszard. *Imperium*. Translated by Klara Glowczewska. New York: Vintage, 1995.

Karavaeva, Anna. *Po dorogam zhizni. Dnevniki, ocherki, vospominaniia*. Moscow: Sovetskii pisatel', 1957.

Kaspe, Sviatoslav I. "Imperii: Genezis, Struktura, Funktsii." *Polis*, no. 5 (1997): 31–48.

Katsakioris, Constantin. "The Soviet-South Encounter: Tensions in the Friendship with Afro-Asian Partners 1945–1965." In Babiracki and Zimmer *Cold War Crossings*, 143–44.

Kenez, Peter. *Cinema and Soviet Society: From the Revolution to the Death of Stalin*. London and New York: I. B. Tauris, 2001.

———. *Hungary from the Nazis to the Soviets: The Establishment of the Communist Regime in Hungary, 1944–1948*. New York: Cambridge University Press, 2006.

———. "Jewish Themes in Stalinist Films." *Journal of Popular Culture* 31, no. 4 (Spring 2003): 159–69.

Kenney, Padraic. "After the Blank Spots Are Filled: Recent Perspectives on Modern Poland." *Journal of Modern History* 79 (March 2007): 134–61.

———. *A Carnival of Revolution: Central Europe 1989*. Princeton, N.J.: Princeton University Press, 2003.

———. *Rebuilding Poland: Workers and Communists, 1945–1950*. Ithaca, N.Y.: Cornell University Press, 1997.

Kersten, Krystyna. *The Establishment of Communist Rule in Poland, 1943–1948*. Societies and Culture in East-Central Europe. Berkeley: University of California Press, 1991.

———. *Narodziny systemu władzy. Polska 1943–1948*. Warsaw: Krąg, 1984.

———. *Polacy-Żydzi-Komunizm. Anatomia półprawd. 1939–1968*. Warsaw: Niezależna Oficyna Wydawnicza, 1992.

Khartmenn, Ann (Hartmann, Anne). "Rukovodstvo kul'turoi i kul'tura rukovodstva v sovetskoi zone okkupatsii Germanii." In *Rossiia i Germaniia v XX veke*. Vol. 3: *Ottepel', pokholadanie i upravliaemyi dialog. Russkie i nemtsy posle 1945 goda*, ed. Karl Ajmermakher, Gennadii Bordiugov and Astrid Fol'pert, 395–421. Moscow: AIRO-XXI, 2010).

Khrushchev, Nikita S. *Khruschchev Remembers: The Last Testament*. Translated by Strobe Talbott. Boston: Little, Brown, 1970.

———. "Speech by N. S. Khrushchev on the Stalin Cult Delivered Feb. 25, 1956, at a Closed Session of the 20th Congress of the Soviet Communist Party." In *Khrushchev Speaks: Selected Speeches, Articles, and Press Conferences, 1949–1961*, edited by Thomas P. Whitney, 204–65. Ann Arbor: University of Michigan Press, 1963.

———. "O kul'te lichnosti i ego posledstviakh. Doklad pervogo sekretaria TsK tov. Khruschcheva N. S. XX s"ezdu Kommunisticheskoi partii Sovetskogo Soiuza 25 fevralia 1956 goda." In *Doklad N. S. Khruschcheva o kul'te lichnosti Stalina na XX s"ezde KPSS. Dokumenty*, edited by K. Aimermakher et al., 51–119. Moscow: ROSSPEN, 2002.

Khudozhestvennaia literatura Pol'shi. Bibliograficheskii ukazatel' knig i statei, opublikovannykh v sovetskoi pechati 1949–1952 gg. i pol'skoi pechati. Moscow: Vsesoiuznaia gosudarstvennaia biblioteka inostrannoi literatury, 1953.

Kichelewski, Audrey. "Imagining 'the Jews' in Stalinist Poland: Nationalists or Cosmopolites?" *European Review of History: Revue europeenne d'histoire* 17, no. 3 (June 2010): 505–52.

Kładoczny, Piotr. *Prawo jako narzędzie represji w Polsce Ludowej (1944–1956): Prawna analiza kategorii przestepstw przeciwko państwu.* Warsaw: IPN, 2004.

Koivunen, Pia. "Overcoming Cold War Boundaries at the World Youth Festivals." In *Reassessing Cold War Europe*, edited by Sari Autio-Sarasmo and Katalin Miklóssy, 175–92. New York: Routledge, 2011.

Kolakowski, Leszek. *Main Currents of Marxism. Vol. 3: The Breakdown.* Oxford: Oxford University Press, 1981.

Kołodziejczyk, Marcin. "Postawy Polaków. Józef Sigalin." *Polityka*, special issue, "Stalinizm po polsku," no. 6 (2012): 107–11.

Kondusza, Wojciech. "'Mała Moskwa.' Legnica i powiat legnicki w latach 1945– 1947." In *W objęciach wielkiego brata. Sowieci w Polsce 1944–1993*, edited by Konrad Rokicki and Sławomir Stępień, 151–83. Warsaw: IPN, 2009.

Konorski, Jerzy. *Conditioned Reflexes and Neuron Organization.* New York: Cambridge University Press, 1948.

———. "Konorski Jerzy" In *A History of Psychology in Autobiography*, edited by Carl Allanmore Murchison and Gardner Lindzey, 183–217. The Century Psychology Series. Englewood Cliffs, N.J.: Prentice Hall, 1974.

Korboński, Stefan. *The Jews and the Poles in World War II.* New York: Hippocrene Books, 1989.

Koropeckyj, Roman. *Adam Mickiewicz: The Life of a Romantic.* Ithaca, N.Y.: Cornell University Press, 2008.

———. *W imieniu Rzeczypospolitej.* Warsaw: Bellona, 1991.

Korzon, Andrzej. *Polsko-radzieckie kontakty kulturalne w latach 1944–1950.* Wrocław: Zakład Narodowy im. Ossolińskich, 1982.

———. "Literatura radziecka w Polsce i literatura polska w ZSRR w latach 1954–1982." *Przegląd rusycystyczny* 9, no. 3–4 (1986): 116–25.

———. "Niektóre problemy polsko-radzieckich stosunków gospodarczych w latach 1945–1957." *Studia z Dziejów Rosji i Europy Środkowo-Wschodniej* 28 (1993): 135–52.

———. "Polska 1957 i 1958 r. w oczach Moskwy." *Dzieje Najnowsze* 34, no. 4 (2002): 185–90.

Kostyrchenko, G. V. *Tainaia politika Stalina: vlast' i antisemitizm.* Moscow: Mezhdunarodnye otnosheniia, 2003.

Kotkin, Stephen. "Mongol Commonwealth? Exchange and Governance across the Post-Mongol Space." *Kritika* 8, no. 3 (2007): 487–531.

Kozieł, Andrzej. "Koncepcje dotyczące prasy i dziennikarstwa w latach 1946–1956." In *Prasa regionalna w 40-leciu Polski Ludowej*, edited by Mieczysław

Adamczyk, 45–59. Kielce: Kielecki Oddział Instytutu Kształcenia Nauczycieli, 1987.

Kramer, Mark. "The Early Post-Stalin Succession Struggle and Upheavals in East-Central Europe: Internal-External Linkages in Soviet Policy Making (Part 1)." *Journal of Cold War Studies* 1, no. 1 (Winter 1999): 3–55.

———. "Stalin, Soviet Policy, and the Consolidation of a Communist Bloc in Eastern Europe, 1944–1953." In *Stalinism Revisited: The Establishment of Communist Regimes in East-Central Europe*, edited by Vladimir Tismaneanu, 51–102. Budapest and New York: Central European University Press, 2009.

Kramer, Paul A. "Power and Connection: Imperial Histories of the United States in the World." *American Historical Review* 116, no. 5 (2011): 1348–91.

———. "Reflex Actions: Colonialism, Corruption and the Politics of Technocracy in the Early Twentieth Century United States." In *Challenging US Foreign Policy: America and the World in the Long Twentieth Century*, edited by Bevan Sewell and Scott Lucas, 14–35. New York: Palgrave Macmillan, 2011.

Krasucki, Eryk. *Międzynarodowy komunista. Jerzy Borejsza: biografia polityczna.* Warsaw: Wydawnictwo Naukowe PWN SA, 2009.

Krawczyk, Andrzej. *Pierwsza próba indoktrynacji. Działalność Ministerstwa Informacji i Propagandy w latach 1944–1947.* Warsaw: ISP PAN, 1994.

Krementsov, Nikolai. "Lysenkoism in Europe: Export-Import of the Soviet Model." In *Academia in Upheaval: Origins, Transfers and Transformations of the Communist Academic Regimes in Russia and East-Central Europe*, edited by Michael David-Fox, 180–202. Westport, Conn.: Bergin and Garvey, 2000.

———. *Stalinist Science.* Princeton, N.J.: Princeton University Press, 1997.

Kremer, S. Lillian. "Introduction." In *Holocaust Literature: An Encyclopedia of Writers and Their Work*, edited by S. Lillian Kremer, 1:xxi–xxxv. New York: Routledge, 2003.

Krogulski, Mariusz. *Okupacja w imię sojuszu. Armia Radziecka w Polsce 1944–1956.* Warsaw: Wydawn. von Borowiecky, 2000.

Kubicka, Grażyna. "Charakterystyka statystyczna prasy ludowej 1944–1949." *Materiały pomocnicze do historii dziennikarstwa Polski Ludowej* 12 (1987): 40–56.

Kurant, I. L., *Khudozhestvennaia literatura Pol'shi. Bibliograficheskii ukazatel' knig i statei, opublikovannykh v sovetskoi pechati i pechati Pol'shi. (1956).* Moscow: Izdatel'stvo inostrannoi literatury, 1957.

Kupiecki, Robert. *"Natchnienie Milionów:" Kult Józefa Stalina w Polsce, 1944–1956.* Warsaw: Wydawn. Szkolne i Pedagogiczne, 1993.

Kurz, Iwona. "Sport to zdrowie." In *Obyczaje polskie. Wiek XX w krótkich hasłach*, edited by Małgorzata Szpakowska, 321–27. Warsaw: W.A.B., 2008.

Kusiak, Franciszek. *Oficerowie 1 Armii Wojska Polskiego w latach 1944–1945.* Wrocław: PAN, 1987.

Kuźnicki, Leszek, ed. *Instytut Biologii Doświadczalnej im. Marcelego Nenckiego: Historia i teraźniejszość.* Vol. 1: *1918–2007.* Warsaw: Instytut Biologii Doświadczalnej im. Marcelego Nenckiego PAN, 2008.

Łapiński, Zdzisław, and Wojciech Tomasik. *Słownik realizmu socjalistycznego.* Cracow: Universitas, 2004.

Lederer, William J., and Eugene Burdick. *The Ugly American.* New York: Norton, 1958.

Lewandowski, Czesław. *Kierunki tak zwanej ofensywy ideologicznej w polskiej oświacie, nauce i szkołach wyższych, w latach 1944-1948.* Acta Universitatis Wratislaviensis no. 1525. Politologia, 10. Wrocław: Wydawn. Uniwersytetu Wrocławskiego, 1993.

Liebman, Stuart. "Les premières constellations du discours sur l'Holocaust dans le cinema polonais." In *De l'histoire au cinéma*, edited by Antoine de Baecque and Christian Delage, 193-216. Paris: Editions Complexe, 1998.

———. "Réflexions sur les Polonais et les Juifs dans le cinéma polonais." In *Juifs et Polonais 1939-2008*, edited by Jean-Charles Szurek and Annette Wieviorka, 171-92. Paris: Albin Michel, 2009.

Liehm, Mira and Antonin Liehm. *The Most Important Art: Eastern European Film after 1945.* Berkeley: University of California Press, 1977.

Lieven, D. C. B. *Empire: The Russian Empire and Its Rivals.* New Haven, Conn.: Yale University Press, 2001.

Lisiecka, Anna. "Działalność Komitetu Współpracy Kulturalnej z Zagranicą w latach 1950-1956." In *Przebudować człowieka: Komunistyczne wysiłki zmiany mentalności*, edited by Marta Brodała et al., 203-60. Warsaw: Wydawn. TRIO, 2001.

Lissa, Zofia, and Elżbieta Dziębowska. *Encyklopedia Muzyczna PWM.* Cracow: Polskie Wydawnictwo Muzyczne, 1979.

Lucas, W. Scott. "Mobilizing Culture: The State-Private Network and the CIA in the Early Cold War." In *War and Cold War in American Foreign Policy, 1942-62*, edited by Dale Carter and Robin Clifton, 83-107. New York: Palgrave, 2001.

Lukowski, Jerzy, and W. H. Zawadzki. *A Concise History of Poland.* 2nd ed. Cambridge Concise Histories. Cambridge: Cambridge University Press, 2006.

Lustiger, Arno. *Stalin and the Jews: The Tragedy of the Jewish Anti-Fascist Committee and the Soviet Jews.* New York: Enigma Books, 2003.

Lygo, Emily. "The Need for New Voices: Writers' Union Policy Towards Young Writers 1953-64." In Jones, *The Dilemmas of De-Stalinization*, 193-208.

Machcewicz, Paweł. *Rebellious Satellite: Poland 1956.* Washington, D.C.: Woodrow Wilson Center Press, 2009.

Madej, Alina. *Kino, władza, publiczność Kinematografia polska w latach 1944-1949.* Bielsko-Biała: Prasa Beskidzka, 2002.

Maes, Francis. *A History of Russian Music: From Kamarinskaya to Babi Yar.* Translated by Arnold J. Pomerans and Erica Pomerans. Berkeley: University of California Press, 2002.

Maiorova, O. N. "Sotrudnichestvo VOKS i OPSD v oblasti kul'tury (1950-1955)." *Sovetskoe slavianovedenie*, no. 4 (1986): 3-15.

Márai, Sándor. *Memoir of Hungary, 1944-1948.* Translated by Albert Tezla. Budapest: Corvina and CEU Press, 1996.

Mar'ina, V. V., and L. B. Miliakova, eds., *Totalitarizm: Istoricheskii opyt vostochnoi evropy*. Moscow: Institut Slavianovedeniia i Balkanistiki RAN, 1995.

Mastny, Vojtech. *Russia's Road to the Cold War: Diplomacy, Warfare, and the Politics of Communism*. New York: Columbia University Press, 1979.

Matsuda, Takeshi. *Soft Power and Its Perils: U.S. Cultural Policy in Early Postwar Japan and Permanent Dependency*. Washington, D.C. and Stanford, Calif.: Woodrow Wilson Center Press and Stanford University Press, 2007.

Mayakovsky, Vladimir. "My Soviet Passport." Translated by Herbert Marshall. *Sputnik*, no. 12 (1982), www.marxists.org/subject/art/literature/mayakovsky /1929/my-soviet-passport.htm.

Mazuy, Rachel. *Croire plutôt que voir? Les voyages en Russie sovietique, 1919–1939*. Paris: Odile Jacob, 2002.

McDermott, Kevin, and Matthew Stibbe. *Stalinist Terror in Eastern Europe: Elite Purges and Mass Reppression*. Manchester and New York: Manchester University Press, 2010.

Mentsendorf, Ia. I., ed. *Khudozhestvennaia literatura Pol'shi. Bibliograficheskii ukazatel' knig i statei, opublikovannykh v sovetskoi pechati i pechati Pol'shi v 1955 g*. Moscow: Vsesoiuznaia gosudarstvennaia biblioteka inostrannoi literatury, 1956.

Mentzel, Zbigniew. *Czas ciekawy, czas niespokojny. Z Leszkiem Kołakowskim rozmawia Zbigniew Mentzel*. Cracow: Znak, 2007.

Mielczarek, Tomasz. *Od "Nowej Kultury" do "Polityki": tygodniki społeczno-kulturalne i społeczno-polityczne PRL*. Kielce: Wydawn. Akademii Swiętokrzyskiej, 2003.

Mikołajczyk, Stanisław. *The Rape of Poland: Pattern of Soviet Aggression*. New York: Whittlesey House, 1948.

Miłosz,Czesław. "Anti-Semitism in Poland." *Problems of Communism* 3 (1957): 35–40.

———. *The Captive Mind*. Translated by Jane Zielonko. New York: Vintage International, 1990.

———. Introduction to *On Socialist Realism*, by Abram Tertz. Translated by George Dennis. New York: Pantheon, 1960.

Mizerski, Sławomir. "Idzie Olchowik po słupkach." In "Polakow portret codzienny" autorstwa reporterów Polityki. Special issue of *Polityka* 9 (2011): 116–20.

Mokul'skii, S. S., and P. A. Markov. *Teatral'naia entsiklopediia*. Entsiklopedii, Slovari, Spravochniki. Moscow: Sovetskaia entsiklopediia, 1961–1967.

Mołdawa, Tadeusz. *Ludzie władzy, 1944–1991: Władze państwowe i polityczne Polski według stanu na dzień 28 II 1991*. Warsaw: PWN, 1991.

Moskowitz, Gene. "The Uneasy East: Aleksander Ford and the Polish Cinema." *Sight and Sound* 27, no. 3 (Winter 1957): 136–40.

Naimark, Norman. "Post-Soviet Russian Historiography on the Emergence of the Soviet Bloc." *Kritika* 5, no. 3 (Summer 2004): 561–80.

———. *Russians in Germany: A History of the Soviet Zone of Occupation, 1945–1949*. Cambridge, Mass.: Harvard University Press, 1995.

———. "Stalin and Europe in the Postwar Period, 1945–53: Issues and Problems."
Journal of Modern European History 2, no. 1 (2004): 28–57.

Naimark, Norman, and Leonid Gibianski. *The Establishment of Communist
Regimes in Eastern Europe, 1944–49*. Boulder, Colo.: Westview, 1997.

Nałęcz, Daria. *Główny Urząd Kontroli Prasy: 1945–1949*. Dokumenty do dziejów
PRL; Zesz. 6. Warsaw: Instytut Studiów Politycznych Polskiej Akademii Nauk,
1994.

Nalepa, Edward Jan. *Oficerowie Armii Radzieckiej w Wojsku Polskim, 1943–1968*.
Warsaw: Bellona, 1995.

Nałkowska, Zofia. *Dzienniki*. 6 vols. (1945–1954), edited by Hanna Kirchner.
Warsaw: Czytelnik, 2000.

———. *Granica*. Warsaw: Czytelnik, 1982.

Naszkowski, Marian. *Lata próby. Wspomnienia*. Warsaw: Ksążka i Wiedza, 1965.

———. *Paryż-Moskwa: wspomnienia dyplomaty, 1945–1950*. Warsaw: PIW, 1986.

Nezhinskii, L. N. *Sovetskaia vneshniaia politika v gody "Kholodnoi Voiny"
(1945–1985). Novoe prochtenie*. Moscow: Mezhdunarodnye otnosheniia, 1995.

Noskova, Albina F. "K. K. Rokossovskii v Pol'she. 1949–1956 gg. Neizvestnye
stranitsy biografii." In *Studia polonica. K 70-letiiu Viktora Aleksandrovicha
Khoreva*, edited by V. A. Khorev and V. K. Volkov, 79–94. Moscow: Indrik,
2002.

———. "Sovetskie sovetniki v stranakh Tsentral'noi i Vostochnoi Europy, 1945–1953."
Voprosy istorii, no. 1 (1998): 104–13.

Nussbaum, Klemens. "Jews in the Polish Army in the USSR 1943–1944." *Soviet
Jewish Affairs* 2, no. 1 (1972): 94–104.

Nye, Joseph. *Soft Power: The Means to Success in World Politics*. New York: Public
Affairs, 2004.

Olejniczak, Maciej. *Polsko-radzieckie kontakty kulturalne po II Wojnie
Światowej. Fakty—problemy*. Wrocław: Zakład Narodowy im. Ossolińskich,
WDN, 1977.

Orekhov, A. M. *Sovetskii Soiuz i Pol'sha v gody "Ottepeli." Iz istorii sovetsko-
pol'skikh otnoshenii*. Moscow: Indrik, 2005.

O'Sullivan, Donal. "'Wer immer ein Gebiet besetzt . . .' Sowjetische Osteuropa
Politik, 1943–1947/48." In *Gleichschaltung unter Stalin? Die Entwicklung der
Parteien im Östlichen Europa, 1944–1949*, edited by Stefan Creuzberger and
Manfred Görtemaker, 45–84. Paderborn: Ferdinand Schöningh, 2004.

Paczkowski, Andrzej. "Communist Poland 1944–1989: Some Controversies and a
Single Conclusion." *Intermarium* 3, no. 2 (1999), www.sipa.columbia.edu/ece
/research/intermarium/vol3no2/pacz.pdf (accessed October 1, 2011).

———. "Jews in the Polish Security Apparatus: An Attempt to Test the Stereotype."
Translated by Claire Rosenson. *Polin* 16 (2003): 453–64.

———. "Polish-Soviet Relations 1944–1989: The Limits of Autonomy." *Intermarium*
6, no. 1 (2003), www.sipa.columbia.edu/ece/research/intermarium/vol6no1
/paczkowski.pdf (accessed June 5, 2012).

———. "Polska droga przez stalinizm." *Polityka* no. 6 (2012): 8–12.

——. *The Spring Will Be Ours: Poland and the Poles from Occupation to Freedom.* Translated by Jane Cave. University Park: Pennsylvania State University Press, 2003.

Panferova, V.F. *Fedor Panferov—moi otets. Ochen' lichnye vospominaniia.* Moscow: Russkoe slovo, 1996.

Paperny, Vladimir. *Architecture in the Age of Stalin: Culture Two.* Translated by John Hill and Roann Barris in collaboration with the author. Cambridge: Cambridge University Press, 2002.

Parker, Ralph. *Zagovor protiv mira: zapiski angliiskogo zhurnalista.* Moscow: Literaturnaya Gazeta, 1949.

Parrish, Michael. *The Lesser Terror: Soviet State Security, 1939–1953.* New York: Praeger, 1996.

Parsadanowa, Walentina (Valentina S. Parsadanova). "Polityka i jej skutki." In *Białe plamy-czarne plamy. Sprawy trudne w polsko-rosyjskich stosunkach, 1918–2008*, edited by Adam D. Rotfeld and Anatolij W. Torkunow, 390–420. Warsaw: PISM, 2010.

Pasierski, Emil. *Miłosz i Putrament. Żywoty równoległe.* Warsaw: WAB, 2011.

Pasternak, Leon. *W marszu i na biwaku.* Warsaw: MON, 1958.

Pavlyshyn, Marko, ed. *Glasnost' in Context: On the Recurrence of Liberalizations in Central and East European Literatures and Cultures.* New York: Oxford University Press, 1990.

Pechatnov, Vladimir. "Exercise in Frustration: Soviet Foreign Propaganda in the Early Cold War, 1945–47." *Cold War History* 1, no. 2 (2001): 1–27.

Pegov, A. M., ed. *Imena moskovskikh ulits.* Rev. ed. Moscow: Moskovskii rabochii, 1979.

Persak, Krzysztof. *Sprawa Henryka Hollanda.* Warsaw: IPN, 2006.

——. "Stalin as Editor: The Soviet Dictator's Secret Changes to the Polish Constitution of 1952." *CWIHP Bulletin*, no. 11 (Winter 1998): 149–54.

Péteri, György, ed. *Imagining the West in Eastern Europe and the Soviet Union.* Pittsburgh, Pa.: University of Pittsburgh Press, 2010.

Petrova, Nina Konstantinovna. *Antifashistskie komitety v SSSR: 1941–1945 gg.* Moscow: Rossiiskaia Akademiia Nauk, Institut Rossiiskoi Istorii, 1999.

Pikhoia, R. G. *Sovetskii soiuz. Istoriia vlasti, 1945–1991.* Moscow: Rossiiskaia akademiia gos. sluzhby pri prezidente Rossiiskoi Federatsii, 1998.

Pinkus, Benjamin. "Change and Continuity in Soviet Policy towards Soviet Jewry and Israel, May–December 1948." *Israel Studies* 10, no. 1 (Spring 2005): 96–122.

——. *The Soviet Government and the Jews, 1948–1967: A Documented Study.* New York: Cambridge University Press, 1984.

Piotrowski, Tadeusz. *Poland's Holocaust: Ethnic Strife, Collaboration with Occupying Forces and Genocide in the Second Republic, 1918–1947.* Jefferson, N.C.: McFarland, 1998.

Podgórski, Czesław. "Zarys rozwoju organizacji Polskich Sił Zbrojnych w Związku Radzieckim." *Wojskowy Przegląd Historyczny* 1 (1966): 1–39.

Pollock, Ethan. *Stalin and the Soviet Science Wars*. Princeton, N.J.: Princeton University Press, 2006.

Polonsky, Antony. "Stalin and the Poles 1941-7." *European History Quarterly* 17 (1987): 453-92.

Polski słownik biograficzny. Cracow: Instytut Historii PAN, 1935.

Pomianowski, Jerzy. "Torowanie drogi do wolności w sferze kultury." In *Białe plamy-czarne plamy. Sprawy trudne w polsko-rosyjskich stosunkach, 1918-2008*, edited by Adam D. Rotfeld and Anatolij W. Torkunow, 515-25. Warsaw: PISM, 2010.

Prokhorov, A. M., ed. *Bol'shaia sovetskaia entsiklopediia*. 3rd ed. Moscow: Sovetskaia entsiklopediia, 1970.

Prokop, Jan. *Pisarze w służbie przemocy*. Cracow: Viridis, 1995.

Pryzwan, Mariola, ed. *Wspomnienia o Władysławie Broniewskim*. Warsaw: Domena, 2002.

Puddington, Arch. *Broadcasting Freedom: The Cold War Triumph of Radio Free Europe and Radio Liberty*. Lexington: University Press of Kentucky, 2000.

Putrament, Jerzy. *Pół wieku*. Vol. 2: *Wojna*. Warsaw: Czytelnik, 1962.

———. *Pół wieku*. Vol. 4: *Literaci*. Warsaw: Czytelnik, 1970.

Pytlakowski, Jerzy. *Fundamenty*. Warsaw: Prasa Wojskowa, 1948.

Pyzhikov, A. V. *Khrushchevskaia "Ottepel'."* Moscow: Olma-Press, 2002.

Ra'anan, Uri, and Igor Lukes, eds. *Inside the Apparat: Perspectives on the Soviet Union from Former Functionaries*. Lexington, Mass.: Lexington Books, 1990.

Ramet, Pedro. *Cross and Commissar: The Politics of Religion in Eastern Europe and the USSR*. Bloomington and Indianapolis: Indiana University Press, 1987.

Reinisch, Jessica. "'We Shall Rebuild Anew a Powerful Nation': UNRRA, Internationalism and National Reconstruction in Poland." *Journal of Contemporary History* 43, no. 3 (2008): 451-76.

Richmond, Yale. *Cultural Exchange and the Cold War: Raising the Iron Curtain*. University Park: Pennsylvania State University Press, 2000.

Rieber, Alfred. "Popular Democracy: An Illusion?" In Tismaneanu, *Stalinism Revisited*, 103-30.

———. *The Struggle for the Eurasian Borderlands: From the Rise of Early Modern Empires to the End of the First World War*. New York: Cambridge University Press, 2014.

Riordan, Jim. "The Komsomol." In *Soviet Youth Culture*, edited by J. Riordan, 16-44. Bloomington: Indiana University Press, 1989.

Robin, Régine. *Socialist Realism: An Impossible Aesthetic*. Stanford, Calif: Stanford University Press, 1992.

Rocznik Demograficzny 2012 / The Demographic Yearbook of Poland 2012. Warsaw: ZWS 2012, www.stat.gov.pl/cps/rde/xbcr/gus/rs_rocznik_demograficzny_2012.pdf (accessed March 27, 2012).

Rokicki, Konrad, and Sławomir Stępień, eds. *W objęciach wielkiego brata. Sowieci w Polsce 1944-1993*. Warsaw: IPN, 2009.

Romek, Zbigniew. "Nauka przeciw ideologii: współpraca historyków polskich i radzieckich po II wojnie światowej." *Dzieje najnowsze* 34, no. 1 (2002): 95-102.

Rosenfeldt, Niels Erik. *The "Special" World: Stalin's Power Apparatus and the Soviet System's Secret Structures of Communication.* Translated by Sally Laird and John Kendal, vol. 1. Copenhagen: Museum Tusculanum Press, 2009.

Roszkowski, Wojciech. *Historia Polski 1914-2005.* Warsaw: PWN, 2006.

Roth-Ey, Kristin. *Moscow Prime Time: How the Soviet Union Built the Media Empire That Lost the Cultural Cold War.* Ithaca, N.Y.: Cornell University Press, 2011.

Rothschild, Joseph and Nancy Wingfield. *Return to Diversity: A Political History of East Central Europe, 3rd ed.* New York: Oxford University Press, 2000.

Różański, Henryk. *Śladem wspomnień i dokumentów, 1943-1948.* Warsaw: PWN, 1987.

Róziewicz, Jerzy. *Polsko-radzieckie stosunki naukowe w latach 1918-1939.* Wrocław: Zakład Narodowy im. Ossolińskich, 1979.

Rubenstein, Joshua. *Tangled Loyalties: The Life and Times of Ilya Ehrenburg.* New York: Basic Books, 1996.

Rubenstein, Joshua, and Vladimir P. Naumov, ed. *Stalin's Secret Pogrom: The Postwar Inquisition of the Jewish Anti-Fascist Committee.* Translated by Laura Esther Wolfson. New Haven, Conn.: Yale University Press, 2001.

Ryback, Timothy. *Rock Around the Bloc.* Oxford and New York: Oxford University Press, 1990.

Schaff, Adam. *Moje spotkania z nauką polską.* Warsaw: BGW, 1997.

———. "O pozytywny program badań społecznych." *Przegląd kulturalny*, no. 45, November 16, 1955, 1-2.

———. "O roli Partii w rozwoju teorii marksistowskiej." *Przegląd kulturalny*, no. 47, November 24-30, 1955, 6-7.

———. *Pora na spowiedź.* Warsaw: BGW, 1993.

Schattenberg, Suzanne. "'Democracy' or 'Despotism'? How the Secret Speech Was Translated into Everyday Life." In Jones, *The Dilemmas of De-Stalinization*, 64-79.

Schatz, Jaff. *The Generation: The Rise and Fall of the Jewish Communists of Poland.* Berkeley: University of California Press, 1991.

Scott, James C. *Domination and the Arts of Resistance: Hidden Transcripts.* New Haven, Conn.: Yale University Press, 1992.

Semler, Helen Boldyreff. *Discovering Moscow: The Complete Companion Guide.* New York: Hippocrene, 1987.

Seniavskaia, E. S. *Frontovoe Pokolenie: 1941-1945: Istoriko-psikhologicheskoe issledovanie.* Moscow: Institut Rossiiskoi Istorii RAN, 1995.

Service, Robert. *A History of Twentieth-Century Russia.* Cambridge, Mass.: Harvard University Press, 1998.

Seton-Watson, Hugh. *The East European Revolution.* 2nd ed. London: Methuen, 1952.

Shore, Marci. *Caviar and Ashes: A Warsaw Generation's Life and Death in Marxism, 1918-1968.* New Haven, Conn.: Yale University Press, 2006.

———. "Children of the Revolution: Communism, Zionism, and the Berman Brothers." *Jewish Social Studies* 10, no. 3 (Spring–Summer 2004): 29–35.

Siefert, Marsha. *"Meeting at a Far Meridian*: American-Soviet Cultural Diplomacy on Film in the Early Cold War." In Babiracki and Zimmer, *Cold War Crossings*, 166–210.

Siekierska, Jadwiga. "Niezapomniane lata, niezapomniana szkoła." In *Takie były początki*, edited by Władysław Góra, 318–55. Warsaw: Książka i Wiedza, 1965.

Skrzypek, Andrzej. *Mechanizmy uzależnienia. Stosunki polsko-radzieckie 1944–1957*. Pułtusk: Wyższa Szkoła Humanistyczna im. A. Gieysztora, 2002.

Skurnowicz, Joan S. "Soviet Polonia, the Polish State, and the New Mythology of National Origins, 1943–1945." *Nationalities Papers* 22, supp. 1 (1994): 93–110.

Słabek, Henryk. *Intelektualistów obraz własny w świetle dokumentów autobiograficznych: 1944–1989*. Warsaw: Książka i Wiedza, 1997.

Słomkowska, Alina. *Prasa w PRL: Szkice Historyczne*. Warsaw: PWN, 1980.

Slonim, Marc. *Soviet Russian Literature: Writers and Problems, 1917–1977*. 2nd rev. ed. New York: Oxford University Press, 1977.

Smolar, Aleksander. "Jews as a Polish Problem." *Daedalus* 116, no. 2 (1987): 31–73.

Śnieć, Jerzy. "Działalność aparatu propagandy 1 Armii Ludowego Wojska Polskiego wśród wojsk i ludności cywilnej nieprzyjaciela w okresie walk nad Wisłą 1944–1945." In *Acta Universitatis Lodziensis*, Politologia 20 (1990): 61–76.

Snyder, Timothy. *Bloodlands: Europe Between Hitler and Stalin*. New York: Basic Books, 2010.

———. *The Reconstruction of Nations: Poland, Ukraine, Lithuania, Belorus, 1569–1999*. New Haven: Yale University Press, 2003.

Sobór, Anna. *Jakub Berman. Biografia polityczna*. Warsaw: IPN, 2008.

Sokol, Stanley S. *The Artists of Poland: A Biographical Dictionary from the 14th Century to the Present*. Jefferson, N.C: McFarland, 2000.

Sokorski, Włodzimierz. *Polacy pod Lenino*. Warsaw: Książka i Wiedza, 1971.

———. *Tamte lata*. Warsaw: Książka i Wiedza, 1979.

———. *Xawery Dunikowski*. Współczesne życiorysy Polaków. Wyd. 1 ed. Warsaw: Iskry, LZG 1, 1978.

"Spotkanie z Dymitrem Kabalewskim." *Muzyka*, no. 1–2 (January–February 1952): 59–63.

Starr, S. Frederick. *Red and Hot: The Fate of Jazz in the Soviet Union, 1917–1980*. New York: Oxford University Press, 1983.

Stefanovich, V. N., and Ia. I. Mentsendorf, eds. *Khudozhestvennaia literatura Pol'shi. Bibliograficheskii ukazatel' knig i statei, opublikovannykh v sovetskoi pechati i pechati Pol'shi v 1953 g.* Moscow: Vsesoiuznaia gosudarstvennaia biblioteka inostrannoi literatury, 1954).

Steinlauf, Michael C. *Bondage to the Dead: Poland and the Memory of the Holocaust*. Syracuse, N.Y.: Syracuse University Press, 1997.

———. "Poland." In *The World Reacts to the Holocaust*, edited by David S. Wyman, 81–155. Baltimore, Md.: Johns Hopkins University Press, 1996.

Stokłosa, Katarzyna. "La vie à la frontière soviéto-polonaise après la création du bloc communiste." In *Frontières du communisme. Mythologies et réalités de la division de l'Europe de la révolution d'Octobre au mur de Berlin*, edited by Sophie Coeuré et Sabine Dullin, 443-55. Paris: La Decouverte, 2007.

Stola, Dariusz. *Kraj bez wyjścia? Migracje z Polski, 1949-1989.* Warsaw: IPN, 2010.

Stoler, Ann Laura, and Frederic Cooper, eds. *Tensions of Empire: Colonial Cultures in a Bourgeois World.* Berkeley: University of California Press, 1997.

Stoler, Ann Laura, Carole McGranahan and Peter C. Perdue, eds. *Imperial Formations.* Santa Fe, N.Mex.: School for Advanced Research Press, 2007.

Stykalin, Aleksandr Sergeevich. "Ideologicheskaia i kul'turnaia ekspansiia stalinizma v Vengrii." *Slavianovedeniie* 6 (1992): 15-26.

——. "Nauchnaia intelligentsia stran tsentral'noi Evropy i ee otnoshenie k SSSR i sovetskoi nauke (vtoraia polovina 1940-kh–seredina 1950-kh godov. Po materialam rossiiskikh arkhivov." In *Intelligentsiia v usloviiakh obshchestvennoi nestabil'nosti*, edited by A.I. Studenikin, 92-104. Moscow: MTsFI, 1996.

——. "Politika SSSR po formirovaniiu obshchestvennogo mneniia v stranakh tsentral'noi Evropy i nastroeniia intelligentsiia: Vtoraia polovina 1940-kh godov." *Slavianovedenie*, no. 3 (1997): 50-62.

——. "Propaganda SSSR na zarubezhnuiu auditoriiu i obshchestvennoe mnenie stran Zapada v pervye poslevoennye gody (po dokumentam rossiiskikh arkhivov)." *Vestnik Moskovskogo Universiteta (seriia X—zhurnalistika)* 1 (1997): 57-70.

Surganov, Vsevolod. *Fedor Panferov. Vospominaniia druzei.* 2nd ed. Moscow: Sovetskii pisatel', 1977.

Surgiewicz, Remigiusz. "Z dziejów prasy frontowej Ludowego Wojska Polskiego, 1943-1945." *Wojskowy Przegląd Historyczny* 8, no. 1 (1963): 33-64.

Świda-Ziemba, Hanna. *Urwany lot. Pokolenie inteligenckiej młodzieży powojennej w świetle listów i pamiętników z lat 1945-1948.* Cracow: Wydawn. Literackie, 2003.

Szaynok, Bożena. *Poland-Israel 1944-1968: In the Shadow of the Past and of the Soviet Union.* Translated by Dominika Ferens. Warsaw: Institute of National Remembrance, 2012.

Szczurowski, Maciej. *Słownik biograficzny wyższych dowódców Wojska Polskiego na froncie wschodnim w latach 1943-1945.* Warsaw: Wojskowy Instytut Historyczny, 1993.

Szporluk, Roman, ed. *The Influence of East Europe and the Soviet West on the USSR.* New York: Praeger, 1975.

Szulzycer, Samuel. "Żydzi w 1 Dywizji Piechoty im. Tadeusza Kościuszki." *Biuletyn Żydowskiego Instytutu Historycznego* 81 (1972): 17-39.

Taranov, Evgenii. "'Raskachaem Leninskie Gory!' Iz istorii 'vol'nodumstva' v Moskovskom Universitete, 1955-1956." *Svobodnaia mysl'* 10 (1993): 94-103.

Taras, Raymond. "Gomulka's 'Rightist-Nationalist Deviation': The Postwar Jewish Communists and the Stalinist Reaction to Poland, 1945-1950." *Nationalities Papers* 22, no. 1 (1994): 111-27.

Taylor, Richard, and D. W. Spring. *Stalinism and Soviet Cinema*. London and New York: Routledge, 1993.

Thompson, Ewa M. "The Katyń Massacre and the Warsaw Ghetto Uprising in the Soviet-Nazi Propaganda War." In *World War 2 and the Soviet People*, edited by John Garrard and Carol Garrard, 213–32. New York: St. Martin's Press, 1990.

Tighe, Carl. *The Politics of Literature: Poland, 1945-1989*. Cardiff: University of Wales Press, 1999.

Tismaneanu, Vladimir, ed. *Stalinism Revisited: The Establishment of Communist Regimes in East-Central Europe*. Budapest and New York: Central European University Press, 2009.

Tobia, Simona. *Advertising America: The United States Information Service in Italy (1945-1956)*. Milan: LED Edizioni Universitarie, 2009.

Todes, Daniel Philip. *Darwin without Malthus: The Struggle for Existence in Russian Evolutionary Thought*. New York: Oxford University Press, 1989.

Tompkins, David. "Composing for and with the Party: Andrzej Panufnik and Stalinist Poland." *Polish Review* 54, no. 3 (2009): 271–85.

Torańska, Teresa. *Oni*. 1. wyd ed. Warsaw: Agencja Omnipress, 1989.

———. *"Them:" Stalin's Polish Puppets*. 1st U.S. ed. New York: Harper and Row, 1987.

Trznadel, Jacek. *Hańba domowa. Rozmowy z pisarzami*. Biblioteka Kultury, vol. 422. Paryż: Instytut Literacki, 1986.

Tumarkin, Nina. *The Living and the Dead: The Rise and Fall of the Cult of World War II in Russia*. New York: Basic Books, 1994.

Ulam, Adam Bruno. *Expansion and Coexistence: The History of Soviet Foreign Policy, 1917-67*. New York: Praeger, 1968.

Urbanek, Mariusz. *Broniewski. Miłość, wódka, polityka*. Warsaw: Iskry, 2011.

Vaksberg, Arkady. *Stalin's Prosecutor: The Life of Andrei Vyshinsky*. New York: Grove Weidenfeld, 1990.

Valkenier, Elizabeth Kridl. "Stalinizing Polish Historiography: What Soviet Archives Disclose." *East European Politics and Societies* vol. 7, no. 1 (1993): 109–34.

Vavilov, S. I., and Boris A. Vvedenskii. *Bol'shaia sovetskaia entsiklopediia* 1949–1958.

Verdery, Katherine. *What Was Socialism and What Comes Next?* Princeton, N.J.: Princeton University Press, 1996.

Volokitina, T. V., and G. P. Murashko. *"Kholodnaia Voina" i sotsial-demokratiia Vostochnoi Evropy, 1944-1948 gg. Ocherki istorii*. Moscow: Rossiiskaia istoricheskaia biblioteka, 1998.

Volokitina, Tatiana V., Galina P. Murashko and Albina F. Noskova, eds. *Narodnaia demokratiia: mif ili real'nost'?* Moscow: Nauka, 1993.

Vucinich, Alexander. *Empire of Knowledge: The Academy of Sciences of the USSR (1917-1970)*. Berkeley: University of California Press, 1984.

Waldorff, Jerzy. *Diabły i anioły*. Cracow: PWN, 1971.

Wasilewska, Wanda, "Wspomnienia Wandy Wasilewskiej (1939–1945)." In *Archiwum Ruchu Robotniczego* 7 (1982).

Wat, Aleksander. *My Century: The Odyssey of a Polish Intellectual.* Translated by Richard Lourie. Berkeley: University of California Press, 1988.

Ważyk, Adam. "A Poem for Adults." In *National Communism and Popular Revolt in Eastern Europe: A Selection of Documents on Poland and Hungary,* edited by Paul E. Zinner, 40–48. New York: Columbia University Press, 1956.

Weiner, Amir. "The Empires Pay a Visit: Gulag Returnees, East European Rebellions, and Soviet Frontier Politics." *Journal of Modern History* 78, no. 2 (2006): 333–76.

Wende, Jan Karol. *Ta ziemia od innych droższa.* Warsaw: PIW, 1981.

Werblan, Andrzej. "The Conversation between Władysław Gomułka and Josef Stalin on 14 November 1945." *CWIHP Bulletin* no. 11 (1999): 134–40, www .wilsoncenter.org/sites/default/files/CWIHP_Bulletin_11.pdf (accessed December 14, 2012).

———. *Stalin and the Cold War in Europe: The Emergence and Development of East-West Conflict, 1939–1953.* Lanham, Md.: Rowman and Littlefield, 2008.

———. *Stalinizm w Polsce.* Warsaw: Towarzystwo Wydawnicze i Literackie, 2009.

———. "Stalins Deutschland-Politik 1945–1949 von dem Hindengrund seines Vorgehens im Osten Europas." In *Gleichschaltung unter Stalin? Die Entwicklung der Parteien im Östlichen Europa, 1944–1949,* edited by Stefan Creuzberger and Manfred Görtemaker, 15–44. Paderborn: Ferdinand Schöningh, 2004.

Werth, Alexander. *Russia at War, 1941–1945.* London: Pan Books, 1965.

Werth, Nicolas. "Soviet Union (1917–1945)." In *A Handbook of the Communist Security Apparatus in East Central Europe 1944–1989,* edited by Krzysztof Persak and and Łukasz Kamiński, 13–36. Warsaw: IPN, 2005.

Wisner, Henryk. "Książka radziecka i rosyjska w Drugiej Rzeczypospolitej." *Kwartalnik Historyczny* 84, no. 4 (1977): 859–70.

Władyka, Wiesław. *Kartki z PRL: Ludzie, fakty, wydarzenia. Vol. 1: 1944–1970.* Poznań and Warsaw: Sens and Polityka -Spółdzielnia Pracy, 2005.

———. "W prasie zapisane." *Polityka,* no. 2821 (August 17, 2011): 54–57.

Wojna, Romuald. "Odrodzenie Polski w 1918 r. w radzieckiej historiografii i publicystyce: do lat osiemdziesiatych." *Kwartalnik Historyczny* 95, no. 3 (1989): 87–106.

Wolfe, Patrick. "History and Imperialism: A Century of Theory, from Marx to Postcolonialism," *AHR* 102, no. 2 (April 1997): 388–420.

Wolff, Richard. "Rokossovsky." In *Stalin's Generals,* edited by Harold Shukman, 177–96. New York: Grove Press, 1993.

Woźniakowski, Krzysztof. *Między ubezwłasnowolnieniem a opozycją. Związek Literatów Polskich w latach 1949—1956. Cracow, 1990.*

Wróblewski, Andrzej. *Być Żydem. rozmowa z Dagiem Halvorsenem o Żydach i antysemityzmie Polaków.* Warsaw: Niezależna Oficyna Wydawnicza, 1992.

Wyszomirska-Kuźmińska, Otilda. *Współpraca Polski z ZSRR w dziedzinie nauk humanistycznych, 1944–1974.* Wrocław: Zakład Narodowy im. Ossolińskich, 1981.

Zalesskii, K. A. *Imperiia Stalina. Biograficheskii entsiklopedicheskii slovar'*. Moscow: Veche, 2000.

Zaloga, Steven J. *Bagration 1944: The Destruction of the Army Group Centre*. Oxford: Osprey, 1996.

Zaremba, Marcin. *Komunizm, legitymizacja, nacjonalizm. Nacjonalistyczna legitymizacja władzy komunistycznej w Polsce*. Warsaw: Trio and ISP PAN, 2001.

Zarycki, Tomasz. "Uses of Russia: The Role of Russia in the Modern Polish National Identity." *East European Politics and Societies* 18 (2004): 595–627.

Zawiśliński, Stanisław. *Wyznania zdrajcy. Wywiad-rzeka z Włodzimierzem Sokorskim*. Warsaw: Andy Grafik, 1991.

Zbiniewicz, Fryderyk. *Armia Polska w ZSRR: Studia nad problematyką pracy politycznej*. Warsaw: MON, 1963.

Żenczykowski, Tadeusz. *Polska Lubelska 1944*. Paris: Spotkania, 1987.

Zezina, M. R. *Sovetskaia khudozhestvennaia intelligentsiia i vlast' v 1950-e–1960-e gg*. Moscow: Dialog MGU, 1999.

Zima, V. F. *Golod v SSSR 1946–1947 godov: proiskhozhdenie i posledstviia*. Moscow: RAN, 1996.

Zubkova, Elena. "Mir mnenii sovetskogo cheloveka. 1945–1948 gody: Po materialam Tsk Vkp(b)." *Otechestvennaia istoriia*, no. 4 (1998): 99–108.

———. *Poslevoennoe sovetskoe obshchestvo: Politika i povsednevnost', 1945–1953*. Moscow: ROSSPEN, 2000.

———. *Russia After the War: Hopes, Illusions and Disappointments, 1945–1957*. Armonk, N.Y.: M. E. Sharpe, 1998.

———. "The Soviet Regime and Soviet Society in the Postwar Years: Innovations and Conservatism, 1945–1953." *Journal of Modern European History* 2, no. 1 (2004): 134–52.

Zubok, Vladislav. *A Failed Empire: The Soviet Union in the Cold War from Stalin to Gorbachev*. Chapel Hill: University of North Carolina Press, 2007.

———. *Zhivago's Children: The Last Russian Intelligentsia*. Cambridge, Mass.: Harvard University Press, 2009.

Zubok, Vladislav, and Konstantin Viktorovich Pleshakov. *Inside the Kremlin's Cold War: From Stalin to Khrushchev*. Cambridge, Mass.: Harvard University Press, 1996.

Index

Page numbers in italics refer to images, those followed by a 't' refer to tables, and those followed by an 'f' refer to figures.

Brzezinski, Zbigniew, 7, 83, 255 (n. 16)
Bubnov, Nikolai: meeting with Popov, 1; refuses to attend Matejko exhibit, 2; and Thaw, 187, 214–15; as editor of *Wolność*, 190–98, 295 (n. 35); Mikhailov and, 218–19; downfall of, 240–41; diaries of, 294 (n. 12)
Bulgakov, Mikhail, 157, 162–63
Bulganin, Nikolai, 72, 196
Burdenko Commission, 37, 38
Bureau of Public Security, 56–57

Cajmer, Jan, 43
Captive Mind, The (Miłosz), 68, 205–6
Catholic Church: communist attack on, 100, 198; materials published against, 136
Caute, David, 212, 240, 256 (n. 16)
Central Bureau of Polish Communists (CBKP): Zawadzki as chair of, 32; ideology of, 35
Central Committee of the All-Union (Bolshevik) Communist Party (VKP(b)), 60, 84–85, 136, 198–99, 300 (n. 23)
Chałasiński, Józef, 216
Checinski, Michael, 267 (n. 10)
Chekhov, Anton, 72, 161
Chervinskaia, Liubov, 151
Chopin piano contest (1949), 122
Chuvikov, P., 291 (n. 43)
Chyliński, Jan, 300 (n. 23)
Civil war, 56–57
Clausewitz, Carl von, 116–17
Club of International Press and Book, 151–52
Coal (Ścibor-Rylski), 178–79
Collective farms, 61, 100, 136, 137–38, 284 (n. 193)
Colonialism, 256 (n. 21). *See also* Empire
Colorado Beetle (Kruczkowski), 183–84
Communist Information Bureau (Cominform), 77
Communists: Sovietization and, 4–5, 7–8, 100; power of, 11–12; perception

of, of culture, 13; cruelty of, 55–56; Jews as, 57, 263 (n. 131); Hungarian, and anti-Semitic fear, 103. *See also* Polish communists
Conditioned Reflexes and Neuron Organization (Konorski), 146–47
Congress of the Polish Writers' Union (1954), 209–10
Congress of the Polish Writers' Union (1956), 232
Connelly, John, 149, 285 (n. 218)
Conspiracy Against Peace, The (Parker), 104
Contemporary fiction: export of, from People's Democracies, 158–59; efforts to publish Polish, 159–61, 164–66, 171–73, 185–86; Mickiewicz Street and, 161–62; constraints on, 163; Polish versus Soviet, 163–64; publication of Polish, 167–68; organizations supporting publication of, 169–72; standards for publication of, 173–79; and "Big Deal," 178–80; and communication between Soviet and Polish literary communities, 180–85, 186; integration of Polish, during Thaw, 221–22; publication of, in USSR, 239; Polish, considered by Foreign Commission, 1947–1953, 245t. *See also* Literature
Cooperation, scientific, 139–49, 215–16, 285 (n. 205). *See also* Cultural cooperation
Crowley, David, 12
Cruelty, as communist tool, 55–56
"Cult of personality," 226–27
Cultural ambassadors, Soviet, 68–76
Cultural cooperation: potential for postwar, 68, 74, 83, 84, 95; effects of, 70; rekindled interest in, 86; between literary communities, 180–85, 186; following Thaw, 231
Culture: tension between Poland and Soviet Union over, 1–2; and debates over censorship, 4; role of, in

Soviet-Polish interactions, 7; Soviet persuasion through, 9–14; in Marxism, 12; communist perception of, 12–14; of Soviet bloc, 241

Currency, printing of Polish, 47

Curzon Line, 38–39, 40

Cyrankiewicz, Józef, 152, 234

Czytelnik (the Reader), 64, 66, 78

Dąbrowska, Maria: on 1953 European Boxing Championship, 124; on *Border Street*, 125–26, 131, 132–33; ideology of, 126; on Boguszewska, 175

"Dąbrowski's Mazurka," 24

Darkness at Noon (Koestler), 208

David-Fox, Michael, 287 (n. 263)

Death to Spies (Smert' Shpionam/ SMERSH), 296 (n. 80)

Decade of Euphoria, A (Friedberg), 289 (n. 4)

De Grazia, Victoria, 240–41

Dejmek, Kazimierz, 212

Dembowski, Jan, 144

Democracy and visions for postwar Poland, 30–35. *See also* People's Democracy

Denisov, Andrei I., 288 (n. 266)

Department of Information and Propaganda, 48

Department of International Information (OMI), 274 (n. 164)

Department of Poland and Czechoslovakia, 60

Department of Slavic Literatures, 170

De-Stalinization: scholarship on, 189; Sokorski and, 208; and scientific cooperation, 215–16; effects of, in USSR, 217; defined, 294 (n. 8). *See also* Thaw

"Distinguished Engineer, A" (Znakomity maszynista), 137

Djilas, Milovan, 103

Dłuski, Ostap, 150

Dluzhinskii, Evgenii I., 104, 283 (n. 175)

Dobrenko, Evgeny, 163

"Doctors' Plot," 188, 203, 207, 218

Dostoevsky, Fyodor: caricaturization of Poles by, 10; rediscovery of, during postwar era, 72; Polish writers' interest in, 115

Drinking, 36–37

Dudek, Antoni, 268 (n. 14)

Dunham, Vera, 178

Eagle as Polish emblem, 23

Ehrenburg, Ilya: in Stalinist cultural landscape, 86; travels of, 86–87; returns to Poland, 89; and World Congress of Intellectuals in Defense of Peace, 89–90; on changes in Polish culture, 114; on Thaw, 187; *The Thaw*, 188–89, 194–95, 213, 293 (n. 7)

Eliot, T. S., 52

Empire: and reflex actions, 149–50; maintenance of, through force, 233–34; source of power of, 240–41; scholarship on, 256 (n. 21)

Engineer Saba (Wirski), 177–78, 179, 184

English Club, 162

Erofeev, Viktor, 12, 242

Ettinger, Paweł, 23, 259 (n. 25)

European Boxing Championship (1950), 125

European Boxing Championship (1953), 124, 301 (n. 27)

Evgenii Onegin (Pushkin), 120

Fadeev, Aleksandr, 89–90, *91*, 195

Farms, collective, 61, 100, 136, 137–38, 284 (n. 193)

Fear: as communist tool, 11–12; as motivation for Sovietization, 102–8, 154–55; as obstacle to scientific cooperation, 144; and reflex actions, 151–54; in publishing contemporary works, 169, 177; Soviet cultural outreach dependent on, 237–39

Fedorov, L. N., 146

250f, 251f, 279 (n. 80); translation of Polish, into Russian, 289 (n. 4). *See also* Contemporary fiction

Lozovskii, Solomon, 97

Lukovnikov, I., 233

L'vov, as cultural capital, 17

Lysenko, Trofim, 140, 144, 217

Machcewicz, Paweł, 229

Madej, Alina, 132

Malenkov, G. M., 80, 153, 203

Márai, Sándor, 236

Marchlewska, Zofia, 170, 291 (n. 46)

Marxism, 12, 125–26, 139–40

Marxism-Leninsim, 142–43, 229, 246f

Maskalan, Władysław, 15, 46, 47–48

Master and Margarita, The (Bulgakov), 162–63

Matejko, Jan, *Bathory at Pskov*, 1–2

Matuszewski, Stefan, 48, 288 (n. 266)

May 3 holiday, 229–30

Mayakovsky, Vladimir, 71, 193–94, 195, 212, 240

Mazowsze, 220, 225

Medallions (*Medaliony*; Nałkowska), 164, 166–67

Medical science, 143–44

Merkina, Regina, 178, 179

Mezhdunarodnaia kniga, 59, 79, 113, 117

Miasnikov, A. S., 115–16

Michurin, Ivan, 148

Michurinist biology, 142

Michurinist campaign, 140

Mickiewicz, Adam: *Forefather's Eve*, 4; *Pan Tadeusz*, 120–21

Mickiewicz Street, 161–62

Mietkowski, Mieczysław, 265 (n. 156)

Mikhailov, Nikolai, *188*, 196, 218–24, 231, 234, 300 (n. 183)

Miłosz, Czesław: meets Putrament, 15–16; as Soviet cultural ambassador, 68; *The Captive Mind*, 68, 205–6; knowledge of, regarding USSR, 71; defects to France, 101; on Putrament, 105, 207; on Soviet journalist, 114; on concepts of freedom in Polish-Russian relations, 239–40; Pasierski on sensibility of, 258 (n. 4)

Minc, Hilary: writes "Theses number 2," 32; and administration of Polish culture, 48; singled out by Soviet diplomats, 150; as chief of Political Department, 265 (n. 160)

Ministry of Information and Propaganda, 48

Ministry of Public Security, 203–4

Młynarski, Zygmunt, 150, 287–88 (n. 265)

Mochalov, V. V., 164–65, 265 (n. 161)

Modzelewski, Zygmunt, 48

Moiseev song-and-dance ensemble, 77, 81, *82*

Molotov, Viacheslav, 195, 197, 274–75 (n. 164)

Motyleva, Tamara Lazarevna, 170, 174, 175, 177

Museum of the Revolution of the USSR, 162

Music: increased popularity of Russian and Soviet, 87; increase in Russian and Soviet, on Polish radio, 112; lack of support for Soviet, 117–18; Western cultural influence on, 121–22; Kabalevskii speaks on Soviet, 151–52; export of Soviet, during Thaw, 220

Musical competitions, as barometer of Polish attitudes toward USSR, 122–23

Muzyka, 152

My Encounters with Polish Science (Schaff), 138–39

"My Soviet Passport" (Mayakovsky), 193–94

My Trip to Russia (Słonimski), 272 (n. 99)

Nagy, Imre, 6

Naimark, Norman, 255 (n. 16)

Pleshakov, Constantine, 99

"Poem for Adults, A" (Ważyk), 187, 201–10, 296 (n. 70)

Poetry, 193–94, 195, 214

Poleski-Szczypiłło, Platon, 22

Polish art and artists: relationship of, with Stalinist regime, 13, 68, 73, 100, 105–7; dilemmas of, 70; compromises made by, 70–71; repression of, 84; socialist realism and, 116, 163, 209; Western cultural influence in, 118, 120–21; hidden transcripts of, 120; freedom of, 164; Jewish themes in, 178; during Thaw, 209, 215; historical themes in, 217

Polish communists: and journey of apostles, 15–20; and recruitment of Polish soldiers, 20–26; and Red Army officers in Kościuszko Division, 28–30; and visions for postwar Poland, 30–35; advancement of, 35–36; and Red Army's push into Poland, 40–41; shift gears in propaganda work, 41–43; Jewish, 44; significance of Sel'tsy and Siedlce to, 50; and Soviet presence in Poland, 53–54, 81–83; political force and popular legitimacy of, 57; cultural symbiosis between intelligentsia and, 68–70; and Poland as Cold War battleground, 76–79; and Sovietization of Poland, 100; fear as motivation of, for Sovietization, 102–8; *Border Street* clarifies complicated position of, 127; *Border Street* and vulnerability of, 132; Soviet Information Bureau and, 135–36; Polish science and, 141, 146–47; Zakrzewski challenges pro-"formalist" bias of, 152; and publishing of contemporary Polish fiction, 160, 171, 178; and Polish October, 228–29; reaction of, to Poznań workers' uprising, 234

Polish Corps, 30, 35–37

Polish intellectuals: as Soviet cultural ambassadors, 68–76; relationship of, with Stalinist regime, 107; Polish science and, 141; and publishing of contemporary Polish fiction, 160; views on World War II, 166

Polish Ministry of Foreign Affairs, 74, 81–82

Polish October, 228–30

Polish Peasant Party (PSL) press, 64, 270 (n. 54)

Polish press: *Wolność*, 54, 57–58, 190–98; Soviet Information Bureau and, 59–67, 134–38, 198–201, 243*t*; and Poland as Cold War battleground, 76–77; and Mikhailov method, 222–23; students' interest in, 230–31

Polish science, 138–49, 215–17

Polish soldiers: recruitment of, 18–26; oath sworn by, 27, *28*; manipulation of newly recruited, 29; problems between Red Army officers and, 29–30, 36–37, 45–46; and visions for postwar Poland, 30–35; advancement of, 35–36; political officers' dealings with, 37–39; Polish communists shift propaganda tactics on, 41–43; significance of Sel'tsy and Siedlce to, 50; and Soviet involvement in postwar Polish culture, 65–66; erasure of, in Soviet film, 74

Polish-Soviet Friendship Society (TPPR), 70, 85–86, 87, 114, 141, 287 (n. 265)

Polish-Soviet Institute, 287 (n. 265)

Polish Stalinism, 101

Polish Workers' Party (PPR), 41, 64–65, 76, 85, 87, 128–29, 164

Polish Writers' Union, 231–32

Political Officer Corps, growth of, 35–36

Ponomarenko, Panteleimon, 216–17, 218

Popov, Evgenii Alekseevich, 286 (n. 231)

Popov, Georgii M.: meeting with Bubnov, 1; refuses to attend Matejko

Street, 130; singled out by Soviet
diplomats, 150; socialist realism and,
153; following death of Stalin,
208–9; on Polish Army, 260 (n. 67);
as member of delegation to Katyn,
262 (n. 99); Kozhushko and, 266
(n. 168); on subjects of postwar
Polish plays, 281 (n. 119)

Sorokin, V., 199–201

Soviet artists: visits of, to Poland, 81–82,
87, 88, 114–15, 151; views on Polish
cultural changes, 116; in music
contests, 122–23; contest cultural
policies of local communists, 152

Soviet cultural ambassadors, 68–76, 110

Soviet embassy: plans for, 3–4; provides
support to cultural institutions, 59;
as nexus of Soviet-operated cultural
forces, 72, 74; and Poland as Cold
War battleground, 79; and problems
of cultural exchange, 85; employees
with diplomatic status in, 272
(n. 104). *See also* Russian embassy

Soviet Information Bureau (Sovinformbiuro): goals of, 59–61; tactics of,
61–63; challenges faced by, 63–67;
and Poland as Cold War battleground, 76–77, 78; Sokolovskii and
subsequent representatives in,
133–38; following death of Stalin,
198–201; articles from, in Polish
press, 1944–1958, 243t; Pechatnov
on western outreach of, 256 (n. 18);
Voslensky on, 269 (n. 31)

Sovietization, 4–5; scholarship on, 6–7,
255 (nn. 14–16); process of, 7–8, 84;
failure of, 9–10, 239–40; through
culture, 9–14, 79; as strategy to gain
control, 99–100; fear as motivation
for, 102–8, 154–55; militant youths as
supporters of, 108–10; friction in,
116–19; Jews blamed for, 129; of
Polish science, 140–41, 148–49; and
reflex actions, 150; enforcement of,
150–52, 154; meanings of, 155;

examination of Soviet side of,
155–56; and Soviet-East European
cultural interactions, 186; as
consistent with Stalin's postwar
policy, 237

Soviet Ministry of Foreign Affairs
(MID), 85, 112–13, 286 (n. 232)

Soviet passivity, 79, 85, 88, 221

Soviet science, 139–49, 215–17

Soviet self-criticism, 221, 224

Soviet students, information spread by,
230–31

Spasskii, V. I., 286 (n. 232)

Sporting events as barometer of Polish
attitudes toward USSR, 122, 123–25

Stalin, Josef: Sovietization and, 4–5;
denounced by Khrushchev, 5; on
Soviet troops, 5; Brzezinski on, 7;
adjusts Marxism to his own needs,
12–13; and Union of Polish Patriots,
18; and visions for postwar Poland,
31; and redrawing of borders, 40;
patronage of, 55; advisory role of, in
creating July Manifesto, 71; takes
increased interest in satellite
countries' internal affairs, 77; and
plan for Sovietization, 84; and
problems of cultural exchange, 85;
Ehrenburg and, 86; speculation
regarding intentions of, 94; execu-
tions ordered by, 97–98; Sovietization and strategy of, 99–100; edits
Poland's new constitution, 100;
leadership style of, 113, 118; anti-
Semitic agenda of, 131–32; purges
Sovinformbiuro, 133–34; on
language and Marxist superstructure,
152–53; and attack on formalists,
159; and war theme in contemporary
Polish literature, 166; Thaw following death of, 187–88; reactions to
death of, 202; and Palace of Culture
and Science, 210; on imposing
communism on Poland, 237; missed
opportunities of, 240; consulted by

Polish leaders, 276 (n. 14); love and respect for, 277 (n. 24); Grigor'ian's letter to, 280 (n. 107)

Stalinism: move from, to Thaw, 1–6; scholarship on Polish, 101; conformity to, 122; science subjugated to, 139, 148–49; and efforts to publish Polish contemporary fiction, 185–86; lost faith in, 202, 205; Woroszylski's break with, 208; critique of, in *The Bathhouse*, 212; Polish October and confrontation of, 228–30. *See also* De-Stalinization; Thaw

Staniukovich, Ia., 174, 177, 183

Staszewski, Stefan, 136–37

State Publishing House of Foreign Literature (Inoizdat), 169–73, 224

Stefaniuk, Zenon, *124*

Steinlauf, Michael C., 129, 268–69 (n. 14)

Stepanov, Boris, *124*

Stoler, Ann Laura, 256 (n. 21)

Students, information spread by, 230–31

Stykalin, A. S., 67, 255 (n. 16), 274 (n. 154)

"Suggestions for Intensifying the Soviet Union's Influence on Cultural Life in Poland, Czechoslovakia, and Other East European Countries," 112–13

Surkov, Alexei, 232

Suslov, Mikhail, 75, 113, 141, 196

Suzin, Leon Marek, 282 (n. 154)

Swearing, 174

Światło, Józef, 203–4

Sytin, Ivan, 162

Szczecin, 99

Szenwald, Lucjan, 25, 43

Szpilman, Władysław, 121

Sztachelski, Jerzy, 146, 150

Szymborska, Wisława, 108–9

Taboos imposed on Polish artists, 70–71

Talyzin, N., 215

Telegraph, 200

Terror. *See* Fear

Thaw: move from Stalinism to, 1–6; hints of, following Stalin's death, 187–89; rate of, in various Eastern European countries, 189; effects of, 189, 229; and Bubnov's *Wolność*, 190–98; Soviet Information Bureau during, 198–201; and "A Poem for Adults," 201–10; World Festival of Youth and Students during, 210–12; confrontational nature of, 212–14; emergence of new trends in, 214–15; Soviet scrutiny of Polish science during, 215–17; Mikhailov as Soviet ambassador during, 217–24; conclusions on, 224–25; varying experiences with, 293 (n. 6). *See also* De-Stalinization; Stalinism

Thaw, The (Ehrenburg), 188–89, 194–95, 213

Theater: and recruitment of Polish soldiers, 25; Russian and Soviet, performed in Poland, 113–14, 244*t*, 279 (n. 86); problems with Soviet, 119; Western cultural influence in, 120–21; socialist realism in, 153; during Thaw, 212; subjects of postwar Polish plays, 281 (n. 119)

"Theses number 1," 31–32, 261 (n. 73)

"Theses number 2," 32

Tikhonov, Nikolai, 114, 115, 120, 222

Tolstoy, Lev, 10

Towards New Shores (Lacis), 153

Tractors Will Conquer the Spring (Zalewski), 180

Translation: of Polish contemporary fiction, 164–65, 167–68, 289 (n. 4); of Russian/Soviet books into Polish, 250*f*, 251*f*, 279 (n. 80); salary for, 290 (n. 8)

Travel: restriction and significance of, 7–8; of Ehrenburg, 86–87; of Bernov, 98–99; of Soviet scientists, 143–44,

Writing, as privileged and prestigious art form, 160. *See also* Literature
Wycech, Czesław, 79–80
Wyspiański, Stanisław, *The Wedding*, 4

Yalta Conference (1945), 40, 94
Yevtushenko, Yevgeny, 214
Youth, as key element of Soviet Thaw culture, 210–12, 214

Zak, Iakov, 114
Zakrzewski, Włodzimierz, 152, 153, 288 (nn. 266, 277)
Zambrowicz, Janusz, 88, 89, 164–65
Zambrowski, Roman, 32, 47–48, 204, 265 (n. 156), 283 (n. 175)

Zawadzki, Aleksander, 32, 265 (n. 156)
Zawadzki, Jan, 28
Zhdanov, Andrei, 87, 137, 151, 159
Zhivov, Mark Semenovich, 170, 172, 176, 177, 184–85
Zholkovskii, Ivan, 159
Zhukov, Iurii G., 33, 261 (n. 77)
Zhurko, F. M., 146
Znieważanie, 281 (n. 117)
Zorin, Valerian, 62, 159–60, 165
Zoshchenko, Mikhail, 75
Zotov, A. V., 280 (n. 105)
Zubok, Vladislav, 8, 99
Życie Warszawy, 137
Żywulska, Krystyna, 167

Patryk Babiracki, *Soviet Soft Power in Poland: Culture and the Making of Stalin's New Empire* (2015).

Sulmaan Wasif Khan, *Muslim, Trader, Nomad, Spy: China's Cold War and the Tibetan Borderlands* (2015).

Margaret Peacock, *Innocent Weapons: The Soviet and American Politics of Childhood in the Cold War* (2014).

Austin Jersild, *The Sino-Soviet Alliance: An International History* (2014).

Piero Gleijeses, *Visions of Freedom: Havana, Washington, Pretoria, and the Struggle for Southern Africa, 1976–1991* (2013).

Lien-Hang T. Nguyen, *Hanoi's War: An International History of the War for Peace in Vietnam* (2012).

Tanya Harmer, *Allende's Chile and the Inter-American Cold War, 1970–1973* (2011).

Alessandro Brogi, *Confronting America: The Cold War between the United States and the Communists in France and Italy* (2011).

Gregg Brazinsky, *Nation Building in South Korea: Koreans, Americans, and the Making of a Democracy* (2007).

Vladislav M. Zubok, *A Failed Empire: The Soviet Union in the Cold War from Stalin to Gorbachev* (2007).

Stephen G. Rabe, *U.S. Intervention in British Guiana: A Cold War Story* (2005).

Christopher Endy, *Cold War Holidays: American Tourism in France* (2004).

Salim Yaqub, *Containing Arab Nationalism: The Eisenhower Doctrine and the Middle East* (2003).

Francis J. Gavin, *Gold, Dollars, and Power: The Politics of International Monetary Relations, 1958–1971* (2003).

William Glenn Gray, *Germany's Cold War: The Global Campaign to Isolate East Germany, 1949–1969* (2003).

Matthew J. Ouimet, *The Rise and Fall of the Brezhnev Doctrine in Soviet Foreign Policy* (2003).

Pierre Asselin, *A Bitter Peace: Washington, Hanoi, and the Making of the Paris Agreement* (2002).

Jeffrey Glen Giauque, *Grand Designs and Visions of Unity: The Atlantic Powers and the Reorganization of Western Europe, 1955–1963* (2002).

Chen Jian, *Mao's China and the Cold War* (2001).

M. E. Sarotte, *Dealing with the Devil: East Germany, Détente, and Ostpolitik, 1969–1973* (2001).

Mark Philip Bradley, *Imagining Vietnam and America: The Making of Postcolonial Vietnam, 1919–1950* (2000).

Michael E. Latham, *Modernization as Ideology: American Social Science and "Nation Building" in the Kennedy Era* (2000).

Qiang Zhai, *China and the Vietnam Wars, 1950–1975* (2000).

William I. Hitchcock, *France Restored: Cold War Diplomacy and the Quest for Leadership in Europe, 1944–1954* (1998).

.